𝕾𝖆𝖑𝖆𝖒𝖎𝖘 & 𝕾𝖜𝖆𝖘𝖙𝖎𝖐𝖆𝖘

LETTERS HOME
FROM A G.I. JEW

Edited and with Commentary
By
STEVE STOLIAR

*For Steve Karras
with MUCH thanks!
Warmly,
Steve Stoliar
P.S. Focus!*

SALAMIS & Swastikas: Letters Home From A G.I. Jew
Edited and with Commentary By Steve Stoliar
Copyright © 2022 Steve Stoliar
No part of this book may be reproduced in any form or by any means,
electronic, mechanical, digital, photocopying, or recording, except for
inclusion of a review, without permission in writing from the publisher
or Author.

Published in the USA by:
BearManor Media
1317 Edgewater Dr #110
Orlando, FL 32804
www.bearmanormedia.com

Perfect ISBN 978-1-62933-877-4
Case ISBN 978-1-62933-878-1
BearManor Media, Orlando, Florida
Printed in the United States of America
Cover design: Steve Stoliar
Book design by Robbie Adkins, www.adkinsconsult.com

TABLE OF CONTENTS

For Dave and Amy
— and Carole Frances

ACKNOWLEDGMENTS

A number of people assisted me in a number of ways as I tackled this challenging endeavor. First, I must thank my dear sisters, Carole Frances Schwartz and Patricia Jane "Pati" Stoliar, for providing helpful feedback all along the way, and for helping to fill in some of the missing puzzle pieces in the lives and chronologies of our parents, Dave and Amy Stoliar. Other family members who helped in the feedback, input, and guidance departments include Jackie Schneider Lipsitz, Jill Newman, Jennifer Kirmse, Lynne Sussman Ballew, and Malcolm Schwartz.

Special thanks to Matt Mackensen, for generously sharing information and memories of his mother, Janine Mougin, and other family members. Heartfelt thanks to Michael Hennarty for keeping me on track regarding all things military.

For her technical wizardry in helping to improve the clarity of some of the more damaged photographs, my sincere thanks to Joanne Lichtenstein. For providing feedback and guidance in getting this book published, I am greatly indebted to Steve Karras. For their encouraging words along the way and thereafter, many thanks to Woody Allen, Joan Antelman, Deb Belz, Dick Cavett, Heidi Dvorak, Bob Garrick, Gerry Kroll, Jerome Lewis, Maeve Meighan, and Stephen Tobolowsky.

Finally, thanks to Dave and Amy Stoliar, for writing and saving, respectively (and respectfully), these remarkable letters – and for having me.

FOREWORD (*MARCH!*)

On Thursday, May 11, 1944, Staff Sergeant David E. Stoliar of the 346th Signal Company Wing, a division of the 64th Fighter Wing of the U.S. Army, wrote a letter from Italy to his wife, Amy, in University City, Missouri – a suburb of St. Louis – in which he stated:

I don't think that my letters are any better than anyone else's – but thanks for the compliment.

There was usually some sort of price to pay for directly contradicting my father, but I think he was dead wrong about this and I'm hoping you'll feel similarly, once you get into these letters.

David Edward Stoliar was born on March 28, 1916, to Elia and Aline Stoliar in St. Louis. He had two older siblings, Sidney and Beulah. As a child, my dad's favorite subjects were History, English and French. He had a special fascination with airplanes and had dreams of becoming an aeronautical engineer, but his education ended with high school, because he needed to find a job – any job – to help his family during the Depression.

Amy Ruth Schwartz was born on February 9, 1920, to Henry and Stephanie Schwartz, also in St. Louis. My mom had an older brother, Joe. She had a natural flair for playing the piano – especially popular songs and Broadway tunes – and she began pursuing a career as a nurse, but gave up it up to become a wife and mother.

Although both of my parents were born into Jewish families – my father's from Russia and my mother's from Czechoslovakia – my parents were fairly secular Jews, only attending temple on the High Holy Days, and embracing the cultural and culinary elements of Jewish life – bar mitzvahs, Passover Seders, matzo ball soup, gefilte fish, and fasting on Yom Kippur – rather than evincing a deep devotion to God, the Torah, or observing the Sabbath. Neither could speak nor read Hebrew, although both spoke a little Yiddish. Our family celebrated Christmas, but it was the Christmas of Santa and Rudolph, rather than the baby Jesus and the Virgin Mary. Likewise, Easter was about dyeing eggs and nibbling at chocolate bunnies, rather than acknowledging that Christ had died and risen.

Dave and Amy dated for a couple of years, especially enjoying going to the movies and dancing at nightclubs. "Their song" was Kern & Hammerstein's *All The Things You Are* – with Cole Porter's *Begin the Beguine* a close second. They were married on January 5, 1941 in the rabbi's study of Shaare Emeth temple in St. Louis, with Chopin's *Nocturne* as their processional.

On June 29, 1942, their first daughter, Carole Frances, was born. By then, the United States had officially entered World War II and men between the ages of 18 and 45 were being drafted in massive numbers to fight the Axis Powers – Germany, Japan and Italy. For some reason, my dad was under the impression that married fathers were exempt from serving, and so, when he received his draft notice, he believed a clerical error had been made and it would all be straightened out in no time. He explained this to the officer in charge, who found it all very interesting. Then he inducted my father into the United States Army.

He barely had a chance to indulge himself in the pleasures of being a doting father before Uncle Sam whisked him away from his young wife and baby daughter. On January 21, 1943, off my father went to Jefferson Barracks in St. Louis and then to Leavenworth, Kansas. From there, he was sent to St. Petersburg and Clearwater, Florida for Basic Training.

(I should clarify that this David Stoliar was *not* the same David Stoliar who was a Romanian refugee and the sole survivor of the sinking of the *Struma*, which was attacked in the Black Sea by a Soviet sub in 1942 en route to Palestine. As far as I know, the two David Stoliars were not related.)

My dad had something of a strained relationship with his parents, who divorced in the early '40s – a rarity at the time. He felt much more of a kinship with my mother's parents, who moved in with my mom and Carole when they purchased a house on Cornell Avenue in University City in 1944. Henry Schwartz took his new son-in-law under his wing and hired him to work at his women's clothing

store – Henry Schwartz & Co. – in downtown St. Louis, where
Joe Schwartz also worked. In a letter written on May 9 of 1943 –
some months before being shipped overseas – my father wrote to
Stephanie and Henry Schwartz – whom he addressed as "Mother
& Dad":

*I've never really told you both how much good fortune I've had in
becoming your son-in-law. You both have treated me better than my
own parents have ever tried. I can only say that I do appreciate it, and
hope that I can make our Amy as happy as you both would like to see her.*

Not surprisingly, the letters contain far more references to my
mom's parents than to his own.

In the spring of 1943, my dad was sent to Camp Pinedale in
Fresno, California for further training and maneuvers. He was
assigned to the Signal Corps and, because he had experience
ordering and distributing wholesale materials at Henry Schwartz
& Co., he was put into the Supply Section, where he was soon
promoted to Staff Sergeant. At first, he gave serious thought to
becoming an officer, but his eventual experiences dealing with the
brass – including helping to court martial his superior officer –
gradually eroded his desire to climb that particular ladder.

Because my dad was going to be stationed in California for a
number of months, he and my mom felt it was worth the money and
the hassle for her and Carole to head west for Fresno and rent an
apartment, until such time as he was alerted to be shipped overseas.
This was a fairly idyllic, if relatively brief, period for the three of
them, because they were able to spend quality time together – after
months of Basic Training separation – and they even found time
to visit fabled Hollywood, where they indulged in such glamorous
pastimes as dancing to Freddy Martin's Orchestra at the Cocoanut
Grove and dining at the Brown Derby.

In the fall of 1943, my dad was informed that he would soon be
sent from Fresno to Hampton Roads, Virginia to await shipment to
the European Theatre of Operations. Consequently, my mom took
baby Carole back to University City and set to work trying to find
a house to move into where she could eventually welcome home
her war-weary husband, as well her parents and any prospective
siblings for Carole Frances.

Although my parents exchanged some letters while my dad was still in the States, they were able to enjoy frequent phone calls – especially on Sundays, when the long-distance rates were cheaper – and a precious few furloughs home – plus that extended stretch together in Fresno – so my mother didn't begin collating my dad's letters into 3-ring binders until he was in Hampton Roads, about to depart for destinations unknown, for a similarly unknown length of time. Consequently, the letters in this book begin with the first letter he wrote her from Hampton Roads on January 5, 1944 – which happened to be their third anniversary.

In order to keep their connection as uninterrupted as possible, my parents vowed to write to each other every day, no matter what. In that way, they would have a sort of ongoing "conversation" that would begin when he departed American soil and end when he returned – whenever that might be. He wasn't able to save my mother's letters for two understandable reasons: 1) Soldiers were not supposed to keep letters from home, because they were uncensored and might contain information that could be useful to the enemy if they fell into the wrong hands and 2) My dad would've had to schlep a big duffel bag stuffed with my mom's letters all over Europe. As a result, we "only" have my father's responses, but because he is so meticulous in his reportage, he takes the time to address specific questions and comments from my mom, and so we get a fairly good idea of what she is asking or telling him in her letters.

About a third of my dad's letters are handwritten, the rest typed, because he had access to a typewriter due to his issuing of endless requisitions. There are also several V (for Victory) mails – hand-written letters that the military photographed and shrank down to a much smaller size in order fit more letters into mail shipments. Except for those few V-mails, none of my father's letters is a single page in length. Some take up quite a few pages – especially on those occasions when he is unable to write for a day or two and feels he has to make up for not having written (as well as asking my mom for her forgiveness). The letters span from early January of 1944 until mid-November of 1945. As a result, there are over five hundred letters totaling over two thousand pages – single-spaced.

This posed rather a challenge when it came to assembling this book. I realized that including every letter – in its entirety – was a fool's errand that would result in a gargantuan volume jam-packed with endless references to St. Louis friends, my mom's card group, distant relatives, and any number of other expansively delineated pieces of information that I felt would be of little, if any, interest to precious few, if any, readers. I also realized that I couldn't even begin to think about what would or wouldn't "make the cut" until I had dutifully "input" *all* of his letters into my desktop Mac. This task required months of diligent, daily typing, handwriting deciphering, and using context to figure out what words had been obliterated by the punch holes and white, circular reinforcements that my mother used when she put the letters into the three-ring binders. (That's not counting words and phrases that the military censors literally cut out of the pages.) Only after I had created a massive, comprehensive Word file could I begin to read through the letters with an eye toward what would make for a book of reasonable length. In most cases, I left out substantial portions of a letter, keeping only those parts that, I felt, made for interesting reading. In many cases, I left out entire letters. What follows, then, are more along the lines of "*Selected* Letters of David E. Stoliar," rather than a comprehensive compendium.

In addition to his granular descriptions of day-to-day army life overseas and the progress (or setbacks) of an ongoing world war – including contemporaneous contemplations on D-Day, the death of FDR, and the atomic bombing of Japan – there are a number of "sub-threads" that I wanted to follow as my dad writes faithfully to my mom from various war-torn cities and countries. One is his frustration with trying to co-parent a baby girl from five thousand miles away. Another is how often he sees movies or hears songs that rocket him back to happier days with my mom – which only fuel the acute homesickness he already feels. Still another is my father's positively uncanny knack for running into people he knows from St. Louis, no matter where in the world he happens to be. There's also his passion for the Cardinals who, in 1944, are doing quite well in the pennant race, as is the other St. Louis baseball team, the Browns. Another sub-thread is my dad's tendency to meet, get to know, and help out strangers he encounters along this long and winding road from war to peace.

My father is also very concerned about where his sister Beulah's sailor husband, Paul, might be sent in the Pacific, as well as whether or not my mother's older brother, Joe, was going to be drafted or if he would be able to continue working at Henry Schwartz & Co. Both families had young children.

There are also his shifting (mis)calculations on how long he expects the war in Europe to last. It's a little amusing – and a little heartbreaking – to see how many letters contain some form of, *"I'm confident this will all be over soon,"* or *"I can now predict I'll be home by Christmas,"* having no way of knowing that he still has another full year overseas ahead of him. I'm also intrigued by his experiences and observations about Judaism and anti-Semitism – not just as it pertains to Nazi atrocities, but in other countries as well, including the U.S. Likewise, there is his ongoing fear that, even after the war against the Nazis is won, he will be sent to fight the Japanese in the Pacific.

I also find it interesting to follow the progress of the war from the perspective of a Supply Sergeant rather than, say, an infantryman. For instance, I'd never stopped to realize that even though tanks are massive, durable, war machines, they instantly become useless hunks of steel if they run out of gas and you can't bring more petrol to them. You also get the point of view of someone who is literally and figuratively "the adult in the room," because he is pushing thirty, while most of the men under him are in their early twenties and, at that age, there's a substantial difference in maturity. Additionally, my dad had a very strong work ethic and was frustrated when others didn't share his dedication to the tasks at hand. Also, his prematurely receding hairline probably contributed to "the boys" referring to him as "The Old Man."

We also follow my dad's adventures with two adopted dogs at different points along the way. These furry friends provide him with literal and much-needed creature comforts and enjoyable distractions from the war, in the absence of his wife and baby. One of them even upstages a Bob Hope USO show.

And then there's the title of this book.

For the record, "Salamis" does not refer to the decisive naval battle between the Greeks and the Persians in 480 B.C. It is, rather, the plural of "salami." It was common practice for soldiers overseas to write home for some special snack or treat they were craving that wasn't part of their regular rations. As I read through my dad's letters, he mentions having a hankering for such Jewish staples as kosher dill pickles and herring, but I was downright dumbstruck by the frequency with which he talks about *salamis*. In the course of his letters, he mentions them *dozens* of times. It starts with a casual request to see if maybe my mom could send him a salami, since some of the other boys are receiving them and it seems like a nice idea. He was hardly alone: New York's Katz's Deli has "Send a Salami to Your Boy in the Army!" as its longtime slogan, because the Katzes had three sons fighting overseas during the war. It becomes a real challenge for my mom – and other relatives enlisted in this Salami Brigade – to ship my dad salamis that won't rot en route from St. Louis to wherever he is stationed. Then he becomes concerned that she is using up too many precious rationed meat "points" indulging his craving and he tells her to stop – only to resume his requests a little later, because he simply *must* have them. My dad's obsession with receiving, sharing, and devouring kosher salamis is as strong a sub-thread as his increasing hatred of the Nazis – which starts out at a 10 and goes up from there – and his strong desire to see every trace of them wiped off the face of the earth, lest they ever get the chance to rise again.

This leads me to say a few words about a few words. I have a strong aversion to political correctness, but worse than that – for me – is *retroactive* political correctness; holding up long-ago comments against current trends and standards and condemning people for not thinking decades ahead to when certain words or phrases would no longer be considered acceptable. I always try to take into account historical perspective and context. It's helpful to keep in mind that during World War II, the pain and fury caused by the devastating Japanese "sneak attack" on Pearl Harbor on that date in infamy was always on the mind of every American soldier and sailor. The Japanese and the Germans were our sworn enemies who were doing everything within their power to *kill* us. American newspapers frequently had headlines about what the "Japs" were doing. This doesn't mean that anti-Asian racists ran the newspapers; it was simply common parlance during the war.

And so, my father freely indulges in what would now be considered "slurs." He, too, refers to the Japanese as "Japs" and "Nips," as well as "slant-eyed bastards;" and to the Nazis as "Jerries" (originally British slang dating back to World War One), "Nazi bastards," and "Heinies" (which also means "buttocks"). He has nothing but hateful things to say about the Japanese and German people who allowed their leaders to rise to power and wage war against us. I do not think that makes my father a racist. Likewise, my dad refers to African-Americans as "Negroes" or "colored" and to Poles as "Pollacks." Again – common, acceptable labels of the era, not "hate speech." Consequently, I have made no efforts to sanitize my father's language, despite the potential discomfort it might cause some readers. I have left his words as he wrote them, for better or for worse.

In terms of annotations, I have added, in [brackets], brief comments and explanations of who other friends and family members are, as well as providing the full names of military leaders, politicians, and personalities that my dad mentions, in case you wish to Google them and learn more. Any words or comments in (parentheses) are my father's own doing.

Beyond those brief explanations, I really should let my dad speak for himself.

1. U.S. &
NORTH AFRICA

1/5/44
[Hampton Roads, Virginia]

Dearest Wife & Baby,

I guess this is about the worst way a couple could possibly spend an anniversary. Darling, we certainly have been separated enough in our 3 years of married life. I guess we were really lucky that we tried to crowd all of our traveling into one big splurge in Michigan. We were together almost 24 hours a day and then we were separated. In St. Louis, I made my frequent business trips, also separating us. Now, our country is the responsible party and we are once more apart. All in all, we really have had a most eventful marriage so far. Gee, Darling, you certainly have had your hands full with you having to carry all the worries alone. I'm glad that we have Carole Frances to help to relieve you and take your mind off your worries. That alone, I guess, is enough to be thankful for our separations.

I suppose you realize that I can't say as much as I'd like to in this letter. It will be censored and all mail coming to us will be censored once we are out of this country. The one thing that I can tell you about this place is that it really is terrifically terrible. To top it off, we have had nothing but a drizzling rain since we arrived. Incidentally, there are a lot of Italian prisoners here and some of the boys here speak with them and we really have a picnic.

Well, dearest, once more – thanks for a very happy three years of married life – regards to all and lots of love & kisses to you and Carole Frances –

With All My Love,
Your Dave

1/8/44 7:25 P.M.
[Hampton Roads, Virginia]

My Dearest Wife & Baby,

I was pleasantly surprised to get my call thru last nite before 12:00. It so happened that I fell asleep and awoke in time to hear my name being called over the P.A. system, calling me to a certain phone booth. I suppose that I did sound rather blue when I spoke to you, but I guess I really was in that mood. This really is a most desolate place and not very cheery. I mailed your anniversary gift special delivery airmail, so let me know if you don't receive the money. Gosh, how cute the baby must be by now. I hope that my call last nite didn't awaken her. You asked me to phone you as often as possible and to phone Sunday morning if possible. That is exactly it – if possible.

Well, darling, I don't know when you will receive this, but send regards to all – love and kisses to Carole Frances and you –

With All My Love,
Your Dave

———

January 31, 1944 [V-mail]
[North Africa]

Dear Amy & Carole Frances,

I finally got across safely and landed in Africa. I hope that this will relieve the tension and strain that you must have been under for the past four weeks. I'm feeling fine and am in good shape. How is our pretty daughter getting along these days? Gee, I certainly would like to see you and her, but not over here. I do miss you so, but don't wish that you were here. Just keep that old chin up and I will be home soon and we will live happily ever after. As you probably realize, I cannot say as much as I would like to, but there will be time for that. So, until a little later, I'll close, with all my love –

Your loving husband and dad,
Dave
P.S. I LOVE YOU VERY MUCH!!!

———

January [CENSORED] *, 1944*
[North Africa]

Dearest Wife & Baby,

We have arrived at some North African port. As you probably know, I can't tell you the exact location, so let's let it go at that. I just found out that only letters that are written on one side of the paper will be accepted. All thru the trip, I had been writing and had 8 pages written on both sides before this discovery came up. I was trying to save on the weight of the airmail letter by writing on both sides. Anyway, I am in good health and feeling fine – except for a nice case of lonesomeness (or loneliness – if you prefer). I reminisced all thru the trip about our courting days – engagement – marriage – honeymoon – travels – and Carole Frances. Gee, we really have had a lot of action, haven't we?

You know, Dearest, that being unable to describe makes it hard to make this a very newsy letter. I can only say that I only hope that all other vessels and men coming over here have as little trouble as we. We had a couple of jukeboxes, or rather record players, on board to keep up that ole "morale." We had records of Tommy Dorsey – Jimmy Dorsey – Artie Shaw and Orrin Tucker. Orrin's were the best.

Well, Angels, I'll close this so that I can get it on the first outgoing mail today. Give my love to all and tell them that I'm thinking of them. For yourself, keep my special, personal love and split it with the baby. Just be patient and just as soon as I can write a more detailed letter, you shall receive it. Meanwhile, if I can't buy a birthday gift for you by the next few days – congratulations and lots of kisses. Also, kiss the baby for passing her 17-month-old birthday. Gee, she's getting to be an old maid already. So – lots of love –

Your loving husband and da-da,

Dave

February 3, 1944
Somewhere in North Africa

Dearest Wife & Baby,

I don't know how many of my letters you have received, so once more I'll say that I am in a port on the North African coast. That is about all the information that I can give you right now. I'm feeling fine and expect to remain that way. Of course, I'm quite lonesome for my family and friends. It is hard to believe that I'm in a foreign land. The buildings all look modern and new (from the outside & far away), but they are just the opposite. The walls about to collapse and the roofs with holes in them. At the present moment, I am writing this by candlelight, in our tent. Right now is the time of the evening when the nite begins to get cold. By 4 in the morning you are freezing. On the other hand, in the afternoon, you just about sweat to death (well, maybe I am exaggerating).

Today we were playing baseball and one of the native boys came up. He was small and ten years old. He was dressed very raggedly and also unwashed. He had on an Army jacket which he must have stolen from somebody. He pulled out 2 pairs of dice and asked us if we wanted to shoot crap. He knew all about the game and when I saw how dirty he was I told him to go away. He called me every name under the sun – could cuss better than an old salt. It was really amazing!!! Well, it seems that the only words that the natives pick up are from the G.I.'s and they usually are cuss-words, unfortunately.

The soldiers really know that they are better off if they stay away from the women. Some of the fellows went to the city today and said that it really is disgusting. Some of the people (quite a percentage, too) are diseased. You see, while under German occupation, just about everything was taken from them and they just about starved. Now, when one walks along the street, the natives from 6 to 60 follow for blocks begging just for a cigarette. The natives teach their children to beg when they first begin to walk. Well, syphilis and gonorrhea are quite prevalent, and we know that one wrong step could just about ruin the whole outfit. I'm content to wait till after this whole thing is over before I have another "party." I know that the feeling is mutual. One of the boys received a letter from his sweetheart telling him that she had married another. Boy! Was he in a daze! You can realize just how these boys feel now. Well, anyway, I'm looking forward to seeing my beautiful family. By the way, one of the Jewish boys who was in town told me that there is a whole colony of Jewish prostitutes there – off limits. Well, I can't believe it until I see it and I probably won't see it. They are all supposed to be refugees from France, Poland, Russia and other European countries – almost unbelievable, isn't it?

Well, Darlings, that's about all the news for now – Oh, yes, I do love you and miss you so very much. It's not that I forgot it either, because everything I see that is new to me, I wonder what Amy and Carole Frances would think about it. Well, some day, in peacetime, we may come here and you can see for yourself. Until later – I send love & regards to those who deserve it – keep my true love and kisses for you and the baby.

With All My Love,
Your Dave

Feb 5, 1944
Still Somewhere in North Africa

My Dearest Wife & Baby,

We haven't gotten paid yet, but I went to town anyway just for the curiosity of it all. It was totally disgusting! The natives run around begging all the time. The refugees are all right. The streets and buildings are dingy and dirty – most unsanitary conditions prevail throughout the town. That's why the camps are outside the town. We did go to a few bars that are recommended by the U.S. authorities. One place was rather modern and had a French "swing band" of 3 pieces. You should have heard them play "Pistol-Packin' Mama!" We had appetizers of cabbage, onions, olives and herring. Then for the entrée, we had egg omelettes and fried noodles. We had real French brown wheat bread, too. To top that off, we had a large bottle of champagne between all four of us fellows. It was probably brewed last year, because most of your old champagnes were confiscated a few years ago for use on the continent. After that, we went to "Joe's Place" – a popular place for the G.I.'s - and had beer. Then we bought a few bottles of cognac at another place and sneaked them into camp. It's really potent stuff – but I haven't gotten drunk yet, so I won't start now. When we got ready to leave, we picked up the 3 lieutenants in front of the Officers Club – pickled to the gills. Don't tell Mary Rodger that, because she may not like the idea – also Lt. Rodger may not like it when he censors this. Anyway, the 3 were like a big, carefree brawl – and did they cuss!

Well, Darling, needless to say that I do miss you and the baby and love you very much – that's about the dope for now – regards to all –

With All My Love,
Your Dave

Feb 7 – 44
Still Somewhere in North Africa

Dearest Wife & Baby,

In the evening, [Sgt.] Fay asked me if I wanted to go to the show at a nearby village. About 30 of us went and saw "The Iron Major" with Pat O'Brien. It wasn't a bad picture at all – except that at times it made me very blue and reminded me of home. It was about the life of Frank Cavanaugh, a football coach. He thought along the same lines as I did about getting into the War and it sort of hit home. He also "bitched" about everything after he got into it, but he also came thru OK in spite of many obstacles. He left his wife with six children while I left my wife with one baby – but the conditions were very parallel. Well, when we got back to our tent, I got out the record player and played some of Glenn Miller's records. They also had "St. Louis Blues" by Ginny Simms. Gee, how I'd like to have been back for a moment. Well, we all get that "ole feeling," but try to work it off. I hope that I haven't made you feel too badly by speaking of my mental attitude. We were told that it was OK to say that we visited Oran, Algeria – so we did. That's all that I can say about it for the moment. It certainly gets hotter than hell here in the afternoon and cold as Fresno at nite – perhaps colder.

There has been a 15-minute lapse since the above – We had a slight fire in the mess tent. The burner from one of the stoves blew up and gasoline sprayed all around, including on the legs of one of the KP's. He ran outside, all excited. One of the fellows who happened to be on hand caught hold of him and threw him to the ground and smothered the flames. They found that he had suffered 1st degree burns and is OK. Most of the company ran up there with helmets (to carry water) but found that the flames were already extinguished. Luckily, it wasn't one of the men in our company.

I was happy to learn that Paul and Beulah had such a great time while he was home on leave. I guess it was pretty hard for Beulah when his time came to leave. Well, we can appreciate both their feelings – can't we? So, until later, give my regards to all and keep the love and kisses for the baby and yourself –

With All My Love,
Your Dave

—

Feb 9 – 44
Still Somewhere in North Africa

My Dearest Wife,

First of all, let me wish you a happiest birthday. I guess you know that I'd certainly like to be there celebrating the occasion with you. This is the second successive birthday of yours that we have spent apart – Let's hope that there will be no more. I am going to enclose a money order for you to spend for your birthday gift – so don't put it in the bank. You know that I'll be sore if you don't buy a gift, so do as I ask. I have kept a bottle of champagne in my tent for this day, so I'll open it and drink to your health and happiness just the same. I'll ask everybody to drop in for a "wee nippy" – as long as the bottle lasts.

So far, I haven't run into Bing Crosby or Bob Hope out here – which road are they on now? I did stop in at the Red Cross Headquarters and see a print of "Sahara," with Humphrey Bogart. We saw it together, back in St. Louis – remember?

Well, Darling, I don't know what else to tell you that could go uncensored, so stay well and take good care of the baby and yourself – give regards to all –

With All My Love,

Your Dave

P.S. I just received your V-mail letter of the 22nd and I certainly was surprised to get it. I had just returned from town where I had been going thru the routine red tape in order to obtain supplies. One could be dying from loss of blood and you couldn't get one ounce unless you had a bona fide requisition signed by all the proper authorities in the right place and at the right time. According to your letter, the baby's nose had been running. It's the first that I have heard of it and am glad it is improved, but sorry that I hadn't known about it earlier. Of course, I couldn't have done much about it, except pray to God to protect her and I do that every nite. So let's wish & pray that she is well by the time this letter is completed.

Well, by now, both you and Mary Rodger have heard that we've landed, so that question is answered. Now if only everybody would stay well for the duration, it would be fine – All we'd have to do is worry about getting this thing over and returning home. That's about all the dope for now – so kiss the baby for me & tell her to get well & stay that way –

Love,

Dave

Feb 11 – 44
Still Somewhere in North Africa

My Dearest Wife & Baby,

Here is another day gone by and a little closer to Victory and home. Just as the French signs read, "Un Seul Fin: La Victoire – General Giraud." After all, Victory is primary now so that we may be able to return to our former lives. It hasn't been too uncomfortable for us so far – we've adapted ourselves very well and are taking all inconveniences into consideration. Oh, we may not be able to get all the chocolates, candy, gum, wristwatches, fountain pens, and just about everything that you civilians are unable to get – so we adjust ourselves accordingly. Mostly, the boys are asking their folks back home to send them some chocolate, but I've got enough to last me awhile as I had bought quite a bit in the States, before leaving.

How is Carole Frances now? Hope that her cold is gone long ago! Gee, I certainly hate to think of a baby, especially our own, being ill. I know that she's getting the best care in the world, but colds are one thing that have baffled the world so far, and I can't help it any by asking "How in the world did she ever catch it?" Just pray that God protects her and yourself and we'll all be satisfied. Now let's get back on the road to Berlin and Tokyo and I'll be home soon.

I bought a native bracelet and am now looking for tissue to wrap it in. It's a little late to wish you a "Happy Valentine's Day," so I'll ask you to accept this little bracelet as my gift – if you'll be my valentine. If you refuse to be my valentine – please return the bracelet – parcel post prepaid. By the way, they are showing two good pictures in town tonite – "Mrs. Miniver" and "Air Force" – Want to go? Just catch a plane and I'll hold the nite open. It won't be long before we will actually be saying that.

Well, Darlings, that's about all of the dope for today and yesterday, so I send regards to all and keep lots of love and kisses for you and the baby –
With All My Love,
Your Dave

———

18 February – 44
Still Somewhere in North Africa

My Dearest Wife & Baby,

It rained intermittently all day. Boy! Does it get cold when that sun goes out. It is sort of muddy around here, but after a few sloshy days of it, you get used to it. We pass the time by playing ball, bridge or poker. In bridge, we have Lt. [Walter A.] *Maddox (a fairly good player), Lt. Micka, Lt. Rodger, Sgt. Mullen (1st Sgt.) and myself. It seems that out of our whole company, these are the only ones who know a little about the game. I played poker this evening, for a change, and I won about $15.00 in a 5-10-15 cent game – Not bad, eh?*

You know, Darling, it is a very funny sight to see the natives running all over this country with their little asses. Naturally, I mean that species of the mule family which is small in stature. These animals draw everything from a load of straw to about a 5-ton load in a tiny cart – very quaint. If only I could send you some pictures of the native people and their typical native costumes – you'd really appreciate it.

It is needless to say that I love you and miss you so very much – but that is precisely the condition that exists. Do something about it – I love you. Swipe a B-17 and fly over with the baby. You can readily see that I am slowly going nuts when I get ideas like that. Well, sweetheart, keep well and regards to all – lots of love & kisses to both of you –

With All My Love,
Your Dave

———

22 February – 44
Still Somewhere in North Africa

My Dearest Wife & Baby,

As to you writing a letter while the President was speaking – that's an insult. And not to be fully attired is doubly so. You ought to be ashamed of yourself. What if he knew that such was the case? Why, he'd probably fire me from my job – I hope! I thought that you knew that Lt. Rodger was the censoring officer – even when you were in Fresno. Anyway, as you can plainly see from my letters, I haven't failed to express my feelings anyway. Of course, he probably did show a little more lenience toward my letters – but I still have not imparted any information that may prove dangerous to me.

Today, I had one hectic day in trying to locate various supply warehouses in the area we're in. You really have to be psychic to find the places. It gets to a point where you are ready to raise all kinds of hell. Luckily, we have a newspaper, which can be obtained in town. It is the "Stars & Stripes," of which you may have heard. It's really right on the beam and up to the minute as far as details on the battlefronts go. They sometimes have "Li'l Abner" or a comic strip drawn by the same artist who draws "Terry & The Pirates." This last named strip ["Male Call"] is really quite popular with the G.I.'s because of the main reason – voluptuous women! Of course, I just open your picture when I want to think about a beautiful woman.

Well, Darling, give my regards to all – keep love and kisses for yourselves.
With All My Love,
Your Dave

———

23 Feb – 44
Still Somewhere in North Africa

My Dearest Wife & Baby,

Today, I received your airmail of January 13th and boy do I appreciate it. I don't know if you realized it, but you must have kept the stationery in the same drawer as your "Toujours Moi." When I opened the envelope, I really started feeling homesick at that elegant odor. If you did it purposely, I do thank you for it – it's swell.

As to any new songs, I haven't heard any radio programs since we left California. The music we do hear is off the records we have – and they aren't too up-to-date. We have radio programs recorded also – but they are of the 1942 vintage. However, even the old songs sound wonderful. For instance, we just finished listening to a program that had Bob Burns and Ginny Simms on it. Along with it was the feature – a dramatization of "Pride of the Yankees" (life of Lou Gehrig) – with Gary Cooper and Walter Brennan and Teresa Wright. Ginny Simms sang "All The Things You Are" – Remember how crazy we were about that song? At this moment, we're listening to a Bob Hope recording at Camp San Luis Obispo in California.

Well, Darling, in the next couple of days, I'll get my first decorations. We are entitled to wear service ribbons for the European-Middle Eastern-African Campaigns. On top of that, seventeen of us are eligible for the Good Conduct Medal (a bar, also) and I'll be among them. As to the kisses on letters, we're not allowed to put any strange marks on mail – so that's the reason for the absence of them. I do send a lot of them, however, and lots of love to you and Carole Frances – regards to all –

With All My Love,
Your Dave

———

25 Feb – 44
Still Somewhere in North Africa

My Dearest Wife & Baby,

I was pleasantly surprised with the two airmail letters from you of the 17th and 18th. That's the best service yet on any mail. You were raving that my mail got to you in 8 days – yours came over in 7 – That's really something. Now we can really correspond with some subjects that are not too old and forgone. I don't know what sort of package you sent – but thanks a million for it. No doubt, it has those cookies with Nestle's chips in them.

However, please don't send any more gum or Lifesavers – We get plenty over here – probably more than you civilians get.

Darlings, it may be a far guess – but we might be stationed in the African area for the duration and six months. That would mean that we'd have very little chance of ever seeing any action and will, without a doubt, all come back in good shape. Your mention of that transport going down with 1,000 aboard was the first that I heard of it. Yes, it was a great disaster – the biggest single loss yet. I, too, am glad that we're on terra firma.

There was another movie across the road so I decided to attend with some of the fellows. We brought along wood boxes so that we could be "comfortably" seated. The picture was "Bomber's Moon" with George Montgomery and Annabella. It was a fair picture – lovely class B. However, it was a movie and that is important. These movies are free so the American soldiers and Italian prisoners all sit together and enjoy it. It's really amazing when you try to realize that there is still a War on and that we are still fighting thousands of Italians in Northern Italy.

Well, sweetheart, that's about all the dope for now – send regards to all – lots of love and kisses to Carole Frances and you.

With All My Love,
Your Dave

———

28 February – 44
Still Somewhere in North Africa

My Dearest Wife & Baby,

Sorry that I didn't write yesterday, because I went into town for a change. Fay and I went together. It was a sunny day for a change and I didn't want to waste it sitting in a tent. We went first to the Red Cross Empire Club, where Fay learned that there was a Lutheran Church in town. He went there for the first time in quite a while. I didn't go in because I'd be out of place. We went to a popular restaurant where we had a meatball and spaghetti dinner. It was really lousy, but nothing in the way of food is any good in this area. We had a few beers to cover up the food and then went to a theatre to see "Across the Pacific" with Bogart & Astor. Unfortunately, the picture didn't begin until 9:00 P.M., so it would be too late for us to see it. Therefore, we went to the Red Cross Theatre and saw most of "Flesh & Fantasy," which wasn't bad. We saw the end and then saw the beginning up to where Charles Boyer refuses to do his jump to the wire 10 feet below *the high one. If you saw the picture, then you'd be able to tell me if I missed anything. After that, we left and hit for "home" – if you can call it that. We had a quiet nite for a change – no wind or rain. But this was too much, because this morning we're having rain and wind and a lot of it. It's pretty cold and we do make use of our woolens.*

Regards to all – lots of love & kisses to Carole Frances –
With All My Love,
Your Dave

———

2 March – 1944
Still Somewhere in North Africa

My Dearest Wife & Baby,

Well, today I was in town and decided to try to locate [St. Louis friend] *Baron Levy. I went to the barracks, then went upstairs and looked in all the rooms, from the balcony. I stopped at the second window when I saw a three-handed game of gin going on. Directly in front of me sat Baron. He looked up at me and stared blankly – then returned back to his cards. About 15 seconds later, he looked up again and you should have seen his lower jaw drop about 4 feet off his face. Well, we sat outside on the balcony and just chewed the fat. I think that he and* [St. Louis friend] *Henry Schlesinger are going out soon with a couple of French Jewesses who are working at the PX at their base.*

If you don't receive any mail for a little while, don't get alarmed. We may ship to another area, but we'll be quite safe and away from harm. I can't tell you where we may go, because we don't know definitely as yet. I can assure you that I'll write just as often as possible, however. So don't be too pessimistic, as you usually are, and think that we're going right up to the front – we are positively not! So keep up your good spirits and remember that I'll be safe and thinking always of you.

This letter was written on the second, but was given back to me today, because I had given out too much information, therefore, I'll just add to it as my letter of the 3rd. We've had beautiful weather the last couple of days. In fact, so good that the rest of the company has been playing ball all day – taking advantage of the weather now, because it will probably get worse. Yesterday, the Radio Section's team played the Teletype Section and Lt. Rodger's protégées lost.

Well, Darling, that's about it for now – so keep that ole chin up and take good care of everybody. I'm looking forward to a helluva big time when we all get together again – and it won't be too long. So say "Hello" to everybody and keep lots of love and kisses for you and Carole Frances –
With All My Love,
Your Dave

———

4 March – 44
Still Somewhere in North Africa

My Dearest Wife & Baby,
    Here it is another week gone and no mail from you in 8 days. I console myself with the idea that the weather is unfavorable for flying between St. Louis and New York. I certainly hope that there is nothing wrong at home to delay your writing. God forbid that there is anything wrong. I'll wait one more day and if no mail, I'm going to try to cable. I may not be here to receive the answer, but I'll get it sometime and be enlightened a little. I hope that you received my Easter card – I didn't have anything to do at the time and decided to try to draw for a change. I don't know what you think of it – but after all, I'm not a Walt Disney. Anyway, I do wish all of you a very happy Easter!
    You know, it certainly is funny – but every time that our company has started to beautify the area, we have had to move. Now we have fixed up this area and we will probably leave soon. Boy, if only the duration of the War depends on our beautification of areas – we'd work like dogs and be home tomorrow. Well, Darling, give my love and regards to all – keep lots & lots of love and kisses for yourself and Carole Frances –
With All My Love,
Your Dave
P.S. I want to remind you that I do love you!

———

6 March – 44
Still Somewhere in North Africa

My Dearest Wife & Baby,
    I was very much disappointed in not receiving any mail from you yesterday – the 8th day in succession with no word. Well, to add to my misery, today 6 sergeants – 4 Staffs – 1 Tech – 1 Master – had K.P. It was a stunt that was cooked up last week. For 4 days, there would be a tent

inspection and the winning tent would have the privilege of selecting K.P.'s for Monday (today). I think that I fried enough hamburgers to supply all Allied Armed Forces in this theatre. Anyway, at noon, I finally received two letters from you – the 20th & 23rd. It was really a great relief to get these letters. I didn't want to cable, because I was afraid that you'd think that something was wrong somewhere.

As to a birthday gift, I guess I can't do much about refusing it. It probably has been mailed already. In spite of all I tell you, you still go ahead and buy something. That's what gets me! No, I don't imagine what it is, because I'm not in need of anything whatsoever. Oh well, I'll be patient and wait to thank you so very much. You probably know that I'd much rather be there in person to show you my gratitude.

That was a very interesting postscript that Carole Frances added. Of course, it was far above me, but someday I hope to be able to understand it. Gosh – what a pair – my wife & baby – I'm pretty lucky. Darling, does she still write on the blackboard and erase? Hold her doll over the toilet? Has she added the word "encyclopedia" to her vocabulary yet? Well, I guess that's the dope for today – just stay well and take good care of the baby and yourself for me – send regards to all – keep lots of love and kisses for the two of you –

With All My Love,
Your Dave

———

8 March – 44
Still Somewhere in North Africa

My Dearest Wife & Baby,

Well, yesterday, I was on the go all day from 8:00 in the A.M. till late in the afternoon. It was everything that dealt with Supply and morale. By morale, I mean new records, baseballs, etc. At this moment, there is a piano version of "Begin the Beguine" – It's really very inferior to yours and I told the fellows who are standing around listening to it. I'm going to hang on to this letter until after mail call, which is after noon chow. If I get mail, I'll have something to add. Oh, yes – we did stop on the road back yesterday and Lt. Rodger wanted me to get up on an old camel so that he could take a snap of me. The camel was acting up a bit and I didn't want to receive the Purple Heart for being bitten by a camel, so some other fellow got up there and the lieutenant took a picture of him instead. That animal was so dirty and flea-bitten that one couldn't tell what you could catch off of it. Right after that, I took a snap of the lieutenant with a group of native Moroccan or Algerian troops. Well, Darling, until a little later – so long.

What a mail! Your letters of the 15th-16th-25th & 26th. It certainly pays to be patient – don't you agree? It is now morning and I want to say that I really had an enjoyable time yesterday. I met Baron and two of his buddies at the Red Cross. We went to the theatre and saw "Du Barry Was A Lady" – Red Skelton & Lucille Ball. You probably have seen it already, but we certainly enjoyed it, because it was new to us. I ran into a couple of the boys from our outfit and we all looked for a nice restaurant to have dinner. We finally found one that had meatballs and spaghetti. It wasn't so bad. After that, we walked around town and had a few drinks at a few bars. We didn't get drunk, so don't be suspicious of that. We got hungry again about 7:00 and found a very pretty little café in one of the arcades.

There is a law saying that all people wishing to dine out must bring their own bread. I asked for some, but the owner insisted that he had none. A couple of French people were sitting at the next table and the man very politely cut off a piece of their bread and gave it to us. That started up a conversation that lasted until 9:00. Fortunately, he was able to understand and speak a little English so that my efforts in French were comprehensive enough. He and his wife have been married for 5 years and were in Paris before the War. He's been in the French Navy and is stationed near here now. His wife asked me what I thought of the War. I told her that, as an Xmas gift, the Allies were going to give Paris back to her by December 24th. That made her so happy and we all agreed to be there when it happened. Of course, if there is any possibility of getting home at that time, I'll just send my regrets on an Xmas card. The couple are 30 years old but don't look it. She thinks that the American women are so very beautiful and dress in good taste. To clinch that idea, I showed her the snap of you and Carole Frances. They were overwhelmed. She started to kid her husband because I had a baby almost two years old and I'm 28 – while he's 30 and doesn't have any. I kidded them and asked if he was any good – he said that his wife wasn't any good. That gave all of us a real good laugh. They asked us to meet them again at the same place the next day – we said that we'd try. We all drank a toast to each Allied Nation, but when we came to England, he wasn't so enthusiastic and told us as much. He thought that the English are not as friendly to the French as they seem and that the Americans were really the real thing.

Well, Darling, that is the news up 'til today and I hope that this letter will hit the spot. Stay well and kiss the baby for me. Give my regards to all – keep lots of love & kisses for yourself and the baby –

With All My Love,
Your Dave

———

10 March – 1944
Still Somewhere in North Africa

My Dearest Wife & Baby,

Yesterday, I went to town and looked around for some souvenirs. I was able to get a small medallion of the Star of David, which I think [Beulah & Paul's daughter] *Jackie would like. After that, I went to the Red Cross Theatre where I saw "Women in Bondage" – Gail Patrick & Nancy Kelly. I enjoyed the picture and then went to that little café where I was to meet this French Naval officer and his wife. They came in about 7:30 and we ate and drank wine until 9:00. They insisted that if we ever get to Paris, after the War, we should be sure to drop in and see them. I, of course, returned the invitation if they should be around St. Louis. The wines that we had were 11 years old and very tasty. That's something that is almost impossible to obtain here now. After all, the Vichy Gov't & Nazi officials just about ransacked all French territories.*

Gosh, how I could use a few hours with you and the baby now. The more we play these new recordings, the more homesick I get. These "new" records are "The Way You Look Tonite" – and others of that vintage. So you can readily see that everybody starts thinking about what they were doing at the time that a certain song was popular. Right now, they are playing "Embraceable You" – gosh, but you certainly are. What's new back home? Has anybody I know been inducted recently? Do you think that the Cardinals have a good chance this year? How's our great big lady, Carole Frances, doing now? Well, Darling, that's about it for today. I hope that all is well again back home. Keep well – give my regards to all – keep a helluva lot of love & kisses for yourself and the baby – They are now playing "Taps" – a nightly occurrence – so – bon soir.

With All My Love,
Your Dave

———

11 March – 44
Still Somewhere in North Africa

My Dearest Wife & Baby,

Here we are at the end of another week overseas and I finally received some mail. Your letter of the 22nd and birthday cards from my dad – your folks – and best of all, you. I was glad that Carole Frances had a hand in sending the card.

Incidentally, maybe I'll get to see Madeleine Carroll. I read in the "Stars & Stripes" that she is at the Red Cross, so maybe I'll see her today. She is an A.R.C. [American Red Cross] worker, you know.

I want you to send my best wishes for a most enjoyable Passover to everybody. I might try to get in on Purim services here. I visited the synagogue, but it wasn't open – so maybe I'll have better luck the second time. Meanwhile, say "Hello" to all – give my regards to everybody – keep loads & loads of love & kisses for yourself & the baby –

With All My Love,

Your Dave

P.S. Je t'aime tres beaucoup et ne l'oublie pas.

(I love you very much and don't forget it.)

———

12 March – 1944
Still Somewhere in North Africa

My Dearest Wife & Baby,

Yesterday, I went to the Red Cross and to my surprise, Madeleine Carroll stood me up. After all we meant to each other and she fails to show up in the afternoon. She was there in the morning, but failed to leave any message for me. Well, someday this War will be over and I won't see any more of her pictures – or if it is with Bob Hope, I'll just not look at her. That ought to hold her for a while. I thought that "Destination Tokyo" was at the Red Cross, so I went to the theatre there. Unfortunately, they had "So's Your Uncle," so I saw about 15 minutes of it and then left for the place where they were showing "D.T." Well, I got in just in time to see the last hour of it. It was very exciting and had good photography in it.

It was about time for evening chow, so I went to a nice restaurant where I was able to get a steak. Don't be alarmed – steak here is a very, very thin slice of meat, which can be mistaken for a platter. Well, I had a nice talk about pre-War France with the proprietor and he broke down in tears when

I told him that on Dec. 24th, we will all be back in Paris for Christmas. You can imagine how that touched him. I walked around to shop once more and ended up by buying a plain, flat-topped, silver ring. I figured that I'd buy it for you or for Carole Frances when she gets a little older. It is impossible to get any gold objects around here, because they have all been taken out of this country by the Vichyites and Nazis. Well, I returned to see the first part of the picture. It was touching because Cary Grant has two children in the picture and he thinks of them time & again. In fact, he tells fellow officers that his most thrilling experience of the past year was not torpedoing Axis ships, but his son sitting in his arms and saying, "That's my daddy." Gosh, how that hit home, because I know that Carole Frances would say the same now. That sort of an incident would be my big moment, too.

Give my regards to all – lots of love & kisses to you and Carole Frances –
With All My Love,
Your Dave

———

13 March – 1944
Still Somewhere in North Africa

My Dearest Wife & Baby,

Your reference to going to a show was the first inkling that I had – Lt. Rodger says that Mary & you saw "Song of Russia" – Wasn't that about the series of battles leading up to the Battle of Stalingrad? If correct, it is supposed to be one of the most thrilling pictures of all time. Last nite, I saw "Flight for Freedom," with Rosalind Russell & Fred MacMurray. It was about Amelia Earhart – if you will remember – a fair, snappy picture. I don't know if I ever told you the sort of theatre we go to – but if you want a good box seat – you have to bring along your own box, or stand. It is an outdoor theatre and many different nations attend – however, only English is spoken in the pictures.

As for an ordinary daily meal – here it is: Breakfast: Cream of Wheat, pancakes with jam, bacon, bread & butter, coffee. Noon: Steak or hamburger, onion gravy, flaked potatoes, bread & butter, string beans, corn, sliced fruit, coffee. Evening: steak or hamburger, onion gravy, sweet potatoes, peas, bread & butter, tapioca, coffee. Now, of course, there are variations, but these seem to be the most popular. I don't eat but two meals a day. In fact, today was the first time I've had breakfast in about two weeks.

Well, until tomorrow, say "Hello" to all – give them my regards – keep my love & kisses for yourself & the baby, because I love both of you so very much –
With All My Love,
Your Dave
P.S. I've got to go now – figuratively & literally – Good nite!

———

14 March – 1944
Still Someone in North Africa

My Dearest Wife & Baby,
At this moment, the tent next to us has the record player and "Blue Rain" is giving out. It is very pretty, but at the same time, it brings back pretty memories when loving did come – remember? Boy, I relive each and every moment not once, but twice and three times. I guess we are about as happy as any family with our ins and outs, petty arguments, parties, and good times, etc. That's the reason for me being so definitely certain that I'm coming back, because you know that I was never the one to miss out on anything good. When we are all back together, we certainly are going to make up for lost time – n'est-ce pas?
Papers tell of Russia taking Lwow, Poland. This is so very close to Warsaw that I'm beginning to think that they will be in Berlin by Xmas for sure. When that happens, unless the Allies absolutely forbid them, the Russians may go on a murder rampage to help to make up for all those innocent Russian civilians who were murdered in cold blood. Well, I don't know if I'm getting cold-hearted or not, but I hope that they do exactly that. It might leave such an impression that the remaining Germans may never ever even think about War again. As you probably know, it is still the Junkers [aristocrats] who bring these wars about and until they can be eliminated, War is bound to return within 50 years. You can easily see how moody I am today – drifting from pretty memories to War. You always did say that I was temperamental. Is Carole Frances also the same? No, I guess she's just a darned good kid full of natural mischief. She'll outgrow it, I'm sure. Well, Darling, that's all for today – sorry it wasn't so very newsy – regards to all – lots of love & kisses for you and Carole Frances –
With All My Love,
Your Dave

———

17 March – 1944
Still Somewhere in North Africa

My Dearest Wife & Baby,

   Last nite, one of the sergeants came into the tent looking for me while I was in the latrine. I came in just after he left and undressed & hit the hay. About 10 minutes later, he came back & said that Lt. Maddox was inquiring about me & I should bring a light into the tent next door – where the lieutenant was. I got up and dressed & brought in a bright light that awoke him. He said that he'd see me in the morning. This morning, he called me in and told me that I was 55 minutes late (he looked at his watch last nite at that time when I went into his tent). I didn't want to argue the difference of 25 minutes, so he spoke to me awhile and then told me that from now on, I'll have to catch the pass truck in every time I go out. You know, if I was a continuous law-breaker, it would probably be the correct thing – but it was the very first time that I have ever gone outside the rules set down in the company. All the while, this sergeant, who was in looking for me, has broken not only company rules, but rules of the Military Police in this area. Absolutely nothing has been done to him. You can see what sort of an effect this sort of thing has on the men. They are reprimanded for things that are more minor than those that this sergeant has done, and he goes scott-free. Well, I'll just forget about it and remember that this thing will be over someday and certain things will not have to be contended with.

   It was certainly a grand ole feeling to read the "St. Louis Post-Dispatch" again. It made me forget that I was even away from the U.S. and made me feel as tho there wasn't even a War on. All those advertisements made me feel lonesome, however. Well, Darling, just to remind you that I love you and miss you very much – Kiss the baby for me and tell her that daddy will be coming home soon. Give my regards to everybody and tell them to keep up the good work back home –

   With All My Love,
   Your Dave

———

18 March – 1944
Still Somewhere in North Africa

My Dearest Wife & Baby,

   Lt. Rodger is sitting here at this moment and I have mentioned some of the things in your letter pertaining to Mary. We still kid each other about the mail situation. If I don't receive mail for some time, he says that it's because you are going out with some other guys and don't have time to write. I tell him the same when the situation is reversed. However, at this time, we are both even. As to the Tollhouse cookies, don't go to any trouble to prepare & ship any. It would only make a mess and the maid would have to clean it up. If there happen to be any around, just "swipe" a few and bundle them off to me.

The lieutenant just left for his rendezvous with Morpheus. I should be there, too, but I want to finish this letter. When I told everybody about Carole's dancing & nail-filing, they were amazed. Has she asked you the secrets of the facts of life? I'll bet that she's going out on dates now – after you put her to bed.

Well, Darling, give my regards to all – keep lots of love & kisses for yourself & Carole Frances –

With All My Love,

Your Dave

———

20 March – 1944

Still Somewhere in North Africa

My Dearest Wife & Baby,

Darling, here I am, 5,000 miles from the States, and you, very mildly, write, "I went to the Chase last night...with Syd Blumenthal." Well, I guess that you have always thought that I'm a broad-minded person – well, sometimes I am. However, you write absolutely nothing to explain why you accepted the date or anything else. Just what in the world prompted you to do that? Certainly, if I ran into a friend of yours over here and took her out dining & dancing, you wouldn't care for the idea either – would you? Sure, Blu is a longtime friend of mine, but I certainly don't relish him taking my wife out while I'm not around. How do you suppose I feel when I read that you had a most enjoyable evening at the Chase with somebody else? Don't you even think that perhaps I long to be back in St. Louis and taking you out? I realize that you'll probably cry when you read this, but it's just as hard to write it – if not harder. You repeatedly write me to let you know everything – Well, that's it right now. I've been waiting since noon (when I received this letter) to let off steam and here it is. I hope that I calm down by tomorrow morning. Oh, I could go out and get lit, but who would I be hurting? No, I've done absolutely nothing out of the way since we've been apart. If you hadn't told me about this date, it would have been better. I'm surprised that your folks said it was OK to go out.

Well, at this moment, my pulse has slackened, because I have read & reread this up 'til this point. If I did cause you to cry, I'm sorry, but please think of this in the future. I'm sure that if you had weighed everything, it probably wouldn't have happened. You don't know one-half of the anguish one goes thru waiting for a nice letter from home, and then to have to swallow something like that. Now please, Darling, don't let anything like that happen again. I'm sure that you, Mary, Bertie, and a few others are able to find a means of recreation other than what I have just written about.

Well, I hope that this finds you, Carole Frances, and everybody else well and enjoying good weather. I'll probably sleep this feeling off, so please do the same after reading this. I'll take your advice of your letter of the 10th and stay in as good spirits as I can, so give my regards to all – keep lots of love & kisses for Carole Frances and yourself –

With All My Love,
Your Dave

———

21 March – 1944
Still Somewhere in North Africa

My Dearest Wife & Baby,

Glad that you received my little Easter message in time. No, there was no other meaning intended than just a greeting. If you want to interpret it fully – It has various things for which Africa is noted – except a rabbit – they don't live here. That why I said – "Don't know what I'm doing here" – which pertains not only to the rabbit, but to me also. Catch on? Also, the rabbit is in a palm tree, which is situated about where I am now. All in all, you understood it correctly.

I just finished reading an article in the "Stars & Stripes" saying that Gen. [Lewis B.] Hershey has urged the Draft Boards to speed up the induction of papas. I never knew what they were going to do with the fathers last year – Where will they put them this year? That may be the answer to a quick ending of the War – n'est-ce pas? Today, the paper says that the Russians are almost all the way thru Bessarabia, which doesn't leave them far from the Roumanian line. Henry Ford is quoted as saying that the War will be over in two more months – That's absolutely ridiculous – He must be going crazy.

I've never told you about this before, so I hope you won't feel hurt. I was afraid to tell you, because the anxiety would probably make you very uncomfortable. Do you remember that American soldier who was married to a girl in the States, who became the father of quadruplets in England? Well – we're going to have little ones also. Now don't blame me – It must have been the moon – the stars – the air – the music - & loneliness. She isn't bad looking – she has coal-black hair, beautifully shaped legs, a little nose, and beautiful nails. When she walks, she has a feline strut. When she lies down, her legs are very pretty, and oh what teeth! Well, it's a cat! Yep, we have a cat in our tent who is about due any day. The big mystery is who is the father, because nobody has ever seen any other cat around, other than this one. I hope that didn't frighten you – I just thought that I'd exercise a little of that subtle Stoliar humor.

Well, Darling, that's about all for now, so give my best wishes to your folks & mine and many others who could be mentioned here – BUT, keep all my love for you & Carole Frances –

With All My Love,
Your Dave

—

22 March – 1944
Still Somewhere in North Africa

My Dearest Wife & Baby,

How's our great little girl doing these days? I haven't the slightest idea as to what she can do now. Of course, I know that she can imitate anyone or anything – but what does she do on her own hook? (Ouch! Those damned mosquitoes!!!) I can't wait until that picture and the snapshots arrive – perhaps I'll catch a C-47 and go back to the States and get them myself. Maybe I'm going nuts – who knows?

At this time, your mother must be getting the house in shape for Passover. How would you like to send me some fried matzos – by television, I guess. Boy, some of those dishes would certainly come in handy now. There I go, thinking about food again. Well, Darling, give my regards to all – keep lots of love & kisses for yourself & Carole Frances – Good-nite –

With All My Love,
Your Dave

—

23 March – 1944
Still Somewhere in North Africa

My Dearest Wife & Baby,

Up until yesterday, all of us were told that we were restricted to our camp because of a couple of cases of smallpox in a neighboring area. Well, after mail call, we were told that we could go out on pass and I had already put in my name that morning for one. So I took the pass and went to one of the approved places to grab a bite to eat. That evening, I went to our celebrated outdoor theatre and saw "Madame Curie." In a couple of scenes, M. Curie is shown with her children and boy, did that make me homesick. It showed one of her children about the same age as Carole Frances and I sort of felt a little lonely when I saw her. Every time I see a similar scene (such as the one in "Destination Tokyo"), I get that same old feeling. Well, I guess I'm in love with my wife & daughter – don't you agree?

Give my regards to all – keep lots of love & kisses for yourself and the baby –

With All My Love,
Your Dave

P.S. What do you think of Henry Ford's recent prediction? It's crazy – but I hope he's right.

---

24 March – 1944
Still Somewhere in North Africa

My Dearest Wife & Baby,

Today brought me one day closer to my 28th birthday and the second which I will celebrate (?) in the service of our country. The announcement came thru today that men of Jewish faith could get passes for Passover. That would give us an opportunity to go to the synagogue here and perhaps be invited to a kosher dinner by one of the families. I think that most of the men are going – I may, too.

Hope that Carole Frances and all the relatives and friends at home and especially you are well – so give them my regards and keep all my love & kisses for yourself & the baby –

With All My Love,
Your Dave

---

27 March – 1944
Still Somewhere in North Africa

My Dearest Wife & Baby,

'Twas the nite before your old man's birthday and all thru the camp not a creature was stirring – not even me. Oh, what a birthday celebration I'm having. No mail today – no nothing! The blues have been creeping up on me for a long, long time. Today it finally hit and boy, am I lonesome! I really was thinking of you and the baby all day long. We had the radio on most of the day and we heard dance music that seemed to bring back our good times at the Chase – Snack Bar – and other places. You probably have also found it hard to fight off – but those blues seem to be right there no matter what you think or do to avoid them. Fay still has a bottle of cognac, which I had given him for his birthday (earlier in the month) and so has Louie Lonigro (one of our Supply clerks). So tonite, we are celebrating my birthday and Louie's (26th) by dunking our blues in drink. I have not drunk anything in quite some time – but tonight, I want to get over that ole feeling. Tomorrow morning, I'll probably regret it, but perhaps I'll be better fitted for anticipating your long-overdue mail.

I never have written you a letter like this, but I just have to get it of my mind. I really do miss you and Carole Frances. I keep thinking of all those things that we used to do and wonder just how long it will be before we're back together, visiting all those places again. Darling, I guess instead of this being a very cheerful birthday letter – it will be just the contrary. I do want to thank you for all the birthdays we have spent together because, without a doubt, they have been the most pleasant to remember. Remember what you said to me one night in November, when you had returned from Columbia? Boy! I just about busted with pride although I didn't show it. Then, that previous Winter, when you said, "Wait 'til Spring comes –." Well, I guess all that waiting really has paid dividends – look at our bright, young daughter. So, perhaps in that line of thought, we will soon be back together – after a little longer wait.

Now, about our expected additions – sorry to inform you that we have none. Yesterday, one of the kittens was born dead. The cat had such difficulties with the others that she also died. Well, I guess it was the best for the cat, because she didn't have any company and it's pretty hard for a cat to raise a family all by herself. Don't ask me how I know – I just imagine it. Well,

*Darling, that's about all the latest news for now – so send regards to all
– lots of love & kisses for you and Carole Frances –*
  With All My Love,
  Your Dave

—

28 March – 1944
Still Somewhere in North Africa

My Dearest Wife & Baby,

  *Today I celebrated my 28th birthday in a most gala manner. With all
the splendor of a Hollywood premiere – the glint and glamour of the Follies
– the lighting of Broadway – the magnificence of Earl Carroll's – the
incomparable descriptions of publicity agents – I did absolutely nothing!
In fact, I wrote you last nite that I'd probably get drunk – well, that didn't
even happen. I took one drink and couldn't even stand that. I just don't care
for anything intoxicating – don't ask me why – I just don't know. Anyway,
I hit the hay just after I finished your letter and had the most comfortable
sleep in quite a while.*

  *This evening, I went to see Claudette Colbert & F. MacMurray in "No
Time For Love" – It really was very good and funny. Some of the cracks
were really risqué – wonder where Hayes was when the film came up for
approval. The funny thing about our theatre is, after it is all over, you see
hundreds of men lifting and carrying boxes – planks about 6 feet long – G.I.
water and gas cans – folding chairs – pieces of board slapped together – seats
out of crashed airplanes – just anything one could use as a seat. Then, to see
the many long lines of men filing out, over the hills, down the slopes, over
the roads, up to their various camps – it looks like a long line of lightning
bugs working overtime.*

  *While walking back to camp with Sgt. Griffith (Mess Sergeant), we
started talking – very casually. He said that he really had the blues – but
good. He also has a baby girl – about one-year-old. He started to enumerate
all the pleasant things for which we are fighting and the list was absolutely
endless. Above all, as you probably suspect, was our wives and babies. We
agreed that after this is all over – there will be absolutely no travel to other
lands by American tourists. If the urge for sightseeing comes up, he'll probably
travel right in the U.S. and see the many things he had overlooked before.
Everybody is too eager to sit at home – before the radio – with his shoes
off – a cool bottle of beer in his hand – reading the latest newspaper's comic*

pages – and being able to go to the latrine without having to go outside – or taking a shower without having to walk a ½-mile – but to top it all off – to have your wife and baby at your side – That's a feeling one could never put into words.

Well, Darling, hope that everybody is well and happy at home – Hope to spend all the rest of my birthdays with you – Give my regards to all – keep an extra huge amount of love & kisses for yourself & Carole Frances –

With All My Love,
Your Dave

———

29 March – 1944
Still Somewhere in North Africa

My Dearest Wife & Baby,

Thanks a million for the delicious candy – it is really something different. I've never eaten caramels with nuts in them before. Yesterday, I picked up the rations of Passover matzos, which each Jewish man is allowed. We each get 3 regular boxes – not bad. It's real American matzos, made in Brooklyn. The Jews over here don't have that type – They have a round, hard matzos, which doesn't look at all appetizing. Anyway, I spoke to the Hebrew Chaplain, who was a captain, and he advised us to bring our matzos to the synagogue with us and we'll probably be invited to dinner by anyone there. So, I'm looking forward to an unusual experience – if I'm able to attend.

As to "catting around" by the men – as I have written you before, a man is foolish to endanger himself physically by engaging in intercourse with the types of women that are around here, so please try to convince the "friends" back home that the men over here don't even think of such things. It may help the single girls back home, who are supposed to be waiting for their "men," to be true blue. You'd be surprised how many girls have forgotten their sweethearts once they are sent over. Men right in this organization have experienced it – but luckily, they are young enough to let it bounce off their shoulders. I'm certainly the happiest guy in the world to know that I've got such a darned nice wife & baby waiting for me. (Hope that you'll excuse the wax drops – one of the candles just dripped.)

As to what sort of casual information I can write – I've written you everything that is possible. As long as no military information is included, I'm OK. That's why I avoid referring to time – places – and things. I hope to be home soon – That's all I can say. You can interpret that as months – days –

or years – or anything. However, I don't think that it will be too long before we're back together – the way the Russians are going. As to what's new in Africa – I can't say, because new developments occur daily. Just sit tight and don't be so inquisitive.

Boy! That must really be something to see Carole Frances reading a prayer book. The amazing thing is that it has no pictures and she still was attracted to it. Well, that's my daughter for you! I guess you had something to do with it, however. Well, Darling, that's all the dope for now – so give my best wishes to all for a most enjoyable Passover and Easter – keep lots of love & kisses for yourself and Carole Frances –

With All My Love,
Your Dave

––––

31 March – 1944
Still Somewhere in North Africa

My Dearest Wife & Baby,

Today marks the end of another month and cuts off the time that it takes to bring us back together again. I guess the time moves slower for you than for me, because everything around here is so new to me. However, I can assure you that my period of time away from you and Carole Frances is altogether too long.

Yesterday, I went into a jewelry store in town, where I bought a couple of Ten Commandment tablets made of silver. They have the Hebrew printing on them and I thought they'd be nice for necklaces for Carole Frances and [Joe Schwartz's daughter] Madlynn. I went to the Red Cross to see "Design for Scandal" – Walter Pidgeon & Rosalind Russell – I thought that it was a new picture, but we had seen it together a couple of years ago – remember? It was enjoyable anyway.

Well, Darling, I'll still be patient & hope that tomorrow brings me a letter from you – hope that everybody at home is quite well and happy – that Carole Frances is getting prettier – smarter – and lovelier every day – regards to all –

With All My Love,
Your Dave
P.S. I miss you very much but love you twice as much.

––––

3 April – 1944
Still Somewhere in North Africa

My Dearest Wife & Baby,

Yesterday, while on pass, I stopped at a synagogue to see what it was like inside. It was a tremendous place and had a very large interior. It had a very high dome and the altar was also dome-shaped. The place where the Torah is kept is in an archway with velvet curtains in the doorway. There were many 7-candled candelabra and very artistic in design. The Cantor's place was in the center of the place. The Chief Rabbi's pulpit was on the side, like the English church. The Star of David was in all the windows and in the ceiling. All around the walls were tables listing the names of the members who had died in World War I. Above the entrance to the synagogue was a balcony for the choir and a very large pipe organ.

Well, when I came, they were just getting ready to perform a wedding. The bride (in bride attire of white, carrying African lilies) and the groom (in full dress) with their relatives arrived on horse carriage. The attendants sat in front or on the sides – the males on one side and the females on the other. The Chief Rabbi placed a taleth over their heads and conducted the ceremony in the French language. In between periods, the choir boys sang – the organist played – and a very excellent singer sang one song. Then, after they were officially married, they received the congratulations in the study of the Rabbi. I told them "mazel tov" – and they understood. After that, I went back to look the synagogue over and helped the second rabbi to clear away the religious bells and cymbals, which are placed over the Torah. Incidentally, they have a very peculiar custom over here. Baskets are passed for donations for the newly married couple – I gave two francs, which was a lot compared to what I saw others give. Well, after that, the couple left in the carriage for their new home. It was certainly a nice innovation for me and it was something which I'll never see again perhaps.

Hope that this finds Carole Frances getting more new ideas (but safe ones) and taking good care of her mommy for her daddy – and you taking it easy and very good care of yourself & the baby – I do miss you so very much and love you even more – send regards to all – lots of love & kisses for you and Carole Frances –

With All My Love,
Your Dave

8 April – 1944
Still Somewhere in North Africa

My Dearest Wife & Baby,

Sorry that the details of your date to the Chase were not in one of the earlier letters – It could have made it unnecessary for that hard letter which I wrote regarding that subject. However, I hope that you have forgotten all about it.

I took advantage of the opportunity given the Jewish soldiers – invitations to homes of native people in town. A couple of other fellows and I were invited to the same home, so we all left together. Our host's name is Mr. Alfred Achache – They have always lived in this area. We met Mr. Achache's mother and his father and their wives – also his sister and her husband. They are all middle-aged people and had young children – the oldest being a 16-year-old girl who spoke English pretty well.

Well, we sat down to the Seder and the ceremony was conducted in Hebrew. The Bible also had a French translation just beneath it. We all had a nice time trying to understand each other fully. I could carry on a passable conversation – but it took a little while to understand everything. They all were very pleased with our conduct and insisted that we return today – if possible. We brought 3 boxes of matzos with us and it is far superior to the native matzos, which was very coarse and round. It is made of a grey flour and is thicker. Anyway, the way we found out that our matzos were better was the young son of Mr. Achache said that it tasted better. You know that a child is not diplomatic, because they always speak the truth. We had muscatel wine and some anisette. I don't care for anisette – You'd probably like it – it tastes like licorice. The meal was not so very good – it all was so strange to us – The only thing we did eat was the meat, dates and oranges. Of course, we hated to leave food on our plates because food is so scarce around here, so I had to force some of that stuff down in order to make them happy. Well, we had to leave early in order to get back to camp on time, so we apologized and departed.

When I got back, the whole camp was under a full moon – Boy, does that get a guy! It makes him want to get back to the States and get out on the road with his best girl. Who do you think is mine? Tune in next week and find out. Of course, that feeling has come up so often now that I'm pretty well used to it. The only difficulty is that it is never relieved. Maybe in a matter of months I'll be back home and we won't ever be apart again – I hope.

Be sure to send my best wishes to all – keep lots of love and kisses for yourself & the baby –
With All My Love,
Your Dave

———

14 April – 1944
Still Somewhere in North Africa

My Dearest Wife & Baby,

Today will probably be a very memorable one in the history of our company. I realize that you always like to have all the information at once whenever I say anything like this. However, this is one time that you will have to wait for the results. Just take my word for it and be patient.

I'll probably never be able to get a grilled cheese until I get back home. It's very true, Darling, that everything is missed and then doubly appreciated. Now that you mention it, a few bottles of Alka-Seltzer tablets really would be the thing. The next time that you send anything, please include a few bottles – Thanx. You dirty skunk! You unthoughtful wretch! You so-and-so! Eating two (not one) barbecued beefs. Well, that takes the cake! Well, wait until I get home – I'll make up for lost time – in sandwiches and "other things."

Do you really think Li'l Abner is now married to Daisy Mae? It's hardly possible – Most of us are going around tearing our hair out – We can't believe it's true.

Sorry to hear about Syd – but he's a whole lot better off in the Navy than the Infantry. At least he'll remain in the States for a little while. If he had gone into the ground forces, he'd probably be at Anzio right now.

As to the radio programs, they were very nice while they lasted – We had mostly recorded programs of name bands from a nearby station. We also received the news from London. However, we've discontinued it for reasons I cannot divulge at this writing.

If you keep on dreaming about me being home – maybe one of these nites, I'll surprise you and really be there. Well, Darling, that's about all the news for now – the bugle is blowing "Taps"– in the far distance – the sky is filled with a million white stars on a midnite blue background – no moon yet – So regards to all – and lots of love & kisses for Carole Frances and yourself – I love you very much –
With All My Love,
Your Dave

2. ITALY

23 April – 1944
Somewhere in Italy

My Dearest Wife & Baby,

I suppose you are really surprised at the above heading. Well, we can't always enjoy just sitting around on one continent all the time. Yes, we're somewhere in Italy – but that's all I can tell you. If you are wondering why I haven't written you since the last letter (about April 14th), it was because it took all that time to get here and for the past two days, I've been working all day long without one minute to spare for myself. Today, I finally got a breathing spell and immediately started this letter. I couldn't write on the way over, because I was unable to find out what was permissible and didn't want to waste a letter by writing something that wouldn't pass the censor. You see, in our letters, they are turned back and not cut out. Therefore, I thought it best to wait until I could say more to you and be certain that it would pass. The trip was very uneventful, except for the 1st nite out when we had a rough sea and I got a little sick, but quickly regained my equilibrium. We were driven out to our new "home" and we had to sweep all the hay out of it before we even went in. We really scrubbed the place up and now you can say that it is almost fit to live in.

I can't say much in this letter, because the censors here are much more severe than from the place we just left. Meanwhile, Darling, don't worry, because I'm very safe and feeling fine – and certainly don't wish you were here. Give my regards to everybody and lots of love and kisses to you and Carole –

With All My Love,
Your Dave

April 25, 1944
Still Somewhere in Italy

My Dearest Wife & Baby,

   I saw my first "Stars & Stripes" over here and it mentioned the fact that soon we will be issued beer – free – Can you imagine that! The brewery was begun by a lieutenant from St. Louis.

   You know, when I see the miserable-looking people around here – I thank God that I'm an American and my family is in America. To just see the shabby kids running around, forever begging something to eat, it just turns your stomach. The smell of the people and the neighborhoods is terrific. Why, to deposit your waste in the gutters of the street is absolutely nothing. Some of these buildings were erected about 300 years ago and people still live there in the original rooms. Now you can understand why I want to stay right in St. Louis and the good ole U.S.A. when I get back.

   Well, Darlings, I want you to know that I love you and miss you very, very much. Give my best wishes to everybody and lots of love & kisses for you and the baby –

   With All My Love,
   Your Dave

   P.S. Max [Sarver] *told me that the Browns won 6 straight games – that's pretty good.*

———

27 April, 1944
Still Somewhere in Italy

My Dearest Wife and Baby,

   Today, I was just summing up the various types of people that I have seen around here. It seems that there have been some pretty well-to-do people here aside from the very dirty and poverty-stricken ones. The former seem to carry the burden of the War pretty well, putting up a front as though absolutely nothing was going on. They even have the good clothing that they must have purchased before the War and make it go a long way. One sees many going around with heel-less shoes that needed repair long ago. The children run around in pretty good apparel. However, on the other side of the fence, it is another story. The people, including the adults and children, all are running around threadbare and badly in need of any article of clothing or shoes. You may see many boys wearing G.I. shoes that they must have stolen. The shoes stick out on their feet like Durante's nose protrudes from his face. For one lump of sugar, they will be your friend for life. Why, at chow time, the women throng around and hold up their rusty tin cans for you to throw your garbage into. I can't see how they exist on things like this.

Now, Darling, you can see why I thank God that we are Americans and you are back in the States. The Nazis must have taken absolutely everything that the people here had. One can still see some of [CENSORED] *of many buildings. The surprising thing is that the people are still able to grow some vegetables and fruits. You are able to get onions galore. I know how you detest the smell of them, so I'm getting my fill of them now, while I'm thousands of miles away from you. Of course, none of them really care if you do buy any as long as you can give them a cigarette or stick of gum or anything to eat. As you probably notice by now, this is written on the machine for a change. I ran out of ink, so I used the first thing I saw. Of course, it is not as good as you can do, so please don't compare it to some of your work, thank you.*

Well, Darling, that's about all the dope for now, so say "Hello" to everybody for me and give the baby a great big hug and a kiss for me and she can return the gesture —

With All My Love,
Your Dave

———

April 29, 1944
Still Somewhere in Italy

My Dearest Wife & Baby,

Today, while I was walking down a street, I came across a woman with a baby boy in her arms. The baby was wailing its heart out as tho it would be breaking any minute. You know how much I like to hear a baby cry — So I walked over and gave the baby a lump of sugar. You should have seen how he shut up — as tho a key had locked his mouth. I've been doing that quite frequently since I've been across, because not only does the child appreciate it, but it helps to build good-will between the natives and the Allies. I give out pieces of candy or gum and it really feels good to see them smile for a change. After all, they have seen so much War that it made deep lines in all their young faces. I'm sure that you'd want me to do what I'm doing, because I'd feel badly if I passed up a crying child.

Well, Darling, regards to all and lots of love and kisses to you and the baby,

With All My Love,
Your Dave

———

May 1, 1944
Still Somewhere in Italy

My Dearest Wife & Baby,

　Today is May Day once more and I'll bet that the Russians really raise all kinds of hell in celebrating. If they continue at the same rapid pace, they'll probably be waiting in Berlin for us before we even enter the Reich. Well, let's hope that the War will be at an end in Europe soon.

　Yesterday, for the first time since we've been over here, I took an evening pass for 3 hours. I had to do something to break the monotony of the steady grind, so Mullen, Okma & I went promenading. We saw many old churches and buildings. After a couple of hours, we ran across an English-speaking native who asked us if we wanted some good wine. We went into a small place that is called a bar (over here) and had a few rounds. This fellow formerly lived and worked in Trenton, New Jersey. Can you imagine finding a guy like that accidentally? He had a couple of friends who also had lived in the States and we had a grand bull session. On the way back, we ran across a couple of French soldiers – so, for the first time, I was able to speak to somebody over here – outside of the Americans & English. When these people start rattling off Italian – I just stand there with a big question mark above my head.

　I haven't seen a "Stars & Stripes" for a couple of days, so I don't know how the flood situation is. It will no doubt bring more mosquitoes to St. Louis than ever before. I want you all to be careful of bites, because it really is easier now to get something like malaria or typhoid than before. If you are bitten, please don't ignore it – but put some alcohol on it at once. You wouldn't want me to worry about you – would you? So take my advice – Thanx.

　That's all the dope for now, so give my regards to all – and lots of love & kisses for you and Carole Frances –
　With All My Love,
　Your Dave

———

2 May, 1944
Still Somewhere in Italy

My Dearest Wife and Baby,

　One of the Italians, who works around here doing odd jobs, brought his little, 17-month-old baby girl down here and is she a chubby thing! The surprising thing is how in the world did she ever get so fat on what little they have around here. She really looks better and healthier than any of the other babies I've seen around. I gave her some candy mints last nite and she really devoured them. This morning, Lt. Maddox and Sgt. Mullen gave her some more candy and her father really appreciated it.

About the only thing we have around to help us keep up our morale is a radio. We get a lot of rebroadcasts of the top programs in the States including Bing Crosby, "Hit Parade," Bob Hope, etc. As yet, I haven't heard any new songs that I haven't heard in the States. Haven't they written any? I know that a new novelty song has swept (?) the nation, named "Mairzy Doats" – or words to that effect. What's it like? I suppose Carole really likes it and can sing it backwards by now. I think that it was taken from a nursery rhyme – wasn't it? Why worry about it when there's a War to be won – eh?

Sorry to read about the Browns finally losing the first game, but all good things soon come to an end, I suppose. It's the first time in quite a while that two St. Louis teams were in first place at the same time – especially the Brownies.

Give everyone all my regards and best wishes. Meanwhile, take good care of yourself and the baby, and lots of love and kisses to both of you –
With All My Love,
Your Dave

---

4 May, 1944
Still Somewhere In Italy
My Dearest Wife and Baby,

Today, I finally received some mail from you. I got letters from April 18-19-22. Gosh, if only you could visualize the relief afforded upon their receipt. I certainly did enjoy that first letter, which you perfumed and now this one – It really is delicious! I let a few of the boys sniff the envelope and they about swooned.

Now that I've been in it a little while longer, I'm afraid that I've changed my mind [about a furlough]. I'm well off and may as well stay that way. Even if it meant going back to the States for a few weeks, I'd certainly be subject to immediate shipment back to a combat zone. It is too hard to take again. You know that it was hard after you left Fresno, but gradually I got used to the situation so that now it isn't too bad. But to go back to all of the hard knocks of [officer] schooling and then have to go away again – no, *none of that for me. Let's just wait this out and be thankful that we're all well and safe. It really isn't worth it all.*

Now for that very personal subject, which you wrote about. As you probably know, this letter goes thru more than one censor's hands now. That makes it rather an embarrassing subject upon which to write. I realize that Carole Frances is growing up, but I never had a chance to think about a companion for her, because nothing ever prompted me to think along those lines. Let's let it go until I get back – There will be plenty of time to talk about it then. I can assure you that I'll be quite interested in cooperating to the fullest extent in that respect. Well, that's about all the news for now, so regards to all and lots of love and kisses for you and Carole –

With All My Love,
Your Dave

———

Saturday 6 May, 1944
Still Somewhere in Sunny Italy

What d'ya say, ya ole hag,

How's that for a new salutation? As you may gather, I received your letter requesting a few different openings, so there is the start. Of course, I don't really think that you are a hag. In fact, I do think that you are just the opposite.

We got our first PX rations today and your Uncle Davie was the unfortunate to dole it out. It took all day. Anyway, the boys finally are well fixed for cigarettes and candy for a while. If these people around here knew how much candy we have, they would probably storm the place. It is really a shame that they don't have anything sweet around here for the children. In fact, the older women shove the small children aside and try to get the candies that are given to the kids. Can you picture something like that happening in America? How thankful I am that we are Americans, you will never know.

As to allowing the Rabbi to read my ideas and impressions of an African Passover, that's alright. However, to have it reprinted in the temple paper – It really isn't that good. Oh, I made a mistake – It dealt with the description of the synagogue and the wedding, but I still don't think it is as good as all that. I'm glad that you finally received the Stars of David. Have you gotten a chain for it yet?

Gosh, you are really a lady of action! Getting 12 bars of soap and 12 packages of blades – That's really something! As to the candy, I'll treasure it and only lick one caramel per day. By licking it, it should last all day. Therefore, a pound should last about a month. Incidentally, Henry Ford's prediction about the War being over in May didn't quite come true – I think. It seems that we are still fighting. He certainly stuck his neck out with a statement like that.

At this moment, there is a recording of "Begin the Beguine" on the radio – by Artie Shaw, too. That song certainly brings us back together in a hurry.

If Carole acted up at the dinner table for a change, you can't help it. She has to let herself go once in a while, don't you agree? Of course, it was unfortunate that she had to pick a time when you would run into a friend.

Say, we are starting to grow strawberries around here now. How would you enjoy coming over and fixing some shortcake? Boy, how I could go for some now. Of course, I'd rather go for you and in a big hurry. What do you think of the idea? Well, that's about all the news for tonight, so say "Hello" to all of our friends and relatives, and give them my regards. As for you and the baby, I love you and do miss you very much. Sorry that there is nothing to be done about it – So, lots of love and kisses to you –

With All My Love,
Your Dave

———

Sunday May 7, 1944
Still Somewhere in Italy

My Most Favorite Wife & Baby,

I received 12 (twelve) letters today, ten of them were yours. Now I'm really behind in my correspondence, especially now when there is so much to be done. This morning, during one of my many trips about the country, I was just covered from head to toe with white dust. You know how much I detest dust in general. Remember how I'd run my hand over a tabletop at home? Well, you can imagine how disgusted I was when I got back here. Luckily, I have found a good "paisan" (Italian for friend or countryman) who launders better than any of the laundresses in the States – and cheaper, too. Should I ship him across to you?

Thanks for proposing a toast to me for my birthday. Sorry I wasn't on hand to help the celebration along. Maybe next time. Gosh, even a Tom Collins over here would be worth $20.00. Can you imagine how I'd act if a mint julep was served up in a foot-tall, frosted glass? Well, that's one of the "things we're fighting for" – I suppose. As to Supply Sergeants not being well liked, I'm not a bit surprised. Darling, there are very few Supply men who are liked. In the first place, they are the ones who are responsible for seeing that money is deducted from enlisted men's pay for any government property that is lost, damaged or destroyed thru their own negligence – unquote. Now, you can readily see that nobody would like someone who would do that – and it takes place every month, too. Before I was assigned to the 346th – I disliked the Supply Sergeants, too – so I can appreciate that feeling. I know that I'm not the best-loved guy in the outfit, by a long shot. It's only because I've babied them along since last May and done everything under the sun for them. Now, if I ask them to do something on their own initiative, they become indignant and think I am pulling my rank on them.

I'll excuse you for not writing a letter on my birthday – but don't let it happen again. I only hope that you won't have to write me again on my birthday. Boy! Do you mean that we've actually known each other for almost six years? How in the world could you stand it? I remember one time when you said that we could never be more than friends – and then Spring came.

Now then, I'm finally going to request something that isn't absolutely an essential item. I have a great craving for a salami or salamis. Some of the boys have been receiving them in excellent condition, so I figure that I could receive some, too. Now many people have asked what I'd like to have – tell them salami and jars of kosher pickles. Gosh, how I'd go after that. I notice that meat points were taken off of some meats – maybe it will make it a bit easier to obtain. Here's hoping that I get some –

Well, Darlings, that's about all the news for now. Meanwhile, I love you and miss you more every day – keep well –

With All My Love,
Your Dave

———

Monday 8 May, 1944
Still Somewhere in Italy

Dear "Claudia" and Jr.,

This evening, we had our first fresh fruitcake. We were fortunate enough to be the lucky ones to get some strawberries today, so the C.O. had some strawberry cake made. It wasn't bad, either. Maybe we'll soon get some *shortcake – who knows? You may already know this – but one can make a whipped cream out of canned milk. All you do is boil it and add a little vanilla and let it set overnight in the icebox. That's one of the many recipes the G.I. cooks learn in the Army. Wouldn't they make good wives?*

Well, another nutty article was released from New York, by one of the executive members of the War Manpower Commission. It said that it looks like men will be released from the service after the European War is finished. That is really a ridiculous thing to say, because there is still the Japs to contend with and that ain't hay. It probably was a propaganda speech to the Nazis and a victory speech for us. So don't place too much faith in those articles that you see in the papers. Of course, I'd like to believe it, but it's too fantastic.

As you probably notice, Lt. Rodger is no longer the censor. He has other duties to take up his time, so Lt. Maddox is taking over. Incidentally, the C.O. really has been a busy guy around here lately. He's really a changed person from the one that we knew over in Africa. Of course, he'll read this, but you know that I usually speak my mind anyway.

I had some pickled herring today and it was really good. I hope that I will be pleasantly surprised with a nice assortment of kosher foods. Gee, if only you could imagine how much I'd appreciate it. We get fresh onions here and that sweet anise, but the Italians don't have the meats to prepare the highly seasoned foods for which they are noted. We used to get some of the Italian salami in California, but that's all gone.

Well, Darling, I don't know of any more to write, so take good care of yourselves and remember that I am still true blue and waiting for that day when we can be together forever. Well, Sweetie-Pie, give my regards to all and keep lots of love and kisses for you and the baby –

With All My Love,
Your Dave

Thursday 11 May 1944
Still Somewhere in Italy

Hi ya, Toots and Little Tootsie,

Well, I had to go to Naples in order to catch the train. Was it packed! The people stand, sit, lay, push, hang, and just any other means of staying on the cars. It is really some experience. I had some of them blowing their breath in my face; others pushing me halfway out the door; and others standing all over my feet. If you think that the transportation is bad in the War-crowded cities of the States, you ought to catch a glimpse of the situation over here.

When you first get off of the train, you don't think that you are in an ancient city. Yes, I was in Pompeii! You first pass thru the newest part of the city (which isn't so new). Finally, I came to the ruins. It is walled off so that one has to buy a ticket in order to gain admittance. It cost only 3 cents to get in, so I could afford that much. The first place of note that I came upon was the tremendous amphitheatre. Darling, I certainly wished that you had been there to see it. Here was a place that had been buried for years – centuries – and the structure was still standing. I entered thru a gateway that was originally used by the gladiators when they came out into the arena. Along the sides are various entrances that lead down to dungeons that no doubt held prisoners who were made to fight the gladiators for their lives.

I came across the main street. The street itself was still of the original stone blocks that the chariots had ridden over. There were stores that lined both sides of the way. Some were in excellent condition and looked like the people had just recently left. There were urns in quite a number of places that had stood in the same spot all this time. There were paintings on the walls, which were hundreds of years old. The colors were in excellent condition and I saw some of the workers washing them with benzene, in order to help preserve the paint. The scenes were mostly those made to represent the gods.

Well, I went on to find of all things, a house of prostitution. Can you imagine a place like that in ancient Pompeii? On the ground, made of stone, was a male organ (complete) pointing to a certain home. All over the walls were paintings of the most imaginative nature. It showed various ways of intercourse. It showed combination man and woman, with female characteristics on the upper part of the anatomy, and male features on the lower. It showed men with two organs. If you think that the present generation is bad, you're all wet. These ancients had it all over us. One Roman even weighed all of his wealth against his .... It did have a humorous aspect to it.

That just about winds up my trip to Pompeii.

Yes, I can appreciate your feeling blue at times. I, too, get that ole feeling and it takes a lot of gulping to get that lump down my throat. Just try to think of something else and to let Carole take up most of your day – That, I'm sure, will help. Yes, we ought to have a lot of good reading matter when we're together, in front of the fire, and Carole out on a date. I don't

*think that my letters are any better than anyone else's – but thanks for the
compliment. You know, yours aren't boring, by a long shot.*

*Well, that's about all for the day, so take good care of yourself and the baby,
and send everybody my best wishes. For you and Carole Frances, a lot of
love and kisses –*

With All My Love,
Your Dave

Saturday 13 May 1944
Still Somewhere in Italy

My Dearest Tuderful Three,

*If you are trying to figure the above salutation, it's a take-off on the Victor
Borge, and I thought that it would be something different. However, in
spite of it, I do think that you both are really wonderful.*

*The C.O. and I have been running around together in the jeep as both
our work runs parallel and we usually go to the same places. The one big
advantage that I have is that I don't have to go over those bumpy roads in
a big 2-1/2-ton truck. For a while, my spine was hurting from that, so I
made as few trips as necessary, so that I could get rid of that pain. Now I
feel pretty good for a change and no pain, so if we continue to ride around
in the jeep, I probably won't have any more spinal pain.*

*No, I'm not coming home for a while, yet. In fact, I don't think that I'll
be home before this European War is over, and that won't be long now. The
Jerries are pretty well all nerves and don't know which way we are hitting
from. So sit tight and keep your fingers crossed.*

*Thanks for the Alka-Seltzer tablets in advance. I probably will be able
to use them when it gets hotter. Pretty soon, I'll be swamped with packages
– soap, razor blades, salami and pickles. Of course, I'm anxiously waiting
for the chocolates, or rather caramels. I agree with you that I, too, would
prefer to be with you rather than have packages sent me. Well, Darlings,
that just about sums up the news for now, except that I do love you so very,
very much and miss you terrifically. Say, write Gen. [George] Marshall –
maybe he'll give me a year off. In the meantime, send my regards to all and
love and kisses for you and the baby.*

With All My Love,
Your Dave

Sunday 14 May 1944
Still Somewhere in Italy

My Dearest Wife and Baby,

Today is another Mother's Day and the second that I have had to write a greetings to you. It certainly doesn't seem like Sunday, either. The days just come and go and one doesn't realize which day of the week it is. The only indication that one has is if he goes into a town and sees the crowds going to church. Well, it is Mother's Day, however, so I do want to have my little say about its commemoration. First of all, I do want to say that I'm a lucky guy for having a wife like you. If that wouldn't have been the situation, then perhaps a baby like ours wouldn't have been possible. Next, I'm thankful that we have such a good, healthy baby. That, as you know, is the most important thing. All this adds up to the fact that you are the mother and a good one at that. Amy, as I have told you many times, you are the best mother a child could possibly have, even tho you may not be the best housekeeper. That last item, of course, is not important, because it can be changed. But to be a good mother, that is something that one must come by naturally. If every child was brought up along the same lines as Carole Frances, it would be a utopian world. So thanks again for being Mrs. David E. Stoliar, and the mother of my baby. I hope that you have a pretty day back home to round out a full day of enjoyment.

Well, Toots, lots of love and kisses for you and the baby –
With All My Love,
Your Dave

———

Tuesday 16 May 1944
Still Somewhere in Italy

My Most Beloved Wife and Baby,

You say that I will be writing to a new address soon. That certainly means that you have not moved as yet, therefore, I will address it to 735 [Leland] until I get definite notice that you have moved. From your description, it sounds very, very, very nice. I know that it is pretty, because you certainly wouldn't rave if you didn't like it. I have thought over all the facts involving the purchase of the place and I agree wholeheartedly with everything that you have figured on. As to the refrigerator, I hope that you have some luck in getting a good buy. I'd hate to hear that you were taken advantage of on account of the War. I know that you are going to have one helluva good time with our furnishings out of storage. I know that you will arrange it very nicely.

So our young lady says that her daddy is a soldier. Maybe he is; I wouldn't know. Anyway, it is rather cute that she is able to say that. I'm glad that she doesn't know what it means, however. As to the War, you read everything that we are able to say, in the newspapers, of course. There are fireside generals who all have ideas on how to win the War in a hurry. The commentators are alright, but if you want real reading, read the accounts of War correspondents who have been around. They see and understand the conditions. Therefore, as to the invasions, you are as qualified as anyone else to guess the means and methods. The one thing that I can tell you is that we are going ahead and will win this War and soon.

One of the boys' wives is expecting and we all got into a jackpot on the hour and day that it would be born. I drew yesterday at 8:00 to 10:00 P.M. The winner will get $5.00 and the balance will go to the baby. There are about 50 men in on it, so the baby will get a nice gift.

Well, Darlings, that's about the dope for today, so as per usual, send my regards to all and for you and the baby, lots of love and kisses –

With All My Love,
Your Dave

———

Wednesday 17 May 1944
Still Somewhere in Italy

Dearest Beloved,

Now that I have been requesting salami and pickles, I'll probably be able to open up a kosher delicatessen somewhere in Italy.

I went to the show yesterday and saw "Action in Arabia," with George Sanders and Virginia Bruce. It was quite interesting and appropriate at this time. If you have a chance to see it, it will be entertaining – but nothing to rave about.

Today, I was able to get away for a shower for a change and it was just our luck that the mobile unit was broke down. However, we asked the British if we could use theirs and they were nice about it. The only thing wrong was that there was no hot water. A cold shower was fine for a change. That was a nice example of Lend-Lease.

Well, Darlings, say "Hello" to everybody at home and give them my best wishes. But for you and the baby, I send all my love and kisses –

With All My Love,
Your Dave

—

Sunday 21 May 1944
Still Somewhere in Italy

My Most Adorable Wife and Baby,

    If you will remember, I said, in Africa, that a certain day was going to be one that will long be remembered in the history of 346th Signal Company Wing. Well, it finally blew up. Lt. Maddox is no longer with us. As you probably realize, there were many things that I couldn't write at the time. In fact, I can't say them now, so let's wait until I get home before giving you all the details. The main thing is that he is gone. Lt. Maddox really felt badly when he told the First Sergeant about him being relieved of his command. He actually cried and told us that he never had more pleasure working with men than with this organization. It was really pitiful to see him. I hope that his wife doesn't take it too hard. It is a dishonor and something of which to be ashamed. So you can see that an officer's life isn't the rosiest thing in the Army.

    As you notice by the newspapers, the Allies are really gaining their stride now. You probably had quite a few nightmares after reading about that sinking in the Mediterranean. You must really have heaved a sigh of relief when you learned that I was safely in Italy. Those fellows were really caught without a chance, but considering all the tonnage that we have brought across the seas, the losses have been very, very insignificant. So you must expect those things once in a while. Why even after the last War, a few ships struck mines and were destroyed. Just rest easily, because there's nothing that will happen to me. I'll be OK and will be home in good shape.

    I could imagine how you must have laughed when Carole threw the ball at your mother. I'm sorry that it had to hit her in the eye. I'd certainly like to see Carole listening to your story of the three bears. I'll bet that she actually understands everything that takes place in the story. I'm really proud of our daughter. Well, Dearest, that is all for tonight, so give my regards to all and for you and Carole Frances, an ocean of love and a boatload of kisses –

With All My Love,
Your Dave

—

Monday 22 May 1944
Still Somewhere in Italy

Dear Tootsie and Wootsie,

Well, today we have a new C.O. and his name is Lonnie C. Temple, 1st Lt., Sig. C. He was the Wing Wire Officer, therefore, he will fit into the picture pretty well. I haven't had much to do with him in the past, so I can't give you my opinion as yet. He seems like a good Joe, and one with whom you can hash things out. If you will remember Maddox, it was always his way or nothing else. I think that the men will hold more respect for Lt. Temple than they had for Maddox. The new C.O. isn't so well acquainted with certain administrative procedures, so he has to rely on Mullen and myself. We'll do everything we can for him in order to have a good and efficient outfit.

Well, Dearest, as you notice by the newspapers, we are on our way to Rome. What shall I send you as a souvenir? Shall it be a column from the Coliseum? Or the King's throne? Well, anyway, it won't be long before we are in there. You can see why the War in Europe will be over sooner than most people anticipated. The only thing that we must expect is mounting casualties, because we are on the offensive now. As it is, we have lost only the barest of a minimum in casualties. So have a lot of faith in the theatre commanders, because they are doing a swell job. As for the columnists back home, they only see a logical side of a problem and today, logic doesn't always hold water. For instance, quite a number criticized the Anzio beachhead and the fact that it was stalled. That was not the purpose to make any great headway, as everybody believed. The landing accomplished its purpose, as you will see in a very short time. The Nazis are in full retreat from the areas South of Rome and the beachhead was very instrumental in helping to bring this retreat about. So, as I have said before, have the fullest of confidence in our generals and we will come out on top a lot sooner.

I'm in good health and good frame of mind for a change. Remember the fellow in our company whose wife was expecting? Well, he is no longer expecting – It was born on the 16th and it was a girl. No, I didn't win the prize. However, I'm glad that the delivery finally came thru, because so many men walked the floor for him. They are going to name her "Patricia." Isn't that a pretty name?

Today, I happened to pick up a few English soldiers on the road and gave them a lift. It turned out that they were Yiddish and from Palestine

– Tel-Aviv, to be exact. So the English have finally outfitted an all-Jewish unit for active duty against the Nazis. Remember, about four years ago, the English refused to listen to such a proposal? Well, these men are really anxious to get at the Germans. They told me that they hold Friday services each week and invited me to attend. If we can get permission from the C.O., we'll probably go. Well, Darlings, there isn't anything else to tell you about the activity around here, but I do want to tell you that I love you and "miss you – more than words can say, dear." However, I still look forward to the happy reunion. Meanwhile, give my regards to everybody and tell them that I haven't forgotten them. For you and Carole Frances, oodles and oodles of love and kisses –

    With All My Love,
    Your Dave

———

Wednesday 25 May 1944
Still Somewhere in Italy

Dearest Beloved Wife and Baby,

    Today has been one of great activity and running around. I was busy all morning and when I got back, an investigation committee was on hand to question certain personnel about Lt. Maddox's activities. I was among them and had to testify. I only told them what was actually the truth and exactly what I knew. There were many others questioned and it still is in progress. I don't know what the result will be, but I don't think it will be good. The Lt. was on hand all thru the questioning and was asked if there were any questions, which he would like to ask – He didn't have any.

    As to the invasion, yes, I do think that we will hit from England, and soon. It isn't talk either. The Nazis know that we are coming, but the question is when. That is having quite an effect on them in worrying about that one thing. They are really having a good case of the jitters now, and that will help to shorten this War. The Japs, too, are having their troubles along the same lines. That is why they are replacing so many admirals and generals who have committed hari-kari.

    Sorry that I wasn't on hand to see the full moon. I haven't seen any over here so far. I'll probably get that same old feeling, too. I really don't need a moon to make me feel homesick. As to the baseball situation, we are kept informed thru the "Stars & Stripes," and at this writing, the Cards are in 1st and the Brownies in 2nd place. Well, Darlings, I can't write forever, because nothing has happened to waste ink on. I do want you to know that I miss you and the baby so very much and love you more than you can imagine. Meanwhile, send my regards to all and for you and the baby –

All My Love,

Your Dave

———

Thursday 25 May 1944

Still Somewhere in Italy

My Beloved Family,

Well, as you have read in the papers, we are really going ahead up in the Anzio sector. We ought to be in Rome for Fathers' Day. That in itself would be a nice gift for all the fathers in this area. The big boys up in the air are really hitting the Nazi-occupied countries with everything but the kitchen sink. The loads will even increase soon. We certainly have a wide superiority in the air. In a few areas, the enemy doesn't even send up any opposition. They just don't have it to spare. The Russians are getting ready for their big push from the East. It will probably come at the same time that we make the big push, and that isn't far.

You know, Darling, it is amazing how the Allies remember the women back home. Wherever you go, there are signs telling you to "Come Back To Them Clean." It's a wonder that there are any men who are infected. If only they would keep their families and sweethearts in mind at all times, I'm sure that V.D. would be at a much lower rate than it is. If men have to go out and satisfy their whims, the Allies provide for their protection before and after, so no man should ever be a victim of V.D. I only hope that more of the young girls at home would remember their sweethearts who are thinking of them. I've heard of so many fellows whose wives write that they are expecting babies; or their sweethearts are expecting, also. You can see that this certainly isn't the sort of thing that would help a fellow's morale. So if you ever hear of any girls going out with a 4-F and raising all kinds of hell, just give her hell and make her feel ashamed of herself.

Today, I read an article in the April issue of "Coronet" about the best way to bring up a sister. It got me to wondering about the method we ought to use in telling Carole all the facts of life – Do you think that she is ready for them now? Of course, I don't mean that at this very minute we ought to plan, but we ought to give it a thought. We will probably have many other baby sisters and brothers for her by the time we are ready to tell her.

I was thinking that perhaps two girls and two boys would be nice – Don't you agree? In this way, all of them would have companionship. Well, Sweethearts, that is all the news for today. To everybody at home, my best wishes. To you and Carole Frances, thousands of hugs and kisses –

With All My Love,
Your Dave

———

Friday 26 May 1944
Still Somewhere in Italy

My Dearest Wife and Baby,

Here we are almost at the end of another month and much nearer to the end of the War. I don't have to tell you what progress we're making, because it is flashed to you immediately and reprinted in the papers. We are very optimistic about the whole thing, however. If the papers back home have printed a late map of the Italian campaign, you will be able to see the important role that the beachhead has played. It has saved us innumerable numbers of men, equipment and other supplies. And at the same time, it has gained us territory in a big hurry, which we would have had to fight for otherwise. Now you can tell those armchair generals that they were all wet on Anzio being a foolish venture.

Now we have come to the end of the day and I miss my family so very much. It is amazing that I am able to stick it out for this length of time. I guess I value my liberty and happiness too much not to be able to go thru a little separation. Well, Sweethearts, that is the dope for today – Nothing new on Lt. Maddox – Give my regards to all and a big, big, biggest kiss in the world to Carole. And if you are a good girl, the same for you –

With All My Love,
Your Dave

Saturday 27 May 1944
Still Somewhere in Italy

My Dearest and Sweetest Wife and Baby,

I arose at the stroke of seven and madly dashed for my helmet, so that I could wash up and shave and be ready for my pass. For one hour and a half, I tried to get a ride to Sardinia or Corsica. Unfortunately, I didn't have much luck, so I decided to take advantage of a Naples pass that I had. I noticed that Bob Hope and Bing Crosby were at one of the shows, so I decided to pass a little time there. I didn't remember whether I had seen it or not – It was "Road to Morocco." After it was on for a while, I remembered that we had seen it while I was in St. Louis on my first furlough. I enjoyed it a second time, however. After the show, I walked the streets for about four miles, just window-shopping. It was broiling hot, too. I had some ice cream, which wasn't bad. It was about 5:00, so I decided to head back to camp. I got a ride with a British officer who is a journalist and is about to start publishing an Italian edition of "Parade," which is the English version of "Yank." He let me off at the airport from which I started this morning. I got another ride almost to camp, but it was still a few miles away, so I decided to hitch another ride. This time, it turned out to be with a few Italians, and in a 2-wheel carriage that was horse-drawn. Can you picture me in that setup?

As to my opinion as to how long the War will last, it is a very hard thing to say. One has to figure all the possibilities and leave room for unexpectancies. However, after thinking it over, you may quote me as saying that the European War will be over by Xmas, if not sooner. (At this moment, we are listening to the "Ride of the Valkyries" by Wagner – your mother would really like this.) As you know, the planes and boats have to bring a lot of supplies up now that we are on the move. Therefore, mail may be a little slow in reaching you and me in the future. As to the present drive, I'm afraid that you don't understand that if we do know where and when our next moves were going to be, we most certainly wouldn't put it in a letter that would possibly fall into the hands of the enemy. At the time of your letter of the 18th, Cassino was not taken, but bypassed and then overrun.

I'm glad that I don't have to see Carole after she has her shots. You know how I enjoy hearing her cry. It's surprising how she remembers everything that you tell her. I hope she remembers me just a little bit. If you think that there is any expenditure that is necessary for the new home and we ought to take care of it, just go ahead and spend our money. We really ought to put a lot into the place if we are to live there. I'm glad that you are playing gin and not drinking it, even tho you are losing.

Well, this is about all the dope for now, so give my regards to all and to you and the baby, all the love and kisses in the world –

With All My Love,

Your Dave

———

Sunday 28 May 1944
Still Somewhere in Italy

My Most Adorable Family,

As you have noticed, I am still typing my letters. I have found that I am able to write more and it takes less paper, thereby lightening the load. I guess you are just as satisfied receiving them typed, because they are more legible, too. No, my speed doesn't equal my accuracy. It takes me a little while longer, but I don't forget what I want to write. In writing longhand, sometimes my thoughts run ahead of my hand, so I forget what I want to write.

You know that the advancement is going full blast now. The Nazis are in retreat and are going fast. There are still quite a number of ancient buildings intact throughout Italy. We will probably see a lot of them as we near Germany. As you know, Lt. Rodger is now the Censoring Officer as Lt. Temple is very busy at this time and isn't as acquainted with the men as Lt. Rodger. However, that doesn't mean that I'll be able to tell you any more than before. I only want you to be certain that I'll be alright and not to worry about anything.

There is nothing new on Lt. Maddox, as far as I know. Just give my regards to all and tell them that I'm thinking of them. So with a great big hug and kiss for you and Carole –

With All My Love,
Your Dave

———

Monday 29 May 1944
Still Somewhere in Italy

My Sweetest Tootsie and Wootsie,

As to India, I never gave it a thought after we left Africa, because we had a good idea of where we were going all the time. I suppose that you were imagining all sorts of places. However, we may still have to go over and take care of the Japs after Herr Schicklgruber is taken care of. Well, let's not look too far in the future.

As to a diary, that's impossible, because I am not patient enough to write daily and it is against Army regulations, too. However, I'm sure that I'll be able to remember all the things that I'll want to remember. There are certain things that one does not wish to remember, not that I have done anything wrong. I mean things that are too gruesome. After this is over, I don't think *that I will even join the American Legion, because I want to forget all about the War.*

Darlings, remember me to all our friends and for you and Carole Frances, a million and one kisses.

With All My Love,
Your Dave

———

Friday 2 June 1944
Still Somewhere in Italy

My Dearest Wife and Baby,

I hope that you will excuse me for not writing yesterday and I can't tell you why. Just believe me that I was unable to write. As you know, many times I would like to tell you things, but censorship makes it impossible. So until sometime later, please don't be at any discomfort over this. I'll be writing you from [CENSORED] *soon.*

I'm using the record player now and some of the songs that have impressed me the most are "Story of a Starry Night" by Hal McIntyre, "Lamplight" by Hal Kemp, "Dance of the Hours" by Toscanini, "Moonlight Mood" and "At Last" by Glenn Miller. They may seem a bit old to you, but they really do remind us of home and all those nice things that we are coming back to.

By the way, have you ever sat out in the woods to have a B.M.? Well, I did. We are having to do that right now and boy, would you be disgusted! After walking thru thorns and bushes for about 300 yards, it is then safe to go – as long as it isn't too near the encampment. You just don't know how much I'll appreciate a good toilet seat again. That is just one of those little things that we are looking forward to coming home to.

I hope that all the packages catch up with me before we go into Berlin. I'll really appreciate those salamis soon. Well, that is all for today, so, Darlings, keep that old chin up and remember that I'll be coming home soon. Give my regards to all and lots of love and kisses for you and the baby –

With All My Love,
Your Dave

———

Saturday 3 June 1944
Still Somewhere in Italy

My Dearest Family,.

I forgot to tell you something yesterday – I have a new love. Only this time, it is a male. I saw a small boy carrying a tiny white dog with black markings on its head, ears, body and tail-tip. It was so pretty that I immediately asked the boy if the pup was for sale. He said that I could have it for a dollar, so I didn't hesitate. It accompanied me all the way and slept most of the time in my lap – just like a baby. He is an extraordinary traveler. He acted very, very good, even when it got chilly at night. When we stopped for a rest, he had a B.M. and passed water. Then, in the morning, he did the same – so you can readily see that he is well brought up. He is the liveliest thing that you have ever seen in the way of animals. I was thinking of what a great combination he and Carole would make. I hope that I am able to take him home with me for the baby. Today, I took him with me to the sea and gave him a bath in the salt water. He certainly didn't like it at all. However, it was probably the first bath he has ever had – judging from the looks of the people around Italy. He sleeps in a box beside my bunk and in the mornings, he whines for me to pick him up and put him into my bunk. That is the first thing that I have had with me to make me feel not so very lonely. He reminded me of the times in Fresno. Well, it won't be long and I won't have to think of them – I'll be living them.

Now that we have landed in Italy for a length of time, I think that it is alright to mention our voyage over. We left Africa in a choppy sea and with a good wind blowing. A little while later, I felt rather groggy. I found a spot to lie down on and went to sleep. I awoke about an hour later and found that I was feeling OK. We had boarded an English liner and it was of pre-World War I vintage, however it has had excellent luck in bringing troops across, so we didn't worry. I can't tell you how many ships were in the convoy, so don't ask. It was really a smooth trip across and not a bit of excitement was to be had. We were on the water for a number of days and finally embarked at a port on the coast of Italy. We were then taken to our area and had to get it in shape in order to live in it. We had a ping-pong table and I beat Lt. Rodger every time but once. (Wait until he reads this.) It wasn't so bad, but the neighbors we had were, as I had already described – filthy.

That brings us just about up to date, so from now on, I'll have to depend on your letters to fill up the space. Send my best wishes along to everybody and for Carole Frances and you, what do you think? Yes, you guessed it – an extra big hug and a kiss –

   With All My Love,
   Your Dave
   P.S. I named the dog "Buck," because that is what it cost.

—

Monday 5 June 1944
Still Somewhere in Italy

My Dearest Amy and Carole Frances,

Well, today has been a most momentous day for the Allies. As you know, we entered Rome officially. It has been the attainment of our objective in Italy and will go down in history as the steal of second base in getting our run into Berlin. The first hit was the African campaign. The next base is the landing on the European mainland from the North. After that, it will be a matter of routine going home. How do you like the ballgame? I have just finished listening to some of the most amusing propaganda, from Berlin. They announced that the German High Command had proposed to the Allied general, Sir Harold Alexander, the recognition of Rome as an open city. It was the German idea to preserve all historical buildings. Can you imagine such outright lies? If anyone gave such consideration, it most certainly has been the Allies. After all, couldn't we go ahead and bomb the civic buildings and civilians in Germany, rather than picking out War targets? Well, they certainly are trying to cover up a most decisive defeat. As you know, they had thrown in many crack divisions from the North in a vain attempt to stall our advance. Therefore, you can see that they are really fearing the next move Northward. I haven't let you down in my letters, saying that we will be in Berlin soon, have I?

As to Buck, he is really getting to be a big boy. He now has a playmate. Another fellow here has a little black dog about the same age as our dog. They play all day long and are worn out by the time the sun goes down. I am giving Buck only bread in a mixture of canned milk and water. I add a bit of sugar to make it taste better. That is one of the many things that I have learned by being a father. Why, even today. I saw a woman with a tiny baby in her arms and the baby was continually crying. I spoke a little (very little) Italian to her and motioned for her to place the baby on her shoulder and burp her. Do you know that that baby stopped at once? Well, I guess we'll have to have another baby to burp when I get home.

Now for the most enjoyable part of the letter, about Carole Frances. As you know, our daughter is now almost two years old. She probably will be when you receive this letter. I think that I will send her a fifty-dollar money order for her birthday. What I'd like to see you do is to spend about twenty-five for odds and ends for her and put the rest in the bank in her name. I think that she will be able to use it later when she needs it for something that she ordinarily wouldn't get.

Now I want you to do me a favor. I made a bet with Lt. Rodger that we wouldn't enter Rome before the 15th of this month. He bet that we would. I figured that if we did, it was certainly worth the loss of the bet. Now then, what we bet was a case of Budweiser beer. So put in an order for the case for delivery when we get home. He's really going to get gypped, because I'll give it to him when we have our party and he will have to let us use the beer for the refreshments. (Wait until he censors this.)

Well, Darlings, that is the news for today, so give the baby a couple of extra big kisses for her birthday. Say "Hello" to all — and lots and lots of love to you and the baby —

With All My Love,
Your Dave

———

Thursday 8 June [1944]
Still Somewhere in Italy

My Dearest Impatient Wife and Baby,

Yes, I can imagine what you have been thinking for the last few days. In view of the fact that you are missing my letters of the 6th and 7th, I had better tell you why. Due to certain matters that demanded my complete attention for the full day, I didn't have a minute to spare for myself. I can't tell you what went on, but I can say that the German language was spoken here not more than four days before we arrived. I have seen enough of the dead Germans lying around to last me a lifetime. They retreated faster here than they did in Africa. There is everything from tanks to bullets lying around here. I have seen German airplanes shot up by the numbers. The stink of the bodies is stifling. The dirty sonsofbitches didn't even have the time to bury their dead, so our forces have to. The damaged towns are not as bad as you see in the newspapers — it is worse! Some of the towns are absolutely nothing but a mass of rubble. There are no buildings intact at all. The amazing thing has been the speed with which our engineers have rebuilt many bridges and highways so that they were passable just a few hours after the Jerries left. If anybody deserves credit for aiding to win this War in a big way, it certainly is the Corps of Engineers.

As long as you have already learned of the invasion from England, I don't have to tell you anything about it. From the reports we have been getting, we will be in Berlin very soon. You don't know what a relief it is, now that we are on that last road home. Remember that baseball game that I wrote you about – Well, this is that steal of third base. The amusing part of the invasion is the propaganda the Nazi announcers are pouring out to the German people. They say that there are only fifty paratroopers left from the original invading number and that the Allies are only 4 miles inland and hold a strip 12 miles long. Well, can you picture a few men holding such a broad stretch of a bridgehead? Then they go on to say that due to bad flying weather, the Luftwaffe was unable to take off to attack the Allied planes. Of course, the truth of it is that they have no planes in that immediate vicinity to send up. At this time, the Allies should be pretty well settled in France and on their way to Paris. Darling, it's beginning to look as if the War will be won sooner than we all figured. That will certainly be one glad day when we are told to get ready to ship home.

As to Buck, I think he has worms, so I am going to try to help him get rid of them. Otherwise, he is just as energetic as ever. He is really an intelligent dog and would make a great companion for the baby. I do hope that I am able to take him home with me.

It is a funny thing, but money is worthless over here to the native people. The Germans took all that the people had and left them to starve. Now when you get some laundry done, they won't take money; they want anything to eat. Lires are nothing to them, because they cannot buy food in the towns.

You have read of booby-traps. Well, I have seen them. The bastards who left them think that all the Americans think of is souvenirs. Therefore, they will place a grenade or bomb under a most innocent-looking object and hope that the Allies pick it up. But none of us even bother with them and leave them for the engineers to pick up. That is another big job for the engineers. I can assure you that the Nazis are certainly getting a surprise in that respect.

Well, Angels, that is the dope for the day, so send my regards to all and a lot of love and kisses for you and Carole Frances –
With All My Love
Your Dave

Friday 9 June [1944]
Still Somewhere in Italy
My Sweetest Itsie-Bitsies,
Things came up necessitating my going to [CENSORED]. *As you know, there is nothing to fear around that sector, so it is a safe trip. I have been*

there before, but now it is alright to mention it. The astonishing thing is the condition of the buildings there. They are in much better shape than the cities that I have seen further North. That is a good indication of our sharp shooting against the poor shooting of the Nazis. The towns that were recently occupied by them are just a mass of rubble. As I went on, there were grave after grave of dead Germans. In one place, there was a cemetery plot with numerous graves. There are still quite a few to be buried yet and the Allies are doing a good job of getting them in shape. One of the men found a German photo-holder and in it was a snap of a big Nazi cemetery. That was the best picture I have ever seen – There will be many more like that one before long.

Well, after a very, very, very dusty trip back to our camp, I was overwhelmed with this batch of mail. The first thing that I saw upon opening your letter was the newspaper clipping that told of preparations for the Italian drive. I admit that in spite of the logic, the Allies are meeting with huge success in their drives. Even if the Nazis do know when and where we're hitting next, there is nothing that they can do about it. They don't have the stuff with which to do it. We can send them a note, saying that at such and such a day and hour, we will strike at Paris. They still couldn't do anything much to offset it and stop it. As you note in the reports from France, the notorious wall of Fortress Europa is a fantasy. The Nazis didn't have the time nor the equipment to put up efficient defenses to counteract the invasion. Don't be surprised to learn the sonsofbitches are ready to ask for peace on any terms. By the time that the Russians get going from the East, the Nazis will be running around in a daze, wondering which way to turn. That is why we are so optimistic over the quick end to the European War. The one thing that has me puzzled is in what way will we do away with Adolf, dot dope.

You said that you had another dream of me. Well, I had one of you just last night and it was so very real, I could almost reach out and touch you. It was our wedding night and you went your way and got drunk and very naughty; and I went my way and got drunk also. A second later, [Uncle] Ben is walking me up the aisle of a large auditorium where we were to be married. He asked me if I had a pair of black shoes to go with my tux. I was all mixed up. Just then, we had to get up, so I don't know what happened after that – I'll have to go back to sleep and continue the dream.

I am not saving your mail, because we are not allowed to do so. In case of capture, those letters that seem innocent to you may be very helpful to the enemy. Don't be so impressed with the way I don't bitch – I do. Only I do it over here and not in your letters. I am proud to say that I am the best bitcher in the European waters. If I see anything about which to bitch, nothing stops me. So you can see that by the time that I am ready to write you, I am out of bitches.

As you have not guessed, the invasion did come off from the North. We'll give you another chance: When will the whole War end? Before closing, Buck sends his regards to all and a caress to Carole. Give my regards to all and keep all my love and kisses for you and the baby.

With All My Love,
Your Dave

———

Thursday 10 June [1944]
Still Somewhere in Italy

My Very Dearest Family,

This morning, I decided to take a little time and walk about and take in the sights. I walked up a mountain about 200 feet higher than where we are. When I got to the top, I could look out for miles and miles. Lakes below me looked like dimes. On a clear day, you can see Rome from here, but today it was hazy. On the way up there, I saw all sorts of equipment strewn all over the roads. The Nazis really did go in a big hurry. While walking down, I noticed a pretty stucco home along the side of the mountain. I stopped in and met the father, mother, sisters and brothers – and a few of the relatives, too. The old man explained to me that the Germans took all their food and clothing and used the people's home to operate from. Meanwhile, the people were supposed to look out for themselves, but the little brother was a clever kid and cut quite a number of communication lines, which were very important to the Nazis. I had a few pieces of food that were in our ration boxes, so I passed them out to the whole family. They were ever so grateful. Then I continued on my way down and saw another town in ruins. There were passageways that were absolutely impassable from the rubble that was stacked three or four floors high. You don't realize the power of the Air Force until you see the damage that it does. I can just about imagine what Berlin looks like now. It must be even worse than the places that are around here and they are completely in ruin.

That is the dope for now – I didn't get to continue that dream of the nite before last. Maybe it will come up tonite. Say "Hello" to everybody and give Carole Frances a big one and a kiss for me –
With All My Love,
Your Dave

———

Monday 14 June [1944]
Still Somewhere in Italy

My Most Lovable Wife and Baby,

We have been instructed that we are not allowed to mention visiting certain cities. I'm unable to say any more about it, so until a later day, we'll have to forget about it. We have been keeping up to the minute on the invasion news. Every hour, the BBC from London gives us the latest dope. As you notice in the papers, we are coming along nicely - not only up in France, but in the Northern part of Italy, also. I hope that you are as optimistic about the end as I.

This afternoon, I read an article in "Life" magazine about the feeling between the soldiers and the civilians at this time. I have heard lots of men say a lot of things about the men back home and know of recent incidents that have occurred. I have, at various times, thought about the time I get home. What will my attitude be towards everything at home? I have wondered if I will be jittery – on edge – Will I find it easy to get back into the life I left? Will I criticize everything that I see? I only hope that I will be able to fall right in with the old routine without any difficulty. I know that I have never mentioned anything like this to you before, but I decided to remark on it, just in case you have read the article and were wondering if it pertained to me. Well, we'll see when I get home.

I spent a few dollars on necessary "refreshments" yesterday. We had no water with us, so we had to use the next best thing – It happened to be champagne, cherry brandy, muscatel wine, anisette and rum, in this case. Oh, yes, there was one more thing – cognac. I hope that you won't be sore about it – I didn't get tight. I remember everything that I did. Next time, I'll remember to bring some water along with me.

This morning, I took a "whore's bath." When you don't have any showers near you and you are on the verge of insanity from not taking a bath, you take your helmet and fill it with ice-cold water. Well, next, you strip and wash with a washcloth all over yourself. Can you picture me standing there in the nude, trying to bathe in a helmetful of water? Well, that, my dear, is a "whore's bath." It is taken from the ancient method of cleaning after intercourse and is still in practice (from what I hear).

Well, Darlings, there is really nothing more to say as far as the news goes – nothing ever happens around here. I am lonesome and miss you and the baby very, very much. So, in the meantime, send my regards to all and lots of love and kisses for Carole Frances and you –

With All My Love,
Your Dave
P.S. I love you very much, too!!!

Wednesday 14 June [1944]
Still Somewhere in Italy

My Most Adorable Family,

I'm happy to know that you are enjoying my salutations, but I am rapidly running out of new ones. Therefore, don't be too disappointed if they start to come in with the same old line as before. (At this very moment, a piano duo is playing "Begin the Beguine" – but not like you can play it.) When I saw that lock of Carole's hair, I knew that it was hers the minute I saw it. I placed it in the folder with her picture and will carry it at all times.

I see that you are well up on the news in Italy, so I don't have to tell you much. Don't worry, I'll try to remember everything that is worth thinking about. We will have many evenings together and I'll try to make it an interesting narration. By the way, did you put lipstick on the envelope or maybe Fay did with a letter he received from one of his girlfriends.

Sorry to learn of the strike in St. Louis. Some soldiers in the States tried to kill [organized labor leader] *John L. Lewis when they got back on a furlough. Those people back home had better get down to earth and realize that an extra dollar won't bring back the lives that are being lost in order to allow them to earn one penny. Amy, at times I get so burned up at the complete blindness of the people. I hope that with the Northern invasion, they will realize that we are in it for blood and not money. Hell, money over here isn't worth a stink if you don't have anyone on whom to spend it and we certainly would prefer our own people to these things over here.*

As to the new C.O., yes, he is much better than the old one and the men seem to get along better, now that he is gone. I do miss you and Carole so very much and love you more, so let's keep that foremost in our minds and not think of us as being separated, but just out to lunch. Meanwhile, send regards to all –

    With All My Love,
    Your Dave

———

Thursday 15 June [1944]
Still Somewhere in Italy

My Dearest Wife & Baby,

    Well, here we are in the middle of the year that will be the last of the War in Europe. It went pretty fast, I should say. Remember when I left last December – and we looked forward to a very long separation? Well, the last half of the year will pass even faster than the first did. Of course, we will get a spell of loneliness, but that goes with true love. As we have always said, it is worth it to have our companionship after it is all over. After we (Carole Frances, you and I) are back home, it will all seem like a nitemare.

    Buck is getting to be a big doggie. Tell Carole that the doggie asks for her and is waiting to see her when we get back. He was such a tiny thing when I first picked him up. Now he is really a young puppy and able to get around for himself. You ought to see him when he hears somebody walking around in the dark – he really lets out a terrific bark. You'd think that he was a Russian wolfhound. He is quite a popular guy around here and everybody likes him. If I am able to stow him away on the boat going home, I certainly will. Carole will like him, I know. Well, Angels, there isn't anything else, so I had better remind you that I love and miss you so very much. Also, give my best wishes to everybody and a lot of love and kisses for Carole and yourself –

    With All My Love,
    Your Dave

———

Friday 16 June [1944]
Still Somewhere in Italy

My Most Adorable Correspondents,

    I heard a flash on the radio last nite, from Washington, that the largest cities, including Tokyo, were bombed by B-29's. That meant that we were finally able to use land bases for bombing missions. Therefore, we will be able to strike at the Japanese mainland at will. That is almost as important as the invasion in France. We were hoping for something like that to happen from the Pacific area. Now the end of the whole War is even closer. As yet, we have had no complete details and I don't think that there will be any for quite a while – at least, until things are secure enough to disclose these facts.

This morning, I was anxiously awaiting further news on that latest attack. At 12:00, after listening to the news, which is good on all fronts, Okie [Okma] and I went swimming in a lake near here. The water was fresh, so it didn't make my hair stiff, and was it warm! In fact, we were told that there is still a sign of it being an old volcano. We stayed in (in the nude) for about 30 minutes and then headed for camp. You certainly don't know the mental effect a bath or shower has on a filthy person – It is the greatest thing on earth! I certainly could have stayed there all the rest of the War. After chow, we had mail call and do you know that I received two letters from you, dated the 8th and 9th of this month? That, my friend, is going some. I immediately went into my bunk and tore the envelopes open. (Buck was asleep and I woke him up with the confusion). As to the censoring of mail, it is now being handled by Lt. Micka, so you will now understand the signature.

As to speaking to Buck in Italian, for a while, I was afraid that I would have to, but he fell in line after a few days. We still say, "vieni qui," which means "come here," and he comes.

Boy, could I use that salami now. I'm anxiously awaiting all packages with them and the pickles. Hope that they stay fresh. Before closing, give my kindest regards to all. You may keep a big, big kiss and hug for yourself and Carole –

With All My Love,
Your Dave

———

Sunday 17 June [1944]
Still Somewhere in Italy

My Most Adorable Wife and Baby,

Yesterday, Mullen asked me if I'd like to go to that city of which I have spoken. We walked for a few blocks, taking in the sights and finally decided to stop for a drink. We pulled into a very nice bar and had a shot of cherry brandy. It was a tiny glass, so we asked for a double-shot glass. After a few of those, we decided that it was also too tiny, so we started on beer-glass sizes. We sat outside and watched the people go by. We ran into a fellow who had been a taxicab driver in Brooklyn and came over to Italy when [Benito] Mussolini came into power. He had hoped to hitch his wagon to a star, but the wagon fell down. Now he is a bootlegger. Well, the bar soon closed and we left. The last thing that I remembered was walking up a highway and feeling awfully tired. I don't remember how I ever got back – I had to ask Mullen. At 8:15 this morning, Lt. Temple asked for me and I was dead tired, but I had to get dressed and go in to see him. If you would have seen me, you would have died laughing. I was all shivers and my legs felt like they were about to give under me. There I stood, speaking in half a stupor. When I got out of the office, I could hardly stand. My head was whirling around and I couldn't get warm. Mullen later told me that I showed the picture of the baby to everyone that we ran across in town. Well, that is the last one that I'll be on for quite a while. I know that we didn't have any intention of getting tight, but we did.

At three P.M., we had the mobile Red Cross unit here for coffee and doughnuts. It is really a wonderful thing that the girls are doing for the men overseas. They really go far up in the fighting zones, too. We had a girl from Cleveland named Dianne Wormsley and another from New York named Gretchen Ahlswede, definitely a German. It was a relief to speak to an American girl for a change. Anyway, they both liked Buck and wanted to take him with them, but he and I are too attached to separate. He is certainly growing up. He isn't afraid of anything – Today, he took on a dog whose paw was bigger than all of Buck. He is just like a baby – plays for about three hours and sleeps about six.

Well, Angels, that is about all for today, so best wishes to all and lots of love and kisses for both of you –

With All My Love,

Your Dave

———

Tuesday 20 June [1944]

Still Somewhere in Italy

My Sweetest Wife and Baby,

Now for some sad news. Yesterday, when we stopped on the road to fix one of the tires, I took Buck out for a walk. I took him across the road so as to avoid him getting in the way of any vehicles going the same way as we were. Well, we were across the street about five minutes when an armored car came along. When Buck saw it, he became frightened at the sight and sound of the car. When I saw this, I said to him, "Buck stay here." I repeated this and as soon as the car got up to us, he dashed out and ran under the wheels. *He was instantly killed. For a few moments, I couldn't realize that it had actually happened. After I saw him lying there, I picked him up and let his body slide down the side of the road. We certainly do miss him. If Carole Frances asks about the dog, just tell her that he went bye-bye.*

We are not at the same place from which I sent my last letter. The only nice thing about packing up is that each time, it brings us closer to home. Darlings, it won't be long before we will have occupied all of Italy. That is the dope for today — Extend best wishes to all; and remember that I love and miss you very much. Give the baby a great big hug and kiss for me —

With All My Love,
Your Dave

Wednesday 21 June [1944]
Still Somewhere in Italy

My Most Darling Wife and Baby,

I was the lucky one to get your letter of the 7th containing the snapshots. Gosh, does the baby look good! She is so big! She looks like you a little, I think. Of course, don't feel badly about that, because you look plenty OK. She looks like a four-year-old young lady. I'm afraid that she will ask who that sad sack is, when I come home.

Well, I finally can tell you that I visited Rome. As you know, I tried to let you know before, but censorship prevented me from giving you that information at that time. Well, the city is a very clean one and really modern in architecture. The only old things are the Coliseum and the ancient walls that were left from Caesar's time. I saw the dungeon walls where the slaves were kept before they were sent out into the arena to fight the professional gladiators. I walked to the top of the Coliseum and looked down, about 75 feet, at the people walking on the streets. It is amazing that the walls have stood as long as they have. I saw the stone maps that Mussolini had made on public buildings, on which he showed the future Empire of Italy (as he wishes it). It depicted the gradual growth, country by country, until he had all of Europe, including England. He really was a great optimist. Then I went to the Vatican City where the pope is. I walked thru St. Peter's Church. Inside, there are statues of all the past and the present pope. About one of the statues, one of St. Someone the 15th, there were sentences in Hebrew. What do you think of that? That was not the half of it — As I walked about the town, I saw a few Hebrew churches with mosaics of the Crucifixion with Hebrew inscriptions on them. I still can't figure it out.

As you know, we are going quite well in the Italian Campaign. Also, the news from the North is quite good. At this time, there is a great sea battle in the Pacific. When you receive this letter, you will have learned the full outcome. At this moment, I am listening to a rebroadcast of a report from the outskirts of Cherbourg. An NBC reporter is speaking and he thinks that the Germans will give up the city any minute. That will mean that we have a tremendously large hold on the coast of France. And that, in turn, means that it won't be long before we are in Paris and then – Berlin. Well, Darlings, let's hope that soon the War will be over and we will have each other to worry about. Before I sign off, I'll thank you again for the pictures and remind you that I love you very much and miss you so very much. Send my regards to all and a great big hug and kiss for you and the baby –

With All My Love,
Your Dave

———

Thursday 22 June [1944]
Still Somewhere in Italy

My Dearest Tootsie and Wootsie,

We have a lot of company around here all day long. If it isn't the bombed-out peasants, it is the lizards. They are really tricky and fast – I mean the lizards. This afternoon, I listened to a propaganda broadcast from Berlin. Darling, you would really have a good laugh if you heard what is sent over their networks. They said that of a recent bombing of Berlin by American planes, 1/3 of the total attack force was shot down. It so happened that we had sent over 1,000 heavy bombers and 1,200 fighters to Berlin and we shot down 49 of their fighters and we lost 43 bombers and 7 fighters. You can see how they exaggerate. Then they go further to say that the losses on the French Coast are so terribly high that some Commanding Officers are having to report the bad situations to their superiors. If that case was so bad, why are the Germans retreating and blowing up everything in sight? They said that the Allies in Italy are stalled, because of weak organization – Why are they still retreating in the North? They said that the Japs shot down a tremendous number of American attacking fighters in this battle in the South Pacific. It seems that the Axis nations are trying to outdo each other in exaggeration. The Nazis then go out on a different angle and tell of newspaper articles in the States that say there is a tremendously high rate of venereal disease in effect at this time. They do not tell of the thousands of women and girls whom they have attacked and left not only in a pregnant state, but also with syphilis or some other venereal disease. You can see girls from the ages of twelve to forty, going around ready to drop a foal. That is what the Nazis stand for – just a great big lie. Well, we won't have long to put up with them – We ought to have this one under our belts by October.

Sorry that I can't tell you more about what I see – Wait until I get home – Regards to all and love and kisses for you and the baby –

With All My Love,

Your Dave

———

Saturday 24 June [1944]
Still Somewhere in Italy

My Dearest Amy and Carole Frances,

Your letter was the first inkling that I had that you had already mailed the first salami. I certainly hope that it makes it here in good shape. Syd wrote that he also mailed his – also, Uncle Ben. So it won't be long before we have a real picnic. Thanks for the salami and Alka-Seltzer – they will both be just what I want.

As you now know, that temporary hold at Terracina was not a big effort. So, in the future, when you read of a holding at a certain point, don't become alarmed, because it isn't much. We are in complete control of the situation and are able to handle anything that may come up. I saw Terracina – it was a mess!

I'm glad that Carole is calling you "Mommy" instead of "Amy." Is she asking, "What's cooking?" yet? I know that you are careful about what you say around her. I never want to hear her say any cuss-word, and I'll do everything that I can to avoid it. To tell you the truth, I didn't enjoy the jokes that you sent this time – they were too crude. I'd better not ask for any more in the future.

The C.O. is boiling mad about the condition of the area and he calls me up on the carpet to answer for the situation. It is the duty of the First Sergeant in the first place, but somehow he has selected me, all of a sudden, to complain to. Now, I have to go around and give the others hell for the laxity. This is the first time that I have ever told you about any little troubles that I have had while overseas – but it finally had to come to a head. There have been too many cases of this going on and it gets you to a stage where you are ready to eat a person up alive. This outfit has certainly gotten to a low degree of efficiency. I am of the opinion that it is all due to Lt. Maddox and his method of running the company. The men have lost all respect for all the officers and just don't give a damn. Now, when anything comes up, it is like pulling teeth to get them to do anything for their own good. I have tried to do a good job of it, but now I am ready to throw in the sponge. I value my wife and baby too much to let the Army get my nerves shattered. So if you receive a letter in the future with a return address of Pvt. David E. Stoliar, don't be surprised. I had hoped that when Lt. Temple took over, that the men would change their attitude and get on the ball. Well, let's hope that this damned War is over soon, so I can throw it all in the ocean as we come across.

That is a load off my chest – so I can rest easier now that you know the truth of the situation. Meanwhile, you don't know how much I really miss you and the baby – It is too much to describe. So say "Hello" to everybody and kiss the baby for me and tell her to do the same to you for me –

With All My Love,

Your Dave

P.S. I don't know what the censor will think – but I don't care.

———

Sunday 25 June [1944]
Still Somewhere in Italy

My Dearest Wife and Baby,

Today, we had a few more officers in, and this time they were representing Maddox. To start with the beginning, it was back in Africa that testimonials were made as to the mismanagement of the company by him. The reports were made to a Lt. Col. in the Mediterranean Base Section. After that, we came across to Italy and, about three weeks later, he was told that he was relieved of his command. Then Lt. Temple was appointed as C.O. Well, then a Major called some of the company personnel in and questioned them. The Major is to be the prosecutor. After about four days of questioning, we moved out and now Lt. M.'s defense is asking questions about what has taken place in the company. They are trying to build up a case against anyone who is saying incriminating things about him.

Darling, I dreaded the day that I was ever assigned to this outfit. It has been nothing but a great, big headache. Now, when one tries to correct

certain things in an outfit, you are getting yourself in for a lot of red tape.
Although Lt. M. had never done anything to me, it had hurt me to see
certain things going on in the outfit that were making it worse and worse
with each succeeding day. Therefore, I was glad to testify that he was not a
desirable C.O. Now we are having a General Court-Martial and all of
us are to go up on the stand next Wednesday. It has been bad enough to go
through all the incidents and then to have to relate them again and again.
I don't know what will happen to him or me or any of the other men who
are testifying, but I don't care as long as the faults can be corrected. He had
made me do certain things that didn't seem right to me, but he was the C.O.
and I had to follow orders from him. Now, he thinks that he is going to place
things in my lap. However, he signed all things and he is the responsible
party and not me. I don't have any personal grievance against him, so I hope
that they let him keep his commission, but take him out of our organization.
I know that you have had enough things to worry about, but I wanted you
to see what sort of things one has to go through in the Army. If only this War
would end soon, I'd certainly be one happy guy. I could go back to my wife
and baby and live a normal life again. Gosh, what a world.

Meanwhile, regards to all and a great big hug and kiss for you and the
baby —
With All My Love,
Your Dave

———

Monday 26 June [1944]
Still Somewhere in Italy

My Sweetest Family,
I am feeling alright now that I have told you everything that has taken
place lately. I was able to get some sleep for a change. In fact, late in the
evening, a group of us went out on the coast and went swimming. It was
such a great relief to most of us who hadn't taken a shower for such a long
time. However, there was one thing that made it bad — It was the refuse
that was washed up on the shores. We only stayed about 30 minutes and it
was growing dark, so we came back.

What do you think of the War situation now? We are doing alright and
soon we ought to have Florence and Pisa and Genoa. After that, the Nazis
will really have a tough time around here. The Russians are certainly
starting to give them hell again. I happened to catch a Nazi propaganda

broadcast this morning, and to hear the sort of stuff that they put out, you would think that they are winning the War instead of losing it. I can't see how the German people can absorb all that hooey. The Nazis stated that the Russians had lost 50,000 airplanes, 70,000 tanks, and about 12,700,000 men. If that was all true, how in the world did they ever get the Jerries to retreat so fast and so far? Another outrageous statement was that the Jewish soldiers in the American Army are receiving 25% more food than the non-Jews. They say that due to Jewish food laws, that difference is in effect – Have you ever heard anything so ridiculous? We all eat in the same mess, out of the same type of mess kits, and are given the same portions that any other soldier is given. That just shows you the type of stuff they are putting out. I'm glad that nobody pays any attention to that stuff.

As I have said many times before, the only thing that keeps me going is the fact that at the end of it all, you and Carole will be there and we can spend the rest of our lives together. I do miss you both so much – but there's nothing to do about it but to do the job and hope for a quick ending. Just remember that I love you and am thinking of you at all times – Regards to all –

With All My Love,
Your Dave

Wednesday June 28, 1944
Still Somewhere in Italy

My Dearest Wife & Baby,

Yesterday, I was on the road to Rome. We were going to a place outside of the city where the Court-Martial is to take place. We took a jeep and a truck down to take care of the first group of men. Today, there is another group coming up to testify. It was quite a drive and we were all worn out and dirty when we arrived. To top it off, nobody thought that we'd need our helmets to wash out of – except one man – so we all had to borrow his helmet. This morning, I got up at 6:00 A.M. and washed and shaved and had breakfast. After that, it has been one game of solitaire after another, waiting for the afternoon to come – that's when the case comes up. It'll be a relief to get this all over with. Last nite, I dreamed that Lt. Maddox threw in the sponge and admitted his guilt to all the charges – maybe? I'll let the rest of this letter hang on awhile, until after the questioning.

Well, Darlings, it is now the next day and about 12:45. Going back to yesterday, about 4:00 P.M., I was called in as a witness. I was in there until about 5:15, when the court was recessed for chow. We came back at 5:45 and continued until about 6:30, when the defense had finished cross-examining me. There were officers from the rank of Colonel to Major on the jury – if that is what you call it. Anyway, I told them the whole truth and what had gone on in the company and that was all there was to it. The most astonishing thing, however, was something that Maddox must have conceived in that wild mind of his. His defense tried to introduce evidence that there had been a plot in effect to oust Maddox and get Lt. Rodger in as C.O.; and me getting the sorry job as First Sergeant. When I heard this, I was amazed. To even get any such notion is the acme of the imagination. Anyway, the judges finally, after a few ridiculous questions by the defense, instructed them to cease that type of questioning, as there was no proof of such a plot existing. I'm afraid that Maddox will not be able to beat the rap.

The unfortunate thing is that while we were back in Africa, there must have been 60% of the company that made statements at one time or another to the effect that they hated Maddox and were anxious to get him out of the company. Now that the trial has come up, they turn right around and tell a deliberate lie, while under oath. They claimed that they never saw him drunk; never saw him gamble with the enlisted men; never saw him borrow money from the enlisted men. Why, there must have been four or five times, at least, that he shot craps in the company street, while 10 or 15 men stood around and either took part or watched. He was seen a few times in a state of being under the influence of liquor. Now when they are under oath, they say that they never saw any such thing – Isn't that enough to get under your skin? I was never so disgusted with humanity as I am now. It will be one grand relief to get home with some decent people for a change. Well, at least there are about ten men who are telling the truth and that ought to bear some weight. We ought to know what the verdict is in a couple of days. The testimony is still going on down there. I don't object to him keeping his commission, because I know how my wife would feel if I lost it. Just let him get out of the outfit, so that we can function efficiently and help to win this War in a big hurry. I guess I nearly hit the nail on the head – Rome was taken near Fathers' Day – so I get my wish. Also, the Russians have launched their attack from the East at the same time as we are pushing in from the West. Say, maybe I'll get to be a military analyst.

As to the future family situation, no, I can't control the sex – but we can control the number. I still think that four babies would be nice. Don't worry about that angle for a while, because I, too, might want to enjoy a "second honeymoon." So that is the dope for the last few days. Darling, you and the baby are even more dear to me than before, now that I have had instances of the types of people who are living in this world. I don't know why I even worry about it anymore – I'm going to forget all about it and concentrate on coming home to my family. I guess that is about all, so send regards to all and lots of love and kisses for you and Carole Frances –

With All My Love,

Your Dave

P.S. In one of the April issues of "Sat. Eve. Post," you will find a story about a Supply Officer – It is really a picnic, because it is so true to life. The title is, "Success is Ruining My Career" – by Capt. Donald Hough. Try to read it – it's hilarious!

HAPPY BIRTHDAY –

Carole Frances

Ask Mommy for a big kiss from me.

———

Friday 30 June [1944]
Still Somewhere in Italy

My Most Adorable Twosome,

I'm feeling pretty good these days – now that the trial is over and a decision reached. I was told that the court found him guilty of four counts, all of which he had admitted. He was fined $50.00 per month for one year. That was all that I found out, but it may have more to it – We will learn later after the case has been reviewed by the Adjutant's Office. It is the general opinion of everybody that he got off very lightly. Well, just so he doesn't come back to the outfit. The men seem to be in much better spirits, now that it is all over.

The War news seems to get better each day – Pretty soon, we won't be satisfied with just gaining 50 miles a day. The Russians are really putting the Jerries to rout at this time. They ought to be in Bulgaria and Poland any day now. When they do get in – it ought to be a slaughter. They will remember the days that the Nazis spent while they were in Russia. I don't blame them one bit if they go on a spree and murder a few thousand of the damned Axis satellites. If we forget all those atrocities that the Nazis were responsible for, we will never come out on the right side of the peace. They ought to pay for every bit of reconstruction in all countries. That would keep them busy for such a long time that they will never have time to think of another War. I hope that not one ounce of consideration is shown them. Why, from what I have seen, it will take at least 50 or 75 years to rebuild what has been destroyed – not mentioning the historical buildings.

I have gotten to a point where I absolutely hate the Nazis and anyone who was or is associated with it. When I saw that picture in the paper of Mrs. Lois de Lafayette Washburn [American fascist and anti-Semite] *thumbing her nose at the court, it made me sick. Just to know that such people are running around loose in the States is enough to turn one's stomach. There are, no doubt, a great many who are starting to plug leniency for the Axis when the terms are to be decided. The government ought to put these away for a while, so that they would have time to ponder their stand. When these people will wake up to the fact that we are losing lives to allow them to live at home safely, I will never know.*

Now that you are so impressed with the second bombing of Japan, do you have 100% faith in the staffs of the Allies and not any in the writings of the armchair generals? We ought to be hitting Tokyo every other day soon.

Well, Darlings, I have given you all the dope for now – Hope that all is well at home and send regards to all. Give the baby a big day-after-birthday kiss and let her return it. So, looking forward to a quick end to this War –
With All My Love,
Your Dave

———

Shabbas 1 July [1944]
Still Somewhere in Italy
My Sweetest and Most Adorable Old Hag, (Excuse me, I meant bag),

Oh well, so I ain't neat. Maybe it is the heat that makes me write so. As you know, I really think that you are the most adorable wife and baby a guy could have.

Well, so you finally know that we are not where you had hoped we would be. I was wondering if you would ever find out. The Germans are way up North this time, so don't worry. I haven't seen any dead Jerries around for quite a while – darn it – They don't stay long enough, they are retreating so fast. Your calculations have been correct so far – up until recently. I am convinced that the War will end very suddenly – possibly before the Allies enter German territory. They do want to keep their lands as clean as possible before surrendering. With the Russians speeding in from the East (they are 575 miles from Berlin now), us coming up from the South (595 miles now) and the Allies pushing thru from the West (600 miles), we ought to all arrive on the border at about the same time. We are the closest to the German boundary and if we ever get in – we'll really wreck that damned country.

I suppose the feeling is mutual on us being apart. I miss you so very much, too. Just remember that I'll be back soon and it won't seem long. Meanwhile, send regards to all and – just to remind you – I love you very, very much – loads of love and kisses for you and the baby –

With All My Love,
Your Dave

Monday 3 July [1944]
Still Somewhere in Italy

My Sweetest Wife and Baby,

Today, I was the proud recipient of a nice, big package from the States. There it was – neatly wrapped (They are playing "Begin the Beguine" right now in London) but for a few cracks on the corners. Well, my stomach swelled with anticipation as I greedily carried it into my tent. I started to undo it and immediately noticed a peculiar odor about. I thought that it was a dog or some wild animal, but after getting the paper off of the package, I was the most depressed guy that you have ever seen. It seems that the lid of the pickle jar came loose and the juice spilled all over everything. The salami was spoiled completely. I know that you are as sorry about it all as I, but let's hope that the others will come out alright. I guess there are more important things than that anyway – don't you agree? Phew, I can still smell it, although it was thrown out long ago.

I don't know what sort of a widow you will be when I get home, but I don't imagine it will be a golf widow – maybe hunting – I have taken a great liking to it. Of course, I won't be able to shoot any Nazis over in the States, but there are some small game that are just as enjoyable to hunt and kill. Maybe you and Carole Frances will care for a long fishing trip for a vacation. Well, we'll see when I get there and have spent about six months at home – and I mean at home. After that, you will probably be tired of seeing me around and get a desire to travel. Why talk about that now – eh?

Darlings, you certainly don't know how much I miss you these days. When the moon comes out so full, I think about those evenings when we pitched *woo up on top of the Muny Opera hill – those were the days. I think of the nights when we showed the baby to our guests while you or I held a flashlight up to the ceiling so as not to awaken her – remember? Then when you and Carole came out to Fresno – it was such a total change. She was a big girl. And the day that she got up off the floor and walked – we nearly keeled over. I like to remember how she'd sit in the big chair and I'd sit on the couch and we would throw the tennis balls to each other. Well, I'm looking forward to continuing those games with her and you.*

I suppose that is all for the day – So, once more, I want to say that I'm sorry about the package – Say "Hello" to all and tell them that I'll be seeing them soon – For the baby and you, loads and loads of love and kisses –

With All My Love,
Your Dave

———

Tuesday 4 July [1944]
Still Somewhere in Italy

My Sweetest Embraceable Two,

I suppose that before going any further, I ought to wish you and everybody at home a most enjoyable Independence Day. Hope that it didn't result in any casualties anywhere in the country.

As you know now, Maddox is no longer with the outfit. Today, I learned that he really fell into a soft spot – as Assistant Special Service Officer for the unit to which we are attached. I am not allowed to tell you who we're with or any of the other units around here – so excuse me. That really is a snap and he's lucky to get in it – There is absolutely nothing to it.

Well, at the rate we are going, it won't be long. As you know, the Russians took Minsk and are much deeper in Poland each day. It certainly is a race to see who gets into Berlin first. Just as long as it is one of us – that is alright with me.

So that just about winds up the news for today and this is your European reporter, Sgt. David E. Stoliar, thanking you for your kind attention and looking forward to seeing you soon – Regards to all and lots of love to Carole and you –

With All My Love,
Your Dave

———

Wednesday 5 July [1944]
Still Somewhere in Sunny Italy

My Most Beloved Amy and Carole Frances,

Say, the French invasion took place about a month ago today. Gosh, how time has flown. It seemed as tho it was only a week ago that the Allies landed. You will probably see a big push now that the channel has quieted down and we are getting supplies into Cherbourg Harbor.

Another fellow received a package that held salami and it also went bad. We thought that it was on account of the cookies that were packed with them. It seems that salami alone comes thru alright, but when with something else, it is ruined. I hope that your other packages are received in good shape.

Well, Darlings, as you know, when there is no mail, it is most difficult to write a long letter. Therefore, please excuse the brevity of this one. In the meantime, send regards to all and a great big kiss for you and the baby –

With All My Love,
Your Dave

—

Thursday 6 July [1944]
Still Somewhere in Italy

My Dearest Wife and Baby,

Some of the boys are getting boxes of chocolates in pretty good condition, so I ought to get a couple of the salamis in good condition, too. I only hope that the pickles don't stick their noses in the salamis' business. At this moment, we are having a showdown inspection and Lt. Rodger and Lt. Micka are checking. Boy, what a headache this job is. You have to be not only a lawyer in order to figure out some of the directives that the War Dep't puts out, but you also have to be a mother to these guys, because they are so damned negligent in watching their clothing and equipment. At times, I get so burned up, I walk out of the Supply tent and try to calm down. I hate this job and told Lt. Temple that. He said that somebody has to do the job now, so I am stuck with it. Well, I'll just carry on as in the past and try not to take these things so seriously. After all, I have to come home to you in good health and a good frame of mind – don't I?

Regards to all and tons of love and kisses for the baby and you –
With All My Love,
Your Dave

—

7 July [1944]
Still Somewhere in Italy

My Sweetest Darlings,

Well, I just hit the jackpot and it really paid off – two packages and six letters. The packages were from you and Syd. Well, I tore at Syd's package like a thirsty person goes for water. I was satisfied that it was wrapped well and protected. When I got all the inner paper off – there lay a moldy salami. I was again disappointed, but got the rest of the contents in good condition – mainly the soap, razor blades, cheese and pickles. I ate some of the sliced pickles and they hit the spot. Right after that, I opened your package, hoping that it would make up for the other two losses. I didn't have to go far – There was that familiar smell and the soft feel to the package. When I got it all opened, there wasn't a bit of it any good. I received the Alka-Seltzer and the soap, however, so thanks for the attempt. I know now that you just can't send salami overseas and expect it to come in alright. From now on, I'll wait till I get home to indulge in those things. If the weather had been cold, I guess they would have come in OK. Oh well – the War won't be lost and I think I'll live. The main thing is that I got six letters – all of them yours. The first was dated The D-Day – 6th June. What a day that must've been in the States. I can picture Washington Avenue with everybody asking the other if they knew that the invasion was on. The idea of praying for all the soldiers was a very thoughtful one – except the workers only thought about them on just this day. They ought to consider them at all times and then there would be no more strikes.

Your calculations were correct on the plans of the Nazis and the Russians for that week. As to the reason for the Nazis not wrecking Rome, it is a matter of opinion right now. Most think that if they should do anything to injure the hub of Catholicism, it would affect the decisions that would be handed down later, when the terms of the surrender are discussed. Quite a few think it will make the Europeans think that the Germans aren't such a bad lot after all, and bring about a little sympathy for them. Of course, as long as they were down in the Rome area and if they'd started the destruction of Rome, there was always the possibility of all Italians, in the North, taking up arms against the Nazis and cutting them off from their homeland. That seems to be the case right now pertaining to Florence. The Nazis say that they want to preserve the art treasures – Did they in Poland

– Belgium – and other territories that they demolished? It is all a protective means of withdrawal.

Sorry to learn about Paul. Don't let Beulah worry, because the Japs are having a hard enough time to protect their homeland without going out and looking for trouble. Even if he is on an island, he is quite safe from air attacks. You'd be surprised how much the Axis air activity has died down. They just don't have the stuff to carry on a very long War.

Well, Darling, that is about all the dope for now, so once more, have a good time and send regards to all – loads and loads of love and kisses for you and the baby –

With All My Love,
Your Dave

———

Saturday 8 July [1944]
Still Somewhere in Italy

My Dearest, Loveliest Wife and Baby,

So you left for your Michigan vacation today. Sorry that I was unable to accompany you; my boss wouldn't let me take any time off. Maybe I'll go with you next time. I probably will get a couple of weeks in Berlin soon. Of course, I hate traveling the continent at this time of the year – but with accommodations as bad as they are now, one can't be particular.

I attended my first traveling U.S.O. show. It took place on Thursday evening and they really had quite a turnout. There were only about three entertainers – a female accordionist, a female vocalist, and a male M.C. He, of course, was a lantzman [fellow Jew] *and had a pretty good line of gags. The singer was announced as formerly a singer with Tommy Dorsey's orchestra – I never heard of her – Vivian Sherman. She was pretty good, however, and so was the other girl. Tonite there is another show – This time, there are supposed to be a chorus of about 50 girls – but you know how latrine rumors are. I think that I'll go anyway, just to get away from this place.*

Wasn't that terrible about that fire in a circus in Hartford, Conn? To think of all those children who were killed in one swift stroke – It's a wonder that the people aren't more careful, now that we're at War. It is things like that that make a fellow think those at home are letting him down. Well, let's hope that another doesn't occur at any time.

As you know, the War is proceeding very well. As I wrote you some time ago, we now know that we are able to bomb Japan at will, so it won't be long before this whole thing will be over. This latest attack, the third one, must have really made quite an impression on the sons-of-bitches. Oh, should I have said sons-of-heaven? So solly. The Nazis are still backing up on all fronts and soon will be dancing cheek-to-cheek with each other. The Russians must be in Lithuania by today, so Prussia will be gotten by the end of the month. Better get my bath ready – I'll be home pretty soon.

Well, I want all of you to have a most enjoyable time and come home well-rested. Don't you go getting chummy with any of those 4-F's up there, either. I'm just kidding – So say "Hello" to everybody and stay well – Lots and lots of love for you and the baby –

With All My Love,
Your Dave
P.S. Just to remind you that – I love you!!!

Sunday 9 July [1944]
Still Somewhere in Italy

My Most Adorable Wife and Baby,

Another Sunday and the beginning of another week that will bring us together again. The time has really flown – It seems that it was just yesterday that I left Fresno. It has now been about six months. If the time goes as fast the next six months as the last, I ought to begin packing right now. As you know, the War in Italy is still pushing Northward, so it is necessary to keep up with the Nazis. Last night, I went to the U.S.O. show – but it wasn't any 50-girl show as the latrine rumor went. In fact, there were exactly five people in the whole affair, including the M.C. He was also a lantzman and was not too funny. There was a girl who spoke one of those risqué songs and she looked like a strip-tease artist. Also a vocalist who was pretty good. There was a fellow who juggled and he was really good. There was also an accordionist who was only fair. It seems that these U.S.O. entertainers are people who were unable to hit a good spot in the States and had no alternative but to go with the U.S.O. I suppose once in a while, we will get to see some really good entertainment.

When we had finished dinner, the Red Cross girls came up again, for the second time, and served doughnuts to the boys. They are here at this moment, but I would much rather write to you than to speak to them. Let the other single guys try their luck. Well, Darlings, I guess that's about all the dope for today, so once more, have a good time, and send regards to all – and an abundance of love and kisses for you and Carole –

　　With All My Love,
　　Your Dave

———

Tuesday 11 July [1944]
Still Somewhere in Italy

My Very Dearest Amy and Carole Frances,

　　As to Maddox, he is being transferred to another company, but we don't know which as yet. Well, we won't have to worry about him for a while now. He certainly did ruin this outfit.

　　As to Rome being cleaner than Naples, it's because the Northern Italians are more modern and closer to the rest of continental Europe than those in the South. Also, the Southerners are mostly from Sicily and the Southern tip of Italy. Those sections always had the reputation as being places from which the bandits and scum came. So that accounts for the differences in the two cities.

　　From the War news, maybe I will be able to write soon that I'm planning to return in a few weeks. The Russians are still pushing Westward and it doesn't look like the Nazis are going to stop them. As you know, the Axis' oil supply is down to next to nothing and no hopes for any more coming in. That is a vital thing, without which a nation cannot wage a winning war. We are finding tanks and other vehicles on roads in France and Italy that were abandoned because of lack of fuel. The bombings of Ploesti don't help either. So from all indications, we ought to get ready to spend Xmas in the States. Or am I being a bit too optimistic? Well, Darlings, I guess that is about all for the day, so keep well and say, "Hello" to all and tell the baby that I love her mommy very much. Also, that I love her as much and am looking forward to that day when I can pick her up in my arms again –

　　With All My Love,
　　Your Dave

———

Friday 14 July [1944]
Still Somewhere in Italy

My Sweetest Darlings,

　　At this time, I am listening to a new record – by Danny Kaye – "Deenah" and "Fairy Piper" – They are really funny. Some of the new recordings that we got are "Star Eyes" – "Besame Mucho" – and a number of others that are new to us. All of them are good.

As to the feeling one has when living in his own home, I can appreciate how you feel. I know that I will try to help to beautify the place as much as possible. You know that I want the best of everything – best wife – best children – best family – and I try to get it that way even if I don't go about it in the most diplomatic way. When I walk home (I should say to camp), I look up at those great big shining stars and wonder if you are looking at them, too. When there isn't any moon, they just stare down at you and make you seem so tiny in this huge world. Well, I guess we are after all. Anyway, I am always thinking of you and looking forward to that day when we will never have to be apart anymore – So send regards to all and tell the folks to take it easy and keep well – A million and one kisses for you and the baby –

With All My Love,
Your Dave

Wednesday 20 July [1944]
Still Somewhere in Italy

My Very Dearest Wife and Baby,

Sunday, I got a pass and started about 8 in the morning for an airport. About 10:45, a plane came in just for a special purpose and I asked the pilot if he had room for another, if he was going to Rome. He said that he could, so I got down there about 11:30. I got a ride in and walked to a Palestine Club for Jewish soldiers. It is sponsored by the British, but they still were glad to help me. I have now flown in three different types of planes – A three-place Stinson; a C-47 such as the one in which we flew down to Los Angeles; and a B-25. Of them all, I like the Billy Mitchell the best – It is by far the smoothest ride of them all. Darlings, you don't know what a feeling it is to be sailing along in the white, wooly clouds and see breaks every now and then where the sea comes thru. I felt nearer to heaven than I have ever felt before – that is, physically. Mentally, it has been on so many different occasions with you.

When I got back to camp, I found nine (9) letters – four from you. If [columnist Walter] *Winchell predicts something – it has a darned good chance to come true. In the case of the War in Europe, not only he and I are optimistic about it all, but a very high Allied officer – Gen.* [Bernard] *Montgomery, commanding troops in France, is of the same opinion. So maybe our hope will really materialize. I read about the big munitions explosions at San Francisco. It's amazing how much carelessness is responsible for tremendous losses of lives right in the States. Don't try to figure what the Army will do next – It just isn't possible – Otherwise, the enemy would be able to solve our strategy. If we continue to do the unexpected, we will all be back in the States again soon. With the Jap big shots and the cabinet out, the Nips will probably try to get out of the War with as much as possible. At least, this is a definite indication that they are breaking within. If you recall, I wrote that now that we are able to bomb Japan from land bases, it will greatly alter the War in the Pacific. Hope that all will come thru as expected.*

I saw a picture the night that I got back – It was "Four Jills and a Jeep" – with Carole Landis, Kay Francis, Mitzi Mayfair and Martha Raye. It was rather amusing and up to the minute. The only thing that all the G.I.'s laughed at was when the all-clear signal was given and a soldier walked along and shouted "All clear! All clear!" That is definitely not done. There was a good song in there, but nobody sang it - "No Love-No Nothing-'Till My Baby Comes Home." How true – eh?

Well, Darlings, say "Hello" to all and tell the folks that I hope that they come back in perfect health. For you and Carole Frances, a great big kiss and a breathtaking hug –

With All My Love,
Your Dave

———

Saturday 22 July [1944]
Still Somewhere in Italy

My Most Adorable Wife and Baby,

Here we are at the end of another week and what a week it has been! The Jap cabinet and heads of the Army and Navy have resigned (demanded); the near-assassination of Hitler took place; and now there are revolts going on in Germany. And to top that, we are on our way to regaining Guam. Now don't you think that we are getting along pretty well? With an admitted defeat by the Nips, we are so very much closer to the end in the Pacific. The incidents in Germany were looked forward to for quite a while and we hope that they will continue and catch hold throughout Europe. If so, it would be only a matter of weeks before this War will end. There will probably be more attacks in the future from other points and with what Hitler has to contend with now, he will really be in hot oil. So let's be a bit optimistic about the whole affair and think of the times we are going to have when I get back.

It is still hot as hell here and I have a devil of a time to keep cool and clean. Lt. Micka went into Naples and got a bottle of beer for each man. It is quite a large bottle and is the first that we will have in Italy. So far, I haven't gone down to claim my bottle – I'm waiting for it to get cold. Gosh, will I gulp it down when I do open it. Well, Fay just returned with the beer and it is almost a quart-size. Gosh, does it hit the spot! We'll have to drink it in a hurry or else it will get warm and flat. We will get some more on Wednesday and also some Cokes and PX rations for the first time in about three months. We had been getting combat rations, which were one package of cigarettes, one package of gumdrops and a package of blades if you needed it. Baron received a package from home that contained five cans of assorted soups. He said that he had been getting them right along, including some chili and tamales. Well, I never did think about that before, but now I'd like for you to get some and send it to me. See if you can get hold of some chicken noodle and clam chowder and tamales and chili.

Well, Darlings, send best wishes to all and a billion hugs and kisses for the baby and you –

With All My Love,
Your Dave
P.S. I did finish the bottle before it got warm.

———

Monday July 24, 1944
8:00P.M. – Monday
[Still Somewhere in Italy]

My Dearest Wife & Baby,

Today, I went thru a town where the former king's palace is located. Outside, there was a long and patient line of traffic that had been held up for about 30 minutes. I stopped and inquired what it was all about and was told that the King of England and a 4-star General (either American or something) were in the palace. I didn't get to see any of it, because I was too late.

At the rate the War is going, we will really be home sooner than expected. The reports out of Germany are really encouraging. However, now, we might push our efforts doubly hard in order to make their defeats felt deeper.

We absolutely must wreck Germany and all her War ideas for the future if we are to rest easily after our Victory.

Tell Carole Frances that she had better not bring back a boyfriend – I can't support him yet. Anyway, have a good time and best wishes to all – a big kiss and hug for you and the baby to tide you over for a while –

With All My Love,
Your Dave

———

Tuesday 7/25/44
Still Somewhere in Italy

My Most Beloved Wife and Baby,

We were issued Cokes (two per man) and I am trying to cool mine in a helmetful of water. It ought to be fairly cool by tomorrow morning. As to rations, we really have been getting the real thing. Yesterday, we had fried chicken and today, we had thick steaks. It has been some time since we had rations like that on two successive days. Tomorrow, we ought to get another week's rations of beer – we hope.

I suppose the War is progressing favorably on all fronts and assume that the Russians are now about 350 miles at least from the German capital. I guess that they are in East Prussia by now. I am almost certain the War will end over here by October 1st. The Russians will no doubt be in Germany by that time and well on their way to Berlin – if not in it. Also, we will be well into France and probably have taken Paris long before. All in all, everything seems to point to a very sudden collapse in Germany and then it will only be a matter of weeks. It has been a known fact that the Junkers were against Hitler, but weren't in any position to break with him until now – when defeats are piling up against the Nazis. Now, they are trying to get a good excuse for the Allies to take pity on them when the terms are discussed.

It has been over seven months since we have seen each other – long, isn't it? Now I am so glad that I phoned as often as I did at our P [oint] *of E* [mbarkation]. *The one thing on which I haven't decided is whether I should phone you when I get back or just walk in. But, of course, you and Carole Frances will be at the pier to welcome me – or will it be an airport? I guess that is about all the news for today, so take good care of the baby and yourself and remember I'll be home soon –*

With All My Love,
Your Dave

Wednesday 7/26/44
Still Somewhere in Italy

Dearest Amy and Carole Frances,

We got another bottle of beer today and this time, I saw to it that we got ice to cool it with. I had mine with some steak sandwiches that we had for dinner. That makes two days in succession that we have had steak – what a hard War! I note in the "Stars & Stripes" that you may soon get rationless meats – true? The War news is pretty good still and, from all indications, it ought to end sooner than previously anticipated. If you failed to catch the drift of my comment the other day about the King of England, you probably know now what I was talking about. Today's paper said that he was in Italy and visited with Sir Henry Maitland Wilson, the Supreme Allied Commander in the Mediterranean area. It was a shame that I was driving the vehicle at the time that we were held up, or else I would have gotten out and looked into the situation myself and gotten to see them both. Well, if I get to see the Statue of Liberty, that will be just the right sight for me any old day.

Well, with each day's victory that the Cardinals are chalking up, we are getting closer to another World Series in St. Louis. I hope that the Brownies are able to keep up the good work – They deserve to win a pennant for a change – if not the Series.

I do love and miss both of you so very much – So, without any more waste of words, say, "Hello" to all and send them my regards – Just keep well and take good care of yourself and the baby –

With All My Love,
Your Dave
P.S. They are playing "Begin the Beguine" right at the moment I am addressing the envelope – Like it?

Thursday – 7/27/44
Still Somewhere in Italy

My Most Adorable Amy and Carole Frances,

I don't know if I have ever told you, but we have some Englishmen attached to us temporarily – It has been for about three months now. We get along pretty well now and we certainly do kid them. We brag about the American cigarettes and the PX rations that the "limeys" are always anxious to get hold of. It burns them up, but they come back with the fact that, in the evening when they prepare tea, all the American boys come around and ask for a cupful. Then, when we have tea to drink with our meal, we all ask for iced tea and they insist that we are ruining it. By the way, today I got hold of a whole truckful of ice and we really have had cool (or cold) drinks all day.

I see that the Cards and Brownies are still playing good ball, so they have a wonderful chance to have a streetcar World Series in St. Louis. However, I don't think that the Browns will be able to stick it out in the stretch of September.

Well, Darlings, keep well and keep all my love warm – I'll see you subsequently – Fondest regards to the folks –
With All My Love,
Your Dave

———

Sunday 7/30/44
Still Somewhere in Italy

My Sweet Embraceable Two,
Darling, as to the exact date of the termination of the War, you know that nobody alive is capable of that prediction. Therefore, when I write that the War will end soon, I don't mean tomorrow or in a couple of days. I mean that, in comparison, it will be soon. It may be a matter of months, but after all, consider the fact that it was planned long before in a matter of years. Therefore, I am not trying to disappoint you in any way; I want you to believe that it will be over in a shorter time than at first anticipated. I realize that you have had one heck of a time trying to figure out what I'm writing, but that's the way it will have to be for the rest of the War, so let's forget about that little detail for the time being. As you know, the Russians are about 15 miles from Warsaw and after that, it is a short distance to Berlin. Considering everything, I know that the Allies are doing OK on all other fronts.

I'm holding Carole to her promise to give her daddy a big kiss when he returns. Also, tell her that I'd appreciate one from her mommy. It's hard to picture her playing with a dollhouse. I'll probably have to get her a real baby when I get back.

The 21st was the day that you learned of the attempted assassination of Hitler. It was a tough thing that the bomb wasn't a bit to the left more – It would have made things so much nicer. Now it means that we will really have to kill him with our own ammunition. As to the idea of Berlin falling, the Nazis won't let it happen – They will capitulate before the Russians can get to the people. They will remember the wholesale slaughters that they had committed on the Russians in Russia and will be afraid of a similar thing occurring in Germany. Therefore, I am almost positive that they won't fight after the Allies are in Germany.

Well, Darlings, that winds up the day's activities – I may go to the show tonight – So stay well and regards to all – About a million hugs and kisses for you and the baby –

With All My Love,
Your Dave

———

Monday – 7/31/44
Still Somewhere in Italy

My Dearest Wife and Baby,

Today, I was honored with a package in which were three nice, juicy, stinky, rotten and moldy salamis – from my dad. I guess that about makes it definite that they cannot be sent from St. Louis in this heat. They were waxed in paraffin and then wrapped in waxed paper, but that still didn't save it. Well, I was able to salvage a jar of sweet pickles out of it. Some of the other boys got packages and their salamis came in OK – I don't get it. One of them got a hard salami – you know, a wurst – or something like that. They seem to arrive OK. Anyway, let's not send any more until the weather's cooler – and I hope that by that time, I'll just have to go up to the corner and buy it.

Earlier today, on my way back to camp, I passed a great number of English M.P.'s (not Members of Parliament) who were standing on both sides of the road in exceptionally clean uniforms. I thought it rather odd and asked about it. I was told that the King of England was coming by soon. Well, I was off that road before he arrived, so once more, I missed seeing him.

I did go to the show last night and saw a pretty good picture – "Follow the Boys" – with an all-star supporting cast to George Raft and, I think, Baronova. It was very entertaining and you'll enjoy it. The only difference in the scenes depicting the traveling U.S.O. shows and the ones that we see, is that we see only the hams. Well, maybe we will get to see the better ones soon. *Well, Darlings, that is about all for today – Give my regards to all and loads of love and kisses for you and Carole Frances –*

With All My Love,
Your Dave
P.S. I love you and the baby very, very much and miss you as much.

———

Tuesday 8/1/44
Still Somewhere in Italy

My Beloved Wife and Baby,

We are at the beginning of another month in our separation and I hope that soon, we won't have to enumerate them. It has been over seven months, but it won't be another seven before I'm home again. The War is coming to its closing stages in this theatre and I'm most confident that it will end suddenly. As you know, the Russians are battling at the gates of Warsaw now and it won't be long before they have taken it. After that, the path to Germany is wide open.

Well, today, we got our first PX rations in some time. It consisted of 15 bars of Baby Ruths, 6 packages of Doublemint gum, 2 boxes of fig bars, 2 boxes of Cheese Tidbits, 1 box of gelatin candy, 1 box of gumdrops, 1 large size nut Hershey bar, 2 rolls of chocolate-covered candies and a package of razor blades. So you see, we are pretty well taken care of in the way of candies. It's those little things like tamales that we miss. Of course, the big things that we all miss are our families and homes – but those will have to be back-ordered.

Remember that I love and miss you very, very much. Meanwhile, regards to all and beaucoup love and kisses for you and the baby –

With All My Love,
Your Dave

———

Wednesday 8/2/44
Still Somewhere in Italy

Dearest Sweethearts,

Beulah wrote of Paul's shipping. I was almost certain that he'd be in the States for the duration. I'm sorry that it had to happen and break up what I hoped would be a pretty period in their lives. Well, I only hope that he is a lucky guy and stays in safe territory.

As to the robot bombs, there isn't so much to get excited about, because they are not accurate in the first place. In the second place, they were only brought out to take away the idea of the Allies' invasion. That was the only thing that the Nazis had to give their people something about which to talk when it all began. Now, I'm sure that it will taper off as we advance into France. They are nothing but bombs with wings on them and do have a great power – but they still are not accurate enough to hit objectives. The evacuation of women and children is just a measure to ease the situation until they have found a good means of doing away with the bombs.

Well, today I got the beer for the outfit and am almost at the end of distributing it. The hell of it is that there are about 50 men sitting around on their fannies, doing absolutely nothing, and not one of them even offered to help the Supply Section. That is such a frequent occurrence that I now pass it off as expected. This outfit is about the lousiest in the whole world – There can't be any as bad. I know that as long as I keep looking forward to that day when I return, I'll keep my wits about me. But if I let this get the best of me – I'm licked. So I'm always thinking of you and Carole Frances and the day when I get back. Meanwhile, I'll send regards to all and a whole lot of love and kisses to Carole and you –

With All My Love,
Your Dave

———

Saturday 8/5/44
Still Somewhere in Italy

My Dearest Amy and Carole Frances,

The weather is still very warm and no sign of rain down here. Of course, we don't want rain in the North where the Allies are advancing so well. According to today's "Stars & Stripes," we are now in Florence. The Russians are going full blast and, of course, the offensive in France is doing well. I know that I've sounded very optimistic in the past, but I really feel that the War will end suddenly in Europe. Of course, the people back home shouldn't think the same way or else their efforts will be relaxed – and that ain't good.

Last night, I saw "Pin-Up Girl" and I thought it sort of stunk. They started with a fair plot, but made it into a hammy picture. Especially, the last scene where Grable drills a unit of girls. The boys see too much of the Army and they introduce drilling into a picture – You should have heard the boys laugh at it – If you have seen it – do you agree with me? Tonight, they are showing "Gaslight" – Charles Boyer and Ingrid Bergman. I know that picture will be good. It's about time that we had a good drama like that. I have seen very good write-ups on it in papers that some of the boys have received from home.

I noticed that [Missouri] *Sen.* [Bennett] *Clark was defeated in the senatorial race – I'm glad, because he was always an isolationist and was one of the men responsible for us not being ready for the Japs. Now that Truman is running as FDR's mate, the Democrats will have the best combination possible. They ought to beat Dewey – However, it will be closer than it has been for quite awhile.*

I suppose that is about all the news from here. So regards to all and take good care of yourselves. You may give Carole Frances a great big hug and kiss for me and she can reciprocate –

With All My Love,
Your Dave
P.S. I do love you and miss you so very much.

Sunday 8/6/44
Still Somewhere in Italy

Dearest Darlings,

I hope that you will excuse the paper if it comes in a bit wrinkled, because there is a high wind and it is rather hard to keep the paper from blowing, especially when it is as thin as this. On top of that, we are really getting the dust today.

That little story that you wrote, on all that the boys over here are giving up in order to live a peaceful life later, was very interesting and I wish that every person at home would feel that same way. They would put more into their War efforts and less bitching about working a little overtime. Wouldn't it be a great War if our men quit at 5 o'clock and said that it was time to stop fighting for the day?

As to remembering the dead Jerries, I've already forgotten all about them. The gov't, after the War, should also try to avoid showing pictures like that.

As to the election, I do think that FDR will win, but it will be a closer race than it has been for some time. He has a well-liked running mate in Truman and should take all. I do wish that the people wouldn't pay so much attention to the election and get down to business – That's one of the big wrongs that we have in our democracy – too much individualism. Every office-holder is scared to death that he will lose out and have to do an honest day's work. At times, Congress looks so stupid when we have a War to win.

Last night, I saw one of the good pictures that I have seen over in Italy – "Gaslight." Did you see it? It is very well-acted. As you know, all good things do come to an end, so this letter is almost at a close. Before I do end it, I want you to know that I am very much in love with you and miss you more and more each day – See if FDR is able to do something about it. Say "Hello" to all and best wishes to them –

With All My Love,
Your Dave

Friday 8/11/44
Still Somewhere in Italy

Dearest Amy and Carole Frances,

I don't know whether to get angry with you or not. First you write that you will absolutely write each and every day, and out of a clear blue sky, you forgot one day. I'd have a devil of a time trying to give you an explanation like that. What's happened to you – is it the separation? I had better get back to you and the baby in a hurry, so that you won't be so absent-minded. Just don't let it happen again – OK? As to hurrying to get off the cans for which I asked, there really is no great hurry – We're still able to digest G.I. food and breathe – don't ask me how. It's just that those other things for which I wrote will add to the variety of the food late in the evening, while we are having a bull session. Those are some of the little things we miss, to say nothing of our wives, children, sweethearts and families. I got something last night that I haven't had in a long, long time – a drink of real American whiskey. Don't be afraid – I only took two tiny drinks. It was really good, too, after tasting the rotten stuff they have over here. Oh, yes, there was a U.S.O. show in the area and I went there. It wasn't bad – There were three girls and a fellow who juggled, whom we had seen before.

Well, it looks like the Allies are really going ahead at quite a gallop in France. Once more, it won't be long. I still wonder what the situation will be when Carole sees her daddy again. I hope that she doesn't get shy. Give everyone my best wishes – lots of love and kisses for you and Carole –

With All My Love,
Your Dave

Saturday 8/12/44
Still Somewhere in Italy

My Sweetest Wife and Baby,

Today, I was rewarded with five (5) very wonderful letters. Gosh, what a haul that was! As to that War, we're not 40 miles from Paris and still going strong. It'll take a major counteroffensive to slow us down now. It's beginning to look pretty darned good all over the world. I hope that [British Prime Minister, Winston] *Churchill's visit here will bring about a quick end to the War. As to the* [General Erwin] *Rommel incident, it is true that he was wounded and is still serious. He has been operated upon twice so far and from the German statements, there are fragments in his brain. A sudden death would come in very handy now, as he was a popular guy with the younger Nazis in Europe. Of course, the Junkers will welcome his death.*

As to the robot-tanks, in the first place, they had been used in Anzio and all of them were fizzles. The Allies blew them up before they could do any damage. When they were switched to France, they had even less effect, because we had known how to handle them in Italy. So don't get so flustrated – it is only something that the Germans are using to try to detract from their defeats. In spite of all their "secret weapons," they are still retreating and having their homes blasted every day.

As to the reported pretty women in Rome, yes, there are some. If a guy goes out looking for something like a pretty girl, he may end up with more than he had bargained for. There is such a high rate of V.D. in Italy, that a guy is a chump to try anything. They do look very nice on the outside, but after all, you can't tell a book by its cover. If you got one look at these girls' legs and saw all the dirt and sores, you'd wonder if they ever washed them.

I've seen a lot of magazine pictures for the picture, "Hitler's Gang" – Did you get to see it? It ought to be amusing, if nothing else, because everybody knows by now just how he arose to power. I did go to see what I thought was a new picture last night – "Big Shot" with Bogart. I had seen it a few years ago with you. Send regards to all and best wishes to the folks, love and kisses for you and Carole Frances –

With All My Love,
Your Dave

Sunday 8/13/44
Still [Italy]

My Dearest Amy and Carole Frances,

I went to the show and saw "Tampico," with Edward G. Robinson and Lynn Bari. Mona Maris was also in the picture, which gave me a thought. They were eating together in the Brown Derby in Hollywood when we were in there. It is quite possible that they were making that picture at that time – do you agree? Anyway, the picture was just about Class BB.

I heard that Roosevelt made a broadcast after returning from his visit to Hawaii. I haven't learned the subject as yet. It'll probably have a bearing on the prosecution of the War in the Pacific. Hope that it is optimistic. I see that all men in the service will get a nice helping of turkey this coming Thanksgiving, Xmas and New Year's Day. I hope that I'm not over here to receive it at that time.

Well, Darlings, send regards to all – lots of love and kisses to you and Carole –

With All My Love,
Your Dave

Thursday 8/17/44
Still Somewhere in Italy

My Dearest Amy and Carole Frances,

We listened to the news broadcast from London. That was the first inkling that we had invaded Southern France. After that, we caught the Nazi propaganda broadcast. That was where we really had a good laugh. They said the invasion was negligible and didn't amount to much. It's really amazing, the way the German people are led to believe that they are actually winning the War. They even gave Tokyo's statement that the Americans are being wiped out, one after the other. Can you imagine such stupidity?

Glad to hear that the people at home are optimistic, but hope that they don't overdo it. Laxity now would mean that we'd be in this a year or two longer. As to just walking in when I get back, I guess that I had better call, because you really would faint. Don't look forward to my being there for Xmas – I'll just try.

Thanks for looking for the tamales – maybe you'll run across some cans in St. Louis. I'll really enjoy the chicken noodle soup and the cheese. Is the tongue smoked? That ought to be good, too. You know I'll like the chili, and if the tamales also come in around the same time, you know what I'll have then.

As to certain passages in my letters, I still am not trying to convey anything but what I actually write in my letters. If you see something definite by what I write, then it is that fact that I'm trying to say. Don't let your imagination run off with you. The one thing that you can be certain of is that we are always very safe.

As to my Italian vocabulary, it's still in the primary stage and soon I won't have to worry about it anymore. I'll be able to get along with the languages that I know. Yes, we are still intact and going along as usual – so don't worry about that.

That's about all the dope for now – Say "Hello" to all and give them my best wishes – millions of kisses and tons of love for you and Carole Frances –
With All My Love,
Your Dave

———

Thursday 8/17/44
Same Old Place [Italy]

Dearest Amy and Carole Frances,

Well, I was well rewarded with a letter from you today dated the 10th – also one from my dad of the same date. He's going to try to send me a hard salami and hope that it arrives in good shape. I was surprised to hear about Paul so soon. Glad that he's in Pearl Harbor – It's a good deal for any sailor to land in. I hope that he stays there for the duration.

As I have already written you a letter this morning, nothing new has happened – except that each man has received twelve bottles of American beer for his rations this week. So, with the same old ending – regards to all and lots of love and kisses for Carole Frances and you –
With All My Love,
Your Dave

———

Saturday – 8/19/44
Same Ol' Place [Italy]

My Sweetest Angels,

I guess you'll have a difficult time reading this. It's my first attempt at longhand for quite a while. I'll be writing for the next couple of weeks, I guess, because the typewriter won't be available. Don't ask me why. Unfortunately, today was another mail-less day. The outfit, as a whole, didn't receive much mail. Of course, this time, I can blame it on the Southern invasion. If we could invade every time we had a delay in the mails – I'd gladly wait months at a time to get mail. As you know, we're doing alright in Southern France and casualties have been held to the barest minimum. We'll do OK there and soon be pushing into Southern Germany. By the time you receive this letter, we ought to be in Paris and controlling the Channel Coast.

We still keep in touch with baseball thru the "Stars & Stripes" and I notice that the Brownies are now 7 games ahead. I certainly hope that they hang on 'til the season ends. That would really be something, to have an all-St. Louis World Series. I wish that I could be there to see the series. I'll bet that we make Carole Frances a baseball fan before she's 15 years old. We'll take her out for the Sunday double-headers and you can take her on Ladies' Days.

Well, Darlings, that's the news for now from Italy, so regards to all, and beaucoup love and kisses for Carole and you.

With All My Love,
Your Dave

Sunday 8/20/44
Still Somewhere in Italy

My Dearest Angels,

I hope that you are now able to figure out why we came back to this area. With the recent actions, that should add up. Don't worry; as far as we know, we're not going to the South Pacific. I still say that I'll be in Berlin soon and am not trying to throw you off. Of course, it will probably be thru another country – but I won't have any trouble with the language. As you know by now, to expect the end of the European War in September is too much. It looks like it could be by Thanksgiving, which would be a very appropriate day.

As to expenditures, don't forget that I wrote if you need anything for the home, go ahead and buy it. As to clothing, you don't have to ask my permission. Go ahead and buy whatever you need – but don't let me have to go over your closet and pick out a million and one things you aren't wearing. If you can't wear them, give it to a relief agency to ship across to Greece or Russia – but not to Italy. I detest these people – First they fight against you and upon seeing that their defeat is inevitable, they are immediately your allies. They have plenty over here if they'd open up all their hidden caches.

As to some letters sounding rather unpleasant and dismal, you ought to know me by now – I'm still as temperamental as always. If the day is dull and mail-less, I'm that way, too. Then again, the environment at times gets you and you have to express your feelings. However, don't take my harshness to heart, because it certainly is not meant. As I have written you before, certain emphasis on words cannot be heard thru writing – so forgive all these letters in the future.

Darling, don't try to figure out military strategy & moves – If I did know, I certainly wouldn't tell you. It involves too many lives to try to put one over on the censors. You know, there is another censor after it leaves our company. Just be patient and I'll tell you all that I'm able to. I'm sure that you have been brilliant enough in the past to continue to gather what you can from my letters and arrive at a good conclusion.

As to the women in Naples – don't worry, I wouldn't take any of them home as my wife – even if I was single. I'd much rather have a nice American-bred female. In a recent issue of "Yank," one page carried answers by various girls, of assorted nationalities, on what they think of the American soldier. They all admit that the G.I.'s are out for pitchin' woo – In fact, one Italian girl said that her boyfriend even promised her a jeep and to take her back to the States after the War. You can imagine the kind of lines they are handing out.

As to the War, we're still going strong on all fronts. There is one detail I want to emphasize – If you will remember our move to Rome, there was a period of 3 days when we destroyed over 2200 vehicles on the roads. After that, we went North in a big hurry. In the last 48 hours (up 'til Saturday) more than 2800 vehicles were destroyed in the West. That does not include armored ones such as tanks and tank destroyers. Therefore, I'm looking forward to a very swift move across Northern France very soon. In the South, we're doing fine and will be enjoying swimming in the Riviera soon. The boys up there really deserve it.

Well, Darlings, that's about it for today. One more thing – I do miss you both very much and am looking forward only to that day when we're back together again for always. So, say "Hello" to all and best wishes to the folks – and an endless stream of love and kisses for you and Carole –

With All My Love,
Your Dave

Monday – 8/21/44
Same Ol' Dump [Italy]

My Sweetest Wife & Baby,

   Okie has a pet dog, Harry, which he brought with us ever since I had first bought Buck. The dogs were great pals right up until the accident. Well, Harry has become the favorite and he hangs around our tent a lot. Recently, we discovered that he's a good hunting dog. He has acquired a taste for lizards. This morning, I finally nailed one that was about 8 inches long that I had my eye on for the past few days. He finally came out of his hole (they live in the ground) and I nabbed him. I brought him out into the center of the road so that it would be easier to catch him again. Well, you ought to have seen Harry pounce around until he finally broke off the lizard's tail. Then the fight really began. Harry kept biting at it and when he finally did pick it up in his mouth, the lizard bit him on the lip or tongue. Anyway, Harry let out a yelp and shook the lizard free. Then he ran off. I called him back and after a few nips at the lizard, the reptile got frightened and started to run away. One of the boys accidentally stepped on it and that was the end of today's hunting. Whenever we start out toward a certain area, Harry is always on the run, ready to hunt. So you see, we do have a little comedy around once in a while.

   I don't know if you read it, but an article came out recently by Lt. Gen. Ben O. Lear who stated that the American troops will return from Europe via the Suez Canal and Tokyo. Well, that statement has not been received any too enthusiastically. In fact, the resentment has been tremendous by way of letters from the G.I.'s to the "Stars & Stripes." That certainly was not a brilliant thing to say at a time like this, when morale should be kept at its highest. Now you can see what I mean by armchair strategists at home. The press had better be more careful with the articles they release in the future.

   Since my last notation on the number of vehicles destroyed in Northwestern France, they knocked off 4000 vehicles and 200 tanks during Saturday and Sunday. You'll be able to see the full effect of this in the next few weeks.

   I never mentioned this before, but we have had to put up with probably the worst-smelling thing in the world. This is a hemp-growing country and, at this time of year, it stinks like a million outdoor latrines that hadn't been cleared for centuries. When I get back, the smell of stockyards will seem like "Toujours Moi" to me. It'll really be a relief to get away from here!

Well, Toots, that's it – so regards to all and loads of love and kisses for you and the baby –
With All My Love,
Your Dave

———

Tuesday – 8/22/44
Still [Italy]

My Sweetest Darlings,

This morning, it was rumored, via BBC London, that we had landed near Bordeaux – If true, it certainly is a big step forward. That would mean that we could bring our boats directly to France all the way from the Channel down to the border of France & Spain. There are numerous ports that could handle all supplies from the States & England. That would eliminate all handling in English ports – except what they ship across, thereby making it a great timesaving factor.

We went to the show last night and saw "Jam Session" – We really should have stood in bed. It wasn't bad – it was putrid. It's bad enough that we have to put up with the stink of hemp around here – and then they send over smelly stuff like that. If the purpose of movies is to help the morale – it's trash like that that will tear it down.

From all indications, there are going to be quite a number of European Theatre men shipped to the Pacific area after we end this one over here. I know that it doesn't help your morale any for me to write this – but it's one of those possibilities that we can't ignore. I certainly hope that they forget about us.

Well, Darlings, regards to all – lots of love and kisses for Carole Frances and you –
With All My Love,
Your Dave

———

Wednesday – 8/23/44
Same Place [Italy]

My Dearest Amy & Carole Frances,

As you note in the papers, the War news is still continuing very satisfactorily. From the reports, we ought to occupy Paris in the next 48 hours. That in itself will be a big moral victory. No matter where the Nazis decide to move the capital, Paris will always remain in the people's mind as their capital and heart of France. With the F.F.I. [French Forces of the Interior] springing up in all the major cities, they will certainly be a big factor in reducing the enemy resistance in the other sections of France. I certainly hope that there is truth to the Bordeaux landing. The Russians' taking of Jassy is a big move, because it is all flatlands beyond and they shouldn't have any trouble with the terrain. Some of the men are saying that the European War will end in September – while others are sure it will be next Summer before it will be over. So you can see, it's just a matter of opinion. I still think that Thanksgiving will be a very nice day.

Well, Darlings I still miss you both so very much – but what to do about it is another thing. Maybe I ought to write Superman – eh? Oh well, I'll wait, I guess, until it's all over. So, meanwhile, say "Hello" to all and exchange a big hug & a kiss with Carole – from her daddy –

With All My Love,
Your Dave

———

Saturday – 8/26/44
Still Someplace in Italy

My Dearest Darlings,

I'm feeling fine and dandy – but lonesome as hell. I read that Xmas packages should be in the mail by Oct. 15th – but there still isn't anything I'd like. I do want that sheet of paper, however, that will allow me to spend the rest of my life with my wife and baby – or babies? I have a watch, pen and wallet and that's really all a guy needs over here.

Yes, I read about the "celebration" that the civilians will put on when the European War is at an end. I can't say that I'm impressed. What they ought to do is all go to church and thank God that it is over and to help us to defeat the Japs with as few casualties as possible. They don't know what belief in God is until they have to call upon him for protection and preservation. Instead of trying to figure out where to be able to get hold of that next bottle of booze, they ought to donate that money to War Veterans' Relief. Oh, well, why write so foolishly – the American worker isn't interested in anything but making money and more money at this time.

Here's your letter of the 15th – the day Southern France was invaded. We've certainly gone a long way in 11 days – haven't we? I was a little lenient the other day when I wrote that Paris should fall in 48 hours – it fell that same day and so did Marseille. Well, Darlings, it's going as good as we want it to go. I haven't seen today's "Stars & Stripes" – so don't know if we entered Berlin yet – or not. The opinions vary over here on who should be sent home first. The best plan of all is the point plan of FDR's. That would give me points on a husband & father and overseas duty. However, it would probably be the majority of the Infantrymen who'd go back first – They deserve it, too.

That's about all for now, so maybe I'll send you something from another place soon. Give my love to the folks and regards to all – a million hugs & kisses for Carole Frances and you –

With All My Love,
Your Dave

Amy Schwartz and Dave Stoliar in their dating days, Lake Michigan (1939) - a favorite vacation spot for Mom's side of the family.

Mr. and Mrs. David E. Stoliar's wedding portrait (January 5, 1941). They were married in the rabbi's study of Temple Shaare Emeth in St. Louis.

FOTODIARY
Trade Mark

It all started:—

Date January 21, 1943

Place United States

From Jefferson Barracks to Leavenworth to St. Petersburg to Clearwater to Fresno to St. Louis to Fresno to St. Louis to Fresno to Hampton Roads. Returned to Hampton Roads - 27 November 1945.

This snapshot and handwritten itinerary of the U.S. cities Dad traveled to before and after shipping overseas were the first images in the scrapbook he assembled upon his return.

Corporal Stoliar in Fresno, California (May 1943). After Basic Training, Dad was stationed at Camp Pinedale for much of the year.

Private Stoliar during Basic Training exercises in Clearwater, Florida (March 1943).

Mom, Carole and Dad outside their apartment in Fresno (May 1943). An idyllic respite before he departed for Algeria.

Dad and Carole in Fresno (May 1943). Mom and the baby left St. Louis and stayed in an apartment near Pinedale for several months.

Dad's Easter V-Mail from Oran (March 3, 1944). The diamond marked his approximate location. He was a fairly adept artist.

Lieutenant Walter A. Maddox presents Good Conduct Medals to Dad's company in Oran, Algeria (February 1944). Four months later, Dad would testify against Maddox during the Lieutenant's court martial in Italy.

Dad on Rue d'Arzew in Oran, Algeria (March 1944). He'd been promoted to Supply Sergeant while still in Fresno. Prior to the war, he'd never been further from American soil than Canada.

Dad and Lieutenant Rodger in front of the Foreign Legion at Sidi Bel Abbes in Algeria (March 1944). Rodger's wife, Mary, became friends with Mom in St. Louis.

Supply officer Lieutenant Micka polishes someone's shoes in Oran (1944).

Dad got out of his jeep to snap this photo of bombed buildings in Naples, Italy (Spring 1944).

Master Sergeant Max Sarver (a friend from St. Louis), a surrendered Italian officer, and Dad in front of bombed buildings in Naples (Spring 1944).

Sgt. Joe Dines, Sgt. Fay, and Dad chat while others enjoy a smoke outside the 346th Signal Company's Orderly Tent in Santa Maria, Italy (Spring 1944).

Dad with a dead Nazi soldier in the Alban Hills of Italy (June 1944). He wrote, "The dirty sonsofbitches didn't even have the time to bury their dead, so our forces have to."

Another dead Nazi near an abandoned German Tiger Tank in Anzio, Italy (June 1944). Dad wrote, "The stink of the bodies is stifling."

Mom and Carole on vacation in Lake Michigan (July 1944). These precious images reminded Dad what he was fighting for – even as they deepened his homesickness.

Dad and two undernourished girls in Southern France (September 1944). He was always trying to help the poor, hungry children he encountered, often with candy, which many hadn't tasted in years.

Actress Madeleine Carroll (The 39 Steps, My Favorite Blonde) autographed the back of Dad's Air Transport Command Ticket in Dijon, France (October 1944). She was actively involved in the Red Cross during the war.

Allied officers in front of the Palace of Versailles (March 1945). Because he had to take a leak, Dad was late, so he rushed to the right-hand corner of the bottom row just in time to make this group shot.

Dad takes a bite of matzo alongside Les Feldman, Bernie Ellison, and Doug Winikoff during Passover services at a damaged synagogue in Nancy, France (March 28, 1945 – Dad's 29th birthday). A photographer from Stars & Stripes took the picture, but because the negative was badly scratched near Feldman's face, it was unusable – no Photoshop back then.

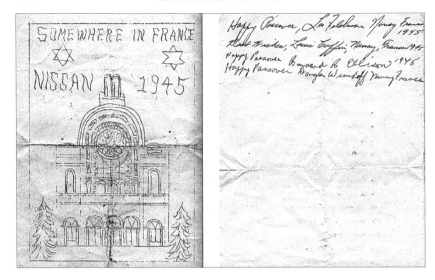

Front and back of the mimeographed program from the Passover service in Nancy (1945). Some of Dad's Jewish buddies signed the back.

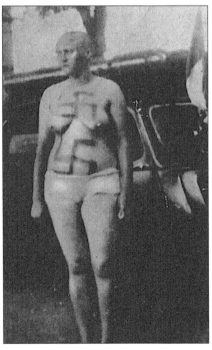

A collaborator in Nancy (Spring 1945). Women who provided "comfort" to the Nazi soldiers that were killing their friends and relatives were publicly shamed with shaved heads and painted swastikas after Germany's surrender.

Another humiliated collaborator, caught by the FBI in France (Spring 1945).

Janine Mougin and Whitey (1945). Dad befriended and provided assistance to Janine and her mother while Mr. Mougin was held prisoner by the Nazis.

Dad and Sergeant Doug Winikoff pose near a bombed bridge between Ludwigshafen (where Mr. Mougin was imprisoned) and Mannheim, Germany (May 1945).

3. FRANCE

Thursday 8/31/44
Of All Places - - - Southern France!

Well, My Dearest Angels,

We have finally set foot on the continent. It took a little while, but we finally got here. As you know, there was absolutely no opposition whatsoever and it was as easy as walking up a stairway in going up the shore. Anyway, I can say that among the cities which I have visited were St. Tropez and Le Luc. There hasn't been any evidence of any opposition for quite a distance inland. We had a very delightful trip over and had recorded music all the way. Included were many pretty songs that were new to us. The crew of this vessel had just received these records from the States. The ones that I like are "Long Ago And Far Away" (very very much), "I'll Be Home For Christmas," and "Good Night Wherever You Are." I think that they are all very pretty, especially the first one. I suppose that they are old to you back home by now. The radio programs that we hear are old ones that still play songs that we were familiar with. At this very moment, we are listening to the news and it is getting better and better every succeeding day. Well, all indications seem to uphold my opinion that it will be over by Thanksgiving. However, I'm afraid that the Xmas dinner will have to wait until later.

Well, Darlings, that's about all the news for now. I'm typing by candlelight now – There is a picture tonight that I had wanted to see (Esther Williams in "Bathing Beauty"), but I'd much rather write to you. So, good night, Darlings, and say "Hello" to all and love to the folks – a great big hug and kiss for Carole Frances and you –

With All My Love,
Your Dave

Friday September 1st 1944
Still Somewhere in Southern France

My Dearest Amy and Carole Frances,

Well, this is my second full day here and it wasn't bad at all. I had to drive around to get some supplies and was able to get a better view of this part of the country. It isn't as up-to-date as the Italians are in the North, but I guess that the Parisians are more modern than those on the coast. The people around here dress in good taste and are familiar with a little English. We don't have any difficulty understanding each other.

As yet, we are not getting any fresh meat, because the troops further North are needing it more than we – and deserve it more. Speaking of the troops in the North, the War up there is coming along pretty well. They are supposed to be beyond the borders of Switzerland. In the Normandy sector, the Allies are having a field day trying to locate any opposition. The BBC reports that it is a complete rout and thousands of Jerries are sitting along the roads, just waiting for the Allies to pick them up. It all seems a matter of time as to when the Allies will march unopposed into Germany. Well, the German people will dread the day that they ever allowed Hitler to come into power. If they try to make war in the future, it will be a surprise. I hope that we do get such a peace treaty written up that they won't have time to think about another war.

There is some talk about us drinking some cocoanut milk before going home – so don't be surprised. Of course, that was always a possibility and we had to consider it. However, if it means that I'll be back home sooner, I won't mind a bit. I know that it's not what we'd like, so let's not count on it before it becomes a reality. The main thing is winning this War and not worrying about the possibility of another in the future.

I guess that's about all the dope for now – so send regards to all and give the baby a great big hug and kiss for me to her and you –

With All My Love,
Your Dave

———

Saturday September 2 1944
Still Somewhere in Southern France

My Most Adorable Wife and Baby,

The radio today said that the Allies are in Belgium and heading for the German border. On the Southern Front, we're going too fast to get an accurate picture of the situation. The Russians are certainly coming along fine and will be in Czechoslovakia soon. Darling, it won't be long now. The small Axis partners are now looking for a way to get out of the War before it costs them too much. Even Japan is looking for an American landing soon, so they are really on the defensive.

I guess Carole Frances is getting ready to welcome her daddy home again. Well, I hope that will be as soon as we had hoped for during the past several months. The Series between the Cards and the Brownies will be starting soon – Hope that one of them wins.

I can tell you that there is a very pretty chateau right where we are. It is the Summer home of the fellow who lives here – his regular home is in Marseille. The one in Marseille ought to be a palace, after seeing this one. The big question today is how did he keep all that he has without collaborating with the Nazis? It doesn't seem possible to us that he could live as he has and not been in cahoots with the Jerries.

Well, Darlings, that's about all the dope for now, so let me remind you that I do miss you and Carole so very much and am looking forward only to that day when we are back together – forever. So meanwhile, send regards to all and millions of love and kisses to Carole and you –

With All My Love,
Your Dave

———

Sunday September 3 1944
Somewhere in Southern France

My Dearest Sweethearts,

This is my first Sunday in France, but it won't be my last, I'm sure of that. The people and soldiers went to Mass today as though there wasn't even a War going on. The religion of the state is Catholic over here. I haven't been able to see any of those old and famous cathedrals about which we have read, as yet, but I hope to be able to. Well, I really didn't come here for an education – so I won't be a disappointed guy if I don't get to see them.

I saw an issue of "Stars & Stripes" in which it had an article on discharging men after the European War is ended. On the basis shown, I'll be among the last to get out. The only things in my favor are being overseas, a husband and a father, and the number of campaigns I have taken part in. The main thing is that so many other fellows have been over here much longer than I and have been in more campaigns and received awards than I. That means that it is almost a certain thing that I will have a good chance of seeing Paul [in the Pacific]. Of course, it is only a guess, so let's not worry for a while. If it is true, there still isn't anything about which to worry, because we will have quite a safe time of it. I'll probably spend all of my time chasing grass skirts and shooting cocoanuts.

Well, last night, I really had an experience. It seems that when I arrived here, the Supply Section was set up in a rock enclosure. It is a very pretty place, but has no cover. After lying down for a while, the rains came. It was the worst rain I've seen since coming across. I had a few pieces of canvas covering myself, but all of a sudden, I felt a pool of water on my cot, under the blankets. Well, I had to get out, so I headed for the Orderly Room, which is in a building. I stayed there until the rain slowed down and then ran out and got another cot from Supply and a few extra blankets. When I got comfortable in the Orderly Room, a big wind came up and blew like hell all night long. You now are pretty well acquainted with the ups and downs of a G.I. overseas. On top of that, there are always certain men with whom you don't get along who are always trying to pester you. It's hell that we have to fight among ourselves instead of just trying to do all to hurt the enemy.

Well, Darlings, take good care of yourselves and regards to all – lots and lots of love and kisses for Carole Frances and you –

With All My Love,
Your Dave

—

Friday September 8 1944
Still Somewhere in Southeastern France

My Dearest Wife and Baby,

I have been on the go for the last four days and was unable to write. For that matter, all of us were unable to do so – so it will make a lot of people back home wonder where the letters are. I do hope that it won't be too long before we are able to tell them where and what we're doing. I can say that we aren't at the same place from which I wrote you last. It was a long way up here and it certainly was a great change in weather, too. When we awaken, there is a sheet of dew all over us. The noted Alps are near, so you can imagine how cool it is around here. This is the closest that many of us will be to God while still alive. We can see the snow on the tops of close-by mountains.

We have seen a lot of happy and relieved people on our way up. It was a thrill for them to see us come thru. They waved to us and offered wine, fruits and vegetables. Many of them threw kisses to us as we passed. All in all, it is like taking a thousand-pound weight from their backs when the Americans arrived. The country is really beautiful up here and the hills look as if they were constantly being mowed and taken care of. An American golf club would go nuts over grass like we see here. The surprising feature is the fact that here, where the Nazis had occupied the country, there is plenty of food, while in Italy, where they were supposed to be Allies, the people were stripped of all food.

The radio didn't have much to say lately, but it is still good news to learn that we are still going forward. At this moment, [General George] *Patton may be entering Germany. With the Russians coming along as they are in the East and Southeast, and us coming up from the South, it won't be long before Baron and I will be drinking that glass of beer in Berlin – that is, if he's over here at that time.*

I'm sorry to see the Brownies falling down so late in the season. It looked like a sure St. Louis World Series, but now it will probably be between the Yanks and the Cards again – with the Cards winning the Series.

Meanwhile, say "Hello" to all the people back home and give them my regards – love to the folks – and millions and millions of hugs and kisses for Carole Frances and you –

With All My Love,
Your Dave

Sunday 10 September 1944
Still Somewhere in Southeastern France
My Darling Amy and Carole Frances,

Here it is – another one of those typical Fall Sundays. It has been gray and dreary all day long, and drizzling off and on. Many of the boys have gone to the native churches and the services ought to be very colorful. From the altars we have seen in Italy and in Southern France, the people are very devout Catholics.

I read that there won't be any popcorn or peanuts available in Sportsman's Park for the World Series – That, my friend, is a major tragedy. After all, what is a Series without those things? It's damned tough that the people back home are going to have to do without these things. After all, we over here are getting whatever our hearts desire. Why bitch about it? It will all be over soon and we'll be driving over to Vic's and Garavelli's again for the things we like. As to getting anything for Xmas for me, don't you think that you had better hold it up for a while and see where I'll be in the next few months? I may even get it in person – who knows? I'll bet that Xmases around here are really going to be tremendous, now that Europe is liberated. The snow up and around here must reach many feet in depth in Winter – Hope that we're not around to see it. There is some talk about us being placed in an army of Occupation Troops, but I don't think much of the rumor.

How time flies! It has already been a bit over 8 months since we have seen each other. Well, it won't be that much longer before we are together again. I guess that is about all the dope for now – so say "Hello" to all and send love to the folks; and for Carole and you, a barrelful of hugs and kisses –

With All My Love,
Your Dave

———

Monday 11 September 1944
Still Somewhere in Southeastern France
My Most Adorable Wife and Baby,

Yesterday, after writing you, about a hundred French peasants came around to visit us. Most of them had never seen an American soldier and it was a novelty for them. They came in families – mother and father and the kids. I was able to speak to them and we all had a good time. One of them brought a bottle of champagne, which he gave me – It was pretty good, too. Most of them brought some fresh eggs as an expression of goodwill. We don't get any fresh things, so the boys certainly appreciate the eggs.

Later in the evening, a dance was held down in one of the villages and there must have been about four hundred people there. The G.I.'s had a pretty good time trying to make the girls. If you remember [Sgt.] Joe Dines – he and I went to one of the farms with seven other G.I.'s and a couple of French people. The girl is 25 and went to school in England. She lives in Paris. The fellow also lives in Paris and was 37. They both spoke English well – so the party was very enjoyable. After the chicken dinner at the farmhouse, we went to a café where we drank about ten bottles of champagne.

I learned this morning that the Brownies are now in second place by one percentage point – Well, I guess they are about finished for this year. It's tough that they had to weaken at this point. Well, we still have the Cards, who are going to win the Series.

Well, Darlings, there really isn't anything much to write about – so I will tell you that I miss you and Carole very much and am still waiting for our reunion so very impatiently. So regards to all and a huge hug and a kiss for you and the baby –

   With All My Love,
   Your Dave

———

Thursday 14 September 1944
Still Somewhere in Southeastern France

My Sweetest Wife and Baby,

   On Tuesday, Lt. Micka and I had to go out beyond Lyon on business and it took us quite some time to finish. After we left Lyon, we stopped at a restaurant at which I ate a few days before in a smaller town. We had French-fried potatoes and steak for a change. We also met some of the other boys in the company. We decided to go out and get a drink at a bar before going back to camp. Well, we finished at the bar and started back for camp. We met some French girls on bicycles who wanted a lift, so we stopped and gave them a hitch to their home. They asked us in to have some wine and dance, as they had learned that all the Americans liked to dance. We accepted and they brought in their sister and brother-in-law and a few others. We also met a Jewish fellow there. There are quite a large number of Jews in France, especially around here. We danced to some old recordings by some ham French orchestras, so you can imagine what a time we had. Well, we finally left at about 11:00 and hit the hay when we got back to camp.

   The next morning, Mullen and I decided to go with a truck, which was going to Lyon. That evening, it was raining pretty hard, so we all decided to get a hotel room and spend the night there. We got two rooms at a place that was formerly occupied by German officers only. We left our belongings in our rooms and went out to eat and drink. At one place, we sat down right next to a group of American officers. When we took notice of them, they turned out to be one Colonel, one Brigadier General, and two Major Generals. I don't know what in the world they were doing there at that time.

   Today, on the way back to camp, I saw the streets lined with people who were waiting for someone to come by. I learned later that it was Gen. De Gaulle who was coming in today. That may have been the reason for the

American generals being there. When I hitched a ride on a French truck, Mullen and the others were ahead of me. I called to them to get on, but there was too much of a crowd to get thru. While on the truck, a woman and her two young sons were also picked up. She told me that her husband was a policeman in Paris up until a month ago, when he was killed during an American air raid. I told her that it was all in the course of the War and she did not blame the Americans, but she was really bitter toward the Germans. All the French hate the Jerries.

Well, when I got here, I found twenty letters awaiting me – that was really some haul, don't you agree? Nine were yours. I'll finish this letter after chow this evening. Which reminds me – I haven't had anything to eat since this morning when we had some French brown bread with cocoa that tasted from manure. For dessert, we had a pear.

As to the setup on Lt. Maddox, he is now with another outfit, but on detached service to us for a while, so he still acts in the same capacity as before. After reading that article in the papers on the invasion of Southern France and you know from where they started, it is no longer a secret why we were in Southern Italy for a while. As to seeing Paris, I'm afraid that is out, because we're not going in that direction as you may see by the newspapers.

Your next letter was the 23rd. That was the day that Paris and Marseille fell to the Allies. As to showing surprise on the invasion of France, I don't know what I wrote to give you that idea, because I even said to Lt. Rodger about a week before the invasion that the only logical spot was right between Nice and Toulon – That, my dear, was the exact place where the invasion took place. If you read about the missions of the Air Forces in Italy and Southern France, you will be able to learn which is ours and anything else about which you may have wondered. I can imagine the gay times in Paris after the Nazis were run out – We've seen a lot of the same thing around here, only on a smaller scale.

Yes, I have often thought about the years we've been married – They weren't long at all. We won't be old either when I get back. Incidentally, are they selling Hershey's tropical chocolate to the public yet? It is a bar that won't melt under hot weather and will also stand up under cold. It's not bad at all.

As to the latest news on the War – I haven't seen a paper for a few days, so I don't know where we are at this writing. Someone told me that we're 15 kilometers in Germany. Over here, we don't speak in terms of miles anymore. Well, it won't be long now. A forward echelon becomes a rear echelon very quickly – that's why all the moving is so necessary for the pursuit of the enemy.

If Carole got some lollipop on the paper, it didn't show. I'm glad that she's in a country where she can get candy. It's hard to see the faces of the children when you mention "bon-bon." They haven't seen it around here for four and five years. Some of them not since they were born. I gave a piece of chocolate to one family at one of the bars and you should have seen the children's faces light up. The women weren't hit hard, but the men had all good tobaccos taken away; and the children their candy. Coffee hasn't been seen here either for a long time. If you mention sugar, they almost have forgotten the existence of it. Well, it won't be long before all those things are back.

As to my suntan, no, it is wearing off with the cool weather. However, the South Pacific will bring it back. I'm almost certain that we'll go to that theatre after this is over. We're too new over here to send back to the States after the European War is won. I know that is counting our chickens before they're hatched, but that's the picture today. I'd rather warn you ahead of time than to have you let down at the last moment.

I want you to know that I miss you very much and love you even more. After all, that's the only thing that gives me hope for the future – being with you and Carole Frances. So say "Hello" to all and regards to all – oodles and oodles of love and kisses for the baby and you –

With All My Love,
Your Dave

———

Friday 15 September 1944
Still Somewhere in Southeastern France
My Sweetest Amy and Carole Frances,

As to your letter of the 29th, that was the day Carole wrote on the walls with the Crayola. Yes, I think that I would have spanked her, too, for doing that. We're lucky that you were able to remove it from the walls. Has she tried it again since that time?

As to that plane that was supposed to have crashed on the 3200 block, it is more than the Jerries are shooting down around here. The Air Force has a hard time finding opposition in the air. I spoke to one pilot on the way to Lyon and he said that he hasn't seen a Jerry since he's been over here and that's been a long time. It's a funny thing, but it is rumored that if we had

had any idea that the invasion of Southern France was going to be so simple, and that we would have taken along much more supplies to follow up the pursuit of the enemy, we would have been in Germany long before this. That is a good thought, because it takes enormous amounts of food, clothing and fuel to attack and pursue. That was the only thing that held the Allies up after landing in the Cherbourg peninsula. It looks like we'll have to just batter down the German cities like we did the Italian before the civilians realize how devastating a land war can be. With a break-thru on a front of over 150 miles into Germany, it won't be long before it will end. Aachen probably has been bypassed already. There are some super-highways from there to other larger cities in Germany and once we have control of these roads, it will be a lot simpler.

As to the subject of poison gas – I don't think that they will use it, because if they do, we have complete air control over Germany and could wipe out all Germans in one day's activities. So the people are just being tugged along with such tripe as that. With the flying-bomb bases out, the propaganda will have to lean to anything [Hitler's Minister of Propaganda, Joseph] Goebbels *can figure out.*

As to your letter of the 2nd, it was in the newspapers that the Americans were in Germany. I think that they didn't get there until this last week – am I right? Maybe I'm getting the news later than you. Let me know if the War is over – I may be a little late. With all the secrecy in the communiqués recently, it wouldn't surprise me a bit.

I hope that your woman's intuition is correct and we don't go to the Pacific. However, I'm afraid that reality this time will overshadow intuition. Well, let's think of more enjoyable things, such as the day when I'll be back for good.

Now comes the time when I shall tell you that I miss you and Carole Frances very, very much; also that I love you two very, very, very much. What will our days be when we don't have to write these words to each other – swell, won't it? Well, that is about all for the day, so say "Hello" to all and love to the folks – a big hug and kiss for Carole and you –

With All My Love,
Your Dave

4. ITALY (AGAIN)

September 25, 1944
[Italy]

My Dearest Wife & Baby,

I guess you have been wondering what in the world ever happened to me and my letters. Well, I'm feeling fine and am well and hope that I haven't caused you too much worry.

To go back to the 14th (the last day I wrote you), I noticed that there was a deep orange color in my urine. Well, I decided to go to sick-call and find out what was the matter. The doctor suggested that I drive down to the closest hospital and have an analysis done there. I had the urinalysis made and they found blood in it and nothing else. Well, I went back to our outfit and told the Captain about it. He said that I should go to the hospital so as to clear up the cause of it. I had to wait until the next day, because it was too late in the day. When I got down to the place where the hospital had been – I found that they had moved about 150 miles North.

I returned to the medics and the Captain said that I ought to go to the nearest air evacuation hospital, so one of the fellows drove me up to an airfield about 65 miles away. There was no laboratory there, so they flew me South to another evacuation hospital. There, the Captain told me that the closest hospital with available means of helping me was in [CENSORED]. *Well, to cut a long story short, I'm now in* [CENSORED], *taking it easy. My doctor is a specialist in urinalysis – also a surgeon in that field. Well, the first day he looked at me and couldn't figure out what was causing the bleeding, because I had no pains. The next nite, I was given a dose of castor oil (first in my life) and about 5:00 A.M., a nice, big enema. Well, I felt like a worn-out dishcloth after that.*

I went over to the laboratories and I was really given the works. They put a large tube into the urinary canal and then two tubes into the kidneys. He placed a light into the center tube and probed – without any success. Then he blew up the bladder and filled the kidneys with a fluid that was detectable under the X-Ray. They took an X-Ray and after that, I was finished. I forgot to say they shot something into my arm that would photograph. Well, all the X-Rays showed a normal setup, so he decided to take a prostrate [sic] smear. That was also analyzed and found to be the cause. He said that that was the trouble, but it wasn't so serious. At first, it was feared to be a kidney stone. So now, the prostrate gland will be treated and I ought to be out very soon.

The reason I didn't write sooner was that first of all, I didn't want to worry you. Secondly, if I did write you sooner, I wasn't in a position to tell you what the trouble was and you'd really worry. Thirdly, I thought that when I got back to the company, I'd write, but you'd be wondering where all the in-between letters were. So now, I have explained everything to you and don't want you to worry, because I'm fine and will be out soon.

We had a movie in our ward yesterday – Edw. G. Robinson in "Mr. Winkle Goes To War" – It wasn't so hot – but his wife's name was Amy and that made me homesick. This ward I'm in is all nose, throat & ear and genital-urinary cases. Most of them are Infantrymen who were hit in action. One fellow right in the next bed volunteered as an ambulance driver with the British Forces last year. He's been across a little over a year and now has kidney trouble. As he is still recognized as a civilian, the Army can't insist on his being operated upon here, so they have arranged to include him in the next air evacuation back to the States. What a break! Get on the plane one day and in the U.S.A. the next.

Well, Darling, that's about all for now, so don't worry and send regards to all – a big hug and kiss for you and Carole Frances –
With All My Love,
Your Dave

———

September 26 – 1944
Still Somewhere in Italy

My Dearest Amy & Carole Frances,

The doctor treated me again and I'm to go to him again Friday. After that, I think that I'll be dismissed. Then I'll really have a headache getting back to my outfit. I think that I know where the outfit is now. We were supposed to move up in a few days after I left France. The War in the West is at a temporary standstill. However, don't let that excite you, because if you will recall, after landing in the Cherbourg peninsula, we had to wait quite a while before starting the offensive. It is the same case now as we accumulate supplies to make the final push into Germany. As long as we are inside Germany now, all that remains is the final drive to Berlin. With the Russians making their push from the East, the War certainly looks like it will end by the end of October. The temporary holding action by the Nazis is a big strain on them to prevent a complete breakthrough at this time. However, it won't be long before we'll be rolling on our way – In fact, by the time you receive this, we ought to be another 50 miles inside Germany.

Tonite they are having services for the Jewish holidays, but I'm going to stay in bed and keep off my feet. I hope that all of you have nice weather and that the temple was crowded to capacity. I've been reading a bit in my spare time and finished a fair book by Louis Bromfield, "Mrs. Parkington" – rather interesting. I've begun on a more humorous one – by James Thurber, "The Middle-Aged Man on the Flying Trapeze" – it's really very funny & typically Robert Benchley type. At times, I just burst out laughing and everybody in the ward is beginning to think I'm a psycho case.

I wish this wasn't an election year. There is so much attention given to political stands that the War is beginning to be a secondary issue. I hope that the people back home awaken to the reality that we're still at War and ignore the speeches of our "eminent statesmen."

Well, Darlings, I guess there is nothing else to tell you except that I do love you both very much and miss you almost as much. Say "Hello" to the folks and the friends at home – give Carole a great big hug & kiss for me and she can do the same to you –

With All My Love,
Your Dave

September 27 – 1944
Same Jernt [Italy]

My Sweetest Wife & Baby,

This is certainly one cosmopolitan ward. Among the patients are Algerians, Senegalese (Africa), Chinese, Moroccan and Americans. We're teaching the colored Senegalese how to speak English – He speaks French because it is under French rule. At times, he embarrasses the nurses, because he cusses in American and doesn't realize what it means.

That was a very appropriate speech that Secty. [of War, Robert] *Patterson made for Yom Kippur. It'll help to remind people that the Jews are also dying for our causes. I also see that the British finally agreed to supply an all-Jewish regiment from Palestine – it took plenty of time. Back in 1939, the Jews there volunteered, but the haughty British didn't take to the idea.*

Well, Darlings, hope that Carole is well and you and the folks are also taking good care of yourselves. Send regards to all and love to the baby and the folks – a great big kiss for you and the baby –
With All My Love,
Your Dave

September 29th – 1944
Still in Italy

My Sweetest Wife & Baby,
Today has been one of the most provoking I've ever gone thru. In the Oct. 6th issue of the "Yank" magazine, I saw letters from the American soldiers that were sent in to the Editor. Among these were a couple that spoke of incidents regarding the POW's in the States. From newspaper accounts, the prisoners were supposed to have been given dances at a number of camps. Some of the prisoners were supposed to have been allowed to go into a public bar and buy drinks with plenty of American money. Then, to top all that, one girl (so far) has announced that she is going to marry a POW. These things are very damaging to the minds of the boys overseas. It makes us wonder just what in the world we are doing over here. Since when must we appease prisoners and try to bolster their morale? It's bad enough that they fire at the Allies and then are given more than humane treatment after being captured.

Another incident was the sit-down strike of POW's when they were asked to work 9 instead of 8 hours per day. Why, in Germany and occupied countries of the Nazis & Japs, a prisoner would be killed for even lesser things. At times, when I see trucks full of Jerry prisoners returning from the front, I do all I can to prevent myself from opening up on them. Darling, the more dead Jerries there are – the sooner the War will end. The damnedest thing is that they are being sent to the States instead of Africa. As a prisoner, we have to see that each Nazi is fed, clothed and paid. We speak of the Geneva laws, but our enemies never heard of them. The people back home had better straighten out these things in a big hurry or the echo will return with a helluva roar. The men don't like it and voice that opinion very emphatically. Now that the atrocities of Lublin are out and illustrated, I hope that people will realize that the Nazis are as savage, or even more so, than the Japs. Just because they are in the European continent doesn't mean that they are civilized more than the Japs. I'm only an individual writing a grievance to his wife. Therefore, there's nothing much to be done by just this one letter. However, if every soldier wrote home the same objection, maybe we'd see a change. Well, that's enough of my bitching – you have enough to worry about.

Well, Darlings, that's about all the dope for today – so regards to all and billions of love & kisses for you and the baby –

With All My Love,
Your Dave

———

October 1st – 1944
Still in Italy

My Dearest Amy & Carole Frances,

This afternoon, the patients were given an exhibition of fencing by about 10 Italians. Among them were the champions of Italy and Europe – who, incidentally, were brothers. The Italians are trying to do whatever they can to amuse us; however, it is still a hard thing to forget that only a little over a year ago, they were in an all-out War against us.

One of the Red Cross representatives just dropped in to get a list of what the patients need. We got to talking, after I requested an honorable discharge, and she asked me if I'd take care of the War maps in the Red Cross tent. I had a map on my bed, which she looked at and that gave her the idea. Being as I don't have anything to do in the mornings anyway, I told her I'd be glad to – as long as I was here.

As to the baseball situation, I've never seen so many Brownie rooters as there are around here. Even tho they are from all over the country, most of them would like to see them win the pennant. With them tied for 1st – they still have a chance. Have you taught Carole who the Cards & Browns are yet?

Well, Darlings, the only other remaining subject is that I miss you and the baby a helluva lot. However, I'm used to that separation by now – so let's just look forward to the day were back together again for good. Meanwhile, regards to all and love and kisses for Carole and you –

With All My Love,
Your Dave

———

October 3rd – 1944
Still in Italy

My Dearest Darlings,

I'm to be moved to another ward where the final disposition of patients are made before being discharged from the hospital. After leaving the hospital, all patients are sent to a Replacement Center to wait for a convoy going to France. Well, from what I hear, those days in the Replacement Center are absolutely lousy. Therefore, I'm going to try to get away to the airport, after leaving the hospital and try to hitch a plane-ride to France. I could save many days, or perhaps weeks, in that way.

I got hold of an August issue of "Esquire," for which I've been looking for some time, and read that first story – about Supply Sergeants. Darlings, if you can get hold of that issue, you will see about 75% of a Supply man's life in the Army. The procedures overseas make up for the remaining 25%. That is a very good article and may help to relieve some of those hard feelings against a Supply Sergeant, if every G.I. got to read it.

How's Carole Frances enjoying her swing – has she lost interest in it yet? I guess she knows all the latest songs by now. Just don't teach her to jitterbug – I still don't like it! Well, Angels, I guess that's about all the dope for today – so say "Hello" to all and a lot of love and kisses for Carole and you –

With All My Love,
Your Dave

———

October 4 – 1944
Still in Italy

My Dearest Amy & Carole Frances,

We just finished listening to the first World Series game, which was broadcast directly from St. Louis. At the beginning, when the announcer described the warm, sunny day in St. Louis, I felt just like I was back in my ol' hometown again. The only difference was that instead of the Sun peering down at us, we had his brother – the Moon. (It's now the next morning, because the night nurse ordered me to bed and wouldn't even let me finish the letter.) That was a tough game for [pitcher, Mort] Cooper to lose – after all, he only allowed two hits – but oh what hits! The Cards still ought to take the Series. We're having a tough time getting the game clearly, because it is broadcast thru the chain to Boston – to Italy and over the P.A. system. However, it wasn't too bad and we were able to catch most of it. It's amazing how such a small thing as a ballgame can take me back to you in such a hurry. The amazing thing is that we didn't count on even getting the game. I was asking the nurse about the hospital putting it on over the P.A. and she didn't think that we'd get far in asking. Well, there was a Captain (also in the same Air Force as I) in the same ward who was also interested in the game being broadcast. After all, there are many bed patients who would like to hear it, so he and I went up to the Special Service section and asked about it. We were told that they hadn't been able to get the station, which was to rebroadcast the game, on their radio. However, if they did succeed, they'd put it on in spite of the fact that everybody is supposed to be asleep by 9:30. So the game came on suddenly at 7:45 P.M. and it was two hours later that I started this letter.

I got hold of "Bedside Esquire" and will begin on that after I finish "I Never Left Home" – by Bob Hope. The Captain gave me the latter and I'll return it to him when I get back to France, because I think he's leaving today.

Well, Darlings, that's about all for today, so regards to all and lots of love & kisses for Carole and you –

With All My Love,

Your Dave

———

October 6 – 1944

Still in Italy

My Dearest Wife & Baby,

Today I have good news – I'm getting out of here tomorrow or the next day. However, I don't know if I'm going to be allowed to get away from going to the Replacement Depot. From what I hear, those in the depot are doing such things as what we did in Basic Training. I don't relish that idea and am going to try to avoid it. It may have me as A.W.O.L., but I'd hate to hang around there just waiting. The nurse said that my prostrate gland had been inflamed and could have been the result of a severe strain. Therefore, I'm going to take it easy in the future.

Well, the baseball game was about to begin and I didn't want to miss it if possible, so I got a chair outside the tent & listened to it until 10:30 P.M., when they turned it off in the end of the 10th inning. It was too late to write, because that night nurse keeps running us to bed. So – now I hope that you'll forgive me for not writing yesterday. That was some game yesterday and I'm glad the Cards tied it up.

What's new with Carole Frances and the rest of the family? Does she listen to the Series, too? I'm completely lost now that I haven't had any mail in three weeks. I know that you've written every day, but it's not coming down here. I hope that I'm able to catch up with all the mail before I get back to France. Well, Darlings, that's about it for today – so regards to all and loads & loads of love and kisses for Carole & you –

With All My Love,
Your Dave

October 7 – 1944
Still in Italy

My Sweetest Angels,

Right now they are playing some old favorite recordings by Bing Crosby – "Please" at this moment. Those songs take a guy back to the States in a big hurry and bring in everything and everybody a guy loves. I guess I'm really suffering from a bad case of homesickness. You know a fellow can't keep pent-up all the time – He has to let off a little steam or he'd blow up.

A statement came out in the "Yank" magazine that just about confirms my earlier letters. It said that the Air Force and its auxiliary units and the servicemen would be the first to be sent from Europe to the Pacific Theatre as soon as the European War is ended. After that, as new replacements are made available, the veterans will be let out. Therefore, it is almost a certain fact that I'm going to that area before I get back. I know that it sort of knocks out all nice anticipations we may have had, but I guess the complete Victory is primary. That's the reason that I refrained from mentioning seeing you this Xmas or the early part of 1945. Darling, you've been toughened up by all of our other disappointments, so let's take it on the chin and look forward to the end of the whole affair. With Carole Frances to keep you company and entertain you, time will pass quickly and I'll be back in no time at all.

The ballgame was broadcast again last nite, but it started to clog up and the static made it impossible to complete the broadcast. However, the damage had been done and the score was Brownies 4 – Cards 1 at the time they shut down. The Brownies are really one surprise after another. I'm still confident that the Cards will win out. Well, Darlings, that's about all the dope for today – Tell Carole that I'll try to take her to next year's World

Series – and if her mother is a good girl, too – I'll take her, too. So, regards to all and beaucoup love and kisses for the baby and you –
> *With All My Love,*
> *Your Dave*

October 11 – 1944
Still in Italy

My Dearest Wife & Baby,

Sunday I was discharged from the hospital. We all had to go to a Replacement Depot to be issued clothing and equipment, which we may be in need of. After that, we were assigned to various depots in another vicinity. I went to one in which most were Infantrymen. It was late at nite when I got in, so was unable to write that nite.

The next day, I had to get back to the hospital in order to get some clothing, which I had given out to be washed. I located the Italian girl who had them and she gave me her address. I went there and sat around chewing the fat with her father and brother until she showed up. She ironed them before she ate dinner and I felt sorry that I had to keep her from dinner, so I gave her $1.50 and 3 chocolate candy bars to make her feel good. When I got back, there was no light, so I couldn't write Monday nite either.

Well, the next day I was transferred to an Air Force Replacement Depot and that's where I am now. I couldn't write all day, because we were told that we were alerted for 24 hours. I didn't want to take a chance on writing and then learning that the letter might be returned. Therefore, I have finally decided to write and let you know that I'm well, but very lonesome.

This evening, they are showing "Atlantic City" – I never heard of it, but hope that it's good. (Just as I had finished that last line – the show began, so I interrupted this letter.) Well, I saw the show and it's nothing to write home about, so I won't. It's almost a month now since I received a letter, so it's getting pretty darned monotonous. Hope I catch up with my mail soon. Meanwhile, hope that everybody is well at home. So regards to all – lots of big hugs and kisses for the baby and you –
> *With All My Love,*
> *Your Dave*

October 15 – 1944
Still in Italy

My Dearest Darlings,

I learned yesterday that our outfit moved up again. Well, that makes it harder to reach now. Therefore, one of the higher officers, in higher headquarters, wired to hold all men who are attached to the same command. There are two fellows who go to the same place as I in this same tent. So it looks like we're here for a little longer than I anticipated. Maybe the War will be ended by the time I get back to France.

Yesterday, I met a fellow who came from Munich. He's been overseas about 3 weeks and is working temporarily at Allied Headquarters. While we were talking, a friend of his came up who had been in the Pacific Theatre for 19 months and had been back in the States for 7 months. Now, he is assigned to this Theatre. So you see – there are others who are worse off than I. On the other hand, there was a large group of men who just left to go back home after being here for 29 months. I guess we'll just have to sweat it out – and hope for a break.

Well, Darlings, hope that everyone is OK at home and the weather good. I know that you are taking good care of Carole and yourself – hope that the folks are taking it easy. So say "Hello" to all and love to the folks – a big hug and kiss for Carole and you –
With All My Love,
Your Dave

October 18 – 1944
Still in Italy

My Dearest Wife & Baby,

I still haven't received any mail since September 15th – but I got some consolation the other night when I dreamed that I got another big batch of mail. Maybe if I keep on dreaming that – it will eventually come true. And also if you keep dreaming that I'm back home – maybe I'll be back, too. However, it's about certain that it won't be before the War is over here and we had been shipped to the Pacific Theatre. For the present, I think I'll be heading for Epinal soon. I may be leaving here pretty soon after all. That's just life in the Army – You don't know what to expect.

This evening, they had "Musical in Manhattan" and it was surprisingly good. It was with Anne Shirley, Dennis Day and a new fellow, Phillip

Terry. We also had about 4 short subjects before the picture and included was a War Dep't one on the Normandy invasion and the entrance into Rome. If you get to see it – then you will see the same sights I saw when I was up there. There was another short on the development of an adolescent girl. The scene was taken in the salon of Richard Hudnut. They showed how a young girl, without a damned thing with which to work, was made into an attractive young lady. It was an amazing picture – but true! I'm glad that my wife and baby don't have to go to such a place – They are beautiful enough.

Well, Angels, hope that everybody is well and business good. Regards to all – love to Mother and Dad – millions of hugs and kisses for Carole and you –
With All My Love,
Your Dave

———

Friday – Oct. 20th – 1944
Still in Italy

My Dearest Darlings,

I guess you all back home were just as surprised and elated as I when I read of the landings, reported by the Japs, in the Philippines. As you know, this is a tremendous step toward bringing to an end the whole War. It was always one of our utmost goals in the Pacific Theatre, but I certainly hadn't expected a landing so soon. This certainly indicates that the raids in that area were very successful. The amazing thing about the report is that they were supposed to have landed in the center of the Islands. This being the case, I hope that we don't have any difficulty in keeping our Supply and Communication lines open and unbroken. Then again, I hadn't expected a move as big as this until after the European War had ended.

Wow, Darlings, I can actually anticipate coming back home. When the complete occupation of the Islands is made (and I know that they will be) it should not be long after that Japan will surrender. The strategy, at this time, no doubt caught the Japs and most of the other people in the same frame of mind and was a complete surprise. It will be a long and hard-fought affair to kill each and every Jap on the Islands – but I'm afraid that that's the way it will be. If you will recall, when we had a very small defending force, we held off the Japs fairly well. Now, on the other hand, the Japs have a large force and fully equipped. In view of the desperate fight that the Jap usually shows, I imagine that it will take until February, at least, to get rid of them in the Islands. After that, it shouldn't take over 6 months more to knock the hell out of the Jap mainland.

So now, I'm definitely planning on seeing you and Carole Frances by Thanksgiving of '45. I tried not to make you too optimistic about my returning this year so that you wouldn't take it too hard if I failed to show up until next. So now you realize just what is ahead of us before I get a chance to return. Of course, there is a very faint chance that an order may come thru to allow us a 30-day furlough in the States, after the European War. However, that's beyond all expectations and hopes now that we've landed on the Islands. Therefore, Darlings, just be a little more patient for a while and soon we won't have to count on the mails.

I read in the "Stars & Stripes" about the points on sugar and butter going up. Has it affected Carole's feeding any? Hope that you're able to get all her foods OK. I guess she feeds herself now. She certainly has brought us unlimited pleasure, especially for you now. She's certainly a good kid. So that's the news for today and hope that you, Carole and the folks are all doing well. Give my best wishes to all and a big hug and kiss for the baby and you —

With All My Love,
Your Dave

———

Saturday – Oct. 21 – 1944
Still in Italy

My Dearest Angels,

Here we are at the end of another week apart. The War is still moving along pretty swiftly and it won't take much longer. From the news, [General Douglas] *MacArthur has landed in the Philippines and that, in itself, is a big step toward the end. I was very happy to read that casualties were very light. I hope that they continue as such. If rumor is fairly true around here, Peace negotiations are in the air. However, I don't have any faith in it, because unconditional surrender is still the basis upon which we will cease firing.*

Of course, Hitler has, at least, told the Germans that the War is lost and all that remains is the killing of as many Allied troops as possible before the Reich collapses. Just how many will follow his demand is to be seen as we go further into Germany. If all the rest of Germany is able to see pictures of Aachen, they'd not hesitate to hasten the end of the War.

I don't know why, but our tent seems to be the point of attraction. The boys come in and we speak of everything from "C" rations to Sinatra. In the last couple of days, I've listened to too many cases of fellows whose wives are pregnant and they hadn't been home in over two years. Some of them had girlfriends who, all of a sudden, write that they married a sailor or something else back home. I don't know what's happening back home, but I certainly hope that the people start to settle down and realize the effect this sort of thing has on the G.I.'s. Don't they know that we are only over here so that we can go back to the persons and things we love? Some of these fellows just say that now they don't give a damn about anything. If they can't trust the girls back home who are their wives and sweethearts – who could they trust? I'm certainly glad that my wife and baby are well taken care of and waiting for me. I'm sorry that it has to take such a long time to get back home.

That just about sums up the dope for the day, so hope that everything's OK still and that Carole, the folks and you are well. Regards to all and beaucoup love and kisses for the baby and you –

With All My Love,
Your Dave

———

5. FRANCE (AGAIN)

Tuesday – October 31 – 1944
Somewhere in France

My Dearest Darlings,

Well, I finally got back here! I'm sorry that I was unable to write you. As you may assume, we were on the go all that time, which made it impossible to get off a letter. I can't tell you all the details about the trip, but we did fly up here and it took us four and a half hours. It's amazing what a plane trip can do. In one country in the morning and another that afternoon. It was not a very eventful trip but it was a little bumpy at times. I can't tell you from where we took off or where we landed – but it's colder than Frankfort in December. The boys told me that I was pretty lucky not to have arrived a few days sooner, because they had been in an area where the mud was up to their knees. The first thing that I asked about was my mail. Now here's the sad part – All of my mail had been forwarded to Italy, including some packages. Now, I'll have one helluva time catching up with all that has gone on in the past two months at home. Luckily, I was able to catch yesterday's mail and in it were six letters, including two from you. It certainly was a great feeling to see your writing again. I got the heebie-jeebies I was so nervous reading. I was wondering when you would hear that I was in the hospital and if you would be worrying. When I saw in the first letter that you didn't know anything about it, I was afraid that some of my mail from Italy wasn't going thru. However, the other letter told me that you weren't worried, so I was relieved quite a bit.

As to the Jews who are still in France, it was only because others were kind to them and kept quiet that they are still here. However, it must have been pretty difficult to get along all these years.

I was out on business with Fay and just returned. We had to go to a large town near here and get some supplies. I was driving and as we were going down one of the streets, I said to Fay, "I think that that's Madeleine Carroll." We stopped and I got out and walked over to her and a lieutenant who was with her. I asked if her name wasn't "Carroll" and she said that it was. I then asked if her first name wasn't "Madeleine" and she said that it was. Then I asked her if she'd do me a favor and sign her signature to something for my baby. She asked how old my baby was and so on. I told her that I was sorry that I had missed her in Oran when she was there. She then apologized for not being able to write better. I had given her my A.T.C. [Air Transport Command] *ticket to sign, because I was keeping it as a souvenir anyway. I can't send it to you, because it has names of cities on it and they wouldn't pass the censors and I'd lose it altogether. What do you think of that?*

My, do I have a most intelligent wife! She spoke of the invasion of the Islands long before it took place. I didn't even think of it possibly coming off until 1945. You are certainly a great gal. As to the nurse who cut out certain words in my letter, she was really an old sourpuss and nobody liked her. The words were "Naples" and "Marseille" as you had figured. At that time, she was of the opinion that we were in a danger zone – What a dope!

I see quite a number of Jerries around here who are working at various depots and it is a great temptation to kill one. Since I last wrote you on that subject, I've sort of let up on it and I guess I'll soon forget all about it. As long as I have my wife and baby to come home to, that's all that counts. And so we come to the end of our letter after a long period of waiting. I hope that everybody back home is well and the weather warmer than what we're having here. Say "Hello" to all – love to the folks – a great big hug and kiss for Carole and you –

 With All My Love,
 Your Dave

——

         Wednesday – November 1st – 1944
           Somewhere in Eastern France

My Dearest Wife and Darling Daughter,

 Believe it or not, I am now going to answer nine (9) of your very nice letters. As to Paul, I hope that Beulah won't worry too much about him on a carrier. The living conditions are unexcelled, but it is the juiciest target in the Navy. I hope that nothing happens to his ship. At this moment, he must be seeing a lot of action around him. In fact, he has probably seen more than I'll ever get to see.

 I have a couple of French kids in here and I'm trying to entertain them by showing them the comic pages from one of the American papers – They're really having a helluva good time. I just gave them some hard candies that I had gotten in the PX while in Italy. It's the first time in about five years that they had any sweets.

As to the Air Force going to the Pacific, I'm almost certain that it will happen, so don't be surprised if it turns out that way. I can see your point of view on our deserving a furlough, but there are a great many more units that have been over here much longer than we. As to Russia declaring war on Japan after the European War is won, that's one point that most diplomats avoid. If you will notice, not many columnists say anything on the subject, because it is like a hot potato. We had better not count on their help.

That was a very nice letter that Carole wrote and I appreciate it a lot. I'd like to have heard her say that she loved me and was going to get a bicycle from Santa Claus. It's really hard to visualize her speaking so well. I, too, feel pretty well licked when I see other couples. However, as we have always done in the past, just stick up that old chin and take it. Just remember that it will be over soon and we'll be together for ever after. The Pacific Theatre is going along very well and without many casualties, thank God! If the weather had only held up a little better for us in the past two months, we would have been deep into Germany. We'll just have to sweat it out.

I want to say that I love and miss you so very much. With all those kisses that you sent me in these letters, I'm overwhelmed. Anyway, send regards to all and love to the folks – a million kisses and a great big hug for Carole and you –

With All My Love,
Your Dave

———

Saturday – November 5th – 1944
Somewhere in Eastern France

My Dearest Darlings,

We are no longer near the place from which I last wrote you, so as you may assume, we were on the go and I didn't have a chance to write. Say, do you realize that today is our 46 months anniversary? Congratulations! May you and your husband be together for all the rest of them.

When I read your letter of the 26th, I was convinced that you were trying to read things into my letters that weren't there, while all the time, the obvious things are there and you fail to read them. What I have specific reference to is that statement that I made while in Italy. I wrote that I thought that I was going to Epinal – Well, that is the name of a city in France. Anyway, I'm not at that place, but a little to the North of it, near Nancy.

Sorry that I am unable to call you on the phone from France. As yet, there are no open lines to America, but if one comes up soon, I'll be among the first to use those facilities. Meanwhile, hope that everybody is well. Give my regards to all and love to the folks – Millions of hugs and kisses for Carole and you –

With All My Love,
Your Dave
P.S. I love you very much.

Sunday – 6 November – 1944
Somewhere in Eastern France

My Sweetest Darlings,

Today was my first venture into American "foreign" territory. I had to go up into the territory, which is under the jurisdiction of the American 3rd Army. As you know, up until our recent move, we were always under the Seventh, which came from Italy. It's sort of unusual to see all the insignias from other units than those that we had been acquainted with all thru the Italian Campaign and the Southern Invasion of France. I had to drive thru the city of Nancy and it is a very pretty city. I hope that I can get a pass to go in and look it over more closely.

Some of the boys are receiving salamis and now they are coming in OK, because it isn't so warm. However, I don't crave any anymore, because I had better start to relax on my eating. In fact, today, I ate only two meals – breakfast and dinner. Of course, I didn't have much choice in the matter, because I wasn't around at lunchtime. Maybe I ought to make my trips at that time every time I have to go out – then I will have to miss one meal a day.

We have finally got a pretty nice setup. We are in buildings and each room has a small stove. Some of the other units in the same command as we are living in tents still and shivering. Fay and one of the other boys have rigged up a double-bunk and we have a nice foursome in our room. Everything is just about perfect, except that the roads are pretty muddy and will get worse as the winter comes on.

Last night, I learned something that I didn't know and something that all the others didn't know either. I can now tell you that we are in the 64th Fighter Wing and have been since we came over. It was under the 12th

Air Force in Africa. In Italy, the 1st Tactical Air Force was formed and known as 12th TAC — We were under that also. It was that unit that shot up all those Jerry vehicles and armored cars in the Italian Campaign and the push from Southern France. Now we are not under the 9th Air Force at all, but in a new Tactical Air Force — The 1st Provisional TAC (Tactical Air Command). It's a pretty big affair and we are playing a big part in it. So now you can rest easily and read about any sorties around here and know that our outfit helped to shoot that Jerry plane down or blow up that railroad in Germany.

Well, Darling, I guess that's about all the news for today — so keep well and take as good care of our darling daughter as you have been doing. Say "Hello" to the gang and love to the folks — A lot of love and kisses for you and the baby —

With All My Love,
Your Dave

<hr />

Monday — 6 November — 1944
Somewhere in Eastern France

My Dearest Amy and Carole Frances,

This evening, I heard a news broadcast and in it was an account of the capture of the 200,000th prisoner in this area. When he was told that he was the 200,000th, he smiled and said that that was a good sign that the War would soon end, because the Jerries are quickly running out of manpower. Maybe there is some truth to the incident, but it still looks like it will go into 1945. It's ironical that Old Man Winter had to be good to Russia when they had their backs to the wall and now he is showing favoritism to the Jerries, now that they are fighting for their lives. Oh well, Victory has always been gained at a high cost, so why be surprised? However, we can hope that Germany will collapse internally and end the War for us.

At the present, the Pacific War seems to have the front lines in the papers. In view of this, the higher authorities must consider the European War just about won and are trying to draw the public's attention to that theatre. It has been said that when the time comes for us to invade Eastern China and Japan, we will do it as we wish. That is, we will be able to handle anything that the Japs will throw at us. There is no doubt that such will be the case, too. Maybe if we wish hard enough, the troops in this theatre will be sent back to the States after it is all over here. Some of the boys kid me that when I get back, Carole will be going steady.

Well, Darlings, hope that Carole, the folks and you are all well and feeling fine and enjoying good weather. Give everybody my regards – love to the folks – and a great big hug and kiss for the baby and you –

With All My Love,
Your Dave

———

Tuesday – 7 November – 1944
Somewhere in Eastern France

My Dearest Darlings,

Around here, the popular song seems to be "Swing [sic] On A Star" – It is different. In the past few days, we have been lucky to get a speaker installed in the Orderly Room, so that we get the recorded broadcasts. In that way, we will gradually get acquainted with the latest songs. We won't get the election results until tomorrow, I suppose. Here's hoping that FDR is back in the saddle.

Have you heard the one about the fellow who went over to see a friend? Upon entering the home of the host, he was surprised to see his host sitting in his easy chair playing chess with his dog, who was sitting opposite him. The guest walked in and exclaimed that the dog was certainly a very smart dog. The host answered, "Humph! Him a smart dog? Why, I beat him two out of three already!"

From the news broadcast, which I have just heard, the Jerries are slowly being cleared out of sectors all over Europe. Soon, all the fighting will be on [CENSORED] and then the people will fully realize that all is lost and that they haven't a chance to survive. Darling, even when we get into German territory, we won't be able to relax. The Jerries are going to try to keep up a guerrilla warfare as long as we are there. There have already been a few such incidents, so you can see that it will have to be a thorough job of defeating the Germans and their ideas if we are to win the War in all respects. I'd certainly like to see the Russians walk in and destroy every Nazi for every Russian and Jew and Catholic that the Nazis murdered. Until that happens, I, personally, won't ever be content. I know that it isn't the American way of thinking, but it is the only way to deal with a Jap or Nazi – the dirty way!

Well, I guess you hear enough of that sort of talk at home – so why bore you with more? I hope that the baby and you are both well and the folks are also feeling fine. Give my regards to all the people back home and love to Mother and Dad – Lots and lots of love and kisses for you and the baby –
   With All My Love,
   Your Dave

———

Wednesday – 8 November – 1944
[Southeastern France]
My Most Adorable Wife and Baby,
   The good part of today was the news broadcasts, which have announced that FDR was reelected and that more Democrats were elected to Congress also. That in itself is as good as a couple of miles advance on the front. Now we can settle down to winning this War over here.
   Tonight they are showing "Hail The Conquering Hero!" at the Wing headquarters. I may go if the rain lets up a bit. It has been given a good write-up in some of the magazines. I'll hold up this letter until later in the evening – so so long. (Just returned) Well, I saw the picture after we had a little trouble with the projector. It wasn't so bad, but it was overrated, I thought. It was funny in spots, but not something over which I could split my sides. Maybe it was because I haven't had any mail and felt sort of dismal – Who knows?
   I suppose that you saw the announcement of the new Air Force in the newspapers. It is about the tops in Tactical Air Forces and will always be the spearhead driving further into Germany. With a little better break in the weather, we'd be much further in than we are. The Philippine Campaign is going along well, so we don't have to worry about their weather.
   I do hope that everybody is well and that Carole and you are in the best of health. Give regards to all and love to the folks – A great big hug and kiss for Carole and you –
   With All My Love,
   Your Dave

———

Friday – 10 November – 1944
Somewhere in Eastern France
My Dearest Sweethearts,
   Last nite, Fay and I walked down to the small village nearby – about 2 miles. It was pitch dark and we had to go thru mud as gooey as melted

chocolate. On top of that, it was freezingly cold. Well, we were invited to the home of a family that included the father and mother and two daughters. One daughter was a brunette named Margerite and the other was a blonde named Andree. Well, Andree's fiancé, named Marcel, was also there. Incidentally, he is also her first cousin. We knew how hard things have been with the people around here, so we brought some cigarettes, tobacco and candy with us. It was the first of these that they had seen in four years, so you can imagine their thankfulness. The whole evening was spent in talking over the War, the election, and trying to get Fay to learn French, while the girls were trying to learn English. Their father was a very intelligent man and we got along well, in spite of my small vocabulary. While there, the mother insisted that we bring our laundry in to them to be washed. At first I refused, but she insisted, so I said that I would.

We left there about 9:30 in the evening and had to walk up that steep and muddy hill. Well, when we finally got back to camp, I was a whipped dog. I hit the hay at once and slept like you do on a Sunday morning. When I got up, I felt like I had gone thru a million years of hard labor. I had to type a lot of requisitions and then waited until this afternoon to go out for supplies. We have to drive with our tops down and this jeep happened to be without a windshield wiper. Well, it rained and sleeted off and on all afternoon, so you can imagine what sort of a ride we had. Out of the whole day of driving, the thing that impressed me the most was the women with their children walking out on the windswept highways in the bitter cold. I thank God over and over again for us living in the States. If we had some room in the jeep, I'd certainly have picked up some of them – but we were full to the brim. I certainly hate to see these poor people having to walk in the cold rain and snow.

As to the Series, yes, I did have five bucks on the Cards – but against the Yanks. Therefore, the bet was void. At the time I made the bet, the Yanks were in first place. The other fellow wanted to pay me, but I insisted that he hadn't gotten a fair play, because he had bet on the Yanks and not the Brownies.

We are going to get one-fifth of scotch and a pint of gin apiece for Thanksgiving. What do you think of that? It will be the first American whiskey we have had in a long time. A lot of the boys are writing to their folks for bottles to be wrapped inside of a bread or something like that – what connivers! Well, I really don't miss it as much as you may think. In fact, all that I have had in the last three months was beer. I guess I'm just an old maid, after all. But why do my ears grow to a point and my voice to a growl when I see a good-looking gal – Am I still a wolf at heart? Who knows – Do you?

Well, that's about all the news for the day, so hope that all's well at home and everybody's feeling fine. Say "Hello" to all our friends, love to the folks and beaucoup love and kisses for you and our darling daughter –

With All My Love,
Your Dave

———

Saturday – 11 November – 1944
Somewhere in Eastern France

My Dearest Wife and Baby,

So today is Armistice Day! Well, so we ain't neat and we are at war instead of peace to commemorate this day. It's tough that we humans are so forgetful and can't remember all the lives that have been lost in the past in wars that have brought us absolutely nothing but grief. Of course, it is hardly possible to think that I can place the Japs and Germans in that same category with us, but they do breathe. This day is just going to pass as another day of the year, because in years to come, there will be another war and wars after that. However, just to kid ourselves, we will pay tribute to our dead and dedicate this day to them, swearing that we will never again go to war. That gesture is just as hypocritical as the Jewish Day of Atonement and the confession of the Catholics. We will remember for that one day and forget for the rest of the year. I really don't know why I should get so philosophical, because, as an individual, I'll never be able to do anything to correct these things that will occur inevitably. So let's let it go as a day which has gone for naught. Personally, it has only added another day to that long list of days we have been separated from each other. On the other hand, it has shortened the number of days we are to be apart.

In spite of the bad weather, the Yanks are doing a darned good job in our sector. With just a spell of nice, dry weather, we will be able to bomb hell out of the Jerries. I hope that each bomb takes at least one Nazi's life with it. Amy, if you will recall what I told you in California – you have to hate the enemy in order to win this War. Today, I hate the Jerries worse than I have ever in all my life. I've seen too many examples of the ruthlessness. They have wiped out complete villages without batting an eye. I spoke to one old

Frenchman who told me that they took a 2-year-old baby and hung it by its neck from a tree. That is just one incident and there are many thousands of other true stories that will startle the world after they are told. We must hate these people as much as we possibly can if we are not to be taken in by their weeping after the War is over. If we soften up when we march in, we will lose everything for which we have been fighting.

That's enough crusading for one day – I hope that you get what I have been driving at. Hope that Carole, the folks and you are feeling fine. Give my regards to all our friends – Love to the folks and lots of lovin' 'n kissin' for Carole and you –

With All My Love,
Your Dave

—

Sunday – 12 November – 1944
Somewhere in Eastern France

My Darling Sweethearts,

Today began another week of War and another step toward home. It began with a beautiful white layer of snow covering all the country around us. The pines looked like white arrows pointed skyward. From our view, it looked like a scene from a typical Xmas card. It was difficult to realize that a War was going on nearby. While on the way to Epinal, we saw people dressed up for church and they certainly reminded me of home. They were all walking in the streets and on the roads and smiling at us as we passed. The only thing that brought us back to the War was an occasional shell-wrecked building or village. Otherwise, as we drove on, the world around us took on a totally different aspect. However, as the roads became more traveled, the snow disappeared and the drab, cold grey of winter took its place. The rains started again and we were soon straining to see thru the windshield, so our little, peaceful scene was gone too soon.

Last night, I heard a rebroadcast of the "Hit Parade." It must have been an old program, because the No. 1 was "I'll Be Seeing You" and from what I have heard, the top tune is "I Walk Alone." We are hearing a lot of "Swing on a Star" – I remember it from Bing Crosby's picture, "Going My Way." At first, I didn't think so much of it, but it is being played up so much that you get to like it automatically. "Long Ago and Far Away" was 5th on the program – It should be higher.

So that is the dope for today as far as the War in Europe goes – and I do hope that it goes. Even if it gets colder, that would be a big help to us, because the roads would harden and allow our tanks and trucks to get thru easier and faster. The Pacific War is coming along well, so all in all, we are on the road to Victory (without Bing Crosby, Bob Hope and Dorothy Lamour). They are rebroadcasting one of Fred Waring's programs and a very delicious arrangement of "Begin the Beguine" has just ended – I guess you and I will always like that song. Just so our likes and dislikes are always the same – we'll be OK. Well, Darlings, say "Hello" to our friends and give my love to the folks and a big hug and a kiss for our darling daughter – Tell her that I love and miss her and her mother very much, too –

With All My Love,
Your Dave

Monday – 13 November – 1944
Somewhere In Eastern France

My Dearest Amy and Carole Frances,

I stopped at that French family's house where Fay and I had visited. They had our laundry ready and it was really a very good job. I thanked them very enthusiastically and offered to pay for it, but they refused very emphatically. They also insisted that I tell my friends to bring their laundry to them to be washed, so I guess they really did appreciate those little things that I gave them. You have to be careful about the people you get acquainted with around here, because many of them are of German descent, and on that account, they are still a little German in their ways and thoughts, in spite of the fact that they live in France today. You may recall that Alsace-Lorraine had always been a problem and will continue to be, so we can't take any chances in getting too friendly with the people as we go further East. In fact, we get more cautious. After all, if we do relax in the Reich, it may be the last time we ever did.

As we haven't had any "Stars & Stripes" for a long while, I'm pretty much in the dark as to the rest of the world. However, the radio did carry a rumor that Hitler must be incapacitated, because he failed to make a personal appearance on two occasions after it was assumed that he would do so. If there is any truth to the rumor (and we hope that there is), it may help to shorten this War over here.

Well, Darlings, that's about all the dope for today, so say "Hello" to all our friends and send love to the folks – and for Carole and you a great big hug and kiss –

With All My Love,
Your Dave

———

Tuesday – 14 November – 1944
Somewhere in Eastern France

My Sweetest Darlings,

I guess we had better begin with your letter of the 21st of Sept. (ancient history for you by now) – the day that you received mail from me when I first hit France. First of all, about 30 men of our company were taken in on the invasion while the rest came in on D [Day]+15. If you read the "Time" magazine of August 28, you read about the landing in the Riviera. Well, our outfit went in at St. Tropez on D-Day. It was above that town that we bivouacked at that chateau. About Sept. 7th, we moved up to a small village of Biol – It is located between Grenoble and Lyon. It was from that area that I left for the hospital. Now you are up-to-date on my whereabouts and the places of the past.

As to the "Time," it states that [Gordon] *Saville is the Commanding General of 12th TAC – so you know that much. Well, General* [Glenn] *Barcus is the C.G. of the 64th Fighter Wing, so that answers all of your questions on who the generals are. Oh yes – the new Commanding General of the 1st TAC is Gen. Ralph Royce, who was famous for leading the first bombing raid on the Philippines in 1942 – so it is really a very illustrious outfit we're in.*

As to the mails being so slow at this time of the year, I think that it is due to the bad flying weather and demand for space for more vital War materials, so don't be too impatient and I'm sure that my mail will reach you in due time. After I have seen so much bad weather, I'd be optimistic to say that it will end by April. However, what occurs inside Germany may change the picture quite a bit, so let's just sit tight and hope for an early defeat.

As to De Gaulle being near me while I was in the Lyon sector, he came in the same day that I left Lyon. He is certainly worshipped all over France. Everybody to whom I have spoken say that he is the man.

As to the article which you read about the Russians diverting their campaign to the Balkans, I can see the reason for that. In the first place, they knew that there weren't many troops left in that sector and a push in that direction would not be as costly as a drive into Germany. Also, after this is all over, a popular type of government will have a big influence on the setting up of governments in countries that are going to get rid of their present ones or ones that were in power at the time of the German occupation. This will no doubt include Greece, Yugoslavia, Hungary, Romania, Czechoslovakia, Italy, France and Spain. If the liberating forces happen to be Red, that will have a great influence in the future of that country. In the case of the Balkans, Russia must make them its friends and dependents after the War, because they are right on its borders. On the other hand, I can also see that this move would look like a definite attempt to allow the Allies in the West to carry the brunt of the War. However, this secondary assumption should be discarded, because if that writer realized just how much the Russians hate the Jerries, he'd not write such a thing. It is the foremost thing in the minds of the Russian soldiers to kill as many of the Jerries as possible and as soon as possible. Therefore, we should have a little more confidence in our Allies and know that each campaign is for the good of all of us.

"The Voice" just finished singing "Long Ago and Far Away." So our daughter also sings "There'll Be A Hot Time in the Town of Berlin When The Yanks Come Marching In" – We had a recording of it by Sinatra when we left the States. She probably does a better job of it than he.

The War in the Pacific is still going along well, but it will be a little while before we are able to clear up all the Philippines. Darling, as to thinking about getting home, at times I think that it is better that we just don't think about it and just know that we will return at some time in the near future – no date especially. Then it will be all the more pleasant when we do come home. I, too, agree that a 30-day furlough would be hard for us. It isn't worth it to go away again.

I just listened to a radio news broadcast and they stated that it is rumored that a run on the banks of Germany is under way at this time. If that is so, it is just the sort of thing about which I just wrote about what will happen inside Germany will determine when the War will end over here. This sort of a thing will be a great help to start an uprising against the Nazis.

While at the Replacement Depot, I saw about a thousand Air Corps men who had just been returned to the American Forces after being liberated by the Russians when they took Bulgaria. Some of these men had just been overseas a short while and were shot down a couple of months after coming over. Now they are sent back to the States, because they have to go to another theatre of War after being a Prisoner of War. There were no doubt a lot of happy parents and wives and sweethearts when these men got back there.

Well, Darlings, just take good care of yourselves. Say "Hello" to all and love to Mother and Dad – Tell Carole to get well real soon and Daddy will try to get back home and take her fishing with him – Also Mama, too, if she is a good girl – Also a great big hug and kiss for both of you –

With All My Love,

Your Dave

Thursday – 15 November – 1944
Somewhere in Eastern France

Dearest Amy and Carole Frances,

I got a letter from Paul dated the 3rd of September. All he said was that he was in the Pacific. As he is in an amphibious unit, it wouldn't surprise me to hear that he was in on the landings in Leyte. I do hope that he is safe, for Beulah's sake. A carrier is really such a nice, big, juicy target. However, it is also one of the most guarded vessels. Well, let's hope that he's OK and will be home soon for a leave.

Your next letter was written the day after Paris was liberated – That is a long time ago. Even with the Balkan countries leaving Hitler, the weather went over to his side and now seems to be better than all of the Axis nations put together. So we won and lost – for the time being.

As to your request to allow my hair to grow out of that G.I. one, I'm way ahead of you – I've been letting it grow for the last two months. Before I got my last haircut, I was beginning to look like Daniel Webster. Well, take good care of yourself and the baby – send regards to all – love to the folks – and a great big hug and kiss for you and Carole –

With All My Love,

Your Dave

Friday – 17 November – 1944
Somewhere in Eastern France

My Darling Wife and Baby,

I just got finished straightening up our room for a very thorough inspection, which we are expecting tomorrow by a colonel from Wing headquarters. From what everybody says, he's a guy to get out of the way from. However,

I've never seen him and I certainly won't shrivel if and when I do. I've seen generals and spoken to colonels and haven't faded away – so why should I begin now?

Guess what? No – you're wrong. We are the possessors of an ancient upright! We got hold of it at a deserted Jerry barracks and hauled it over here. A couple of the boys are able to pound the ivories pretty well, too. The other night, someone said that it was tough that you weren't around to play the piano for us – See how they remember how well you do play? Anyway, if you were here, I certainly wouldn't let you spend your time in playing the piano – comprenez-vous?

Do you remember that dog that Okma got at the same time that I got Buck? Well, he is really starting to be a big dog after all these months. The other day, a stray brown dog, of the opposite sex, came into camp. It is a pretty dog and has nice fur – but it is a younger dog than Harry. Well, Harry has been trying to jump from being a boy to a man in one easy lesson. However, the other dog has other ideas on the subject and Harry always ends up with the other dog snapping at him. Maybe when Spring comes, he will be a little more successful.

Now then – you just take extra good care of both yourselves and don't let anything give you a cold. So that's about all the news – Say "Hello" to all and love to the folks and lots of love and kisses for the baby and you –

With All My Love,
Your Dave

———

Sunday – 19 November – 1944
Somewhere in Eastern France

My Sweetest Wife and Baby,

Well, today, I certainly can't kick, because I was the proud recipient of three packages and three letters from you. As to the packages, I got two this morning – one from you that you sent from Michigan with the chili, cheese and tongue. That was a long time in getting here, but it was forwarded to Italy after getting to France the first time. Now for the surprise – I got a nice, big, Xmas package from the Levys – Baron's folks. In the package was a jar of herring spread, a jar of deviled Smithfield ham spread, a package of Pabst-ett [cheese] and carton of crackers, and then the most delicious-looking 1-lb. nut and fruit cake. It also had a box of peanuts in it. It is so good looking that I am going to keep it until Xmas with nearly all the other packages that I get, and with those that Fay and the other two Supply boys get, and with our allotment of liquor, we ought to have some party.

I haven't eaten any of the soups either as yet. It is all too precious to do away with at one time. The third package was from [Amy's] Aunt Mary. It had a few packages of assorted-flavor Lifesavers in it, a box of Beechies [chewing gum], a tube of toothpaste, a tube of shaving cream, a tube of hairdressing (I never did use it), a package of razor blades, a rubber comb, a box of Blu-Jay foot plasters, and what do you think? Yes, a salami! It was the neatest wrapped one that I ever received as yet. It was paraffined about ¼-inch around the salami itself. Then it was wrapped in waxed paper and dipped in more paraffin. When I opened it – it was as fresh as if I had taken it out of a delicatessen. I ate a huge piece of it at once and gave Fay and Louie a piece and you'd be amazed at the way that they raved. Louie receives Italian salami that doesn't taste quite the same – and he raved. Also another Italian boy who usually gives me some of his salami when it comes in good – He said that it was perfect. Well, I saved most of it after the first hour. I wrapped the open end in paper and left the paraffin on the rest of it. Boy, it is good, tho.

I was thinking that it may be a good idea if you could send me a box camera, if you can get hold of it, so that I could send you some pictures that you'd like. See if you can get hold of one.

Today we really had a most perfect day for Sunday. It was warm and the sun was out all day long. Best of all, it gave us a full day for flying and I can assure you that the air was occupied.

Take good care of yourselves. Send my regards to all and love to Mother and Dad – and tell Carole that I love her and miss her very much and would like to be there to say it in person – also her mother – and that I send her and Mommy a great big hug and kiss –

With All My Love,
Your Dave

———

Monday – 20 November – 1944
Somewhere in Eastern France

My Dearest Darlings,

Lt. Micka and Capt. Temple went out and got some schnapps, wine and beer – so we have a little something with which to start our bar. Another thing that was decided was that each bottle of liquor that the officers and sergeants were authorized would be donated to the bar, so that the other men could also get a drink of something good for a change, so that will put a damper on our little Xmas party that Fay and I had planned in our room. He is still pretty well discouraged over the idea of giving up our allowances – and so am I, as we both voted against it. Well, it's really a very minor thing compared to our winning this War.

From what we hear over the radio, the Allies are really on the go all along the Western Front and the Jerries are retreating at a fast pace. The few days of good bombing weather certainly did have its effects. If we continue at the same pace, the Nazis will be running around in horse-drawn wagons soon. It's been pretty optimistic-looking lately, but I guess it will still take until next Spring to get the job over with. The natural defenses are still pretty tough to contend with, which will aid the Jerries in holding out a little longer. However, as I have written before, just a few breaks in the weather and we could blow them all to hell. I wonder, at times, if there is a wall standing in Cologne and some of the other Ruhr cities. If so, they certainly don't have all four walls attached. Berlin must really be a mess by now, too. The policing of that country after the War will be a very touchy thing and I hope that we get home before they decide to include us in.

Well, Darling, say "Hello" to all our friends and send love to the folks – a great big hug and kiss for Carole and you –

With All My Love,
Your Dave

———

Thursday – 23 November – 1944
Somewhere in Eastern France

My Dearest Sweethearts,

To begin with, I will wish you a very Happy Thanksgiving Day. This afternoon, we had our dinner of dinners. I don't suppose we will ever have anything as nice as this in the Armed Services again. At least, I hope that I won't be in uniform to indulge in it. Anyway, we had sliced turkey – dressing – mashed potatoes – corn – peas – cranberries – apple pie – chocolate cake with chocolate icing – raisin bread and coffee. Then on the tables were bowls of hard candies and packages of cigarettes. It was really more than any one person could possibly eat at one sitting – but we all weathered it well. Everything was prepared to perfection. Some of us decided to save our cake until this evening, as we were full enough.

That night – to my complete surprise – there was a batch of letters waiting for me stuck in my field desk. There were exactly twenty-eight (28) from you. Well, I decided to have dinner before I dove into that stack – so I went over and had a carcass of one of the turkeys for my meal. That was enough to fill me up. Then I settled back in a chair in the Orderly Room and began reading at 5:30. When the clock hit 8:00, I had just finished the last letter and was pretty well pooped. I decided to eat the piece of cake that I had set aside and it was really good. Then, in order to brace myself to answer all this, I went up to the bar and had a couple of beers.

I will begin with the November 7th letter – the day that we brought Roosevelt back into office. So the Nazis are telling the American soldiers that the Jews reelected him – Do they think that after all the years of fighting them that we will believe anything that they tell us? I'll trust only a dead Jerry in the future. As to the War, it looks like all of France will be liberated as soon as you receive this letter. The Allies are in Strasbourg at this writing, so we're doing pretty well. It wasn't long ago that we could see the flashes of the guns – but the War has moved on at a fast pace. Even with all the rains that we have had recently, we are doing splendidly.

When I read about Paul being in on the invasion of the Philippines, I thought of something that I had written you some time ago. That was that he'd see more action in one day than I'd ever see in all the time that I am overseas. From his letter, he has already done so. That must have really been a hot spot for a while. I do hope that his ship came thru OK. I hope that you have been able to console Beulah and try to buck her up a bit. She'll probably be thinking the worst from here on in.

I was invited out to the home of some people with whom I visited last week. I guess if you are kind to people, they will try to reciprocate, even tho they don't have much themselves. I know that they don't have such an easy time of it, because the woman's husband is a prisoner in Germany and the girl is an only daughter. The daughter is attending the university in town and is studying to become a math professor. They have a home in town, but when the War was so close to them, they decided to move to a close-by village and this is it, so until the War goes further away, they will live here. Meanwhile, their home in the city is closed. The father had been a Venetian blinds manufacturer and they seem quite wealthy, so maybe Fay and I will go down there tomorrow night.

Well, Darlings, I do hope that you are both well, also, that you have received my Xmas gifts to you by now. So send regards to all – oodles of love and kisses for Carole and you –
With All My Love,
Your Dave

———

Friday – 24 November – 1944
Somewhere in Eastern France

Dearest Amy and Carole Frances,
It looks like the War is coming along pretty favorably in this area. From late reports, the French have been fighting in Strasbourg and have captured a bridge intact. This would allow passage of supplies on into Germany without any trouble. If that hadn't been possible, we would have had to build bridges, which would take valuable time and lives. As long as the Jerries are on the go the other way, we will continue to pursue them until the end. When we pushed up from Italy, we kept at their heels; after Rome fell, we were right after them; when we landed in Southern France, we kept after them; then when they retreated up the Rhone, we were on their tails – So if they continue to retreat toward Berlin, we will continue to follow all the way. I wonder how the Rhine looks from Strasbourg or any other point on the French side of the river.
I'll bet that our daughter really ate herself silly yesterday at the dinner table. It was tough that it couldn't have been a happier Thanksgiving dinner – Maybe next year will bring a different picture.
Regards to all – love to the folks – lots of love and kisses for Carole and you –
With All My Love,
Your Dave

———

Sunday – 26 November – 1944
Somewhere in Eastern France

My Dearest Darlings,
Fay and I walked back down that hill and were enthusiastically welcomed by our hostesses. They hadn't eaten as yet, as the custom is to have dinner about 7 or 8 in the evening, so they were very happy to get the few little things that we brought with us. The people still have to have ration points for everything, and even if they do have points, the desired items are not to

be had, so when we bring some chocolate, cigarettes, candy and other things, they are really grateful. Fay wanted to take the daughter to see the movie that was showing last nite – I had seen it in the hospital – but they said that they were expecting another visitor – a fellow whom I had met the last time I was there, so Fay went alone. The other fellow came up at about 7 and at 9, I decided that I had better leave, so I had to walk up that damned hill once more in the dark. You can imagine how I felt when I finally hit the hay – I was really all in.

Well, Darlings, say "Hello" to all and love to Mother and Dad – Lots of love and kisses to Carole and you –

With All My Love,
Your Dave

———

Monday – 27 November – 1944
Somewhere in Eastern France

My Sweetest Darlings,

I went into Epinal this morning and it took me about 1-1/2 hours to get one item and then waited for the requisition to be filled. It was about two when I began my return trip. On the way, I saw one of the most disgusting accidents. On the left side of the road was a truck – you couldn't tell what sort of a truck it was, because it was so mashed up – and three Americans lying on the ground with dirt and blood all over their heads. The ambulances had already been called, so there was nothing to be done but wait for them. I didn't spend any time there – but that one moment was enough. It's tough enough to know that men are being killed thru carelessness – then to add up the huge number of vehicles that we're running by the same method. The Jerries would be proud of themselves if they could strafe ½ of all these vehicles. Well, I guess considering all the driving that is done, it is only a small % that is wrecked. However, it still adds up to a large number that could be used for future purposes.

When I got back to camp, I had to line up all the radio, telegraph, teletype and other Section Chiefs to get their requirements for next month's supplies.

Well, Lassies, my thoughts are only of you two – so regards to all – love to Mother and Dad – lots of extra hugs and kisses for Carole and you –

With All My Love,
Your Dave

———

Wednesday – 29 November – 1944
Somewhere in Eastern France

Dearest Darlings,

I received three huge packages and two very nice letters, which were dated the 14th and 15th of November. The first package that I opened was from Beulah and it had a very well preserved salami in it. Also, a jar of tamales in sauce, and a jar of wine jelly. I immediately opened the salami and found it in even better condition than Aunt Mary's. In fact, after dinner, I ate a piece and it's delicious – Am I giving you a taste for some now?

The next package was yours and it contained clogs, games, caramels and handkerchiefs. Everything came in very well. The caramels were in excellent shape and also the games. Thank Carole for the candy and tell her that I send her an extra big kiss for it. I hope I can get enough patience to play the games. So thanks for all the nice surprise Xmas gifts.

The last package was a nice big box of snacks containing assorted Lorna Doone cookies and some assorted jellies. At this very moment, we're indulging in consuming the package. So you see, we have really hit the jackpot in the mailbox today.

As to your question – Where do I think Hitler is? Well, I really don't care, because it is the German people themselves whom we are fighting now. Even if Hitler is dead or in hiding, the people are still the same ones with whom we went to War and who put Hitler in power anyway, when he promised them "Der Velt"["The World"]. Now, with [SS leader, Heinrich] Himmler and Goebbels at the head of the government, it certainly doesn't make it any easier for the people. We've still got to kill that certain feeling that has been instilled in their minds for the past twenty years. From the looks of the prisoners, they are realizing that "Der Superman" is a thing long forgotten. The German people are grateful when the Americans walk in to capture a town. They are afraid that if it were the French or Russians or Belgians, they would be murdered, just like the Nazis killed the innocent people they found in conquered countries. If only the Russians would hurry and push on into Germany and wipe out towns and villages like the Nazis did – there would be a lot of very happy people – and people who are most certainly not barbaric. Even if we must show that we are from a democracy and that criminals shall be given a fair trial, it hurts to know that not long ago, he may have raped, burned and murdered innocent people without even flinching. Maybe the people back in ancient history weren't so wrong when they believed in an eye for an eye. Well, the sooner that this is all over with, the better all of us will be.

Well, I guess that's about the sum of the day's events, so say "Hello" to all our friends – love to the folks – and a thousand and one kisses for Carole and you – you get the one –

With All My Love,
Your Dave

———

Thursday – 30 November – 1944
Somewhere in Eastern France

My Darling Wife and Baby,

Now for the big news – We received the liquor rations today, but most of the sergeants had voted to donate it to the bar that we have. I voted against it, as did a number of others, but the majority ruled in this case.

The weather during the past week has been the kind that you see in movies of London. It is so thick at times that you could reach out and cut it with a knife. It is cold and damp at all times and I wear my scarf, which Aunt Mary knitted for me three years ago, all the time. At night, I sometimes wear my long woolens. This sort of weather isn't the best for advancing, but we're doing darned well. There is only a very small part of France in which there are still Jerries. We're inside Germany on a front that extends from Holland to a point just North of the French Line running along the Saar region. The climate has certainly been against us the past two months, but we're doing OK in spite of it. I'm still of the opinion that the War will go into next Spring. Of course, Russia could always spring a surprise at the last minute. Well, just as long as we win and return to America soon, everything will be OK with me.

Well, Beulah's box of snacks is about finished and so is the salami that she sent. Aunt Mary's was finished a long time ago. Now that we are getting cool weather, I wouldn't mind getting a salami every so often from you, too. Also, try to include some more pickles. By the time the warm weather returns, I hope to be home. Those little snacks that we don't get from our Uncle Sam add so much to a lonesome evening.

I suppose that's about all the news for now – except that I do love and miss you and the baby so very much. Maybe I won't have to write that one of these days and will be there speaking to you – let's hope. So say "Hello" to all and send love to the folks – A million hugs and kisses for the baby and you –

With All My Love,
Your Dave

———

Friday – 1 December – 1944
Somewhere in Eastern France

My Sweetest Darlings,

We now begin the last month of the last year that we will be separated. It has been a long time, but I think that we both have come thru it pretty well. Our letters have certainly shortened the time we have been apart, so I guess we can put up with a few more months of being apart. Just think – Next year, we will be back together again for good. I sincerely say that we went thru a very fast year and the coming months will go by just as fast, so let's just keep on writing the daily welcome letters and I'll be seeing you in no time soon.

Today, we finally won out on the decision on shall the men authorized to get liquor keep it. Well, Fay and I got two nice, big bottles of the Johnnie Walker Red Label Scotch and one bottle of Gilbey's Dry Gin. With the three bottles, we ought to have a darned nice party on the 25th. From all rumors, it will be the last time that we'll get the issue – but we'll be optimistic.

A couple of the boys are going to Paris for schooling - one of them being Joe Dines. The men will be gone for three weeks schooling, so they ought to have a real stay there. I certainly wish that I were able to take off like that and see Paris. From all reports, things are quite high and it takes a bankroll to live there, so just one day would just about bust me flatter than a pancake.

By the way, that little female dog that was here a week ago returned today and Harry is still trying to get into the "men's" class. He certainly tries hard enough. Gosh, it makes me homesick.

Well, Darlings, send regards to all and love to Dad and Mother – a lot of love and kisses for the baby and you –

With All My Love,
Your Dave

———

Tuesday – 5 December – 1944
Somewhere in France

My Dearest Darlings,

This morning, I drove over to one of the depots and then we drove to one of the finance offices where Mullen had to turn in the money that was collected for this last bond drive. While there, I stayed with the jeep and listened to the radio that is installed in it. It was Temple's jeep and was the only thing around that we could use. Well, about that time, school let out and I was swarmed with small children who clambered all over the jeep, listening to the music. They were amazed to hear the sound coming from the speaker that was attached to the floor – under the dashboard. Well, there were two small boys who hung around longer than the others and I gave them some chewing gum that I happened to have at the time. After looking at them awhile, I started to think of Carole Frances and you. Damn it! Every child I see reminds me of the baby and it sort of chokes a guy. I thought I had that feeling nearly licked, but I guess I'm very much mistaken. It was that way when I left the station in St. Louis and also that way when I left the P.O.E. I suppose that the War hasn't hardened me too much, to get that ol' feeling about my wife and baby. Well, it won't help matters any by telling you about my feelings, because you experience them, too. So I'll just keep on seeing children, talking with them, and let them remind me of you.

One of the passing thoughts while driving today was the impression that I got of the older women. It's amazing the endurance that they all have and display. You can see numbers of them walking on the roads every day, carrying huge bundles that would ordinarily weigh the average girl in the States down. They don't sag or show any signs of fatigue, but, on the other hand, look as tho they were at it all their lives. The surprising thing is their pride that each seems to take in her makeup. They all do their hair up in the most attractive manners and it makes it hard to tell if they are young ladies or old women. Why, while waiting for Mullen, one old woman walked out of a building and she must have been as old as my grandmother and she had a very smart hairdo. I guess that what is said about France and its styles is really true after all. Oh, well, I'll still take you any day of the week – even in the morning when you awaken.

That, my darlings, just about winds up my day's activities and thoughts for the time being – Hope that all's well at home and that Carole is getting bigger and better each day. Regards to all and love to the folks – a great big hug and kiss for the baby and you –

With All My Love,
Your Dave

Wednesday – 6 December – 1944
Somewhere in Eastern France

Dearest Amy and Carole Frances,

I finally broke the ice and received a package from Uncle Ben. It was a very nice can of Busy Bee Chocolates – sweet and bittersweet hard centers. It's really a delicious box and I'd hate to see it by tomorrow. We have already hit half of it, so the other half ought to be gone by the next day.

Last nite, after I wrote you, I read the October issue of "Coronet" and it had an article on the possibility of Europe going Communist after it is over. He, the author, stated that he didn't think so. His reasons were that [USSR dictator, Joseph] Stalin and the Russians had their own problems to figure out after the War and will be too occupied to look for bigger boundaries. However, he failed to see the popular impression the Russians made on these old monarchies. In African colonies such as Oran, I saw Stalin being posted on the billboards and walls as often as De Gaulle. In Italy, it was even more so – The people are very much in favor of Communism. And now in France, I have seen and listened to many people who like the Soviets and their form of government. However, the old loyalists are the ones who definitely don't like it and want the monarchy or republic back after the War. Now then, the popularity of the Russians has risen to such a point that even if the Russians don't influence the people directly, they will still select Communism as their form of government after it is over. That was the reason for the English desiring to be the liberating force in Greece. If it had been the Russians, the English would have lost all influence that they ever held in that section of Europe. As it is, I do agree with the writer that Greece is sort of disgusted with the English after the way they left the Aegean area in 1942. Anyway, it will take a lot of diplomacy on the part of America and England to divert the Balkans and France and Italy and even Spain to any other type of government than Communism. Well, it is just my guess anyway and I am entitled to that.

So much for current events. Tell Carole that her daddy misses her and her mother very very much and wishes that he was with you. However, we'll just be a little more patient and know that we'll be together next year at this same time. So until later, regards to all – love to the folks – and a great big hug and kiss for the baby and you –

With All My Love,
Your Dave

Thursday – 7 December – 1944
Somewhere in Eastern France

Dearest Darlings,

Your first letter was of the 16th of November – the day that Beulah received a letter from Paul that he was on the high seas on the 8th. That must have been after the invasion of the Philippines. I hope that he's on his way back for a leave. It would be good for her and Paul. Of course, I'd like to get home too, and as soon as possible, too.

So! You found a grey hair in your head. I guess that is the end, you old hag. It's a little grey hair in the nest – a parody of "A Little Grey Home in the West." Anyway, don't worry about it and you won't see any more of them – It was probably from some flour that you spilled. As to mine, I guess I'm not any too well off, as it had continued to creep back on my forehead and it's really not a bushy head of hair. Anyway, it doesn't worry me, because now, when it is more important to worry about just living, the condition of one's coiffure isn't important. When I get back home, I'll worry about it – and then I may not.

From that newspaper clipping, you really got a bird's eye view of one of the roads where the fighting took place lately. It is the very same road that I passed a couple of times while going for supplies. As to the map on the other side of the paper, you did make a guess, but it was way off. First of all, you must consider the scale of the map. Then you would have to consider how often I had mentioned a certain place – namely Nancy. In that case, we must be very close to Nancy – yes? Well, you had us between Metz and Nancy and on the other side of the battle lines, in German territory. I wouldn't care to be there – at least not at that time.

I'm glad to see that you are so optimistic about us not going to the Pacific after it is over here. Maybe it will turn out as you hope and I'll be coming home next summer. At least, we can hope for it. If there is one spot I don't care to go to – it is the Pacific Theatre. As to the invasion of France, half of our outfit made the invasion and the other half, including myself, came in on D [Day]+15, which was the 30th of August. However, don't worry about the danger of it – You have read all about it in the papers by now.

Just three years ago today, you and I were listening to our radio, to Sammy Kaye's Sunday Serenade. Well, here I am, thousands of miles away on account of what happened that day. Of course, we don't know whether or not Hitler would have dragged us in sooner or later, but it did separate us a *little sooner than we had ever imagined. Since that day, however, we have come a long way and now have just about gotten rid of Hitler and will have one enemy to fight next year. I don't want to celebrate this day as an anniversary, but to dedicate it to those who died due to carelessness.*

Well, Darlings, say "Hello" to all and love to the folks — lots of love and kisses for the baby and you — I do love and miss you both so very much —

With All My Love,

Your Dave

Sunday — 10 December — 1944

Somewhere in Eastern France

My Darling Wife and Baby,

I just finished reading the "Stars & Stripes" and there is a controversial subject in it dealing with the Jerries going in for underground work after the Allies walk in. Whether they will or will not go underground makes no difference, as the Allied soldier will still have to be more alert than ever before. There will be nobody for them to trust, because they all, one time or another, did back up Der Heel.

I also just finished reading about "Prisoner 339, Klooga" in the Oct. 30th issue of "Life." I had seen an article on that same incident on the deliberate shooting of the prisoners and after reading the actual facts, it makes me even more tempted to shoot the next damned bastard of a Jerry that I see, even tho he is a Prisoner of War. I don't know what prevents some of the infantrymen from just killing the sons-of-bitches off instead of taking them prisoner. It only means that we have to feed and clothe them after they are taken. We ought to do the same as the Nazis have been doing the past ten years and let them know that we mean business. At times, I think that we are so softhearted that we'll awaken to another Pearl Harbor sometime in the future. If only the people would go thru one day of battle and see all the unscrupulous and underhanded things the Jerries are capable of, they would wake up to the fact that the present world's security is not at stake, but the one of the future. The gravestones of the last War just laugh at the Allies as more and more bodies fall. Won't the civilians back home wake up and see that the peace has to be of the most drastic nature in order to hold up? I don't know — Maybe we are beating our heads against the walls.

Last night, I had a very unusual dream. I dreamed that the Americans made another landing at the island of Bohol, in the Philippines. I could see it so clearly, because I pointed to it on a map. Well, this morning, I was discussing it at breakfast and was told that no such landing took place – so I was sort of left hanging in mid-air until I realized I must have dreamed it. It was so clear in my mind that I could have sworn that it took place – Who knows? – Maybe it will take place soon.

Well, I guess that's about it – I do love you and the baby and miss you more than this typewriter can say – so regards to all and love to the folks – a big hug and kiss for you and the baby –

With All My Love,
Your Dave

———

11 December – Monday – 1944
Somewhere in Eastern France

My Darling Wife and Baby,

It is the practice of the Wing to distribute to the children each year, some of the things that the G.I.'s receive from the States. In this case, most of them receive candy, so the Special Service Officer has asked all men to cooperate and donate some of their candies to this cause. I think that I will go to Nancy and give mine out there, as there aren't many outfits stationed there and there are many more children there to be taken care of than are in this small village. It will really make me happy to be able to bring a little joy to some of these kids after such a long period of suffering. This will be one Xmas that all the French will remember for years to come.

Back in Oran, when I'd meet some Frenchman on the street and strike up a conversation with him, it would invariably end up with when I thought we would be in Paris. To be optimistic and polite, I'd say that Paris would be in French hands for Xmas and it would be received with tear-filled eyes by the person to whom I'd be talking. Well, now it has happened and it will be the first Xmas in four long years that will be celebrated so vigorously. In Paris, the people ought to really raise hell.

Did I ever tell you that I do miss you and Carole Frances more and more every day? At times, I wonder if it will all suddenly come to an end, but after seeing the past couple of months of fighting that the Germans have displayed, it is hard to see the War ending before next Spring. Well, it will mean not going to the Pacific area – perhaps. Anyway, let's thank God that everybody is well and that Carole is getting to be such a very darling baby of whom we should be the proudest parents. It won't be too long before we'll be back together and then we won't worry about a thing.

Well, regards to all – love to the folks – and lots and lots of hugs and kisses for the baby and you –
  With All My Love,
  Your Dave

———

  Tuesday – 12 December – 1944
  Somewhere in Eastern Europe

Dearest Darlings,

While out today, I stopped by the APO [Army Post Office] and asked what was the delay in the mail and was told that it was on account of the transportation shortages. So it looks like it won't be earlier than January before I get my packages. I guess that there are more important things than our mail – After all, we can't shoot a damned Jerry with a piece of paper. Well, we'll continue to sweat it out as before.

Early this morning, it was raining, but as the day grew older, the clouds broke and the sun came out to make it a very nice day for the airmen. Just about a week of this sort of weather and the Jerries will be on the run. As long as the roads stay hard and it doesn't rain or snow too much, we'll be OK.

Yesterday, I spoke to one of our fellows who is attached to a forward unit up front. He is billeted with a German family and he said that they are treating him pretty well. I told him that I don't care how well they treated him, they are still not to be trusted. However, he didn't seem to see it that way. I hope that most of the boys don't feel like him. If they get too lax, we may see a few things that we'll regret.

At the present time, we are listening to Glenn Miller and the G.I. band that he brought overseas. He's somewhere in Europe, so maybe we'll get to see him. An earlier program, just before Miller, had some of the old-time favorites, such as "As Time Goes By" – "Hands Across the Table" – "The Man I Love" and many more that we have liked and danced to many times. Each date that I had with you was very enjoyable and full of fun. I guess we were just made for each other. Carole is a good basis of argument on this point. Well, there's not much more to say – so, regards to all and love to the folks – and millions of lovely hugs and kisses for you and the baby –
  With All My Love,
  Your Dave

———

Wednesday – 13 December – 1944
Somewhere in Eastern France

My Sweetest Darlings,

    Lately, I've been asking people where is the best place to distribute candies for the children at Xmas-time – in the schools or in front of the churches on Xmas Day? So far, nobody seems to know or give a damn – as long as they get some bon-bons. Well, I have definitely decided to give it out to the kids anyplace I find them on that day – I certainly wish I had more to give them. I shouldn't have eaten what I did; then I would have more. I'm sure that the folks back home would want me to do so, if they knew that it was all going for a good cause. It will be the first time in years that the kids have had any chocolate. Some of them never knew what candy was – as they were born when the Jerries moved in. I wish that there was more that we could do for them.

    I saw that recent article in the "Stars & Stripes" about a WPB [War Production Board] *member saying that the Navy had told him that it was their opinion that the War with Japan will go on for five more years. Even if that were the case, it wouldn't do the Armed Services any good to hear or read about it. Morale should be picked up and not knocked down at this time, but it is the same old thing – those damned armchair strategists who are "in the know." If they would keep their big mouths shut for a while and pitch in with a little War production, the situation would be a thousand percent better off than it is. In fact, the European War might have been brought to an end if those back home would have concentrated on production and not the election. If you will recall, there was a definite lag in War production at the time of the campaigns. After the election, the people got back down to business. However, all that material will never be made up. That's the reason why I harp so much on why the civilians don't awaken and see the reality of the situation. The Germans definitely need a strong arm to watch over them after it is over.*

    Well, Darlings, hope that everybody at home is well and that you will have a white Xmas. So regards to all and love to the folks – beaucoup love and kisses for the baby and you –

    With All My Love,
    Your Dave

Thursday – 14 December – 1944
Somewhere in Eastern France

My Dearest Amy and Carole Frances,

The mail brought us some more Special Service magazines and I just finished looking at the pictures of the World Series in "Life." That shot of the scoreboard in Sportsman's Park really made me homesick. There was a very clear and appetizing sign advertising "Alpen Brau." I guess those little things are really big after you miss them awhile. Then "Esquire" sent some miniature calendars for 1945 that are really terrific – especially the month of June, mmmmmmmm. Of course, I'd rather be with someone else I know. However, a picture is also rather nice to look at, once in a while.

Today, the sun came out so that there was plenty of air activity. With breaks like this, we can look forward to some rapid advances all along the front. It looks like the damned Jerries are realizing that we aren't going to stand still during the Winter. They have shifted quite a number of armor to the South to meet Gen. [Alexander] Patch, thereby taking it away from a sector up North. I certainly do hope that the roads stay hard and we get enough material from the States to end this thing next Spring.

From all appearances, we do have to admit the Asiatic situation does not look so rosy. On the other hand, the Pacific area is looking as rosy as could be expected. If there is any one person to blame for the condition in China, it is Chiang Kai-Shek. If he had reached a compromise with the Communists long ago, he would have their cooperation now instead of the two separate armies fighting each other and the Japs. That was the big thing that [General Joseph] Stilwell was trying to clear up while he was over there. However, Chiang was too big to allow a foreigner to walk in and take over command of the Chinese and show up the Commander in the eyes of his troops. So now, we all are having to pay for such a stubborn resistance. Well, maybe we won't have to chase the Japs out of that country – They may do so themselves by getting the hell bombed out of themselves.

So now that my little lesson on world conditions is over, I want to tell you that I miss you and Carole Frances so very much – and love you even more. So I guess my family will always keep me looking ahead until this is over. Hope that the folks are well and that you have received all the packages that I sent. Say "Hello" to all and love to the folks – a great big hug and kiss for the baby and you –

With All My Love,
Your Dave

Friday – 15 December – 1944
Somewhere in Eastern France

My Dearest Darlings,

Last night, the old man who lives above us with his family asked me to come up to see him this morning as he had something I'd like. Well, I went up there and he poured out two glasses of a drink called "Mirabelle," which is really potent. It has the appearance of schnapps, but is stronger. He, his wife and their children were there and we had a long discussion on France and what it will do after the War. They told me all about the Jerries when they had occupied the very same quarters that we are now living in. It was really hell. The old woman told me that it was nothing for the Jerry soldier to call an old woman over and rape her. That is just a minute incident compared to some of the other atrocities.

I went up to the home of those people I've told you about. I got there about 1:30 and stayed until 4:00 – just batting the breeze. I brought them some chocolate and some of the caramels that Carole sent me and a piece of raisin pie that the cook made yesterday. They were very pleased with it all and were ever so thankful. We spoke of the possibilities of a Communistic France after the War, the prices of furs in France and the States, what news I had from you lately, and most every other thing under the sun. I also told them of my plan to distribute some candy to the kids in Nancy next week and asked if they would accompany me at that time. The mother explained that since her husband was a prisoner in Germany, she nor her daughter had ever gone out to have a good time. I told her that if her husband knew about it, he would probably insist that they go out and enjoy themselves instead of grieving themselves to death. She answered that she doesn't even know if he is still alive – let alone hearing from him, so I didn't insist on them coming along, as the people who would see them out with an American soldier may get the wrong idea. They, in turn, invited me to have dinner over at their home in Nancy next Saturday, so I guess that will be the case. First I will give out the candy I have at the elementary schools and meet them for lunch at their home.

We also discussed the Jewish situation. She said that the French had always felt for the Jews and when the Jerries were here, they would defy the Jerries on the streets. She also told me of one incident when a young mother was walking down the street in Nancy and a Jerry soldier stopped her and *told her to go across the street for something. She started to take her baby with her, but the soldier told her to leave the baby in the buggy. She went across the street and when she returned to her buggy, there lay her baby – strangled to death. It was only two months old. That is just one of the many atrocities they are all guilty of. This woman told me that she had many good Jewish friends before the War and even now. All the big department stores were owned by Jews and one at which her sister worked before the War had treated her generously when her sister was ill in bed for months. So she was really emphatic in her admiration of the Jews and said that they would all soon return and enjoy France once more. When I told her that there were instances of anti-Semitism in the States, they were both surprised. I explained that most of it was due to propaganda and jealousy. They said that in France, it was also true that many of the gentiles were envious of the Jews, because they were successful in business and noted doctors and lawyers. Well, all in all, it seems that the French treated the Jews better than the Americans. At least, that's what I gathered from the little talk we had. I told them that the Jewish problem was not the big thing after the War – but the Negroes. Maybe it will be true and take away some of the anti-Semitic feeling and toss it on the Negro. As much as I hate to admit it, I do dislike the Negro and would like to see him in Liberia with his own government. However, it is talk just like that that is responsible for the prominence of the Jewish feeling. Yes, it isn't democratic, but it is true and there are many who are of the same feeling, but would never publicly say so. Anyway, I do hope that we will be able to iron out some of our difficulties after the War.*

Now I suppose I have come to the most important part of the letter – telling you that I love and miss you and Carole very very much. I guess you know that by now, but it keeps popping up, especially when I see other small kids with their mothers. I picture you with Carole, taking a walk in the sun. So I guess that's about all for now – so regards to all and love to the folks – lots of love and kisses for the baby and you –

With All My Love,
Your Dave

———

Sunday – 17 December – 1944
Somewhere in Eastern France

My Darling Wife and Baby,
It has been one thing after another all day. I just finished one of the reports and it really took a lot out of me. If we would spend one-tenth of the time

in firing at the enemy that we do in making out these damned reports, we'd probably be on our way back home. At one time, Patton said, "The hell with reports – I want action!" How true that is.

Darling, I realize that you don't know why in the world I have to go to distant places, but some things are hard to write. However, I'll try to tell you. In our case, the War moves along so quickly that the Supply Depots are left in the rear in a hurry. That makes it necessary to have to go there for things you need in a hurry and can't wait until the depots move up – Now do you understand? Not only that, I have to pick up supplies that we expend daily – These are called expendables and we get these twice a month. There are many other things that come up during the day that we may have to make a trip for that will take a whole day's traveling. With Strasbourg taken, the depots near the Nancy area are now as far back as the ones to which we had to go when we first moved up to the area near Lyon. It is no doubt very difficult for you to understand this, but I have said too much already.

As far as the Army encouraging drinking, they don't, but it is more of a morale builder than a destroyer. You see, the English had been issuing it for hundreds of years and we hadn't, so as long as we are Allies and the soldiers do mix, they decided to make an exception of the rule.

So you'd like to be up here playing our upright. Well, I'd like to have you here, but not with all these wolves around. Even the other night, Mullen said that he'd like to hear you play the piano, as you could certainly tickle the ivories. By the way, you know that mother and daughter I had visited recently – well, the daughter also plays and she said that she'd play for me if I go to their home Saturday. I told them about your ability and they were really impressed.

I was surprised to read about the strikes in St. Louis. Now can you see how it makes a guy feel when he is out here and hears about something like that going on outside their own little circles? Here it is hard enough to bring this War to a close in Europe and they are holding out for more money. What if we all just got up and demanded more money and stopped doing our jobs? It just makes me cringe to read about it – especially in my own hometown. They are just as guilty of prolonging the War as each German War-worker. It's amazing that the soldiers who have returned home from overseas don't take some of these strikers by the collar and just beat the daylights out of them and tell them to get back on the job. God help us to clear up all this after we return.

England will first have a problem on its hands after the War. Why, just today's "Stars & Stripes" carried an article on her agreement with Russia to allow her to keep the Eastern part of Poland that she took in 1940. In return, Russia will "allow" Poland to take over Danzig and East Prussia. Why, even if England didn't approve of it, Russia would have taken it over anyway. Right now, England is at its weakest state of influence. Even in Greece, although the strike of the Elas is over, England will have very little effect on that country after the War, except perhaps to aid the people. As you wrote, there are more intelligent people who are working on that than us, so why worry? Glad that one of the strikes was ended by the time you finished that letter. Maybe it will all be over by the time you get this.

That idea of posting all the letters in chronological order is a good one and the late letters will make more sense to you when you receive them. It will be nice to go over them after fifty years of married life – Could you stood it?

What do you think of my dream about that landing in the Philippines? I just read that it did come off in the island of Mindoro. Well, I missed it by a few miles, but I got the right islands. Well, Darling, the most important thing in the whole letter is that I love you and Carole very much and am keeping it well implanted in my mind. In spite of our being apart, I still feel close to both of you at all times and know that, in reality, we aren't away from each other at all. So say "Hello" to all and send love to the folks – lots of love and kisses for you and Carole –

With All My Love,
Your Dave

———

Monday – 18 December – 1944
Somewhere in Eastern France

Dearest Darlings,

Thanks for the congratulations on my 47th-month anniversary – I really never did figure it in a matter of months. Anyway, I want to return the same to you, although it will be time to be the 48th month by the time that you get this. I agree with you that it is very inconvenient for us to have to spend half of our four anniversaries apart – However, as the French say – c'est la guerre. I'm positive that we won't have to spend any more apart, so let's look forward to next year with a little more anticipation. After all, who ever even thought that we'd be in Germany a year from last year? So even as slowly as we are going now, we are still doing damned well. From the recent broadcast, the Germans are making a last desperate stand and are counterattacking as a measure of bringing some hope to the people who are now seeing their cities being slowly crumbled to bits. After [General Courtney] *Hodges takes care of this effort, he will probably have an easier time of it in going deeper into Germany. It is just a repetition of what we have seen before – so don't become discouraged. They have always made a terrific stand just before retreating, and I think that this is exactly the same as before.*

Your letter of the 7th was the third year after the bombing of Pearl Harbor and I was glad that you didn't write about it in your letter. It's something we had better try to forget.

Yes, it would be a better idea to put up the Xmas tree the night before and let Carole think that Santa has brought it during the night. I'd like to be the one to climb down the chimney and leave the toys this year. I wouldn't even mind getting full of soot. See if Santa could use a helper.

So I am getting some gefilte fish. Well, I guess I'll like it, even tho it is canned – thanks for it and the camera. Well, Darlings, that about sums up the day's activities and I want to tell you that I love and miss you very much. So I'll keep your love warm and you do the same – also send regards to all and love to the folks – lots of love and kisses for Carole and you –

With All My Love,
Your Dave

———

Tuesday – 19 December – 1944
Somewhere in Eastern France

My Darling Babes,

I see that they are reviving "Louise" – Is it because Maurice Chevalier was found not guilty of being a collaborateur? There seems to be a varied opinion on that subject, in spite of the fact that he sang recently for the American soldiers in Paris. Oh well, why worry about one man? We'll have our hands full when we walk into Germany.

Don't become discouraged at what you read in the papers recently as I'm sure that it is the last effort of the Jerries in order to effect as many casualties on the Allies as possible before the final crash. From [Field Marshal Gerd] *von Rundstedt's own request that each Nazi make his best last effort, you* can see that he has already given up any hope for the Jerries to be able to continue to keep up the fight. With that in mind, perhaps the War will end sooner than it seemed a month ago.

We are pretty lucky in one respect around here – We have a lot of wild Xmas trees, so the Mess Sergeant took one and placed it on top of one of the tables in the Mess Hall and trimmed it with some silver and gold paper that he had gotten in his rations. Then he cut out a star and covered it with silver paper and placed it on top of it. He then cut out "Merry Xmas" and "Happy New Year" and covered them with silver and gold letters. So we have a slightly ornamented tree for Xmas so far. As some of us receive packages, we will add to the colors on the tree. For our room, we took some branches of the Xmas trees and wound them with some wire and made a nice wreath out of them. It is now hanging on our door and makes the hall smell just like the holiday season. Well, our imagination can do wonders. We plan to add a ribbon or two if we get one in a package. Maybe a candle, also.

Gee, I do like that picture of you and Carole that you sent. I can't make out who Carole takes after – Is it the iceman? I hope that she takes after you, because you are more beautiful than I – don't you agree? Anyway, thank God that she is a good and healthy baby. Gosh, how I'd like to be with you two now and forever more. Well, I guess that about winds up another day's bull session – Don't you ever get tired of reading all this tripe that I write? So send regards to all and love to the family – a great big hug and a thousand kisses for Carole and you –

With All My Love,
Your Dave

———

Wednesday – 20 December – 1944
Somewhere in Eastern France

My Sweetest Darlings,

The bulk of the afternoon was taken up with listening to the radio programs. We heard a very good broadcast by Glenn Miller's band. They're still doing up "It Could Happen To You" in a big way. From an article in today's "Stars & Stripes," "I Walk Alone" is the leading record in sales back home.

The War is really at a pitched peak and I'm glad to see that no news is being given out by us. It's a lot better that way. I still don't have any fear of us being thrown back any great distance from this recent flare-up of Jerry *armor. It is still a last breath before the death. One thing it has done for us is that it brought out of hiding the Luftwaffe that had been missing for a long time, so our boys have had a proper picnic lately in knocking them out of the air. Now the reserve is definitely in the air and fast diminishing, so keep up that old chin and don't get excited at newspaper accounts.*

Well, Tooties, regards to all and love to the folks – and if Carole is as angelic as she appears in that photo, you can give her a great big hug and kiss for me and you also – that ought to be something to see – you kissing yourself –

With All My Love,
Your Dave

———

Thursday – 21 December – 1944
Somewhere in Eastern France

Darling Amy and Carole Frances,

This evening, we heard that "Till We Meet Again" was at the Wing theatre – so I got dressed and took off for the show. The Red Cross girls were there to serve those doughnuts and coffee – They were the same ones who had, on two other occasions, served us the same. In fact, one recalled the drink that I had given her in Italy and she said that she'd like to have another. I told her that the boys are having a little party on the 24th and if she were able to – to come up for a drink. I'm not counting on seeing her – but we were polite about it. The picture was very good and it was the first decent one that I had seen in some time. As you know, I do like Ray Milland's acting anyway – so he was good. The one scene where he starts to tell the French sister about his wife and baby boy is one that really touched me. He was trying to explain to her what marriage was like – and there were some phrases in his dialogue that hit the nail on the head, so I really did like the picture.

Now that the shortest day of the year has passed, we will start looking forward to staying out later. It will also help us in our pushes into Germany. I suppose you have been getting a little jumpy at what you have been reading in the papers – but I still repeat that it is nothing over which to get excited and it will all be over soon, so don't worry about us over here.

I hope that you get a white Xmas – After all, what is Xmas without snow on the ground? It's like me without you – hard to see. Well, Darlings,

regards to all and love to the folks – a million and one hugs and kisses for the baby and you –
      With All My Love,
      Your Dave
      P.S. I may attend services in Nancy tomorrow afternoon.

———

Friday – 22 December – 1944
Somewhere in Eastern France

My Sweetest Wife and Baby,
      After lunch, I remembered that I had planned to attend services. [Bernie] Ellison came running down saying that he'd go along and that he had a ride for us down to Wing headquarters in a jeep. Well, we got to the synagogue at about four and stood up all the time that prayers were said. It was colder than a Nazi's heart there. The place had lost a lot of its former beauty due to the Germans' destruction when they had occupied Nancy. There were still a number of Jews in the city who turned out for the services – so they must have prayed doubly hard.
      The rabbi was a chaplain and the whole service took only about an hour. After it was over, he announced that he had a number of mezuzahs – that small metal tube with the Ten Commandments in it. So I went over and got one. That was the first time that I had gone to services since I left the States – It was sort of uncomfortable at first. However, after I concentrated on the prayer book, I fell right into the thing. As you may have guessed, we read the Friday evening services and those who found it necessary said Kaddish. There were mostly G.I.'s there and a lot of them brought along some candy for the children who happened to be around. Well, it was about five when we got out and six when we got back to H.Q. That was too late for our Mess Hall, so we ate at the 64th Mess. Well, after dinner, we had to walk back up to our area, which was really an ordeal. We were all fagged when we reached the top.
      Well, Darlings, I guess it is just a matter of hours now before Santa drops down your chimney and leaves all those nice toys for our darling daughter. When she awakens, she will probably forget all about eating and spend her time playing with everything. I'd certainly like to be around when it happens.
      Our anniversary is only about eleven days from today – and so I want to wish you a very happy fourth anniversary and hope that you and your

husband will be together for the fifth and all those following. So, Darlings, that's about the dope for now – say "Hello" to all and give my love to the folks – and for Carole and you a hundred million hugs and kisses –
  With All My Love,
  Your Dave

—

                    Saturday – 23 December – 1944
                    Somewhere in Eastern France
My Darling Angels,
  This morning, I went over to a Kindergarten in Nancy and went on in. I introduced myself to the teachers and asked if it would be OK for me to give out the candies to the kids. They were very grateful for the gesture and said that it would be just fine – so the class was called to order and I went around offering the box to each child. It was really wonderful to see them take only one piece and say "Merci, monsieur" – There were kids from two to six in this class and I got a little lonesome with all those children there. After I had given all the kids candy, I offered some to the teachers and they were so overcome that it was hard to get them to take a piece. Two of them asked me to return soon and have Xmas dinner with the kids in the school – but I know that they have a hard enough time getting food for themselves – so I replied, "Perhaps..."
  When I walked away from the school, I felt as if I had done one good thing in my life and like I was a few years younger. Well, it was about noon then, so I went over to the apartment of the people with whom I had an appointment today. As I reached the front door of the place, another French woman approached and rang the bell that I was going to ring. As soon as the door opened, out came the young girl, Janine, and she hugged and kissed her visitor. Unfortunately, she didn't do that to me. Anyway, she welcomed me and explained that this was her cousin who lived only a few blocks away – She is married. So we went in and her mother was so glad to see me – We went into the kitchen first, as that was the only room where there was a fire going. We talked about everything under the sun. Well, when the food was done, we opened the door leading from the dining room to the living room and carried the table in so that we'd be warm while eating. Heating facilities is something that is hard to get around here – so they have two stoves – one in the kitchen and the other in the living room. So we had a nice meal, which included cold beets, cold sliced potatoes in some sort of oil, peas

and carrots (the radio is now playing "Long Ago and Far Away" – pretty, isn't it?), hot roast beef (I think) and brown French bread. I had red wine with my food and they drank a concoction of lemon soda and beer – I didn't go for it.

After the meal, the girl played the piano. She did rather well. I told them how well you played and what our favorite songs were – They also don't like jitterbugs. Well, we then had coffee with some of the G. Washington coffee that I brought them. That is, indeed, an extra-special treat for them and they liked it. The mother had managed to scrape together some ingredients and made a honey-cake without the honey – It was pretty good. With the cake, we had some fruit that looks like cherries, but is called Mirabelle – and a very potent drink is made from them. Well, after chewing the fat for exactly five hours, it was time for me to take off, so I excused myself and they said that they were so very grateful for the few things that I brought them – a package of laundry soap that I had bought while in the Replacement Depot in Italy, a bar of face soap, a couple of packages of cigarettes, a can of tuna, and a couple of bars of G.I. chocolate. Also, that can of coffee – so it was also a Merry Xmas for them – I guess I'm an old softie at heart.

So now Xmas draws near and I still would like to be taken on one of those trips with Superman where he carries me to you for one day. That would really be a nice visit – Wouldn't you like that? I really would like to be there the day after tomorrow when Carole gets up. I will be there with you in mind and I really don't mind. So, my Darlings, that's about it for today – regards to all – love to the folks – and oodles of hugs and kisses for Carole and you –

With All My Love,
Your Dave

Xmas Morn – 25 December 1944
Somewhere in Eastern France

My Dearest Darlings,

I want to wish you and Carole Frances a very Merry Xmas and hope that everybody had an enjoyable one. It's about four in the morning back home right now, so it is still too early for Carole to see all that Santa has brought her. Anyway, about the time that we are having our Xmas turkey dinner, she will be playing on the floor with everything, so I'll be thinking of her and you all the time and imagine that I'm right in the same room with all of you.

Now to go back to yesterday: After we ate dinner, I had to get everything in order so that we'd have everything ready for the evening, so I got a few pots and pans together from Ellison and he brought over some frying grease. I opened some cans of Heinz Vegetable Soup and got it to a boiling point. At that point, I added an envelope of Lipton's Noodle Soup, which really made it taste delicious. Then I opened the cans of chili and heated it, and then added the tamales. Then I took the potatoes that Ellison brought over and sliced them for French fries. The first three batches were excellent, but the last time, there were too many in the pan, so they got soft and soggy. Meanwhile, as everything was either cooking or heating, I made hors d'oeuvres out of salted crackers with tongue, ham spread, and cheese. We also had some raisin bread, which I cut into squares and put tuna on that. We had an upper half of a mess kit for our appetizers, which were anchovies and salmon. We placed the crackers and bread on other mess kits on which we placed sheets of paper first to act as doilies. Then we took some vanilla wafers and spread Welch's Grape Jam on them. I put them in the tin can that came from Busy Bee. After all that was ready, I cleared off the desk that is in our room and spread out a clean mattress cover that acted as our tablecloth. Well, it was really a very attractive layout and everybody was impressed with it all. The party started out at six and I was able to locate some lemon soda in Nancy, with which we mixed the scotch and the gin. So as the fellows came in to pay their respects and extend their best wishes for a Merry Xmas, the party got higher and higher. I also got some shot glasses from our bar and highball, too, so I had everything necessary except the ice, and it was cold enough without it.

Well, as the evening grew older, Louie, one of the Supply boys, got stiffer and stiffer. He got to the point where he didn't know what he was even doing. Finally, we were able to put him to bed. Well, about eleven, some of the boys brought in Louie de Fillipo, the guy who has all the money and who bought that 1000-dollar bond in Pinedale and also one over here last month. He had fallen down and broken his leg, so we let him lie on the floor in the Orderly Room until the doctor came up with the ambulance. He looked at it and placed it in a steel frame in order to keep it quiet and diagnose it as a fracture of the fibula. That was about midnight when he was taken away and that incident sort of sobered up everybody and they all went back to their rooms and went to sleep. So there, my Darlings, is the reason why I didn't write you yesterday – Excused?

Well, this morning, it is quiet as a cemetery as everybody is either at work or sleeping. Louie awoke with a terrific headache and dizzy as well. I gave him a couple of Alka-Seltzers and he came out OK. At the time when de Fillipo was here waiting for the doctor, our Louie got so sick that he stumbled out and vomited, so he must have really been a sad sack this morning.

So that brings us up to the minute – 10:35 Eastern Gaslight Time. So once more, Darlings, have a very enjoyable Xmas and remember that I'll be with you next year at this time. Send Season's Greetings to all our friends and love to the folks – a great big holiday kiss for you and Carole –
With All My Love,
Your Dave

———

Tuesday – 26 December – 1944
Somewhere in Eastern France
My Sweetest Darlings,

It was such a pretty day – snow on the ground and nice and sunny. With weather like this, we ought to really go ahead in our advance into Germany. In the last four days, we have had bright, sunny days, but very cold. It has helped us a great deal as it keeps the roads hard for an offensive. Also, the visibility for planes is just the type we want. So it has been ideal – Maybe it is God's gift to us for Xmas and the New Year. Your excellent description of the holiday spirit downtown was very effective and impressive. I felt as tho I was down in front of Famous-Barr [department store], looking at the windows.

I really don't have a terrible time of it as far as Jerries are concerned. In fact, the only ones I have ever seen are those who are dead or captured. So rest your mind and be assured that I'm as safe as an egg in a nest. You mentioned the slow progress the Russians were making in the East. Well, I read an article in "Time" magazine. It dealt with the great influence that Russia is having on the nations of Europe in setting up a new government. It is exactly as I had written you awhile back. Also, there was another article on Stilwell and China, which also brought out the points that I wrote you sometime ago. So you see, I'm not really talking thru my hat when I write about politics in Europe and Asia. As to Austria allowing the Allies to walk right thru their country, it is something that we'd like to see but is also impossible as the Jerries have too much control over them. The only way we are going to get into anyplace will be through our own initiative and power.

As to your letter of the 10th – That night before must have been a bad one for you, with all the other girls' husbands either on their way home or in the States. Well, you know that those things are bound to happen. After all, there are a helluva lot more wives and husbands who have been separated longer than we, so do not let others' good fortune get you down so easily. You've been a pretty tough cookie to take it as you have in the past year. Considering all that has happened at home and abroad, you have done better than any other person could have done. I guess it is about time that you broke down and got a lot of accumulated things off of your mind. So I'm not sorry to read about your gripes and ideas – however, I can't say that it is what I'd want or that it is as easy as you think. I really do think that you agree with me and that you'd want it that way when we win the War, so let's keep that old chin up. Remember that our love is much stronger than any break that I could get.

As to OCS [Officer Candidate School], *I'm not so hot over the idea. I've seen too many things that walk around with bars on their shoulders to ask for them. After you have seen as much as I have over here, an officer isn't worth the money spent to get him his commission. There are too many who have found a home in the Army and would hate to see their good times end with the Victory, so I'm content to remain an enlisted man and wait for my discharge, so I can go home to my family and forget all about the Army.*

So the baby had a time in the snow! I was wondering if she'd like it. Don't let her play too much in it, as it is too dangerous. I remember how I would play all day and get wet and catch cold from it. Did you build a big snowman for her? Sorry that I'm not around to do so. Boy! I'd like to have seen you shoveling snow – it must really be a scream. I can assure you that I'd like to be there to do it rather than let you.

Fay told me that the people with whom I had lunch in Nancy last week came all the way up here to visit me. They told him that they'd like to have me visit them this evening or tomorrow afternoon or evening, so I guess I'll go over there tomorrow in the afternoon. From what Fay said, the boys who saw them really whistled – but don't be frightened, as I still love my wife and baby too much.

So, with that in mind, I want you to say "Hello" to all of our friends and send love to the folks – a great big batch of love and kisses for the baby and you –

With All My Love,
Your Dave

Thursday – 28 December – 1944
Somewhere in Eastern France

My Dearest Darlings,

Yesterday, about noon, Capt. Temple called me up from headquarters and asked me to come down there. I went down and we had a little discussion and it rose to a tremendous argument in which the climax was that I banged my fist down on his desk and told him that if he didn't have any confidence in me as his Supply Sergeant, he should have gotten rid of me long ago. He had just previously said that he realized that I didn't have such a high opinion of the company and that if I had any desire to get a transfer out, that I should go ahead and ask for it. I told him that it didn't make a bit of difference to me and I just wasn't taking any knocking around from anybody – an officer or an enlisted man. I was even surprised at the way that I spoke to him and we really raised our voices down there. In fact, a number of other officers stuck their heads in to see what it was all about – but I certainly didn't want to take any unnecessary lip if I didn't have to do so. It involved some supplies that I had picked up the day before. I had taken out some items that I thought were for us and he didn't seem to agree that that was the way that I had figured. Well, after that nice, long argument with Temple, I guess it won't be long before I am a nice and unworried private. The only drawback will be that the fifty-dollar allotment will be discontinued, as I wouldn't be getting paid that much. Anyway, I'm not worrying about it – It does not make a damned bit of difference to me. Well, in the afternoon, after having lunch, I phoned Temple and told him that I was taking the afternoon off and he said that it was alright. So that takes us into the second phase of the story.

As you know, I had an invitation to visit those people who had been up here the day that I was away, so Okie and I walked down to the village and went in. By the way, I don't think that I had ever told you the name of the people I had been visiting – It is Madame and Janine Mougin. Just before I left, Mrs. Mougin told me that she and Janine would like to have my opinion on a very serious matter. She asked me what I thought about a sergeant whom I had met at their home the first time that I was there. I told her that it was rather difficult, as I had only seen him for perhaps 30 minutes at a time and didn't speak to him very much at that, so I really couldn't be able to pass an opinion on him at this time. Anyway, she told me that Janine had received a letter from this fellow, asking her to marry him.

I told them that they ought to wait a little while and sleep on it and perhaps in about a week, they would be able to come to a more intelligent conclusion. It was a very great compliment they are paying me in asking my opinion and what they should do.

Here is the whole picture: They are all that each other has in the world and it would be a great decision if they decided that she should become engaged to him. Her father is still unheard from in Germany, which makes it all the more important to figure it right. They asked me if he spoke correct English and impressed me as an educated fellow – so that they could both be sure that he was as intelligent as they wish Janine's husband to be. I said that he was OK and asked what he did in civilian life. They told me that he was a veterinarian; that his father was a naturalist; and that his mother was a pianist. His hobby was a bird fancier. Well, if his parents were as stated above, he may be an educated fellow, as it is necessary to go to college for his degree. However, I really didn't think that he was something out of this world, but I didn't tell them that. I promised them that I'd think about it and also mail Janine's letter to him. I figured that I could take Sunday off, so I told them that I'd see them again Sunday afternoon.

Okie wanted to go to another town and get a few beers, so we took off and walked about five miles to the next village. We went to one place where there was a one-man band playing an accordion and the drums. We went to another place where we found a wedding celebration in progress. Well, one of the persons introduced herself as the mother of the bride and asked us to stay for the evening supper. We accepted and went in to the main dining room, where there were about fifty more people. There were many there who spoke a bit of English, so with my bit of French, we got along quite well. When it came time to serve, we sat down at the guests of honor seats – Okie to the right of the bride and I between the parents of the bride and groom. It was a very happy affair and the first time that such a gathering was held in four years as the Nazis had forbidden such meetings. Well, in between the courses of the meals, they danced and some played the piano and sang. Okie and I gave out with a few of the old-timers that we thought they would recognize and they did.

Well, about one in the morning, the party was broken up and everybody went home. Okie and I started to go back to camp, but figured that it was too far and too cold to go all that distance. Therefore, we called to the bride's father, with whom we had gotten along very well, and he took us to a hotel not far away. He walked in, went behind the counter, and took a key, walked upstairs, opened the door of #5, and lo and behold, there was a very beautiful room. He gave us the key and told us to sleep well. I asked him who we pay and everything else and he told us to forget about it – so we thanked him. It was a very cold night, but with all the covers, we slept warm. In the morning, we got up and were out by eight and back in camp by nine. Nobody even knew that we were gone – so all was well. So there, my Darlings, you have the story up until this morning.

The third phase was this morning's trip into Nancy on business with Okie. We went to the Red Cross and I learned that they couldn't do anything towards learning anything about a French civilian prisoner. They told me I'd have to go to the French Red Cross, as that was the right channel for this case. So now, I'll tell the Mougins and see what they want to do.

As to the snow and road conditions, take extra care if you are driving. If you must leave the house in bad weather, be sure that you are cautious. It is very easy to slide on ice and break a bone – so be careful. Speaking of breaking bones, that fellow who hurt himself Xmas Eve broke his leg in two places and was evacuated to England – Some break, eh? Say, maybe it could happen to me! As to the jeep being open at the time of my letter of the 28th of November, it was an order around here so as to avoid a strafing by an enemy plane. Also, your windshield was not supposed to be up when the sun was shining on account of the glare. However, since then, the weather has changed a bit and we are allowed to have tops and windows up.

Well, as long as you are going to send some jars, send some herring and pickles. I liked those that you did send, but I only received two bottles of them, so send salamis and pickles and some pickled tomatoes – if possible. Also, some shrimp and oysters and a jar of horseradish and chili sauce – or a jar of regular seafood sauce. One of the boys actually received a jar of Miracle Whip.

I was surprised to see that you were alarmed at what the radio and newspapers carried about the push by the Nazis. It was not a surprising thing when the Jerries pushed thru at the point between Northern Luxembourg and Belgium. There was no great concentration of troops and materials at that point at that time, because it was not a very strategic sector. The 1st and 9th Armies were above and below this point and engaged in advancing toward Germany. Well, von Rundstedt had a lot of men and materiel in reserve and each time that he retreated, a certain amount of it was lost thru wreckage or capture. Well, it is just a theory, but he probably figured that it was foolish to keep retreating and lose men and materiel without gaining something. Therefore, he selected a spot where it would be the easiest to penetrate and he pushed in all that he had in a sudden thrust. As there wasn't any concentration in that sector, he was able to gain quickly at first, without any trouble. The reason behind this push could be that he's to cause as many casualties as possible so as to try to get a better issue for the final surrender. There certainly cannot be a possibility of him ever getting thru to the coast in order to isolate one of the armies. Now on our side of the ledger, I think that this move will certainly shorten the War as it has given us an opportunity to get at his planes, armored vehicles and reserves. Heretofore, they had always been held in the rear and made only spasmodic appearances. Now we'll be able to knock it all out at once and bottle up the men that are now in Belgium. Well, at least that is my way of seeing the whole affair – so it will have to be seen when it is over.

As to the bombs they are using, don't get jumpy, as it is only a jitter propaganda item out of Goebbels' bag of tricks. It isn't of any great military value and never will be as long as it is uncontrolled, so don't take in that Jerry propaganda and have confidence in our generals and our armies. Yes, it is alarming as it hits without notice, but still isn't as bad as one of our directed blockbusters. The whistle of a dropping bomb is certainly more startling than a sudden explosion.

So there, my Darlings, you have the news for the day. It's pretty late now and I'm tired after writing these ten pages. So regards to all our friends and love to the folks – and oodles and oodles of hugs and kisses for Carole and you –

With All My Love,
Your Dave

———

Friday – 29 December – 1944
Somewhere in Eastern France

Dearest Amy and Carole Frances,

As to making a distinction between officers and enlisted men, Darlings, the U.S. Army is the most undemocratic in all the world. They certainly do and it is a major grievance between them. That is another reason why I don't care to go to the trouble to try to become one. It certainly isn't worth the trouble, unless you planned to stay in the Army after it is all over. As to the Pacific Theatre, I have since changed my mind. The reasons are that this European War has taken longer than I had figured on. Therefore, we have been tied up here while men are being poured into the other theatre. Even when this is ended, it will take a long time to transfer the men over – Meanwhile, the Pacific Theatre will be going along at a pretty good pace. So all in all, it is beginning to look as tho we will return to the States first, even if we are slated for the Pacific. I hope that we get a break and get stationed at one of the bases in the States.

Now that you know that I would like salami every so often, you can send the pickles also. You don't have to send them both in the same package – You can send all the jars of pickles in one and the salamis in another – OK? Will it set you back on points too much? Well, Darlings, give my regards to all and love to the folks – lots of love and kisses for the baby and you –

With All My Love,
Your Dave

———

Saturday – 30 December – 1944
Somewhere in Eastern France

My Dearest Sweethearts,

Well, Darlings, it looks as tho the Nazis' thrust has come to an end. God seems to have given us just enough good weather to knock their planes and armor to pieces. We had about six good days and took advantage of each hour in them. Now they are in retreat and will be badly mauled by the time we reach the German borders again in that area. That is why I still say that von Rundstedt has shortened the War by his effort. Who knows – maybe he did it with that in view. He's probably as tired of War as anybody and never did care for Hitler, as he is a Prussian. Anyway, they did lose heavily and are unable to replace any of it, so now as the New Year draws close, we can actually look forward to the end of the European War in 1945.

Tomorrow, I am supposed to visit the Mougins. They probably are sitting on pins and needles waiting to hear from their husband and father. I'll ask them if they want me to see the French Red Cross – It may help.

Well, Dearests, regards to all and love to the folks – a million hugs and kisses for Carole and you – Flip a coin to see who gets the first –

With All My Love,
Your Dave

———

Sunday – 31 December – 1944
Somewhere in Eastern France

My Sweetest, Darling Wife and Baby,

   Here we are at the end of another year! It will be a memorable year for historians to record. Certainly a year ago, this same time, very few of us had any idea that we'd be this far into Germany and ready to finish the War in Europe. In that year, two large-scale invasions were effected and we have cleared out the Nazis from 99% of France in less than seven months. Also, we have driven them from most of Italy and have taken the capital. The Russians have liberated the countries of Romania, Bulgaria, Latvia, Lithuania, and Hungary is almost completely taken. Czechoslovakia and Greece are included on the almost list also. The other countries have been Holland and Belgium – so you can easily see that much had been accomplished in 365 days. Look at the Pacific area – Whoever thought that we'd be in the Philippines and bombing Japan at will? So if next year will be as successful as the one that is fading out, we will be at peace with the world. At least we know one certain thing – the War in Europe will definitely end in 1945. That is the New Year's greeting that the little image of 1945 is bringing with him. He'll have to go fast in order to fill the shoes of the old man of 1944.

   Well, this afternoon I visited my friends down in the village. They were very happy to see me and were impatient to hear what I thought about the prospects of Janine becoming engaged. I spoke with them for a long time and we finally decided to wait until they receive another letter from this G.I. and see if it wasn't possible for him to spend more time with them. Anyway, I think that they will wait until he is able to get back here and when the father and husband will return. It is a most critical decision to make, as they are all there is for either of them. If Janine marries, they will be separated for the first time in both their lives and it will be pretty darned hard to get used to. Anyway, they both say that they value my advice very much for, after all, I am an American, married, and a father and have "good common sense." There is still the possibility of Janine's father returning soon, which would be very important in deciding the situation. Well, I hope that I have given them the best advice – At least, down deep in my heart, I feel as tho I have done so. Madame Mougin said that she had a gift for you – I don't have the slightest idea what it is. It certainly is nice of them to give us something, considering the conditions around here. She said that if I were able, to stop by next week for it.

So that about winds up another year of correspondence. I can't truthfully say that it has been boring, because it hasn't. Your letters are really enjoyable and make our separation seem like a vacation. I'm sincere in my thoughts when I say that I am looking forward to being with you next year at this time – So with a fond mental caress, I wish you, Carole, the folks and our friends a very Happier New Year. As a special deal, give the baby and yourself a big kiss –

With All My Love
Your Dave

———

Monday – 1 January – 1945
Somewhere in Eastern France

My Darling Angels,

Here we are at the christening of the New Year – 1945 – and I hope that we will spend the future first days of the year together. We have been lucky to get a little sunshine along with the cold, so it sort of makes up for the discomfort. When our planes can fly, we don't care what kind of weather we are having. It also means that our tanks are able to navigate on hard surfaces, which result from long cold spells. So let's hope that the sun and cold will stay with us long enough to wipe the damned bastards off the face of the map. Darlings, you probably never thought that a person could hate anybody as much as I do the Nazis. Well, I can readily understand that – but that is certainly the case. If there is any room in my physical makeup for any more hate – it would be for the Jerries. After seeing what has happened lately to some of our men who were taken prisoner, one cannot be too lenient with them when we have finally won this War. It is not only the soldiers and SS, but the people also who are to be blamed.

I suppose you are wondering what I did to welcome the New Year last night. Well, I could have been in the company of about five nice, sociable fellows, eating salami, herring and drinking scotch and schnapps. However, I went to bed at about 8:30 and read until 11:15, when I couldn't keep my eyes open any longer. I had planned on seeing the New Year come in, but I just couldn't stay awake, so as I slept, our diapered friend made his appearance. A number of the boys got high and made a little racket. Louie, one of the boys from Supply, was among them and he was one sad sack this morning. The first thing that he asked for was an Alka-Seltzer tablet. He didn't recall much of what had taken place last night. The fellows who had invited me down to their room for the New Year sent up a salami sandwich anyway, so that I could have a snack. I suppose you certainly had a much more exciting time than I.

Then came our New Year's Day dinner – lunch to you. We had turkey again for a change and it was good. In fact, there was much too much to eat and everybody was filled to the gills. I got two large slices of meat that must have weighed at least four pounds. There was dressing to go with that; mashed potatoes, cranberry sauce, peas, custard pie and coffee. We can't say that the food is sad up here. I wonder what you civilians are having, with all this good food coming over here. Well, I asked the Mess Hall for a couple of carcasses and they gave me some nice ones. I wrapped them and a couple of wings and brought them down to these people who I had been visiting down in the village. They were amazed at the thought of my bringing them this – but so grateful for it.

Today, we received some PX rations that included two bottles of American beer and some chocolate bars. It wasn't much, but it all helps. This evening, I was still full from our lunch, so I didn't go to dinner. When I got back here, I was sort of hungry, so I had a bottle of beer. There is definitely a difference between the European and the American beers. Louie is warming some canned corn now as he, too, missed dinner.

Well, Darlings, I hope that Carole enjoyed the New Year's Day and that it was a warm and pretty one. Just so she and you and the folks stay well – I'll be happy. So regards to all our friends and a great big hug and kiss for Carole and you –

   With All My Love,
   Your Dave

———

Tuesday – 2 January – 1945
Somewhere in Eastern France

My Dearest Darlings,

   I went to St. Dizier on business. It was a beautiful day – the sun shining all day and not a cloud in the sky. However, it was cold as all something or other. Then, on top of that, it was slippery as our Winter Garden [skating rink]. If it isn't the mud, it's the rain or the ice – so that's the story of the trials and tribulations of warfare. At least it did give us a golden opportunity to knock the hell out of the Jerries. God is certainly good to us, from all indications the past two weeks, so we must be on the right team after all.

The company is planning an anniversary dance this coming Saturday in one of the villages nearby – Can you make it? It will be held in a regular dance hall and we will get a six-piece band from among the G.I.'s. The G.I.'s will either bring their own dates or the girls from nearby will drop in – from what I hear. I don't expect to bring a date, let alone even go. I don't crave dancing with anybody that much. Now if you were there, I'd change my mind in a big hurry. So I think that I'd much rather write you a letter and hit the hay early. You know – my beauty sleep is necessary, too. Speaking of beauties, how is our darling daughter doing these days? Did she have a hot New Year's Eve? I had better not hear of her coming in drunk.

Well, as long as I have spoken of celebrating, I have already made plans for celebrating our fourth wedding anniversary. While I was in St. Dizier, I bought a bottle of real French champagne. It is a good brand, as I had heard of it before the War. It wasn't too expensive - $5.00 – so I will do my celebrating in good taste. I'll be very sorry that you are not with me – or rather, I am not with you, which is certainly the more desirable situation. So far, I haven't decided just what to do in the way of celebrating outside of the champagne. Maybe I will go in to visit the Mougins and let them celebrate with me. After all, they miss their husband and father and I miss my wife and baby – so there is a common grievance there. Anyway, it will be one anniversary that I won't want to repeat – away from you.

Oh yes, I forgot to mention that the New Year started me off wrong. I bet that Southern Cal would beat Tennessee in the Rose Bowl game – and, as you know, I lost 13-7 and also five dollars. So that set me back another ten dollars so far this month and it is only the 2nd – what a guy you married! In other words, I think that you had better send me a few kopeks to get by on.

Well, Darlings, I guess that's about all for now – so regards to all our friends and love to the folks – millions of hugs and billions of kisses for Carole and you –

With All My Love,
Your Dave

———

Thursday – 4 January – 1945
Somewhere in Eastern France

My Dearest Darlings,

Ellison and I went to town about 10:00 A.M. and it was a long and busy day. I saw a very pretty department store there, named "Galeries des

St. Jean." I got to talking to a fellow there and he turned out to be the merchandise manager and he was so happy to find some American soldiers. He lives only a few miles from us and invited us to his home for Sunday's dinner. I thanked him and told him that I'd let him know in advance if I was unable to be there. Ellison was nuts over a girl who works there and wanted to take her with him, but she said that she was engaged – so he was one sad sack. After that, we went to a few more bars and had some more beer. All during the day, we had a little of everything, including white whine, schnapps, beer and something called kirsch, which isn't bad at all. As we went out, I saw my friend, Janine, across the street. She said that she and her mother were back in Nancy and wanted me to have dinner with them Sunday. I explained that I had another invitation for that day and thanked her and her mother anyway. They will be living in Nancy now for a little while due to some unfortunate accident in which Janine, her mother, and her aunt were cut a bit. If you remember to do so, ask me about it in about a month or so – I can't tell you now.

That so-and-so who told me that Southern Cal lost to Tennessee in the Rose Bowl later told me that he was only kidding, as he did not even know what the result was at the time, so now that we have found out that S.C. won 25-0, I won the five bucks, which pays for our wedding anniversary bottle of champagne. Gee, maybe I'll try to send it home to you and we can drink it when I get back – It would really be an occasion! I'll really have a job figuring out how to mail it so it doesn't pop on the way.

So regards to all – love to the folks – lots and lots of love and kisses for Carole and you –

With All My Love,
Your Dave

———

Friday – 5 January – 1945
Somewhere in Eastern France

My Dearest Wife and Baby,

I suppose we could have a more pleasant day and condition to celebrate our fourth anniversary – however, in view of all our inconveniences, I still want to wish you a very happy wedding anniversary and many, many more to follow. As I look back at the past four years, it certainly has been filled with pleasant memories. We both know that there were times when we had little, insignificant tiffs, but I can never recall them or the incidents.

On the other hand, all that I can remember are the pleasant experiences we have had together. I guess those are some of the things a couple retains when they are happily married. Of course, the War interrupted our life together, but I am still as close as ever to you and Carole. As I have said on other occasions, it is only a temporary thing that we will forget about just as soon as we are reunited – Carole Frances, you and I. After all, even space and time will never keep us apart, so I want to thank you for being my wife and for helping me to have such a pleasant life in the past and in the near-future. So-o-o once more – A happy flower anniversary!

Today has been a very clear and cold one, with ol' Sol out in full bloom – In other words, a very good day for knocking the hell out of the Jerries. (They are playing "Begin the Beguine" now.) It is icy on the roads, so we have to take it sort of easy while traveling. It snowed a bit during the night, which made it a very pretty sight when we awoke this morning. This afternoon, we received some more PX rations. We each received a bottle of American beer, some chocolate bars, a box of vanilla wafers, a couple of cartons of cigarettes (which I give to the boys when they run low) and a few other small items. It all ran up to $2.00 – but that fellow paid me the five that he lost on the Rose Bowl Game. Incidentally, he is the same one with whom I had made that bet on the World Series if the Yanks had been in it – so it was inevitable that I win his money.

In yesterday's letter, I wrote that I'd try to send you that bottle of champagne – Well, just after closing that letter, I found some excellent wrapping equipment and sent it out today. When you receive it, be careful in unwrapping it, as there is a large piece of paper that should be interesting to read in it. It has the trademark of one of [Hitler's second-in-command] *Herman Goering's factories on it. Anyway, I did a pretty good job on it and I don't think it will break very easily.*

Well, Darlings, say "Hello" to all and love to the folks and a big anniversary hug and kiss for the baby and you –

With All My Love,
Your Dave

———

Saturday – 6 January – 1945
Somewhere in Eastern France

My Sweetest Angels,

This evening is our anniversary dance, in honor (?) of our first year overseas. Well, I suppose all the boys at the dance are having a good time and will remember it. I don't care to celebrate such an affair, as I don't think it is something that we should celebrate. It is a damned shame that we have been over that long. Anyway, they are in full swing by now and will probably make a lot of dates and friends there. I'm really not very interested – I'd much rather have you and Carole Frances with me. Incidentally, last night, I dreamed about you and Carole and I could see you so very plainly. The funny part of it was that you were pregnant – Hmmmm. Anyway, I was taking you and the baby out for a sleigh ride. When I awoke this morning, I was cold and felt as tho I had been out all night in the snow. It seemed as if I spent the whole night with you – Gee, I wish that it was true. Well, I'll be seeing you sometime this year and it will come true.

Well, Darlings, I'm sorry that I'm spending some of the best years of my wife in the Army, but I'll be home soon and we can forget all about it. So say "Hello" to all our friends and send love to the folks – and a big hug and kiss to Carole Frances. Lots of love for the baby and you –

With All My Love,
Your Dave

———

Monday – 8 January – 1945
Somewhere in Eastern France

My Dearest Darlings,

Today, I had to do a lot of driving around the Nancy area and it was really cold on the road. When I got out on the main highway, I saw Janine walking toward Nancy, which is some hike in this weather – in fact, any weather. So I invited her to get into the truck and I drove her to her home in town. It is forbidden to pick up civilians over here, but I couldn't see a friend walking that far in this weather, so I was in luck and was able to take her all the way in without being stopped. On the way home, I had to go up a steep hill that was very long. At the bottom, I saw an old woman trying to make it on foot. That got me – so I asked her to get in and I'd take her as far as the main road, which was ¾ of the way to where she was going. She was so grateful and she couldn't thank me enough – It was the least that I could do. At times, I say to myself – What if it is a spy and I am caught for carrying one? – Then again, I think that as long as my intuition is good, I don't have to worry. But I certainly can't stand to see them walking on icy roads with a gale blowing in their faces. I guess I'm not cut out for war.

As to your letter of the 17th of December – You had packed up a box and couldn't fit in the pickles. By now, you should have figured that you can send two packages at the same time. Anyway, I'll enjoy the salamis with or without pickles. You don't know how I crave potato chips – just like a girl craves something when she is pregnant. From the way in which you wrapped the salamis, they ought to be as fresh as when you sent them. They will come in handy as a birthday gift. Your figuring was pretty accurate as to the time when I'd get this letter. You said that it would be about the 5th and it was the 8th, which is a darned good guess. So thanks for your congratulations on our anniversary – sorry that I wasn't around to get them in person. As to trying to get rid of you when I am home – brother (I know you're not my brother) I can assure you that that will be the most remote thought in my mind.

Well, the latest was the nite before Xmas and all thru the house, all of you were stirring, trying to make Carole believe in Santa. Well, there is no doubt in my mind that she does, after all the gifts that she received. There is probably no greater person than he in her mind. Anyway, I hope that the baby, the folks and you are well and not taking any unnecessary trips out in bad weather. Also, that you all had a happy New Year and are looking forward as eagerly as I to that day this year when we are all back together again.

So regards to all and love to the folks, and millions of hugs and billions of kisses for the baby and you –
With All My Love,
Your Dave

———

Tuesday – 9 January – 1945
Somewhere in Eastern France

My Dearest Sweethearts,
This morning, I went to town on pass. I can tell you that it was cold. I took my scarf and put it over my head and ears and then put my helmet back on. I went to the department store where I received that invitation to dinner from one of the buyers. I saw him and his wife and explained why we didn't show up at their home last Sunday. She was very much put out at first and told us how she had prepared a big meal and then waiting two hours for us to come. I begged her pardon and told her that I understood how she felt. Anyway, it finally ended with them inviting me again – This time,

I told them that Monday would be easier as Fay is out on pass on Sunday. They have no children and both look to be about 35 or 38 years old. They said that they were married just before the Nazis invaded and didn't want to do anything about it as long as they were there. Now, they are waiting for the War to end before even trying.

About 1:30, I thought that I had better take off for the Mougins. I got there about 2:00 and found Janine at the university and her mother & aunt at home. We sat around awhile and talked – then Madame Mougin excused herself. She returned with a very pretty piece of hand-crocheted work. She told me that she had gotten it in Milan, Italy, before the War. I insisted that there was absolutely no reason for them to give us that gift – but they insisted. Janine returned from school and we talked some more. About 4:00, I looked outside and saw that it was starting to get dark – so I hit for home & walked along the street, thumbing, and finally a nice, big, open truck stopped – so I got a ride all the way into the village. However, I was a solid cake of ice when I jumped off the truck. Now came the toughest part of the whole day – walking back up that damned hill. When I finally got up there, I was puffing like the Paducah 9:15.

Well, Darlings, I'll wrap the gift and the perfume and some pictures and send it off tomorrow, I think. By the way, I never heard "Don't Fence Me In" – but see that it is up on the "Hit Parade." I still like "Long Ago & Far Away."

So meanwhile, regards to all our friends, love to the folks and beaucoup love and kisses for Carole and you –
With All My Love,
Your Dave

———

Wednesday – 10 January – 1945
Somewhere in Eastern France

Dear Carole Frances and Amy,

I just got finished giving out most of another issue of PX rations and feel pretty tired. Each man got 15 packages of cigarettes, two bottles of Ballantine's Beer and a package of candy mints. It cost each man 50 francs, so it is a bargain. The reason that I get the cigarettes is because Fay or one of the other boys may run out of smokes, so I give them some. I also bring them with me to friends when I visit them – so it isn't too much of an investment for good will. I'm still waiting for your package of cookies that you sent last

August – They ought to be really aged by now. I really don't need any candy or chocolate – but a snack like sardines, salami or potato chips is a handy thing to have around at about eleven at night. Joe Dines gave me a piece of salami the other day and I really took good care of it in a big hurry. Of course, those pickles that you sent will come in nicely, too.

Well, soon, we won't be around this village, as we expect to move to another location closer to the city. From what I hear, we will really have a wonderful setup there. Mullen and I will be in one room – along with steam heat. Can you imagine what a deal that is? We will have separate rooms for our reading and writing, a room for our War maps, a room for our PX and a room for our entertainment. Also, there will be one for the barber – isn't that something?

Well, Darlings, say "Hello" to all and send love to the folks – and millions of hugs and kisses for the baby and you –
With All My Love,
Your Dave

———

Thursday – 11 January – 1945
Somewhere in Eastern France

My Sweetest Darlings,

I just got back from our new home and am slowly thawing out. Mullen, the Mess Sergeant, and I went along with Lt. Micka and the driver to look over the place. It is a very pretty and new place that had been a university. Mullen and I are sharing a room and we have really fixed it up so far. We got two nice modern beds, equipped with springs, and also two, deep, innerspring mattresses. Then, to top it off, we got hold of two pillows – European style – that is, they are in the shape of Tootsie-Rolls. Then we got hold of two new chairs that are upholstered. Then we brought in a good desk with a lamp on it. The room is in nice enough shape to do credit to any room in any American dormitory. In fact, it will be damned hard to leave. The bad thing about it is we will have to be mopping the halls and our rooms all day long. The place will have to be spotless at all times, if we are to hang onto it. I think that it would be a lot cheaper if we just walked on our hands, so as not to get the place dirty. Oh well, we can't have everything – After all, there's a War going on – I think. When we see this place, it is hard to believe that a War is going on not far, in Germany. At least we will be right close to everything in town and won't have to worry about getting a ride back to camp if we go on pass. Also, that ol' hill won't have to be walked up anymore.

Well, Darlings, what do you think of the latest landings in the Philippines? They have pushed well into Luzon and should complete the occupation of the whole thing by the end of March. This latest effort caught the Japs off-guard and they have had to race enforcements up that way from the South. I saw a late teletype resume from the Pacific Theatre and it had a communiqué from [Admiral Chester] *Nimitz in which we were supposed to have knocked off 626 planes and about 348 ships in four or five days – It is hard to believe that, even though it is our Navy. If it is true, it will make our eventual landings on the Japanese mainland a much easier task. So, all in all, our War is coming along quite well. I hope that you have not been worrying too much about the recent Nazi effort to break thru – It is about all over for this round. However, they are still able to fight and in strength – so we aren't too optimistic about a quick Victory in the next couple of months. However, we are sure that we will win this year and before the Summer is over.*

Well, Darlings, hope that the baby and the folks are well and feeling fine – give my regards to all our friends – love to the folks – a billion hugs and kisses for the baby and you –

    With All My Love,
    Your Dave

—

                Saturday – 13 January – 1945
                Somewhere in Eastern Europe

My Sweetest Darlings,

Today has been a very pretty one. After starting with being very cold and cloudy, the sun came out this afternoon and the planes were up in huge numbers. It was the first time in some time that we have been able to get any decent flying weather. I saw large numbers of four-motored bombers overhead and they must have really given the Jerries hell. If we can only continue to get that type of weather, we will be able to knock them out a lot sooner. From reports, the Nazis are well on their way back into Germany from Belgium, after that "push." It certainly was a costly affair for them.

One of the Supply boys got a package containing a jar of herring spread and another jar of ravioli, which spoiled and stunk to high heavens. The herring is still good, so I guess we will dig into that. The letter situation is still lousy, but I hope that you are receiving my letters in spite of it. There is no doubt that it must be on account of the bad flying weather. Then again, during the recent Nazi effort, there must have been a lot of more essential supplies flown over that didn't leave so much room for mail.

When we get to our new spot, I'll place your Xmas picture right on top of our desk where it will shine as big as a full moon in July. Well, Darlings, say "Hello" to all our friends and send love to the folks — and beaucoup love and kisses for the baby and you —

> *With All My Love,*
> *Your Dave*

———

Sunday — 14 January — 1945
Somewhere in Eastern France

My Sweetest Angels,

I forgot to tell you, but on the 12th, we celebrated being overseas a year, as that was the day that we boarded the boat in the States. So since then, our overseas service began. I can recall almost everything that happened that day. We left the camp and marched to the trains. There, we were issued box lunches, which we ate on the way to the docks. We got to the water about 1:00 in the afternoon. As we walked up to our ship, there was a band playing and some Red Cross workers serving coffee and doughnuts. We boarded our ship and stayed on it for the next 21 days. The first Friday out was the beginning of the storm when I got so sick. Now I can tell you that I had volunteered to be one of the gunners on our ship. There was one time when we had a gun drill and our gun was a new one that was just fitted on the ship before we left. We had just fired it once and it was fine. The second time, it jammed and we were unable to get it out. Finally, after the drill was all over, one of the sailors was able to extract the shell and threw it overboard, so as not to take any chances on it going off. That was our first of two scares. The other was a sub scare, but we never did know if it actually was there. So you see, it was a most uneventful trip.

The next was the trip from Naples to Southern France, when we had a couple of sub scares and dropped ash cans [depth charges] for about 30 minutes. Nothing ever happened and we continued on unmolested. When we sailed from Africa to Italy, there were a number of our boys who went along ahead of us with our vehicles on another boat. It so happened that their convoy was bombed and torpedoed, about which you have read in the paper some time ago. There were a couple of sailors wounded and one killed,

I think. We sailed just after that happened. While over in Italy, we had a number of air raids, but we never suffered any casualties. Most of them were nuisance raids and never amounted to much. There was one time, however, that a Jerry came swooping down at night and we thought that he was headed right for us, so we ducked along a wall. We heard a loud swish and the next morning, we learned that a dud bomb had gone thru a three-story building. That was as close as we had ever come to an explosion. However, there were some of the boys who came into France on D-Day who saw one plane bomb and strafe our ships. Luckily, nobody was hurt and since then, we haven't been near a raid to speak of – at this time.

Yesterday, I stopped by to see our Jewish friend, who is the manager at that department store. I realized that it would be impossible to have dinner with them tomorrow, so I told them that we are moving and would they prefer any other day. We finally agreed on next Sunday – so Fay is taking Saturday off and I'll take Sunday. Their home is very modern and nicely furnished. While there, I met some friends of theirs who were eating with them. Mr. Hosansky showed me some places where the Jerries had shot into his walls before they evacuated the city.

Today's news was pretty good if true – that the Jerries were retreating out of Italy on account of the manpower shortage in Germany and the high cost in food and supplies for those troops down there. It was a very successful stalemate on our part, as we tied up quite a number of divisions with a bare minimum of troops. Now, we too will be able to send those in Italy up to the Western Front to finally slaughter those damned Jerries. With the Russians on the move now, the Jerries will have their hands full soon. I hope that everybody at home is now satisfied that Russia is not laying down on the job. After all, if you will look at the map, you will see that she is fighting on a front that extends from the Baltic to the Adriatic and Aegean. Then again, she has to bring up supplies from Moscow and other manufacturing areas that are hundreds and hundreds of miles from the fronts. All that takes time and careful planning – So now it has begun and you will see the result soon.

Well, Darlings, that is about the dope for today – hope that the baby is doing fine and getting prettier, smarter and more lovable each day. Say "Hello" to all our friends and send love to the folks – and a million hugs and kisses for Carole and you –

With All My Love,
Your Dave

Wednesday – 17 January – 1945
Somewhere in Eastern France

My Sweetest Sweethearts,

I just got finished marking up the new changes on the maps since the recent pushes of the Russians and the Allies on the Western Front. It has been some time since we had any changes to make – going Eastward. Also, going Westward. However, I'm sure that both pushes are synchronized to bring about the quickest destruction of Germany that the world can ever realize. Now that we are once more on the offensive, and the Jerries have lost irreplaceable tons of materiel, you will see a quick advance into Germany, not only from the East, but from the West. The Russians are practically in Vienna, let alone Budapest, Cracow and Koenigsberg. With the materiel and manpower that they have brought up, there will be a tremendous push thru the German Silesia – I think. Anyway, the main thing is that the War is certainly a lot brighter than it was three weeks ago. Now you can see what a few weeks of good, clear weather can do for us.

Then the new landing on Luzon is certainly going to hasten the end of Japanese dominance over the Philippines, do you agree? To add to all the good news, I noticed an article in the "Stars & Stripes" quoting Gen. [George] Marshall, that there will be a lot more men sent home on rotation this year and soon. Well, as yet, this does not affect us. However, when June rolls around, we will all be eligible for it and I certainly hope that we are home by then or that I get a break first in our outfit. Gee, it sounds funny talking about coming back home as an "almost" reality. This is the first time that I ever seriously said that I had even a slight chance of getting home. The other times, as you probably knew, I was hoping and trying to talk you into the same idea. However, now, I actually do mean every word of it. After all, in earlier letters, we were overseas only a month – then two – then four – then eight – and now a year. Well, as you know, a man is eligible after 18 months over – if he has a good record – so it could happen to us. Anyway, we can hope for a break with the New Year.

So – regards to all, and love to the folks – and barrels of hugs and kisses for Carole and you –

With All My Love,
Your Dave

Thursday – 18 January – 1945
Somewhere in Eastern France

My Dearest Darlings,

After getting my supplies earlier in the day, I got back to our new place about three in the afternoon. Then I had to go to another place for more supplies. Well, after getting back here, I found five nice letters waiting for me. Two of them were from my dad and the other three were yours – Nice, wasn't it? Your first letter was from the day after Xmas. You certainly did have your ups and downs with that Nazi effort in Belgium. It had to be costly to the Jerries, as they didn't have the necessary supply lines to keep it up for a continuous time. Anyway, I'm sure that you are no longer alarmed at what took place up there. The one thing that I hope for is that the people will retain that feeling of total vengeance on the Nazis when we are deciding the surrender. As to any publicity that the 1st TAF may get, it will be very little. There are certain things about the Air Forces over here that most people don't realize and which cannot be made known at this time, so just be content to know that we are all doing our part in knocking the hell out of Jerry.

I got the first inkling of what you did on Xmas from this letter – Hmmmm, drank wine, eh? Well, I hope that you didn't take too much. I'll introduce you to a lot of different wines when I get back. Gee, I hope that the champagne arrives in good shape. Be sure to keep it upside down, in the basement somewhere, in the dark if possible. I didn't know that you had a white Xmas, but I was happy to read about it, as it's so much nicer to have a white Xmas – especially with a baby in the house who is looking for Santa to arrive in his sleigh – and it would be tough sledding without snow – Hmmm, I remember the first time you pulled that on me.

As to coming to New York when I return, that is definitely out, because the traveling facilities are not sufficient to allow it. I'd like for you to be there, but there will be thousands of others who live right there to greet their home-comers, too, so just take it easy and I'll see you in St. Looie.

I have seen so many good reviews on "The Robe" that I am deep into it by now. It's about 450 pages long – so it will take me quite a while. I doubt if the Special Service will get a pocket edition of "Forever Amber" – It's a little out of line, n'est-ce pas?

Well, Darlings, hope that everybody is well and that Joe is still at home, so regards to all and love to the folks, and tons of love and kisses for the baby and you –

With All My Love,
Your Dave

———

Friday – 19 January – 1945
Somewhere in Eastern Europe

My Most Adorable Darlings,

Today, I received just one letter – from the fellow who asked Janine Mougin to marry him. He just wanted me to tell her he has received the letters that she has sent – if she was wondering about them. So I may get a little time to see them and I'll relay the information.

As to the War situation, what do you think of the Eastern Front now? I'd say that the Russians are, by far, the most effective force and will bring this War to an end sooner than we or the British. From what I heard this evening, they are in Germany already – in Silesia. As there is nothing but plains on into Berlin, the going ought to be a little easier than that which they had in the Carpathians. However, at the same time, the Germans' supply lines are shortened and enable them to put up a stronger resistance. After the Russians are well into Germany, there will probably be another lull to get their supplies up to the front and decide the final punch that will carry into Berlin. Meanwhile, the Rhine will still be a line of defense for us and will take a big push to cross it in sufficient strength to allow us to push on to central Germany. That, no doubt, is the reason that the British are trying to make a push around the Northern end, so as to avoid the crossing. Well, we'll have to let time take care of the probabilities that I have written.

Well, Darlings, regards to all and love to the folks and lots and lots of love and kisses for the baby and you –

With All My Love,
Your Dave

———

Saturday – 20 January – 1945
Somewhere in Eastern France

My Sweetest Toosie-Wootsies,

This afternoon, I had to drive about twenty miles. The distance was absolutely nothing – but the conditions under which I had to drive were terrific. The ground was worn from yesterday's warming up and then it started to snow late in the evening. That caused ice to form on the roads. Then all day, it has been snowing very hard, so that it was twice as hard to get the tires to grasp the roads. Then, to top it off, I had no windshield wiper working, so I had to stop every five minutes to wipe the snow and ice off the glass. It was even worse when I got off onto the side roads where the snow covered the roads and sides so that you didn't know whether or not you were driving on the road at all. I did take a few minutes on the way back to stop by at the Mougins' house and give that letter that I received from this suitor. They wanted me to stay for a while, but I explained that I hadn't the time and that perhaps I would next week.

I received a package from you. It was the camera, film, and the gefilte fish. I put the fish away for a rainy day, as I haven't been too hungry lately. As to the camera, boy! What a camera! Do you really think that it will work? Anyway, I'm going to try. Those films won't last very long if it does work, but I think that I'll be more successful in getting more than you would in the States.

What do you think of the War now? It's a little different than a month ago, isn't it? See, if only we all have a little more confidence in our armies and their commanders, and the home workers will buckle down to getting out the materials, this War will end a lot sooner. There doesn't seem to be anything to stop the Reds, so they ought to be well into Germany by now. After all, Stalin doesn't say too much and when he does, it is about two days later.

That, my Darlings, is about all the news for today. Say "Hello" to all our friends and give love to the folks – carloads of love and kisses for the baby and you –

With All My Love,
Your Dave

Monday – 22 January – 1945
Somewhere in Eastern France

My Dearest Darlings,

You had better not look for a letter of the 21st as I went to that dinner and was unable to write. At about 11:15, Dines and I took off for this place. Ellison couldn't go, so I asked Joe to go along. On the way, we saw a bakery, so we decided that it would be a nice gesture to buy some snacks – so we bought some small custard cakes and pieces of honey-cake. When we got there, they were so happy to see us. We sat around in the living room for a while and talked. Joe is able to speak Yiddish and Mr. Hosansky is able to speak German, so they were able to get along. His wife isn't Jewish and speaks only French. The first thing on the table was a platter of cold meats. They tasted like salami and we liked it. There were also urchins and pickled onions with it. They, of course, served the French brown bread, which tastes very much like our pumpernickel. After that, there was potato salad made with eggs and onions. With that, we had some red wine, which wasn't bad. Then she served something that looked like a pie and was made of dough and cheese. They said that it was "chinkin-something" – You know the first word – "chinkin," like in chinkin-flakin. So I ain't neat. Anyway, after that, I thought that the meal was over and that we were ready to leave – but in she came with a big platter of steaming roast chicken. She gave me the rear end, but it was very good with the gravy. With that, we had French-fried potatoes and string beans, also some better wine. Then we had another bottle of wine, which was the oldest and the best of all. After that, she served some cake she had made and also put out the snacks we had bought. With that, she served coffee and some schnapps. It was really a meal to be remembered. I couldn't get up from the table, I was so full. Anyway, we finally left at about five in the evening.

Today, we received the first issue of the Nancy edition of the "Stars & Stripes." We are always in the first issues, it seems. So far, we have received the Rome, Strasbourg and Nancy issues. Maybe we will also get the Berlin issue soon – that is, if the Russians don't start their own paper when they get there before us. At this time, they are 210 miles from Berlin at two different points. As yet, there doesn't seem to be anything to stop them in their drive up the Silesia area. They ought to take Polsin this week, which would place them about 125 miles from Berlin – so it won't be long.

Today was really a beautiful day for the boys upstairs – They poured it on the Jerries all day long. It was the same yesterday, too. There was nothing but a steady roar of motors all day long. I often wonder what we will find when we get into some of the larger cities in Germany – There can't be much left.

Well, Dearests, that is about all the news for today. The one thing that isn't news is that I love and do miss you both very much. Hope that you both are well and enjoying warmer weather lately – also that the folks are well. So say "Hello" to all and lots of love and kisses for Carole Frances and you –

With All My Love,

Your Dave

Tuesday – 23 January – 1945
Somewhere in Eastern France

My Darling Amy and Carole Frances,

I heard that two of the mail boats had engine trouble in the Atlantic and had to be tugged into port. If true, that would account for the delay and we ought to expect a lot of it soon. The story goes that there were 30 million letters on the two boats. I certainly must have some of them.

Well, what do you think about the European War now? I read many opinions as expressed by some of the newspapers back home and they were all very optimistic about the Russians. I don't like to see that, because I remember what happened when we were going along so nicely in the autumn of '44 and the people were betting on the War being over by Xmas – which caused a helluva lot of overenthusiasm. This resulted in a big letdown in War production and we lost a lot of equipment that we otherwise would be using against the Jerries right now. So I'd rather not see them so optimistic at this time, in spite of the beautiful picture that we see today. After all, it looked the same when we were approaching the borders of Germany and they made a damned stiff stand. Of course, we all would rather see the Russians when they march in and do the same to the Nazis as they did to the Russians when they marched in in '40. I truthfully would like to see them burn and murder as the Jerries have done for so long. So many French people have asked me why the Americans are so humane in our kind treatment of the Nazis – What can you tell those who have had fathers, brothers, relatives and sweethearts murdered by the Nazis? If we were to allow the Belgians, French, Dutch and Russians (and the Greeks) to walk into Germany, they would give the Germans a treatment that would make them regret the day they ever thought about War. The Poles would probably wipe the country completely off the map as the Jerries did them. I sincerely say that I absolutely hate the Jerries with all my heart.

Well, that's about the news for today. Say "Hello" to our friends and love to the folks – beaucoup hugs and kisses for the baby and you –

With All My Love,
Your Dave

Wednesday – 24 January – 1945
Somewhere in Eastern France

My Sweetest Carole Frances and Amy,

The roads are still very icy and difficult to travel, but we came out OK earlier today. At the same time, the sun came out and the clouds broke a bit, so our planes were out in full force. They probably gave the Heinies hell. Speaking of the War, I heard from some of the boys in the Radio Section that the Russians had crossed the Oder River and had taken Koenigsberg. There still is not any indication that the Nazis will make a stand, as they are, from all reports, in full retreat. In fact, there is a story going around that the officers in this Wing have been given two weeks notice to move out of their hotel rooms – as the Russians are due about then. It is a very appropriate gag at this time and I hope that they do pour thru as far as the French Front. It would save a lot of lives. If the Germans have not drawn up a line of resistance from Breslau, Prague and Dresden, they may withdraw from the Western Front to a point East of the Rhine and make us cross the Rhine. In the past, large river crossings have been pretty difficult and costly, so this would give them a breathing spell and shorten their lines quite a bit. Cologne and Coblenz would be the only cities of any size to be lost and they would probably keep snipers in there to act as nuisance rear guards.

The "Stars & Stripes" are a bit behind the radio and teletype reports that we get each morning. However, it did say that in the Ardennes sector, we had destroyed over 3200 vehicles including tanks. There is the thing about which I wrote you some time ago – that this "effort" of the Nazis would give us the opportunity to get at their materiel that had previously been stored up behind the Rhine. They took St. Vith already and the Southern part is about retaken, so it was a most costly venture for von Rundstedt. I noticed that [Kurt] Dittmar, the German commentator, said that the defense may be from the Western side of the Oder, which is similar to the possibility that I have stated, that is, in regard to the Western Front.

I also note that there is a meat shortage cropping up – Are you also having difficulty in getting fresh meat? If so, perhaps you had better not be sending me salamis so often, as you need the meat for the baby and folks more than I. Well, Darlings, I guess that's about it for today – so regards to all and love to the folks – and billions of hugs and kisses for the baby and you –

With All My Love
Your Dave

Saturday – 27 January – 1945
Somewhere in Eastern France

My Dearest Darlings,

I just finished "The Robe" and it was really terrific. I don't know if you are acquainted with the story or not, but it really sets one's mind to realizing things that go on, even today, that can so easily be corrected. If only each of us would try to be a little more considerate and thoughtful of the other, and it was practiced throughout the world, what a great improvement it would be. The book is a very powerful affair and will, no doubt, have the same impression on most of its readers. If you are able to pick it up anyplace, do so, as it is one of the best of all time.

Yesterday evening, Mullen and I had dinner together and after we had finished, he and the Mess Sergeant asked me to join them for the evening and stop in at a few restaurants and listen to the music and have a few drinks. We went to one place, then another and then another and then another. The second-to-last place was the largest in Nancy and had the best orchestra that I have heard since leaving the States. Well, we stayed there until it closed, which was about 8:30 and then went to one more place. It was there that we found some champagne. After drinking schnapps, Mirabelle wine and beer, this put the finishing touches on the evening. We stayed until the place closed also, which was about 9:00. We walked home in snow that was up to our knees and Mullen met a girl whom he walked home. I went in and right to bed and he came in about 15 minutes later. It was right about that time that I felt pretty putrid and headed for the door. I found a large garbage can right outside our room and there I was – one sad sack, heaving everything up that I had eaten. When I finished, I went right to bed, and after the room stopped swirling around, I fell off to sleep. In the morning (today), I felt like a beaten rug and was definitely not in the mood for work. I didn't go to breakfast, which isn't so unusual, so I was really hungry as a bear this afternoon. So you can see that I was in no position to write letters last night. It was the first time since we were in Italy that I got lit, so I hope that you will excuse me – OK?

Yes, I can agree with you that our worries, after this is over, will be very trivial, in comparison with what we are going thru now. You asked if I really think that men will be sent to the Pacific after seeing action here. Well, to tell you one thing, all Air Force units, having non-technically trained personnel, have had all men under 31 and under Staff grades physically *examined for possible transfer into the Infantry. In our outfit, Fay and Angelo have been examined and may have to go. Louie failed on account of his eyes. It's bad enough that a lot of men have served over here for two and a half and three years and should have been sent home on rotation, let alone being transferred into the Infantry. There are so many men back in the States who are shirking their duties, while others are in the service are doing their share of the fighting. So far, nothing has happened, but it looks more and more like it will as Gen. [Ben] Lear is now over here and it was originally his idea. So there is no doubt that it will go into effect – However, with the speed of the Russian offensive, we can hope for the end of the European War before any of these fellows are sent up there. I hate anyone who shirks his duty and you know it. That same principle can be derived from the book I have finished, as it certainly is not being thoughtful and considerate to say, "Let the other guy do it." Just such a thing is helping to create and enlarge the feeling between the men overseas and those back in the States. That will definitely be one sore spot after it is all over.*

As to the type of schooling Joe Dines took while in Paris, it dealt with telephone installations, which he has always been in, but this was something that wasn't taught him before – so he and another fellow went. He said that he had a most enjoyable time, but it cost beaucoup gelt to stay there. From all indications, we will be unable to see Paris until the War is over. They ended all passes to Paris when that last Nazi "effort" started.

Well, Darlings, I suppose I have given you all the news for now and hope that I am forgiven for not writing yesterday – Say "Hello" to our friends and love to the folks – for Carole and you a billion hugs and kisses and a good, mental necking –

> *With All My Love,*
> *Your Dave*

———

Sunday – 28 January – 1945
Somewhere in Eastern France

My Most Adorable Wife and Baby,

Ellison told me that he was going into town for an hour or so, as we have a curfew. I decided to go along, so we went to a nice bar and listened to the music and drank beer. By the way, Ellison also gave me some Jewish salami that he had received in the mail, so I have a snack every now and then.

The teletype news came in this morning and was very optimistic. The Nazis have already conceded Posen, while the Russians haven't said a thing about it. Also, the Russians are supposed to be about 100 miles from Berlin. Also, that Hitler has given up any hope of holding Breslau. About one-half of Silesia has been occupied already, which is quite a loss for Hitler's industries. There will be immediate effects very soon as his coal and iron ores are sorely needed to offset the bombings the Allies have made in the West in the Ruhr Valley. So it looks like the War will be over pretty soon. I would certainly like to follow the Russians into Germany and Berlin and watch them as they repay an old debt. I notice that the list of Germans killed is much greater than that of those captured. That is exactly what we all expect and would like to see. In fact, there shouldn't be any captured.

Well, regards to all and love to the folks – a great big extra tight hug and a big kiss for Carole and you –

With All My Love,
Your Dave

Monday – 29 January – 1945
Somewhere in Eastern France

My Dearest Darlings,

This evening, after supper, I decided to go down to that bar where the good orchestra is and meet Fay and Ellison there. On the way back towards our area, we met a man, his wife and their baby. We started talking to them and gave the girl some gum. Well, after we had gone about 50 yards, they called us back to come into their home. We went in and had a drink with them and sat around awhile and talked. Their baby is seven years old. The wife said that she had relatives in Kentucky from whom she had had no news since before the War. I offered to try to find out if they are still alive and if it is possible to get some news of them for this family. They live in Owensboro on Roost Road – probably a farmer. I'll try to drop them a line and perhaps be able to do them a favor. You don't think that I'm going out of my way too much for these people – do you? After all, if I placed myself in their position, I'd certainly be grateful if somebody were to do the same for me.

Today was a very bright and sunny, but very cold, day. The sun was out in full and the skies as clear as a bell, so you can assume that the planes had a field day with the Jerries. The latest rumors are that the Russians are less than 85 miles from Berlin and still going strong. At that rate, the War will be ended even before my birthday – I hope. You can imagine how the situation will be when the Russian planes no sooner take off than they are over Berlin and bombing and strafing it at will. Their missions wouldn't take them over an hour now and still have plenty of gas left for strafing. It won't be long now.

Well, Darlings, regards to all and love to the folks and a lot of lovin' and kissin' for the baby and you –

With All My Love,
Your Dave

—

Wednesday – 31 January – 1945
Somewhere in Eastern France

My Most Adorable Darlings,

I received all your holiday letters together – unusual. You wrote your Xmas letter at a late hour, so you must have really been tired from all the activity. I'm sorry that I was unable to be there with you when Carole Frances walked downstairs and saw all the pretty things that Santa left for her. She must have to sleep outside her room in order to make room for the toys.

I take it that not many people spend their stamps on catsup and chili sauce, as they are so high in points. Gee, I'm glad that we don't have to worry about points over here, but I'd much rather have to worry about them and be over there with you. It will be very hard now that canned soups are rationed again. What do you do for the baby now – prepare all her foods from fresh foods? Of course, she could live on cod liver oil alone. If the meat situation is getting to be so tight now, you had better forget about sending me salami, as it would only add to my weight. Tell the others the same thing. There is no reason to put you out just to satisfy a craving of mine, so you do that and everyone will be happy.

The other letter was the New Year's greeting – the day after. Gee, you must have really had a lot to talk about if you stayed up until 5:00 A.M. If I stayed up 'till midnight, I'd get so sleepy that I'd fall asleep standing up. Say, don't you go making my daughter a nite-owl – allowing her to stay up until all hours of the night. Well, as long as it was only for that one night, I'll forgive you. Those snacks that you had for midnight lunch sound very appetizing. However, eight girls altogether sounds even more appetizing – Am I getting to be a wolf? I hate to think of you back home with a few oil points left and the weather so cold. Hope that you are able to make out OK. The coal situation is getting serious from the news. As to building a fire, I'm afraid that I won't want to do a thing but sit back and enjoy automatic heat for the rest of our lives.

The War is really getting brighter as the time goes by. From the latest news, the Russians are within 40 miles of Berlin. Can you imagine just how close to the end of the War that is? Even though the Nazis may decide to move their government to a city further South, it would mean that it would be only a matter of mopping up. Well, we can thank God that we are all on the winning side.

So now I had better close and get some sleep – Regards to all and a great big hug and kiss for the baby and you –

With All My Love,
Your Dave

Thursday – 1 February – 1945
Somewhere in Eastern France

My Sweetest Angels,

Today, I was the very surprised recipient of a package that was postmarked the 18th of December and also a V-Mail from you that was dated the 7th of January. I didn't hesitate a moment in opening the package – and there, before me, was the nicest set of salamis. They were surrounded by a box of potato chips, a can of tomato soup, and a can of fruit cocktail. Everything came in very nicely – except that there weren't enough of the chips. I had expected a great big box, but I see that it wouldn't have fitted into that box you used, so maybe you will be able to send some more in the next package. As to the condition of the salamis, I opened one and it is really delicious. In fact, I have already paid back Joe Dines that piece he had given me last month when I didn't have any. Mullen and Louie have already had some, and now Fay and Angelo are still to be taken care of. With what I have left of the first one that I opened, that ought to take care of them. As you had figured, the V-Mail is coming over, whereas the regular airmail is being detained. As much as I hate to write on those things, it looks like I'll do it anyway.

By the way, if you will recall, I told you that I read a book while in the hospital – "Mrs. Parkington" – and thought so much of it. Well, I noticed in "Newsweek" magazine that they are making it into a picture with Greer

Garson and Walter Pidgeon. It ought to be very good. We are still waiting for "Since You Went Away." There haven't been any good pictures around here – so I haven't seen any.

The streets are water-filled and in spots full of ice; if it isn't one thing, it's another. As to the War, the news is still about 36 to 48 hours behind and we know that the Russians are less than 40 miles from Berlin. The Reds are still pushing on ahead and there is still no indication that the Jerries will be able to make a stand. The popular opinion of the boys around here is that the Nazis will transfer the gov't from Berlin to some city further South – perhaps to Stuttgart, which is in the South-central part. However, that would just mean a little longer mopping up period. I still insist that the War will be over by April.

Well, Darlings, hope that everybody is well and feeling in tip-top condition – regards to all and love to the folks. You may give the baby a huge hug and kiss and let her do the same to you – for me –

With All My Love,
Your Dave

Friday – 2 February – 1945
Somewhere in Eastern France

My Dearest Darlings,

As to your latest package, the potato chips are all gone and so is one salami. I still have the other salami and the cans of soup and fruit salad.

Here's the sad part of this letter – Two of the men examined for transfer are slated to leave on the 6th and one is out of Supply – Angelo. It is not that it means taking a man out of this section, but he was so afraid of going and now he is going. I hate to see him being transferred, but there is nothing to be done about it. Also, they are taking a fellow who is married and has a baby. That's one thing that I can't see. They could have certainly selected a single fellow in his place. Damn this War! I hope that it is ended before they are assigned to a division. Well, I can't worry about everybody else – I have my own family to think about and hope that they are well and safe.

I suppose that article on expecting flying bombs in New York this month sort of frightened a lot of people. I don't know why they allow such stuff to be printed. It is a shot in the dark by the reporter, and if he happened to hit it, he'd be in a position to say he had predicted it. Such wild guessing shouldn't be allowed in the papers at a time like this. It doesn't take a genius to imagine that a bomb could be propelled from a sub into New York, but it is also almost fantastic, as it would only be a negligible bit of satisfaction on the part of the Nazis, to shout to the world that they have bombed New York. I wouldn't put any faith into the idea, as right now, they are too occupied with trying to protect their homes and themselves.

With the Russians building up a front of almost 200 miles inside Germany (not by John Gunther [author of the "Inside..." books]), they are getting ready for that final push into the capital. If there is a slowing down soon, it won't be because the Germans had stopped them – It will be because the Russians had stretched the supply lines too far to keep up a steady push. That was the same case as we had when Patton was approaching the German line last Fall – The supply lines were far behind him and we hadn't anticipated such a deep drive. It is possible that the Russians hadn't figured on going so deeply also, and may have to pause to catch up. After all, from Warsaw, they have pushed almost 300 miles. Anyway, personally, I hope that it carries right on in and the damned thing is ended very soon. Of course, that would mean that Stalin would have the upper hand in the surrender negotiations – but as long as the War ends, that's OK with me. Let England, France and Russia decide the main points of the surrender – We don't have to take too much interest in it. No matter which way it ends up, we will have to supply the poor and suffering nations with food and clothing.

I guess that's about the dope for today – so say "Hello" to all and love to the folks – and billions and billions of hugs and kisses for the baby and you –
With All My Love,
Your Dave

———

Saturday – 3 February – 1945
Somewhere in Eastern France

My Dearest Darlings,

I have already started on the second salami and I guess, by the end of the week, it will also be gone – Ain't I hoggish? It isn't that – It's just that in the evenings, after reading or writing letters, I'd get a hankering for it and there it goes. The second one isn't as good as the first, as the skin was loosened in some manner. It may have been due to the hot wax after cooling – It tightened it up and loosened it. However, I skinned it and it is pretty good.

So far, about ten different guys have partaken in the delicacy, and they are all crazy over it. What gentile isn't?

Well, this evening, Dines and I went to the Red Cross Theatre and saw "Rainbow Island" – with Dorothy Lamour and Eddie Bracken. It was putrid and I'm sorry I wasted my time there. It was the first picture I have seen in quite a long time.

Well, Darlings, give my regards to all and love to the folks – beaucoup love and kisses for the baby and you –
With All My Love,
Your Dave

Sunday – 4 February – 1945
Somewhere in Eastern France
My Sweetest Sweethearts,

This may come as a surprise to you – but Xmas comes more than once a year. How do I know? Well, yesterday, I received two Xmas packages. The first was from the Block Marble Company in Philadelphia. The other was the pretzel sticks and potato sticks you sent. Here's the funny deal – I don't know anybody in Philadelphia by that name. I have the return address, so I'll write a thank-you letter. That package contained everything from soup to nuts. It had a ½-pound fruitcake, a box of raisin cookies, assorted tea cookies, six pieces of 5-cent candy, a baseball-bat-shaped pencil, a calendar, a cigarette lighter, a pair of wooden dice, a deck of cards, a box of leads for a pencil, a blotter, and a very risqué collection of pinup pictures. That's a lot of stuff to send somebody with whom you aren't so well acquainted. Say, maybe some other David E. Stoliar was supposed to be drafted? That would really be something. As to your package, I have already devoured two of the packages of pretzel sticks and rye squares.

This evening, I thought that it was about time I visited the Mougins, as I hadn't been there since right after New Year's. I brought over a few candies and things and they really appreciated it. I told them about the book I had just finished, "The Robe." I told them that if it is translated into French, to try to get it. We spoke of some of the films that dealt with Christ, such as "King of Kings" and "Ben-Hur." Then I brought up Paul Muni's portrayals in "Life of Louis Pasteur" and "Emile Zola." Madame Mougin told me that her parents forbid her to read Zola's books when she was single, as he and his books were banned in France for a long time – They exposed all the wrongs of the government, which was too much for the gov't officials to take. Anyway, after she was married, she read his works and she said that he is her favorite author. It all ended up with an invitation to dinner next Sunday.

Otherwise, there's nothing more to say — except that I do love and miss the baby and you very much. So regards to all and love to the folks — many, many hugs and kisses for Carole and you —

With All My Love,
Your Dave

———

Monday — 5 February — 1945
[Eastern France] *V-Mail*

My Darlings,

Well, here is my first attempt at V-Mail since Africa and I hope that it gets to you in a big hurry. As you had figured, the regular airmail was slowed down due to bad flying weather and the V-Mails were getting through. So far this month, I have received only V-Mails — but I'll get the rest sooner or later. I've been writing you daily and I hope that my letters are arriving in fair time. As this is only a supplement to my regular letters, there won't be much to say. I did get the news this morning that the Russians are only 30 miles from Berlin now, so that side of the War is still looking pretty rosy. We're also getting up steam and pretty soon, Adolf will be looking for rooms. From the reports, we knocked the hell out of the main headquarters in Berlin Saturday.

In the Pacific, we have entered Manila, which is a lot sooner than a lot of us had expected. If the War continues at that same pace in both theatres, we'll get the damned thing over with in a hurry. I'd like nothing better for my birthday than the end to the European War.

Meanwhile, I miss and love you and the baby very much — regards to all —
With All My Love,
Your Dave

———

Monday — 5 February — 1945
Somewhere in Eastern France

My Sweetest Darlings,

Believe it or not, I got 16 letters today and nine of them were from you. I don't think I'll answer all of them at once, because it would mean one, big letter, while tomorrow, I may not have anything to answer. Therefore, I think I'll break it down to answering three letters each night – just to make it more interesting.

You really flew up in the air to see that we regarded the Nazi "push" so lightly. I suppose now you can more readily understand why we weren't so alarmed by it. The papers are always looking for a headline – no matter if it is good or bad. After all, you can imagine how many more papers they sold when they spread out the news that they were pushing into American lines. Now, they are only going one way and that is backwards. That is one phase of the War that we are not up on and one that the Nazis could teach us very well. You now have found out all about what took place and what we gained. All the territory has been won back and we have taken more on top of that. However, the main thing is all the men and materiel that the Nazis have lost will certainly help in bringing this thing to an end.

Glad that you have given me an honorable pardon on the drinking charge. Why, even the beer that we drink around here is so weak that we drink it as a chaser after drinking water, so don't worry about me getting drunk . Have you had an occasion to say ___-damn it or are you extra careful? If you will recall, I never did care for you to say that. You had better be more careful now, as the baby can say anything that she overhears. Gosh, what if she hears us at night when I am back?

Glad that you now know that we are doing something to help win this War – as noted in the clipping about the 1st TAF. I am glad to see that you went to that book review to hear about the problems facing the world after it is all over, however, there should have been a few men there who are well versed on the subject to give the ladies a better picture. It's good for one to realize just what is going on outside of just winning the War. A year from now, you will see almost every government in Europe change from what it was before the War.

As to seeing New York or Los Angeles – both of them are out for right now. All that I want to do is to sit down in my room and rest and if I want an ice cream, all that I'd have to do is to phone or get in a car and drive. I don't want to do a thing! We can go visiting after a year or so – but immediately after, I want to stay put. Now you know my plans for our homecoming.

I was surprised to read that Joe got a defense job. I had often thought about it, but never did want to mention it for fear of offending him. Now that he has taken it, it is the best thing that he could have done. If I had the same opportunity, I'd have done the same thing. At least, he is not in the Armed Forces and is home with everybody and is still able to handle his business.

As to your postscript regarding the French girls, I certainly can't walk down the street without seeing them – I'd be bumping into everybody. Anyway, don't worry. Even though a lot of them are attractive, the American girls still have a certain something that the French lack. Don't ask me what it is – I haven't gotten that familiar with them.

Regards to all and love to the folks – lots and lots of hugs and kisses for Carole and you –

With All My Love,
Your Dave

———

Tuesday – 6 February – 1945
Somewhere in Eastern France

My Dearest Darlings,

Those men who were assigned to the Infantry were shipped out this morning. It was very early – about 8:00 – and I didn't know about it, as I had wanted to wish Angelo a lot of luck. Well, the 1st Sgts. of the organizations and the Commanding Officers were all there – all except the 346th Co. There were even other officers on hand to wish the boys luck – but not one officer from this outfit. Perhaps this will help you to understand that feeling I have against them. As far as they are concerned, these two men can die and it would never even phase [sic] them a bit. Gosh, how I long for this damned thing to end, so that we can all go home and let these "officers" stay in the Army, as they never had it so easy as they do now.

You mentioned that one of my letters spoke of my going to a synagogue – It's funny, but that was the one time that I went. I haven't had any desire to go since. As to praying with the mezuzah, no, I just pray with my mind and heart.

Now we come to another situation on post-War plans – This time, you ask if we can visit the Mougins when we "tour Europe." Well, as far as I'm concerned, I am going to stay right in my own backyard for about two or three years and then, if I get an urge to travel, we'll drive to the West Coast or North. After seeing all that I have seen over here, I do not have the slightest idea why in all the world any intelligent person would pay a lot of money to go thru the inconveniences that one does over in these backward countries. The Mougins are still without any information on Mr. Mougin, however, the Mrs. told me that she now has more hope than ever that he will walk in one of these days. That is a lot of confidence for a woman who has taken care of her daughter without her husband being there for about four years – especially after the city where he is supposed to be prisoner was bombed so often by the Allies – Ludwigshafen.

As to de Filippo, the fellow who was injured on Xmas Eve, he is supposed to be in a hospital in England, I think. He had a double fracture – not a compound – so it will be a long time before he will be able to walk again.

You asked if the 5-day furloughs are still in effect – Well, they were discontinued when the Nazis started to counterattack. Today, a new deal was brought out, whereby a fellow gets his transportation and lodging paid for and a two-day pass in Paris – I was the first to apply for it, but I don't know if I'll get it. Two men are allowed to go at a time from our company. That ought to be a good deal, as I wouldn't want to spend more than two days' worth of francs there.

I'm afraid that I gave you the wrong impression about the food situation here in Nancy. There is definitely a shortage. Lately, a lot of restaurants are turning away American soldiers, because they don't have enough to feed the civilians. You really can't blame them either. There is a great shortage of milk for babies.

Well, as long as we are no longer at the place from which we moved, I can tell you that we were not in Luneville. You were too far Southeast. We were only about five miles from Nancy, in a village that you would never find on a map.

The only new thing to bring up is that I am starting on a new book – "Der Fuhrer," by Konrad Heiden. It is supposed to be one of the best books brought out dealing with the birth and rise of the Nazi Party.

Well, hope that everybody is well – love to the folks and regards to all our friends – and lots of love and kisses for the baby and you –

With All My Love,
Your Dave

———

Wednesday – 7 February – 1945
Somewhere in Eastern France

My Sweetest Sweethearts,

This afternoon, I decided to take my day off and I went into town. When I got back here, Fay told me that Temple was on the fire again. He was asking for an item that he had told me to forget about. Now he wants it and wants to know where in hell it is. I phoned him and explained it to him – but he'll wiggle out of it as he always does. At times, he is as bad as the rest of the officers. This is not only my opinion – but most of the men think the same. As to your suggestion to keep some of my opinions to myself at times, you know that I never have, and when I see something that I think is wrong, I speak right out, even tho it may hurt me in the long run. It's just that I never did like to see injustices done. I can assure you that everybody knows just what I think of them, as I don't speak of them behind their backs.

As to the Mougins, you were mistaken about Janine being almost swept off her feet by an American. She was definitely not and has thought this over for a long time. I think that Janine will become engaged to him and wait until after the War to marry. As to her beauty – Yes, she is quite attractive – blonde, blue eyes (I think), about 5'1" and about 100 lbs. However, don't let that give you the wrong idea – We have never been more than friends to each other. So don't let that green-eyed monster get you anymore.

As to the order on having the jeep tops down in the Summer – or any other time when the sun is shining – the sun reflects on the windshield and gives away its position – so the glass is always covered. The top is down so that if you do see a plane coming, you can stop and get out into a gully or something.

Well, that's about it for today – so regards to all and love to the folks and lots and lots of love and kisses for Carole and you –

With All My Love,
Your Dave

———

Thursday – 8 February – 1945
Somewhere in Eastern France

My Darling Sweethearts,

This morning, Temple phoned me to come down to his office. I went down there, expecting a nice, hot bawling out and an argument, however, it was just the opposite – Everything was nice and hunky-dory – don't ask me why. I showed him what I have been doing and he seemed satisfied that I was doing my job – and that was all. He gets some very funny spells at times.

Say, do you know that we've already been in France as long as we were in Italy? Five months apiece and two and a half or three in Africa and in transit. So you see, the time does move swiftly. As you probably now know, the rumor is very true about the Russians fighting on German soil. In fact, it looks like they will go thru the defenses at Frankfurt and that town North of it. After that, it will be a miracle if the Nazis are able to keep the Reds from Berlin. (The fuses just blew and I am writing by flashlight.)

No, "Meet Me in St. Louis" hasn't shown around here – but if it does, I'll be right there. I just finished counting the pages that you have written during the month of December – How many do you think there are? No, you were close, tho – There are 78. (The lights just went back on.) Well, I am just finishing that box of celery-flavored pretzel sticks and they were good! In fact, the only thing that is left out of that package is the can of fruit salad. That will probably be a has-been soon. You can send me some more potato chips and sticks and pretzels and cheese-crackers if you wish.

Well, Darlings, I guess that is about it for today. Send regards to all and love to the folks – and beaucoup love and kisses for my two best gals –

With All My Love,
Your Dave

———

Sunday – 11 February – 1945
Somewhere in Eastern France

My Dearest Darlings,

Today has been a very typical blue Sunday. It started out to be a very nice day, then it clouded up and began to rain and it got colder in a few minutes. Since then, it has continued to rain for the rest of the day. I was supposed to take today off and go to the Mougins' house for dinner, however, Fay left for Paris last night, so I couldn't leave here, since either he or I are always here at one time or another. So I didn't get my day off and I didn't get any mail, which also helped to make the day a very dreary affair.

I hope that you will understand the note I wrote on that Easter card to Carole last night. I meant for you to prepare the eggs and place them under her pillow that morning, so that she will find them and think that the Easter Bunny really did leave them for her. I suppose that life itself is nothing but one deception after another, so try to explain that Easter is just a day for her to get all dressed up and go for a walk in the park. You ought to get this a long time before Easter – so I'll hold off on my greetings. In fact,

Passover greetings will be in order soon. I remember the Pesach that I spent in Oran with that French family. Their name was Achache. I still have his card and may drop him a line one day soon.

So far, it seems that it is just a matter of days before the real drive to Berlin has begun. From reports, the Nazis are really having a helluva time, with our advance in the West going so well. They certainly cannot take troops from one front and transfer them to the other without causing a major weakness. Also, their communications systems don't warrant such sudden shifts of troops – so it won't be long now.

Send my regards to all and love to the folks – I'd like to express my wishes to you and the baby in person – so until then, a lot of hugs and kisses –

With All My Love,

Your Dave

—

Monday – 12 February – 1945

Somewhere in Eastern France

My Sweetest Angels,

After chow this evening, we had mail call and I got only twenty letters – yes 20! Twelve were from you, however, I'll do as I had done last week and answer about three at a time, so as to let it stretch out through the week – Don't you agree?

Well, well, so our "darling" daughter scribbled all over her bed with Crayola – Were you able to wash it off? I can imagine how you felt to see that – so I won't ask what you did to her – but I'm sure that she won't do it again. I guess it is just her artistic ability coming out in her and she can't hold it back – just like her singing and dancing.

As to you being so worried about what was going on around Strasbourg, you shouldn't have done so. After all, you know where I have been all this time and we were never in any danger at any time, so please don't worry, because when I tell you that we're OK, we are really OK. From a news report, the Russians have pushed across the Oder towards Dresden. If that is true, it will be pretty hard for the Nazis to move down to Munich and make a stand, as Dresden isn't far away from Munich. I notice that the subs have become active once more around Canada. With what they are faced now, one would think that they'd call in all men to fight with the ground forces, as the few ships that they might be able to sink certainly won't nick the supplies that we have over here or those that will arrive. However, after all, there have been quite a lot of things that we have never been able to figure out about the Nazis – so why worry about this one?

So Carole Frances remembers the songs from "Meet Me in St. Louis" – I wish that I had been there to see and hear her when you gave the records to her. That incident about her asking if the little children in France wore overalls if they hadn't any clothing was priceless.

I don't know if I have ever told you, but I really and truthfully get more thrills out of giving something to another person than if I received a gift from him. It's not that I'm a little Jesus or anything like that, because you know that I'm not. It's just that there is a certain amount of feeling of doing something good in this world by helping somebody else. No, it wasn't caused by my reading "The Robe" – I have felt that way for quite a long time.

So the War Widows have decided to start a bridge club – well, that is a good idea and I hope that it continues with much success until the War ends and the other kind of partners are all back in bed with the women where they belong. Ain't I filthy?

Well, Angels, I guess that's a lot for one night – so say "Hello" to all our friends and send love to the folks – and as for you and Carole Frances, give her a great big kiss and hug for me – she can't give you what I'd like to, so let it go for the time being – I do love and miss all of you –

With All My Love,
Your Dave

—

Tuesday – 13 February – 1945
Somewhere in Eastern France

My Dearest Darlings,

This afternoon, I got as busy as a butcher giving away rationless meat. The weather was as good as we could possibly want it to be and we really took advantage of it. There must have been every plane up in the air today and giving the Nazis a helluva time.

As to that picture that Max and I took in Naples, don't be misinformed by that background. Naples is not as bombed out as you may think. In fact, there is very little that is destroyed in comparison to the number of buildings there are there. The best part of it all was the airfield where all the buildings were smashed to bits, while just across the street, there are tenement houses that weren't even touched. It was a very good example of precision bombing. The towns that really were smashed were Civitavecchia, Terracina and

Littoria. Those were fair-sized cities that were smashed to bits by us. Those pictures of the female collaborationists were very mild to what I have been told about others around here.

I guess you were a little too optimistic in your guess that Breslau would fall in a few days. It still is fighting hard and will probably take as long as Budapest as it is a large city. With Budapest out of the way now, the Russians can send those troops on up forward. By now, you should have gotten over the frightened feeling due to the action that was around Colmar. As you know, the Nazis have been cleared out and we took a lot of prisoners – more than we should have taken.

So you sent me a B-29 kiss – Well, over here, we don't see many of that type, so it is a scarce and precious item. So you can see that I'll treasure that kiss a long time. I, in return, send you a P-47, P-51, P-38, P-61 and a nice Beaufighter kiss. Those ought to hold you for a little while.

Well, my Darlings, say "Hello" to all our friends and love to the folks – a great big hug and a twice as big kiss for Carole and you –

With All My Love,
Your Dave

———

Wednesday – 14 February – 1945
Somewhere in Eastern France

My Dearest, Sweetest Darlings,

After dinner, Fay asked me to go over to his girlfriend's house so as to explain why he hadn't been there in some time. We got there before his girl returned from work at the postal telegraph office, so we sat around and chewed the fat with the rest of the family. Well, I explained that he had just returned from Paris and was very busy, but would be back as soon as he had caught up with his work. After that, we decided to go on home – so we started out and were hailed by a voice in the dark. It turned out to be a G.I. who was sky-high and lost. He asked us the way to where we were going and we told him to hang on and we'd take him there. I don't know how in the world he would have found the place if somebody from there hadn't happened along. He hung his arms around Fay's and my shoulders and every 25 yards, he'd pass out and we'd have to revive him. Well, we finally got him back and had to haul him up four flights of stairs to his room. He'll probably be one sick Joe tomorrow.

I note that you have sent another salami, so thanks a million in advance. Are you sure that you aren't being too inconvenienced with the ration points to be buying a salami so often? I'd really not like to see that happen as, after all, there are many more than just me to consider – mostly the baby, who likes hamburger so much. So take it easy on the points for me.

As to the unfortunate incident that involved the Mougins, you certainly came close in your guess – How did you do it? As yet, I can't give you the full details, but it was an explosion and many were killed and injured – mostly due to glass. However, it was definitely not a flying bomb, as you had believed. At the time, I was on the road, far away from it – so I was really surprised to hear about it when I got back.

As to the new song, "Saturday Night is the Loneliest Night of the Week," I haven't heard it, but can appreciate it. Over here, we don't keep tab on the days – just the date and month and year. One day is just like all the rest to us.

(I just returned from the John) As to writing the Mougins a thank-you letter, there isn't any mail going to civilians yet, I don't think – that is, from the States. You may ask at the post office, however, and write to Madame et Mademoiselle Mougin – 33 Blvde. De Jean Jaures – Nancy, France. I'm sure that Janine would be able to understand your writing. As to your hope that she isn't too pretty, I'm afraid that that was up to Mother Nature and she was there ahead of you – Yes, she is attractive. However, I explained all about me being a married man with a very attractive wife and a very pretty daughter – so who'd want an old used man like me? As to all the French being so kind, I can't say that all are – but a good many of them are. If you show good intentions toward being kind to them, they will do the same for you. It may seem funny to you, but ever since Lafayette's time, the French and Americans were always friendly and had an unexplainable like for one another.

I guess that takes care of today's news. The War is still going along favorably and will continue to do so until the end. So regards to our friends – love to the folks – and tons of love and kisses for Carole Frances and you –
With All My Love,
Your Dave

Thursday – 15 February – 1945
Somewhere in Eastern France

My Most Adorable Wife and Baby,

There was a picture at the headquarters that sounded pretty good – "Yellow Canary" – an English picture with Anna Neagle and Richard Greene. However, the main reason for my going was that they also had a short subject that is put out for the G.I.'s dealing with our invasions and campaigns. They are really quite interesting and I often wonder if they are shown to the civilians also. There was another shortie that dealt with our invasion of Munda and showed how the workers in a medicinal supply firm aided in the campaign. It is quite effective if shown to the public.

So that story about me playing "ball" with the Passover eggs is still going strong – Well, at a time like this, it wouldn't be so funny – would it? Well, now I have another salami on the way – Hope that it gets here soon, as the warm weather will set in soon and they may begin to rot again in the hot holds of the ships. As to French fries, I never got them, but I did get some potato sticks – Are they the ones you mean? I'd like some more – if they aren't rationed. The oysters ought to hit the spot, as I haven't had any seafood since we left the States. Oh yes I did – on the Atlantic. One night, I snitched a can of shrimp from the steward and we did have a picnic.

Gee, I hope that champagne gets to you OK, as it is something that we are going to look forward to. That is indeed a good type and one of the best in France – so be careful when you open it and place it in the cellar – upside down or lying on its side.

War itself is bad enough, but even in peacetime, there are altogether too many tragedies. I recall one picture of a mother looking at the body of her 8-year-old son who was killed by a truck while riding on his sled. That picture really hit home and I couldn't stand to see it for any length of time – Perhaps you have seen that same picture in the papers. So please be as careful as possible and don't take any unnecessary chances in anything.

As to the stubborn resistance of the Germans, that is a subject that not many people know how to analyze, so I won't try. All that I'm interested in is the absolute defeat of those damned bastards and a permanent peace. With the Russians also pushing into the Southern part of Germany, there will be little left for the Nazi Party to flee into. I was pretty lucky, inasmuch as I guessed that the Big-3 were meeting on the Crimea somewhere. I had figured Sevastopol, as I hadn't even heard of Yalta.

Well, Darlings, that's about it for today – so regards to all and love to the folks and lots of love and kisses for Carole and you –
With All My Love,
Your Dave

———

Saturday – 17 February – 1945
Somewhere In Eastern France

My Most Adorable Wife and Baby,

As to that nurse's aid position, I'm dead set against that, as there are still so many single girls who could do that same job without calling on mothers with babies to take care of. So you keep on taking care of the baby and soon we'll all be together again and forget all about this separation.

This afternoon, I was kept busy with some paperwork and having to go on a supply run. In fact, this time it was very profitable, as I got all the campaign stars that we are authorized to wear now. We now have four stars in the theatre ribbon. There is a slight possibility that we may get another, according to reports. I'd just as soon be home without any stars and ribbons.

So you went to the Chase for a change – The last time that you were there was when Blu took you and your husband raised such a stink about it. Well, hope that you had a good time and enjoyed the dancing.

Well, Darlings, I guess we have reached the end of another day – so regards to all – and love to Mother and Dad – and I wish that I could tell you in person what I am wishing for you – a thousand hugs and kisses for Carole –
With All My Love,
Your Dave

———

Monday – 19 February – 1945
Somewhere in Eastern France

My Most Adorable Wife and Baby,

While at dinner this evening, I saw that there was to be one of the outstanding pictures this evening – so I went directly to the show from chow. I can truthfully say it was one of the best pictures that I have seen overseas – but not for all time. In fact, the acting by Ingrid Bergman was superb! Yes, it was "Saratoga Trunk." Gary Cooper was, of course, his usual self. So if you haven't seen it, try to do so when it comes to your neighborhood theatre or a reasonable facsimile. After it was all over, I felt a lot better than I felt before the show. This morning, I awoke with a clogged nose and a slight cough – so I hit for the nose drops, which I had taken the previous evening, and took them again. Also, this morning, I went to the medic who is attached to our outfit and he gave me some of our celebrated elixir of terpin hydrate of codeine. Well, all day, I had a clogged up head and nose, but after the show, it was a lot better. I'll take the drops again this evening and in the morning, I ought to be as good as almost new.

Tomorrow ought to be very good for flying. Incidentally, that was a shame that [Ivan] Chernyakhovsky was killed in Prussia. He was the youngest of all the Russian generals and a Jew. He certainly didn't take many prisoners either. After Koenigsberg would have fallen, he probably would have been made a marshal. Well, those are the unforeseen events of the War. There will no doubt be great tributes paid to him, now that he is dead – That is so common for public sentiment. If all tributes were paid during the time a person was alive, just think how much better it would make that person feel. Well, the Russian advance will go on in spite of it, and we will soon smash the Nazis to bits – so what is the difference of one man more or less? That is War – and there's not a damned thing to be done about it. I wonder what some of those people in the States, who had anti-Semitic feelings, will say about him and his ability. I suppose just as much as they say about the great Jewish physicians and lawyers.

Well, I guess that is about all for today – so regards to all – love to Mother and Dad – and a great big hug and kiss for the baby and you –

With All My Love,
Your Dave

Tuesday – 20 February – 1945
Somewhere in Eastern France

My Darling Amy and Carole Frances,
Well, the War news in the Pacific is sort of pressing the Russians on the front pages. With the new landings on Iwo Jima almost completed, we will be within range of Japan and we will be able to bomb and strafe her even more than we did in our recent, carrier-based attacks. Flying from land bases means so much more to a flyer. Even if the Japs decide to come out and attack us on those islands, it would expose their ships to attack and that is exactly what we'd like for them to do. So it remains to be seen whether or not they will place their remaining fleet in danger or allow the invasion of

the Volcano Islands to go on unopposed from Japan. I don't think that they will bring out their fleet until we approach the Japanese mainland again. So the War over there is fast approaching the attacking stage, instead of the regaining period through which we have been fighting since Pearl Harbor. I certainly hope that we get sent home for a rest after this European War is ended. At least it would be a vacation for those who deserved a rest long ago, and also for those who may be sent to the Pacific afterwards.

As to going to Paris, I still don't know when I'll get to go – but I do hope that it is nice if and when it happens.

Well, Darlings, say "Hello" to all our friends and love to the folks – a million hugs and kisses for Carole and you –
With All My Love,
Your Dave

———

Wednesday – 21 February – 1945
Somewhere in Eastern France
My Sweet Embraceable Two,

I awoke completely cleared of my cold – so that was a good start. This morning, an inspecting officer came in from the 64th headquarters and asked to inspect the Supply installations. I took him downstairs and showed him around. After we were all finished, he commented that everything was very nicely arranged; therefore, I suppose we passed the inspection.

This evening, I heard about a stage show that was in town this evening and tomorrow – so Mullen and I decided to take it in. It was held in the opera house and I must say that it was a very pretty place. Before the War, the opera must have been the place. They had a G.I. as the Master of Ceremonies and he was pretty good. The orchestra and all the entertainers were French, however, that was not a handicap, as all of them spoke English and were talented. There were four chorus girls, a few soloists, a couple of ballroom dancers, and a number of comic dancers. All in all, it was a very entertaining evening and it was the first ballroom dancers that I had seen since we were at the Chase together. The place was full of G.I.'s and a few nurses and Red Cross workers. I just came back from the show and I want to thank you for the very, very attractive Valentine card, which also came today with the letters. It was well-worded and I liked the postscript that you added, so after reading it over, I guess I'll be your Valentine – that is, if Carole Frances doesn't mind.

With all those things that you sent, including the Miracle Whip, cucumber pickles, herring spread, green tomatoes, shrimp and French fries, I ought to really have quite a time. I suppose the salamis are on their way also, so thanks a million in advance for all of it.

As you know by now, that champagne was originally bought for our little celebration over here, but that at the last minute, I changed my mind and sent it to you. Yes, it is forbidden to mail bottles of liquor – but I wanted to take that chance. Have you received it yet? As to receiving bottles – lots of men get them inside of loaves of bread or cake – so where there's a will, there's relatives.

As to that air attack that the Nazis put on, it never came near us – That was why I didn't have any comment to make. As to the War news, it seems that every commentator is of the same opinion that the Nazis will leave Berlin and set up the government in Munich. After all, Berlin is only an administration city and not one from which the Nazis are drawing a lot of War materials. In the South, they will have the Ruhr Valley closer to them and be able to continue to produce, even if Berlin did fall. Well, it is just a guess, but a better one than most.

Well, it is now about 11:00 P.M. and time for your ardent admirer to bring this letter to a close. So say "Hello" to all and love to the folks – and a great big hug and kiss for Carole and you – I do love and miss you two very much –

With All My Love,
Your Dave

⸻

Friday – 23 February – 1945
Somewhere in Eastern France

My Dearest Darlings,

Mmmmmmmm – That is good! What's good? Why, the kosher green tomatoes that I just received in the package that you sent. In fact, they will be gone by tomorrow at this same time. So far, I have given about eight fellows a helping and they all went for it in a big way, except the new fellow in Supply – George. I still have a few of the other Jewish fellows to give some to – So you can see that it will be gone before you even hear about my receiving the jar. It came in very nicely and everything was just as though they were brought in from the delicatessen. In fact, the dinner this evening was lousy, from all reports, so I stayed in and decided to eat the

French fries and some tomatoes. Gee, what a great treat those things are!
I'm saving the can of shrimp until I get the cocktail sauce – then it will be
gone in a jiffy, so if it isn't too much trouble, please duplicate the packages
that you have sent – the other two that you sent at the same time ought to
get here tomorrow.

At this time last year, we were in Oran and getting acquainted with a
War. To tell you the truth, the only thing we ever saw that had an inkling of
War to it was a reconnaissance plane that came over and the ack-ack drove
it away. However, in Italy, things got a bit warmer and we saw and heard
more as we were there longer. Just before the invasion of France, there was
a recon plane that came over the harbor at midnight each nite for about five
days. You could set your watch by the time that he came over – but he never
got anything, as he was driven off by ack-ack each time. That's about all that
I can tell you for the present.

As you have read in the papers, the invasion of Southern France was
comparatively easy and not much opposition met. Since then, you have been
getting good service from the newspapers on news coverage. So now we
are all waiting for the Russians to break out with a tremendous drive to
Berlin and cities to the South. It's beginning to seem that even my March
prediction is too soon for the War's end over here. With the rivers swelling,
a lot of unforeseen things come up and make it necessary to alter plans.
Anyway, we do know that it won't be too long before we will be stepping on
each and every Nazi. Today was a very pretty day and we gave Heinie hell.

So, my Sweethearts, we come to the end of another day and I am still
thinking of you and missing you more each day. Say "Hello" to all and send
my love to the folks – and a million hugs and a billion kisses for the baby
and you –
With All My Love,
Your Dave

———

Saturday – 24 February – 1945
Somewhere in Eastern France

My Sweet Embraceable Two,

I see that you had a nice blanket of snow recently at home, while in the
South, the rivers were climbing from the yearly thaws. I certainly hope that
Congress will provide some money for building levees along all those large
rivers, so that billions of dollars of damage won't be done each year. After

what has been spent on destruction in this War, a billion for a good purpose would be only a drop in the bucket.

As you see, we are advancing along the whole Western Front and it won't be too long before we will be on the banks of the Rhine. The crossing will be something of a major project and we'll do it. In the Iwo Jima islands, I was sorry to read about the high list of casualties that we suffered. However, I guess we had to take a chance to get as precious a land base as that – with three airfields. Well, when it is all over, we can look back and say that it wasn't all in vain.

Well, Darlings, regards to all and love to the folks – and lots and lots of love and kisses for the baby and you –

With All My Love,
Your Dave

———

Sunday – 25 February – 1945
Somewhere in Eastern France

My Darling Amy and Carole Frances,

It looks as though we are getting our Spring weather rather early this year, or else it is making up for the premature Winter that we had last Fall. Either way, it is a great break for us and we are really taking advantage of it in a big way. You have probably seen the results in newspapers in the number of planes that the various Air Force units are sending over. If the weather holds from now until Spring, we may end this thing in a big hurry.

So our darling daughter has another two teeth. She has been the best baby at all times – even when she was in pain. I still recall the time when she burned her leg on that hot pipe in Fresno – She didn't say a thing until that evening, when she tried to lie down in bed and it irritated her. She is a great kid and I'm very proud of her and the way in which you are bringing her up. It is a shame that there will be such a difference in her age and her brother or sister's.

Lt. Rodger may go to England soon – on pass. We are sending two men each week and he has put in his name to go next. As to me ever going, that is impossible, because Temple has the last say-so, and after the differences that we have had, I guess I'll be lucky to see Paris even. Well, what the hell's the difference? As long as I get home soon, I don't give a damn if I ever get to see either one. As you probably have heard by now, there is a lot of brown-nosing done in the Army – but here is one cookie who is not going to stoop to please anybody, just to get a favor. If he decides to place me on the England list or Paris – OK – If not, the hell with it.

Well, say "Hello" to all and love to the folks – and millions of hugs and kisses for Carole and you –

With All My Love,
Your Dave

———

Monday – 26 February – 1945
Somewhere in Eastern France

My Darlings,

I just got back from seeing "Mrs. Skeffington," [sic] with Bette Davis and Claude Rains. Amy, I thoroughly enjoyed it. The producers, a couple of Jewish brothers [Philip and Julius Epstein], *really took a chance in presenting the problem of the Jew into a motion picture. It is a delicate situation and it was handled very, very well. In fact, when Claude R. tries to tell his daughter about the advantages she would have by not following the Jewish faith, he is all tangled up. However, it is a forceful scene that should have impressed a lot of people who had anti-Semitic feelings. It made a deep impression on me, and I suppose on a lot of other Jewish people. I wonder what the effect was on others in the States. When Rains sits and plays with young Fannie, I nearly burst into tears, as it made me think so much of Carole Frances. She was about that same age in that scene. Then he said that a baby girl is always nice to have, as you can always kiss a girl – but when a boy gets old, you shake his hand. It was a very good picture.*

As I was going out of the show, I looked at this fellow and then looked away – Then I looked again and then I looked away – Then, the third time, he said, "Stoliar – what are you doing here?" He was a fellow whom I had known back home, but I couldn't remember his name. We stood around and talked for a long time. He was in Africa for a year with the G.I. Film Service. He lives outside of town, but works at the "Stars & Stripes" Building. He took me up there and showed me around the place where they show the pictures before releasing them to the various theatres. I was surprised that he remembered my first and last name, as I didn't ask him his until we said goodnight – Les Feldman. Anyway, we made a date to meet the next evening and make the rounds of the town. I guess I'll run into somebody everyplace I go. Gee, what price popularity! He asked me if I had fallen for any French girls yet. That was a laugh, as I explained that

I was married and had a baby girl about two years and eight months old. I showed him that portrait that I carry in my pocket and he was amazed.

It has turned warm again, but rather a bit misty and cloudy – just like Spring. With the good weather, you have probably noticed that our raids have been tremendous. We'll flatten every single military installation in Germany, even if it is a wall.

Well, Sweethearts, that is about the summary of the news for today and it was an unusual one. Say "Hello" to all and love to the folks – and lots and lots of hugs and kisses for the baby and you –

With All My Love,

Your Dave

———

Tuesday – 27 February – 1945
Somewhere in Eastern France

My Dearest Darlings,

I haven't received those other two packages that you mailed at the same time that you mailed the one that I have already received. I still have the can of shrimp, but no sauce as yet. Well, there are more important things in life than feeding my face.

In the evening, after chow, Fay and I decided to go down to meet Les Feldman. I was supposed to be at his place about 6:15 or 6:30 and I didn't show up until about a quarter to seven. Well, he had gone to chow and I didn't know whether he had figured that I couldn't make it or not, so we decided to go on to a show and try to call him tomorrow. I enjoyed "To Have Or Have Not" [sic] fairly much, but wasn't exactly impressed with the new star (?) Lauren Bacall. As for her singing, she should have stood in bed. I really don't care for her voice at all – It just doesn't have any appeal to me and I don't think that she'll stick, as it is just a passing fancy. Bogart, as usual, was good, but I'm getting tired of that same type of part. He is really getting to be typed. Gee, what a life! All I have to do is worry about the movies that they are showing here. Tomorrow they are having "Rhapsody in Blue" with Joan Leslie and a newcomer. We tried to get in this evening to see that, but the theatre was packed to capacity and men were standing all around the back. It must be a pretty good picture. Have you seen it as yet?

From the War news, we are doing OK in our drive to the East. Say, by the way, I saw a couple of Russian officers in town this evening and it's beginning to look like they mean business this time. Well, just as long as

they are on our side, everything's OK. I haven't seen a paper since Monday,
but I suppose that the War is still on. I have been reading a few articles on
the atrocities of the Japs and the Nazis from various magazines. At times,
I get so very hot at the very thought of these things that I want to shoot the
next Jerry prisoner that I see pass by. I have seen quite a lot of them lately,
too. We really do treat them far too humanely, as they don't appreciate that
sort of treatment and don't understand it. If we ruled them with an iron
fist, then perhaps they would realize that they have actually lost the War. I
also saw an article in the January issue of "Readers Digest" on the coddling
of German prisoners in the States, so it isn't just mine or other soldiers'
opinions on that same subject, but those in the States also.

It is a bit foggy and cold – so we may not have much aerial activity. The
news in the Pacific is still coming along satisfactorily – I hope that Paul
is safe, as he probably has seen quite a bit of action during the past three
months. Has Beulah been hearing regularly?

Well, Darlings, I guess that's about the news for today – so regards to all
and love to the folks – and millions of hugs and kisses for Carole and you – I
do love and miss you very much –
With All My Love,
Your Dave

———

Wednesday – 28 February – 1945
Somewhere in Eastern France
My Darling Wife and Baby,

I guess I had better give you my impression of "Rhapsody in Blue" before
I do anything else. It was a shame to end the picture, as we were always
looking further for something else to happen – But, after all, the hero did
die. The story is the life of George Gershwin and it is a very interesting one.
Each part was well acted and, at times, it would make you cry. The lead was
taken by a fellow named [Robert] *Alda, of whom I had never heard before.*
He turned out to be pretty good, too. If he can play the piano, he does it very
well. If not, it was a good cover-up.

I decided to go over and see the Mougins and explain why I hadn't been
over in a long while. Mrs. M. was the only one home, as Janine was at
the university and the sister in town. She told me that the plans for the
marriage are being put through at this moment. She also told me that
Janine must really be in love with this soldier, as the other day, a French

chemist, who comes from a well-to-do family, asked her to marry him and she refused. I hate to get involved in something like a marriage, but I suppose they have a lot of confidence in me and what I think and say about Americans and the States. We have even discussed the Jewish problem and they are intelligent in expressing their personal views. Anyway, they are getting pretty impatient now that the Allies are near Ludwigshafen, where her husband is a prisoner. I always insist that he will be coming home soon, which tends to brighten their lives a little more.

Well, when I got back here, I found that there was some mail and included were two packages for me. Everything came in very nicely and I have already opened one jar of pickles and offered half the contents to friends who went into ecstasy. I also opened the herring spread, as Ellison came in this evening (as I was writing this letter) and said that he was hungry and wanted a snack to eat. So we ate a bit of the herring and also opened the jar of Miracle Whip and had bread with that – not bad either. I'm going to hang on to the cans of shrimp until I get good and hungry at night – then I'll really have a picnic. I suppose that you have already taken for granted the fact that the package of potatoes has been devoured – Well, you can, as it is.

Incidentally, Maddox was over here today and passed right by me without saying a single word. He also went into the Orderly Room where Mullen was sitting and didn't say a word to him. That, I would say, is certainly a stupid thing for an officer to do. He ran into Micka at the Finance Office, where Micka was picking up our payroll – Maddox was picking up his for the outfit he is in now, so Micka invited him over for lunch. They are still very friendly with each other. Also, Micka made 1st Looie the other day and he is the thing now, so in spite of himself, he made 1st.

As to the packages, the next time that you send the funnies or magazine section, please don't tear it all up, as I'd like to read it. I like to see familiar scenes from St. Louis – It brings me right back there in a big hurry. I guess that about brings us to the end of the day – in news and time, as the clock just struck twelve in the steeple – so regards to all and love for Mother and Dad – beaucoup love and kisses for Carole and you –

With All My Love,
Your Dave

Thursday – 1 March – 1945
Somewhere in Eastern France

My Darling Sweethearts,

The first day of the new month started out like a typical Spring morning and the sun was out and blue skies above with a few white clouds. As you may have guessed, it was almost a perfect day for aircraft – and we did see plenty of heavies from England on their way to Germany. They just kept on coming, hours at a time. The fighters looked like tiny mosquitoes in Summer trying to get into the screen doors. It certainly is a fine spectacle to witness – especially if we are the ones who are doing the dropping. Then, in the afternoon, it clouded up a bit and the roar of the motors echoed more thunderously as they started for home. Well, it seemed as though God gave us just enough time to get up there and drop the bombs and get back, as it turned very cloudy later in the day and started to rain, so we were able to get in a good day's work after all.

Now for your letter – the day that the papers carried the story about the carrier attacks on Tokyo. I hope that Beulah has heard from Paul and that his ship came thru OK. As you had reasoned, it was a pre-invasion attempt. It was just a good beating, to let those damned slant-eyed bastards know that we mean business and will never rest until they are thoroughly defeated and driven back to their islands. As you know, we are nearing Cologne and Duisberg and Dusseldorf – all important manufacturing cities upon which Hitler is depending very much for munitions and other materiel for carrying on the War, even if Berlin does fall. If we push through that area as fast as the Russians took Silesia, the War will certainly come to an abrupt end. The reason that I think that we may be home this year is that even if we are transferred to the Pacific, we would probably get a thirty-day furlough back home – I hope. Perhaps Paul will be home even before I will, as after a certain number of months in action and on the sea, they are sent home for a rest. However, it would be nice if we were home at the same time.

As to those new songs, "Rum and Coca-Cola" and "Are You Livin' Old Man" – no, I haven't heard them or any other pieces in a long time. We don't have a radio anymore, because the officers need them in their quarters. Now do you see what I mean when I say that I don't want to be an officer? Why, just about two months ago, a letter came out from [General Dwight D.] Eisenhower, addressed to all officers, telling them to be more interested in the welfare of their enlisted men and then see about their own personal comforts. Well, that didn't apply to these officers, apparently, as it made them even more indifferent.

Thus we come to the end of another day. It was a happy one as long as I get mail from you and the planes are knocking the Nazis around. Hope that all is well back home. Say "Hello" to all and love to the folks – a great big hug and kiss for the baby and you –

With All My Love,
Your Dave

Friday – 2 March – 1945
Somewhere in Eastern France

My Darling Wife and Baby,

This morning it was beautiful out – the sun shining brightly – white clouds floating by – and a very pretty blue sky for a background. It was fairly warm and the planes were up in all their glory. As the day went further, it turned cooler and cloudier. In fact, at about five, it was grey and started to snow – That was really something. Well, it cleared up a bit in the evening and the sky was clear and each star was as bright as a Xmas-tree ornament. The moon was as bright as a flashlight and it was hard to even think that it had snowed only a few hours before.

In the afternoon, I decided to go over to the Mougins and tell them that I'd be there tomorrow evening instead of this evening, as I wanted to go to the show and see "Laura" with Fay. It was a pretty good picture and I liked it. It was a little different from the usual run of mysteries and it was amusing at the same time. If you will recall, the villain was Clifton Webb. He was an old musical-comedy star on Broadway and very funny. It was a different sort of a role for Dana Andrews and he did it well.

We're quickly doing away with the pickles, herring spread and one can of shrimp already. Everybody enjoyed it all and they are all, in turn, writing home for more of the same. So now the parents of a lot of gentiles are going to be surprised when they receive request after request for kosher foods from their sons who left eating only foods which they had always eaten. They'll probably think that the Army is starting to convert them. Oh well, c'est la guerre.

Well, be careful and take good care of yourselves – Say "Hello" to our friends and love to our folks – and a million hugs and kisses for Carole and you –

With All My Love,
Your Dave

Saturday – 3 March – 1945
Somewhere in Eastern France

My Most Adorable Darlings,

I just returned from visiting the Mougins and the time really went by in a hurry. Mrs. Mougin told me that Janine went to a doctor for a complete physical the other day and he found that she was anemic. He told them to try to get some milk, so as to fatten her up – but that is something that is very hard to find in the larger cities. The farmers just don't bring it in, as they haven't the means and don't want to go that far just to try to help the civilians in their cities. There is a definite feeling between the people who live in the country and in smaller towns and those who live in large cities – just as in the States, we'd say that one was a hick from the sticks. I was able to get a couple of cans of milk from the Mess Sergeant, which will be of some help to her. Mixed with water, it will be almost as good as fresh milk. She can add some chocolate to it and make it richer.

Well, we sat around and had schnapps and then cookies and coffee. Janine played the piano and she wasn't so bad. Her favorite composer is Chopin – I told her that our favorite was his "Nocturne," which was our wedding march. Incidentally, I meant to tell you that that was played by "George Gershwin" in that picture the other night. When I heard it, it made tears come to my eyes – I guess that I'm just an old softie after all. Well, after that, we discussed the military and political situation of the world. It seems that the people who were at one time well-to-do are fearful of France going Communist after this is over. On the other hand, the poor people are all for it. Therefore, the former want to have a republic in a hurry. They don't especially want De Gaulle, but as he is the only logical man for them at this moment, they will accept him as their leader. Since De Gaulle's visit to Moscow and Stalin, the leader of the Communist Party in France has returned to Paris and is one of the most popular men in the country now. That is a definite asset for that cause. So as the picture looks today, there will be a big discussion as to the future government of France after this is over.

I explained that you had asked if Janine was pretty, so they gave me a snap to send you, which I am enclosing. It is a fairly good one of her during the good days. So now you can judge for yourself. Anyway, it is purely on a friendly basis.

I guess that is about all the dope for today – so say "Hello" to all of our friends and love to the folks – oceans of love and barrels of kisses for Carole and you –

With All My Love,
Your Dave

————

Sunday – 4 March – 1945
Somewhere in Eastern France

My Darling Wife and Baby,

Fay and I just got back from the show, where we had gone with Les Feldman. We met him in front of the place at which he works and tried to get in to see Bob Hope in "The Princess and the Pirate," but the theatre was packed to capacity. Well, we then saw that "Bowery to Broadway" was also playing in town, so we went there. It was an amusing picture, but not extra-gigantic. Well, after the show, we all decided that a beer would come in handy – so there was a new G.I. place open where they had a band – so we went there and sat around until about 10:00. I got sleepy about then and so were the others, so we called it a day. When we got out, there was a nice drizzling rain to greet us, so Fay and I were soaking wet when we got back here. To offset the miserable weather, we made some hot chocolate and heated some cans of meat and spaghetti, which was really good. It is one of the new type of C-rations that the G.I.'s are getting. Other types are frankfurters and beans and meat and stew, which was one of the old favorites.

This morning, Lt. Micka called me in and told me that we were having a meeting with him, Capt. Temple, Mullen and the Motor Sergeant. Well, we all were wondering what it was all about and finally Temple arrived and we had our bull session. It was a result of the inspection that was made by one of the officers at headquarters. The list of discrepancies was read off and each man was asked to explain them in connection to his section. Well, when he came to Supply, the statement was that the Supply was found in excellent condition. It was at that point that Temple said that he usually calls me in to argue with, but this time, he was glad to hear that my section was on the ball. He also said that probably at times, I must have thought that I was on his ---- list and that at other times, he must have been on mine. I explained that I'd take him off mine if he'd give me a pass to Paris or England. Well, that was a humorous subject to him at that time, but I'm going to ask again.

Well, Darlings, I guess that is about the dope for today, so hope that all is well at home and that the buds are coming out on the trees in front of the house. Say "Hello" to everybody and love to the folks – a great big hug and a thousand kisses for the baby and you –

With All My Love,
Your Dave

———

Monday – 5 March – 1945
Somewhere in Eastern France

My Darling Amy and Carole Frances,

Today, I had occasion to go down to Temple's office and, while down there, I asked him about going to Paris. He said that his latest instructions to Mullen were to draw the names out of a bag – so it looks as though I'll not be going to Paris – You know what luck I have on drawings. I tried to get Mullen to consent to picking out my name in the next batch to go there, but he couldn't be influenced. With each and every succeeding thing that comes up in this Army, I get more and more impatient to get back home as a civilian again. There is just too much distinction being made between the officers and enlisted men to call ourselves a democratic nation or Army. It is just disgusting at times. The only ones to whom this does not apply, however, seem to be the men in the Infantry, who see that one's life is worthless without another man's consideration and respect, so one will go out of his way for the other, whether he is an enlisted man or an officer.

As you know, we are now perched on the Rhine along a front of about forty miles. With the cities of Duisberg, Dusseldorf and Cologne in our immediate advance, the Ruhr is almost around the corner. Of course, the bombings have about knocked out the industry, so the actual taking will only give us the possession of that area and a good opportunity to knock the Nazis out for good. So if we coordinate our drive from the Rhine with that of the Russians in the East, this thing ought to come to an abrupt end.

Well, Darlings, send regards to all and love to the folks – Hope that all is well back there and the weather better – love and hugs and kisses to Carole and you –

With All My Love,
Your Dave

———

Tuesday – 6 March – 1945
Somewhere in Eastern France

My Sweetest Sweethearts,

This morning, I happened to be in the Orderly Room when I was informed by Mullen that Temple had asked that I be sent to Paris in the next group going, which will be the 13th – next Tuesday. So it paid to speak to him after all. If it all goes thru, you can't say I didn't see Paris in the Spring. Of course, there won't be that old honk of the taxicab as there isn't gas to get them around, I don't think. Now I'll have to pinch each and every penny until I leave.

I decided to look up a tailor and see about getting my blouse tailored to fit and have it shortened to the new type. I found a shop and went in and asked if he could do that sort of work. He said that he could and I asked him in Yiddish, "Vee feel?" ["How much?"] Then he smiled and asked if I was also Jewish and we got to talking and it ended up with an invitation to dinner at any time that is convenient for me. I refused, as I wasn't able to tell them that I'd be there any certain day – so he said that any time that I decide to drop in, it would be OK with him. He also invited me to Passover dinner with him, so perhaps Les and I will go over there and visit him.

Well, what was your impression of that snap of Janine that I sent? Are you jealous or have you been convinced that she will be one of your friends in the days to come? I think that I know you well enough to be sure that you have already recognized her and her mother as good friends of the family, so if they do come to America after the War, you will be one of the first to ask them to visit us.

Hope that all is well back home – regards to all and love to the folks – Lots of love and hugs and kisses to Carole and you –
With All My Love,
Your Dave

Wednesday – 7 March – 1945
Somewhere in Eastern France

My Darling Angels,

This afternoon, we got in another Special Service radio for one that was on the bum due to bad tubes, which are irreplaceable over here – Isn't that just like the Army to pull a stunt like that? Anyway, it is a German radio and works very well. We just heard a "Mail Call" program that is a special program in which the artists are all requested by the G.I.'s who write in asking for them. This evening, it was Bing Crosby and Dorothy Lamour and Jerry Colonna. It was very entertaining after such a long time without hearing a radio. They just finished playing "At Last," with Glenn Miller's band. It's tough that he was lost at sea in that plane crash.

I still have the address of the Naval Officer who I met in Oran last year and he may be back in Paris at this time. It's a funny thing, but last year, at this time, we were sitting at a table in one of the better restaurants in Oran and he and his wife, in a joking manner, asked me when I thought we'd be in Paris. I thought for a moment and then, to make them feel good, I answered that Paris would be theirs for an Xmas present. Now that it has been returned to France, I suppose they may have remembered my guess. Anyway, I'll try to find them. (They are playing "Sweet Lailani" with Bing as the vocalist now – Mmmmm.)

Darling, you don't know how much I miss you each succeeding day. I know that you're not any too happy about it either, but I guess I have to let out steam every once in a while. I see French civilians out with their girls and I get that ol' feeling for you. In fact, when I saw "Guest in the House" the other day, it reminded me so much of you and me when we used to play around in the bedroom. Remember when we used to dance around without shoes? Well, Ralph Bellamy and Ruth Warwick did the same and I felt as if I was right there with you. I don't know – maybe I'm going nuts slowly.

Well, Darlings, I guess there isn't anything else to mention today – Take good care of yourselves and I'll be seeing you this year – lots of love and kisses for Carole and you –
With All My Love,
Your Dave

———

Thursday – 8 March – 1945
Somewhere in Eastern France
My Sweetest Darlings,
Your package arrived and I really tore into it. Everything in it came in perfectly, including the cans of oysters and tomato juice. Of course, the main thing was the well-preserved salami that looked as though it was taken out of a magazine advertisement. I, of course, couldn't wait to see if it was OK or not – so I cut off one of the ends and it was delicious. Now that I have it, I'll have to be a little more stingy with it. So far, Ellison was the only one

who has gotten any of it and what he cut off could take care of him for the rest of the year and a little over. Well, I guess I do have to share our good fortunes with each other, now that we are in the Army. Anyway, thanks a million for it and I hope that you weren't inconvenienced too much in ration stamps.

Last night, I was in the dayroom and was approached by a few of the fellows to get into a poker game. It was a small game – 10-15-25. After thinking about it, I decided to try to win some money for my Paris trip. Well, I got in and sat down and started to win at first, which was my usual bad luck sign and I ended up losing 18 dollars. I hope that you will excuse me, as it was the first time that I gambled since we landed at St. Tropez in September, so that isn't so bad, is it? Well, now I'll be a bit more sensible about it and forget about winning money. I'll just have to earn mine, I guess.

So we now have another White Castle from which we can get our ten-for-a-quarter specials on Friday nights – I can't wait to get home so that I can get in line. It's surprising that they were able to get building materials – Where will they get the meat now?

Well, Darlings, I love and miss you and Carole very much – Hope that all is well at home and that the weather is better – regards to all and love to the folks – hugs and kisses for the baby and you –

With All My Love,
Your Dave

———

Friday – 9 March – 1945
Somewhere in Eastern France

My Darling Sweethearts,

Do you recall my writing a letter to a party in Owensboro, Kentucky? Well, today I received an answer to that letter and they are in Evansville, Indiana now. The husband had moved from Kentucky about two years ago and the husband is now working in a P-47 plant. They were so very grateful to receive that letter from me that the writer of the letter started to write in French and English at the same time. You don't know how good it felt to have been able to reestablish contact with persons who may have been given up as dead long ago, when the Nazis marched into this area. It would be the same as if I arranged for your parents' folks to write to a relative in Hungary. Now I feel as though I have done some good in this War, if not *shooting a Nazi. I know that these people are going to be amazed that they have finally received a letter from their relatives.*

So you have finally received the bottle of champagne – officially. Now then, do you think that you will be able to set it upside down instead of on its side? I thought it over and I'm afraid that it may pop open from the heat in the Summer – what do you think? I'd hate to lose that, after getting it that far.

As to the clipping that you enclosed pertaining to the poisoned liquor, we were way ahead of the authorities, as we were warned a few days before that happened not to drink anything but beer – and I can assure you that we don't take any chances even now. We don't love liquor that much to endanger our lives.

As to Mal Kaufman's death, I can't picture it yet, as I always see him as a devil-may-care guy. I can imagine the shock that the parents felt when they were informed of Mal's death. I had known him a long time – about 14 years. In fact, he was in our old U. City fraternity. We were charter members. Mal is the second fellow who I have known to be killed – Darell Iskowitz being the first, on December 7th at Pearl Harbor.

Well, now that you have heard about my experiences overseas – you can see that it is pretty safe around here. It is really a shame that we may have to move out of here – and soon. After all, the War has moved up and we are behind too much now.

Take good care of yourselves, as you are my only wife and baby that I have for the time being. Hope that everybody else is well at home – regards to all and love to the folks – lots and lots of love and kisses for Carole and you –

With All My Love,
Your Dave

———

Saturday – 10 March – 1945
Somewhere in Eastern France

My Darling Amy and Carole Frances,

I went over to those people's home to give them the letter. You cannot picture the joy and gratitude that these people felt when I gave them the letter. They asked me to come up for a dinner sometime, but I refused, as I have felt that it is a great hardship on them and we have enough food for the G.I.'s without going to the civilians for food. I told them I would come back Monday evening for a chat and drink.

Today was my day off, so I went over to the place where I bought that champagne and got a bottle of Moet-Chandon again. I wrapped it up in paper and walked over to the Mougins' house. Janine seems to be a bit better now that she has had a bit of milk and chocolate. I will see them before I leave for Paris and also after I return. I gave them the bottle of champagne and told them it was for the family for the day that Mr. Mougin returns.

Well, so our baby has started to answer back! I was surprised to hear that she had told your dad that only her mother could spank her. Please be careful and don't let her get out of hand, now that she is such a likeable child. Thank you for excusing me for getting tight that night when I heaved – It was the last, too.

As to those men who were transferred to the Infantry last month, they were Angelo and the married fellow with a child. We have received a letter from each and they are both feeling OK and in training at this moment – I hope that the War ends before they get up front. Incidentally, we have sent two more this month who are leaving Wednesday. They are both single and young, which isn't as bad as the other two. Anyway, I hope that none of them ever gets to see real action. It's just like waiting to be drafted again.

I knew that you were being shown some films of the various invasions, but didn't know if they were the same as the ones that we see. The ones that you mentioned sounded very familiar to me, so I think that I have seen them.

Hey, today I asked the wine dealer if it was better to stand the bottle of champagne on end or on its side and he said that on its side was the best – so please turn it back over on its side again, as you had it before – I am very sorry that it happened; it won't happen again.

Well, say "Hello" to all and love to the folks – millions of tons of kisses and a great big hug for you and the baby –

With All My Love,
Your Dave

———

Monday – 12 March – 1945
Somewhere in Eastern France

My Darling Wife and Baby,

Yesterday was Fay's birthday and I wanted to help him celebrate it before I left. We are leaving this evening, which made it impossible to go with him to dinner, so instead, I went out to this place where I bought the champagne and got another bottle. I explained that I had a small party planned. We *would go over to the Mougins' first, as I told them I would drop in before I left for Paris. After that, we went to a bar and had a couple of white wines and then went to the Red Cross. They weren't selling coffee and doughnuts at this time, as the machine was broken down – so we listened to a G.I. play the piano for a while. It was about time for the show to begin, so we went in and saw "None But The Lonely Heart," with Cary Grant and Ethel Barrymore. It was a difficult type of story to understand, as it was Clifford Odets. It was a very philosophical picture in which Odets spoke his own thoughts about life and its burdens. That was not the type of picture to send overseas to men who are looking for enjoyment and light stuff. In the States, it may have been a great picture, but over here, I'm afraid that it was a stinkeroo. The acting was good, but the story was too deep.*

Well, we got out about 11:00 and walked back here. We met in the Supply Office where I made a couple of healthy salami sandwiches with some white bread that we had picked up at the Mess Hall on our way back here. That was our evening celebration, with the bottle of champagne thrown in as the washer-downer. We sat around and talked until about 12:30 and we were both ready for bed – so I congratulated him on his twenty-second birthday and we hit the hay.

Your letter said that it was now confirmed that the new offensive by the Allies was under way – Well, you now know how far we have pushed. That taking of that bridge at Remagen was a godsend and will shorten the War a great deal and save us a lot of lives. So it looks like this is it from both sides. The Russians will burst thru any moment and go right into Berlin. With the attacks on Tokyo mounting, we're at the best stage of the War we have ever been.

Well, Darlings, that is about it for today, so send regards to all and love to the folks – a million and one hugs and kisses for Carole and you –
With All My Love,
Your Dave

———

Friday – 16 March – 1945
Somewhere in Eastern France

My Dearest Darlings,

Well, here I am, back in the old corral and trying to recuperate from our recent trip to Paris. I can tell you in one sentence that there is, without a doubt, no other city in the world like it. I had no idea that a city could be so beautiful, modern, old, lively and refreshing. In fact, if I were to ever leave the States to live somewhere else, that would be the only place to go.

There were three of us who went from our outfit and I was in charge of them, as I was the highest in rank. We got our reservations at the best hotel in Paris – The Grand Hotel – and it was gorgeous! During peace times, it must have been the place. Well, as long as there were three of us, we got a room with three beds and a bathroom. As a rule, the single rooms don't have toilets – just douche basins, which are standard equipment in all homes in France. We were lucky enough to get a toilet and a tub in ours. Well, after we got all washed up, we went to the quay along the Northern side of the Seine and drove along until we came to Champs Elysees, where we drove down until we came to the Arc de Triomphe. We got out of the bus and saluted the Grave of the Unknown Soldier, which lies directly under the Arc. There are fresh flowers on the tomb each day and an ever-burning flame above it.

From there, we drove over to the Isle de la Cite, where the Notre Dame Cathedral is located on an island in the Seine. I had no idea that it could be so ornate. The original gargoyles are there, sticking their heads and necks out from the pillars as you may remember from the picture, "The Hunchback of Notre Dame." Bishops of great renown are buried there, along with some of the Kings of France including St. Louis. He seems to have been the one who was the most responsible for the beautiful churches and artistic decorations all over Paris. We got back just in time to get some late lunch at the hotel. We went into the dining room, which is absolutely beautiful, and sat down at tables with white tablecloths on them. We were served by waitresses and ate each thing off of plates – Ah, what remembrances of home! The food was delicious and we were able to get seconds on anything – and we did.

The next morning, we drove out to Versailles. On the way, we passed the Renault factories. They were the ones that were producing so much materiel for the Nazis when they occupied Paris. The plants had been bombed time and again, and were very good examples of precision bombing. The houses on the opposite side of the street weren't touched at all, except from the concussion. Well, we arrived at the palace grounds and parked in front of them. We all got out and stood behind the statue of Louis XIV, which is shown mounted on a great base just as you get there. The guide had a picture made of the group that was on tour at that time. It so happened that I was down in the lavatory when they all assembled to take the picture and was the last one up – That explains why I was on the end.

Well, we went back to the hotel, where we had dinner and then washed up, so as to be ready for the show that night – the Casino de Paris. We had some very good loges seats, so that we didn't have to stretch our necks to see the things we wanted to see. There they were – well-developed breasts dancing around before your very eyes. The chorus always came out with nothing over their breasts except when they did a high-class number, which wasn't often. There was one act where the woman had nothing on except a very, very small G-string. She danced with a couple of men, who threw her all over the stage and had their hands all over her body – It was really something to see. Well, there was also an act that showed a couple of lesbians, too. You know, women who were queer – and one marries a man and the other dies of a broken heart. We got back to the hotel at about midnight and hit the hay.

The next morning, we got up and I decided to try to locate that fellow and his wife whom I had met in Oran. I took the subway out to that section of town and walked a few blocks until I located the address. However, nobody knew of him and I asked a number of neighborhood stores, but they didn't know of that name either. At least I tried. About that time, we all had to vacate our room as all rooms have to be cleared by 11:00 of the morning that you leave – so we left our things at the checkroom and ate lunch. After that, we went out to Le Borgiet Field where Lindbergh landed in the Spirit of St. Louis in 1927. It was bombed to bits and now is being fixed up to look like new.

Well, we found that there was a plane leaving in about thirty minutes for a town North of us about 65 miles. My feet were killing me, as it had turned very warm during the time that we were in Paris and from all the walking, I had a couple of blisters on the bottom of my left one, so I took off my shoes in the plane and was so comfortable that I went to sleep, lying across three seats. I awoke just in time to see him buzz the field just before landing. If you've ever seen a plane swoop down and almost hit the ground and then all at once go up into a steep climb – that is a buzz. Anyway, it was a very neat landing after that. We got a ride with a French civilian about twenty miles and then we dropped off to wait for another ride. We caught a G.I. truck and really froze, as it was wide open and we had to sit in the back. We got here about eight in the evening and had to walk from the edge of town up to our area.

So it took us only an hour to get from Paris to this place North of us and three and a half hours to get down here. We were one sad sack lot of boys when we finally got in. We were dusty from the roads and hadn't eaten any dinner that evening, so I immediately washed up a bit and heated some frankfurters and beans and made some hot chocolate to go with it. That really hit the spot! Then I went down to the shower room and washed off all the dust of the day's traveling. From there, I immediately hit the hay and didn't awaken until this morning. So there you have the events of the past few days.

Well, until later this evening, I guess I'll say "So long" and send you all my love and beaucoup hugs and kisses –

Forever Yours,
Dave

———

Friday – 16 March – 1945
Somewhere in Eastern France

My Darling Wife and Baby,

As to you being pregnant via a dream – I really can't say that I'd relish the idea. After all, there is nothing that can replace the real McCoy. As to the list of possibilities of what will happen after the War in Europe is ended, I think that we have a good chance to go back to the States first for a 30-day furlough and then go to the Pacific Theatre. That seems to be the best guess – and the second would be to go directly to the Pacific. Of course, anything could happen in the Army and it wouldn't surprise me one bit, so don't put too much faith in anything and just take things as they come. I wish that I could tell you when we will be back to normal life – I was just thinking about that the other day. It is something that everybody is thinking about and waiting for, but nobody can answer correctly. As to entertaining you next year in a better style than that which you were entertained in this year for your birthday, I can assure you that if I am in the States, you will absolutely have a better time than you had this year.

Your letter spoke of Manila and Berlin burning – What do you think of Japan's main cities and how they are really blazing? Gosh, I hope that every square inch of the island burns down to the sea. The effects of our bombing are probably far better than we ever anticipated. When they have to evacuate five of the largest cities – there must have been some great damage done. When this is all over in Europe, they will get even a larger-scale bombing than they ever figured on. Why, the Berlin bombings will seem like child's play. Can you picture about 4,000 bombers and about 5,000 fighter-bombers over Japan at the same time? Why, it would just about wipe Tokyo off the map, if they bombed that target at one time. So, with a concentration on the Japs after this War, it shouldn't take over a year to finish them off in a hurry.

Meanwhile, say "Hello" to all of our friends – love to the folks – and a lot of hugs and kisses for you and the baby –
With All My Love,
Your Dave

————

Sunday – 18 March – 1945
Somewhere in Eastern France
My Darling Sweethearts,

It seems that everybody was out today walking around in their Easter outfits. I suppose we'll be wearing the same matching ensemble that we wore last year – and the year before that. Well, it can't last forever. Anyway, while driving thru town, I decided to pass the Mougins' home to see if they were in. I saw Janine on the sidewalk and I told her that I'd be over this evening for a visit. Then I came back here and saw that woman who has a relative in Indiana and to whom I had given that letter. She asked me when I was going to drop in and visit – so I decided to take her up on it for tomorrow evening. Gee, what a social lion I'm getting to be!

As to that batch of Tollhouse cookies that you sent from Michigan, I'm sorry, but they never did get here. Maybe the package is still somewhere in Italy being forwarded to various Replacement Depots. If you want a request now and not at the end of the letter – here it is: Some jars of pickled tomatoes and kosher pickles; cans of shrimp and oysters; jars of barbecue sauce; and potato chips. Is that enough for one time?

Holy smokes! Do you mean to tell me that you had to pay a fellow a dollar to brush the snow off the walks and driveway? That's outrageous! I remember when a quarter was good pay for that type of work. He must have really made a haul that day.

Has Beulah received any more mail from Paul since the Iwo Jima landings and fight? She must go thru hell every time she reads about another great air attack or invasion in the Pacific. As to the War situation, you can see how very important the Remagen crossing is from the attention that the Nazis have paid to it by their air attempts and counterattacks. It was the luckiest break of the War since the invasion of Normandy. Without that, we would still probably be seeking a potential spot through which to break – let alone land on. As we are already on the superhighway, it won't be long before we are attacking the Ruhr from that side of the Rhine. As to the Russians, don't think that they are laying down on the job – They are just as anxious to get this over with as we and are doing it their own way. However, as far as getting Victory for you as my birthday present, that seems impossible, as the 28th is only 10 days away. However, I'll gladly accept it as a Father's Day gift, as we did in Rome.

I hope that all is well at home. I know that you are doing wonderfully with our daughter – so say "Hello" to all and love to the folks. Lots and lots of love and kisses to you and the baby –

With All My Love,

Your Dave

———

Monday – 19 – March – 1945

Somewhere in Eastern France

My Sweetest Wife and Baby,

Well, I just got back from an afternoon show – I saw "Song to Remember," with Merle Oberon and Paul Muni. It was in Technicolor and very enjoyable. Muni was very good, as usual, and Oberon was good, too. The fellow who took the part of Chopin [Cornel Wilde] *was fairly good, too. So all in all, it was entertaining.*

Last night, I went to visit the Mougins as I had planned and got there about 7:30. Mrs. Mougin asked me if I wanted another souvenir of France – a piece of one of the stars of France. I was in a daze for a moment, and then she explained that while they were down in Nice, they met a friend who had seen a meteor fall in that vicinity. He picked up some of the pieces, which I have wrapped up and sent on to you. She told me that a professor at the university at Nancy has been anxious to get hold of one of these pieces to have on display in his department – but they have refused to give it up. However, he did an analysis on it and found that most of it consisted of sulphur and iron. Then came the surprise of the evening. Janine opened a package and gave it to me, saying that it was a remembrance for Carole Frances. I was speechless, as I hadn't expected anything like that to happen. It is a very pretty, tiny-linked necklace made of gold. Here is the amazing thing – In order to buy some object made of gold or silver in France, one must have the same or in some cases twice as much of that metal to trade in, so they must have given some gold article in exchange for the necklace. I couldn't thank them enough for it and was sorry that they had to make a sacrifice in order to get it. We had a cup of coffee and a dish of pudding and then I had to leave. It was 11:00 – the curfew time for G.I.'s, so I really had to step on it to get back here before the M.P.'s picked me up.

Did you enjoy seeing Jose Iturbi? I'm sure that you must have. Did he play Chopin's "Nocturne"? Whenever I hear that, it brings duck-bumps all over my body – You, too? I guess all our moments together will always bring a sensation to us. When he played it in the picture this afternoon, I was having a hard time seeing the picture clearly. Are they showing "Saratoga Trunk" yet at home? Don't miss it. I see that Bergman got the Academy Award for "Gaslight" – Well, she will give them a run for their money from her performance in this one also. However, as to Crosby and Fitzgerald for their picture, I can't see it. Somebody pulled some strings somewhere.

Thanks for your permission to go out and get "stinko" when the War comes to an end – I doubt if I'll take advantage of it, however, as you feel so bad that morning after. So I'll take a rain check on it for the time when we are together back home.

Well, Darlings, that bring us to the close of another day and I have to get ready to go over to that house to see those people for whom I wrote to the States. I told them that I'd be there this evening at eight – so regards to all and love to the folks – lots and lots of hugs and kisses for you and the baby –

With All My Love,
Your Dave

———

Tuesday – 20 March – 1945
Somewhere in Eastern France

My Dearest Amy and Carole Frances,

The War news was certainly good today, as we have pushed the Nazis completely out of France and we are now fighting completely on German soil. That, in itself, is a very important psychological factor. From now on in, all the damage done through land battles will be that much more of a reminder to the Germans in the future that they lost this War. The 3rd Army is really pouring it on them and it will not be very long before we will have pocketed up another army or two between the Rhine and Saar Rivers. With the 7th pushing up towards Ludwigshafen, perhaps Mr. Mougin will be home before long. I know that these recent advances have brought a lot of *hope and enthusiasm to the Mougins. It would be nice if he was found there and in good health. I do hope, for their sakes, that he is still alive and will be back here soon. There are so many different opinions lately about the end of the War that I don't want to say a thing on that subject. There is no doubt in my mind that it will be over within two months, so by the time this letter reaches you, it will be a month and a half.*

When I opened the envelope of your letter, it smelled of perfume and it still smells nicely – Did you pour any on it purposely? As to the packages that you sent, I appreciate them very much – however, I was sorry to see that you sent some soluble [instant] coffee, because we can get as much of that as we please. Of course, you didn't know that – but try to get the things that I ask for. As to tuna or salmon, don't send any of either in the future, as I don't like it. Also, if possible, send potato chips instead of the pretzels, as we can get pretzels over here. It isn't that I don't appreciate these things – it's just that the same space could be used for something that I'd want more.

Well, so I have a double! That gives me an idea. Maybe he can take my place in the Army and serve out the rest of my time, while I take up butchering. I hope that you didn't tell him that he looks like your husband – That would certainly be a good excuse to get acquainted. However, as long as he is a butcher, he has as many women trying to gain his favor, in order to get some steaks, as he can handle. I'm only kidding – but that is a coincidence.

Well, say "Hello" to all and send love to the folks – and for the baby and you, a thousand and one hugs and kisses –

With All My Love,
Your Dave

———

Wednesday – 21 March – 1945
Somewhere in Eastern France

My Dearest Darlings,

Today, I left here at eight and drove in a drizzling rain for about forty miles Northward. I drove thru areas that were battlefields not so long before. There were fields all pocked with bomb craters, broken field pieces, tanks, and pillboxes. When you see all the materiel that the Nazis have lost just in this little sector, it is difficult to believe that they are still putting up a fight. Why, there were even frozen cows lying all over the area. As I approached the village, the people would look at me as though I was a criminal who had purposely destroyed their homes. You see, when the Nazis were in control, they didn't even see the farmers, except occasionally to take away some milk, butter, cheese, cows, and vegetables. All the other times, the farmers were left alone to take care of themselves – so these farmers had no grievances with the Nazis. On the other hand, in the cities, it was a lot harder, as the people couldn't get out into the country to buy the necessities of life from the farmers – the Nazis tying up all the gas and automobiles. When the Nazis left, they took all stocks of food that they had stored away just for such a day and shipped it to Germany for all the soldiers and civilians there.

This, of course, made it doubly hard on the Allies when they arrived. We have had to build up a food stock and try to get the farmers to go into the cities to sell their products to the civilians there. Well, the farmers have since found that they can get more for their products on the black market, so it doesn't make a bit of difference to them if they ever get back into the city again. So as I went into the small villages, that was the types of people I would see staring me in the face. That is what is wrong with them – They don't care one iota for the rest of the French people. They just see that their homes were shelled and destroyed and their lands torn up and want to blame the ones who had done it – not the ones who had caused it to be done. That is why France will have to be educated in the post–War plans. The schooling will have to include the children of the farmers, so that they can understand what is taking place in their country and around it. I can't help but feel that they are right in their attitude towards us, but at the same time, if they only knew the real truth about the War, they would cheer us as we came thru, instead of looking incriminatingly at us.

I say this only about that part of France that I had gone thru today, as it is right near the German border and the Germans have always been a great influence on them. In fact, the buildings are not even French in design, but German. The people don't speak French up there, but German. They don't even look like French, but like Germans. They are the most dismal-looking people you have ever seen. I don't know what it is – but they are as different from the French as the people here are from those in Paris. Their dress is drab and dark, while the French always go in for colors. Now you can see why the Saar region has been such a problem and will remain so until the people have been educated.

Well, to get on with my story, I got to my destination at about 11:30 and then had to go to Metz. I was about 25 or 30 miles from the front at the place I had to go – but I didn't hear a thing as the War is going along much too fast. In fact, the radio just announced that the 3rd Army is only four miles from Ludwigshafen – You can imagine what a feeling the Mougins are experiencing at this time. Perhaps they will have Mr. Mougin back long before they had anticipated. I do hope that I will be able to see him before I leave here.

The headlines in the "Stars & Stripes" said that Worms had fallen – That was some drive, as the last I had heard was that they were in Mainz. If the advance continues at that rate, we will have the whole Western side of the Rhine cleared by Saturday, the 23rd. You probably haven't noticed that nothing has been said about the British and Canadian armies lately, however, don't forget that they are still up there and will soon be on the move as quickly as we are going. [Field Marshal Bernard] *Montgomery is nobody's fool and when he is ready to take off, you can rest assured that he will really go. So, all in all, the War news is getting better and better each succeeding day. Now if the rumor factories at home would stop giving out with what will happen to the troops in this theatre after the War is over, we'd all feel a lot better. When that time comes, we will worry about it, so why can't they let it alone for a little while?*

It's beginning to look as though your bridge club is on its last legs, with you always having such a difficult time getting the girls together. If I had known far enough in advance what you were going to serve, such as egg salad sandwiches on finger rolls, potato chips, pickles, tart and Pepsi-Cola, I'd be there to take a place in the game. Gee, what a time I'd have with seven women whose husbands weren't around! Do you mean to tell me that you are still able to get Pepsi-Cola – by the case, too? Holy smoke, what I wouldn't give for a Pepsi-Cola! Say, send that in to the bottlers and they may decide to send me a case each week – prepaid. You don't think that I'm going batty, do you?

As to commenting on your way of bringing up our brilliant daughter, I wasn't trying to hand you a compliment. I really meant it and it was the truth – so why try to get away from the truth? I have often thought about the difficult times you must have in being both a mother and a father. It is a job that I wouldn't relish and would probably boob up. So thanks again for the very incomparable manner in which our daughter is growing up. If you think that I'll mind when you turn her over to me for the day – you are as badly mistaken as you will ever be. There used to be a different meaning to "Just wait until I get my hands on you" – but it is another thing now. So thus, we come to the end of another day and we will be seeing each other sooner than yesterday. What a mathematician!

Well, say "Hello" to all and love to the folks – and a whole boatload of hugs and kisses for the baby and you –

With all My Love,

Your Dave

P.S. The 3rd has taken Ludwigshafen according to another dispatch – so I'll drop in on the Mougins tomorrow, as it will be an occasion.

———

Thursday – 22 March – 1945
Somewhere in Eastern France

My Most Adorable Darlings,

On the way back from where I had to go this morning, I decided to stop in and see the Mougins and extend my heartfelt wishes for a very sudden return by Mr. Mougin. They, of course, were all atwitter and getting the house in shape – giving it a real Spring cleaning. It will be a very great disappointment to them if he doesn't get back within the next month. I told them that I expect to be on hand when he gets in and they said that they will go out and drag me in to celebrate the homecoming when it comes off. It will make a difference in life and despair to them, I'm sure.

Well, this evening, I decided to take in a show, so I went to see "The Thin Man Goes Home," which was not any too good and I think that that one will probably be the last of the "Thin Man." It was very corny in places and not as interesting as their other pictures had been. I suppose that we have to expect that, as they aren't getting any younger. On the way back from the show, I met another fellow from our outfit who lives in Kansas City. We got to talking and I happened to mention the fact that I didn't get any mail today and wondered if he had. He said that he hadn't received any in a month, as he doesn't write often. That sort of surprised me, as he is single and young, and I asked him if his parents don't worry about him. He answered that he wrote them about the sort of work he does and that now they don't worry about him, even if it means only one letter per month. I then asked him if he didn't have a girlfriend and if she didn't ask him to write more often. He said that it was a very delicate subject and that he didn't want to speak of it – so I let it go at that. It's amazing how infrequently some of these fellows write. If I was one of them, I'd be in a helluva mental state. I don't know what their conditions were at home, but one would certainly think that just a letter a week wouldn't be too much to ask of them. Oh well, I have my own worries.

By the way, I finally heard that "Hit Parade" leader, "Don't Fence Me In" in one of the movies and I thought that it absolutely stunk. I can't see how in the world it could have possibly been a hit, but maybe that is one of the reasons that they are bringing back the old but good ones.

I just heard over the radio that they haven't quite taken all of Ludwigshafen – so I may have been a little premature in my visit to the Mougins. In spite of that, the 3rd Army will have taken it by tomorrow or tonight – so I won't worry. The War in the Pacific has been really good lately. With that recent carrier attack on Japan, Beulah was probably wondering what shape Paul was in. I hope that his ship came thru OK and he also. That was a terrific blow to the Jap navy, as they had already suffered such great losses in their attempt to prevent the landings at Leyte. Well, it can't be too long before it will end over there, too. Of course, it will be long after this one is over.

I have an American station on the radio now and am waiting to hear which station it is. It is the first one that I have heard since we were in the Naples area last April. Gee, of all the breaks in the world! It is from New York and they just began a new program dedicated to men in different cities. All of a sudden, a voice piped up, "Are you from St. Louis?" They are having this evening's program for us – Can you imagine me getting to hear this? They started from Grand and Olive and went on downtown past the Missouri-Pacific Building, the Auditorium and so many other old favorite spots of ours. They are in the mayor's office now and he is giving us all the old sales talk about how welcome we will all be when we come home. They stopped at Tune Town to broadcast some music by Bunny Berigan's orchestra, which is there at this time. Of course, it was all a prerecorded program from St. Louis, as it would take them too long to go around town and broadcast on the way. [Sportscaster] France Laux is now speaking about the baseball prospects. The cab driver is supposed to be taking them to the Union Station after it has been redecorated. They just went from the Statler to the Chase. They went up to the Zodiac Room, then they mentioned going to Garavelli's for a roast beef and a bottle of beer – a hamburger at Bill Medart's – and introduced the Washington Hatchet Queen, who said that the song fellows from St. Louis would want to hear the most was "St. Louis Blues" – so Ben Feld played it. I still can't get over it.

*Well, it is now midnight – so I had better get to sleep – so regards to
everybody – lots of love and kisses for the baby and you –*
With All My Love,
Your Dave
P.S. I do love you very much.

———

Friday – 23 March – 1945
Somewhere in Eastern France
My Darling Sweethearts,
    *As to us having a honeymoon all over again – that is not a bad idea at
all. In fact, think it over and maybe we will. We could take the baby with
us without any difficulty at all. Gee, what a time she would have with us!*
    *So you thought Janine was a bit big in the hips – Well, she is anything
but that, as she weighs about 100 lbs. at the most. No, I didn't pick her up.
As to building up her strength, no, they aren't able to get any liver around
here – let alone meat of any kind. They are allowed 50 grams of meat each
week per person – That isn't much. It is just a tough situation and one which
they will have to work out. As to her going to see that movie dealing with
the life of Chopin, I'm afraid that that is something that will never happen
until Mr. Mougin returns. They have just declined all sorts of recreation
and amusements until he comes back. I have been trying to talk them out of
that idea – but it's a delicate subject.*
    *Yes, the Navy men do get home sooner and more often than the Army men
– Don't ask me why. Paul ought to be home pretty soon. That will be a tough
nut to crack – going back to the Pacific Theatre after coming back home.*
    *Well, so my birthday is to be on the first night of Passover – I didn't know
that. So far, I have received three invitations to have Passover supper at
different homes – however, I don't know if I will take advantage of them.
Joe Dines and Ellison want to go with me if I do go.*
    *Well, well, so our daughter is starting to notice things – such as two sexes.
That is sort of rushing things a bit – isn't it? Maybe you ought to tell her the
facts of life. She'd probably come back with something like – "You can't kid
me – I wasn't found in a rosebud."*
    *Well, Darlings, love to the folks and regards to all our friends – and lots of
love, hugs and kisses for you and Carole Frances –*
With All My Love,
Your Dave

———

Saturday – 24 March – 1945
Somewhere in Eastern France

My Most Lovable Wife and Baby,

*It looks like this is the push that I had told you about – Montgomery's. He is on the Eastern side of the Rhine and not having too much trouble. Now that we have three or more armies on that side, it will not be too long before we can write this one off the books. The Russians are just starting to pick up momentum and it won't be a matter of over a week before they are nearing the Austrian border and pointing towards Vienna. Along with the satisfactory gains in the Pacific, we aren't doing any too bad at all. We are still enjoying very wonderful weather and the planes are taking advantage of each and every good flying hour. It's a great and wonderful feeling to see them going over to bomb the Heinies day after day. One thing is definite – The Germans will know that they have lost the War of destruction after seeing their cities in ruins. Of course, the after-effects of the War are still to be seen. However, as far as we are concerned, I can assure you that I won't even spit on them if they are dying of thirst. There is no death too bad for all of them – the dirty *@&#X&Z.*

Well, Darlings, regards to all and love to the folks. A million and one hugs and kisses for the baby and you –

With All My Love,
Your Dave

———

Monday – 26 March – 1945
Somewhere in Eastern France

My Beloved Wife and Baby,

Last night, Fay, Dines, Les and I met at Les' place and decided to go to see "A Tree Grows in Brooklyn" with Dorothy Maguire and Joan Blondell. Well, we had to stand in line and wait for the earlier show to let out. The next show was to have begun at 8:00. We waited until about 8:30 and the show still wasn't over, so we pushed our way into the show and found seats. We got in at about the halfway mark, so it wasn't as entertaining as it might have been. Well, after the picture ended, we had to wait for the second show to begin – That was about 9:45 and it was very warm there. Well, as you may have suspected, I had one heck of a time staying awake and my head nodded time and again until I couldn't do a thing but close my eyes for a moment, which was, in reality, a few minutes. When the picture came to the point where we had come in on the first show, we decided to get out and in a hurry. To add to our discomfort, the film broke at one time or another or the power went on the bum – so it was certainly not a good show.

We got back to our place at about 11:00 and we immediately went into the Supply Office and sliced up some bread and had some butter and Joe Dines brought down some pickled herring that he had received. Then came the real celebration – We opened a bottle of champagne and Louie, Dines, Fay and I bid Louie and Dines a very happy birthday and may they not celebrate any more in the Army. We sat around and listened to the radio and then hit the hay at about 12:30 and I was tired. So there you have our evening and the reason why I didn't write you last night. Am I excused? Thanks.

Well, today, we received some assorted liquors including Benedictine, white wine, eau-de-vie, cognac, Armagnac, vodka, and I guess that's about all. We received this all from captured Nazi stocks and it is to be used only for entertainments, so we are going to have a dance next Thursday or Friday and serve the intoxicants. However, we have to figure out a way of giving each man enough to enjoy himself, but at the same time, enough not to allow him to get drunk. We have had other dances, but I have never gone to them – so I'm going to this next one just to see what they are like.

This afternoon, I received a package from Beulah. I looked at the postmark and noted that it was mailed in July and was sent over here – to Italy – and back here again. It was en route about 8-1/2 months and I finally got it. Luckily, there were a number of cans of sardines in it, which couldn't become rotten. Included was a box of mixed nuts, which were as old as the trees from which they were picked – from the time that they were on the way. I tried to help them by roasting them in salted butter – but even that didn't help any. However, the other fellows liked them and now they are all gone.

You wrote that Carole always says her prayers now and I'm included in each and every one of them – I'm glad and want to thank her. That is indeed a great honor to be placed as No. 1 on her list of those to be blessed.

Our weather has been a bit cloudy lately, but not enough to prevent us from sending up ships. I just heard a news bulletin, which stated that [former Prime Minister David] Lloyd George died – He was a great old man. The English were lucky to have Churchill around or they would have had to call on George in their critical moments. In the same broadcast, they announced that Patton had pushed past Frankfurt and had taken Aschaffenburg, which is about 20 miles further East, and are bypassing the former for the time being. Later, I heard that tanks had entered the outskirts of Frankfurt – so it looks as though it is another one of Patton's cooked gooses. He is almost halfway across that section of lower Germany to Czechoslovakia. Maybe he'll meet the Russians yet. And when they do meet – I hope that they raise all kinds of hell with those damned Nazi bastards. In today's "Stars & Stripes," there was an article on the prison in Cologne, which had killed thousands of persons thru Gestapo torture methods. After reading that piece and thinking about all the others that we have read about, we can see that each and every Nazi will have to be wiped out altogether, if we are to have peace in our generation and that one to come. I'm getting to hate them more and more, each and every day. If it comes to a point of fraternization with the Germans, I'd rather put a bullet thru them. As you know, there are severe penalties for soldiers who do get friendly and we can't blame them for being punished. That is the only way to be rigid in the occupation and show them that we mean business.

Well, Darlings, I guess that is about all the dope for now. By the way, try to send some boxed cookies, such as Hydrox and other sandwich cookies. I had some today and they were really good and fresh. Try to get all chocolate – ahem!

So regards to all and love to the folks – a million hugs and kisses for the baby and you –

With All My Love,
Your Dave

———

Tuesday – 27 March – 1945
Somewhere in Eastern France

My Darling Amy and Carole Frances,
Your latest letter was delivered in five days, which is really something! That was about the best service we have had since we have been apart. It may not be too long before I'll be sprechen deutsch, so don't be alarmed if the letters start getting slower in about a couple of weeks. Yes, you were right in saying that at this time, all a clear day means to us is a good chance to bomb the Nazis. And I also agree that it will be a great pleasure to come home and wash the car and go for a ride on such days as those. I guess we'll automatically look up in the air when the days are nice.

As to the matzos issue for the men for Passover, it is out now. They were unable to get enough of it across in time, so just those who go to service at the temple will be issued them. So we won't go to the home of those who invited us. I don't like going to a home and not bringing something. I think that Les, Dines, Ellison and perhaps a couple of others will go to the synagogue – including me.

As to [Amy's Aunt] Otty wanting to aid her relatives in Southern France – money is worthless. The things that she should send them if she wants them to really appreciate it are canned goods, including foods, fruits and vegetables. Also, as much sugar and coffee as she can spare. Then, also some new clothing and shoes, as they haven't been able to get any clothing around France for a long time. Now that they are for sale, the people need points and the prices are terrific, so the amount of money that Otty would want to send them wouldn't last over five minutes.

I received a package of salamis from my mother – two of them – and at first, I was afraid that they weren't any good, as they all stunk to high heavens as I opened the package. After I washed them off, however, they were as good as new. In fact, I ate a sandwich for dinner instead of going to chow. Now I do have a real delicacy with which to celebrate my birthday. Just think – tomorrow I'll be edging on the 30 mark. Well, I don't feel any older and that is a very important thing. In fact, I don't think that I look and act that old. I wonder what I'll be like when I get home.

The War news is especially good this evening as Patton has pushed Eastward into Lohr, which is about 50 miles East of the Rhine – That's really going some! The Rhine River is now the rear echelon they are going so fast. With all the reports of landings on those islands South of Japan, maybe this damned affair will be over long before we think. Anyway, it all looks so very good to us. Just keep on praying and hoping and pretty soon, we will be back together again for good. Well, Darlings, I guess that is about the news for today – so regards to all and love to the folks – a billion big birthday kisses for the baby and you –

With All My Love,
Your Dave

Thursday – 29 March – 1945
Somewhere in Eastern France

My Darling Sweethearts,

As you know, yesterday was a day that I should ordinarily remember, as I was born twenty-nine years before. However, as I was just a baby, I can't seem to recall a single incident regarding my entrance into the world. So as I grew up (i.e., grew older, because I really didn't grow so very tall), I began to think of the time when I will be a man – twenty-one years old. Well, it came along, as all the other days of my birth, and I didn't feel any older than when I was twelve or two. Well, now, that I am bordering on thirty, I begin to think how old a man is at that age, and I find that he isn't really old at all. In fact, the saying, "You are as old as you feel," is absolutely right. At this time, I feel fine and like a two-year-old ready to run its first race.

Most of my birthday was a routine day in which I was kept busy marking up my map. Patton has been moving so fast, I ran off the map that I have and will have to get another. The other armies are also doing well and linking up at various points to overrun quite a bit of Western Germany. Just think, only a few years ago, we were looking at a world being overrun by a mad man and wondering if anyone was going to stop him. Now we are fighting on German soil on all fronts. Well, this will be one War that the German people will remember for years and centuries to come. It will take a hundred years to rebuild the cities that have been wrecked. By that time, they ought to be educated enough to realize that peace is the best of all conditions to have in this world.

Well, last night, I got three men to go with me to temple – Les, Ellison and Doug Winikoff. We found a great turnout there – about three thousand people, including civilians. They had a Seder, which I didn't expect as I ate regular chow at camp. However, they didn't have much to eat, so I could go to the Seder, which didn't have much to offer either as far as stomach-filling foods go. We all sat together along one end of the temple and there were G.I.'s galore there. The only ones who were allowed to sit at the Seder were the soldiers, and the civilians stood and served. The whole medical staffs of the hospitals must have been there. If any emergency operations had come up, it would have been a tragedy.

There was a Jewish chaplain who carried on the services. He introduced a one-star General who is stationed here in town, who gave a very enjoyable speech. He told us a story about a Jew who gave Washington all his money and possessions to help in the Revolutionary War. After that, he went to France and borrowed two million more dollars for the Colonies. After the War, he died in poverty and was forgotten. Now, he was a great factor in helping to build the nation which we have now and which is now defeating another movement which had tried to wipe out the Jewish race. So we ought to be very proud to say that a Jew was responsible for our great country. It was a nice story and I felt very proud. After the General finished, a gentile chaplain was introduced, who gave us a strong speech in which he asked us to live as Abraham and Moses wanted us to live. After those two left, the Seder began. We had about a third of a glass of white wine, a few bitter herbs, horseradish, and English-made matzos. The first thing they served was gefilte fish – then potatoes – then buttered asparagus. It was a very nice thing to do, but there were so many men there and it was so noisy that it really wasn't a well-carried-out Seder.

We saw Les to his bus and walked back. When we got in, Fay and Louie were waiting for me, and we went into the Supply Office and I prepared salami sandwiches. Fay had a bottle of champagne left over, which we opened and we really had a midnight snack. Well, we listened to the news and then decided that it was time to hit the hay. So there you have the reason that I did not write last night – OK?

I hope that your thought about shipping all these men to the E.T.O. is being made to relieve those already over here, after Victory Day, is correct. You mention the crossing at Remagen – that seems so long ago now. In fact, it is over a hundred miles behind Patton at this time. It is a surprising thing, but at some points, we are meeting absolutely no opposition and at others, we are meeting stubborn resistance. The latter is up in the English area. However, the Ruhr is probably what they are trying to save out of this terrific retreat. I don't know how much they can still get out of that industrial area, however, as we have bombed it to hell in the past three years, but they are opposing us there. I think that Montgomery will break out and go East in a big hurry.

So you have found another sweetheart – Van Johnson – Well, [Robert] Taylor will never rest now that he has lost out. As I haven't seen either "Winged Victory" or "Thirty Seconds Over Tokyo," I can't pass judgment on it. I suppose that Spencer Tracy was good in the small part that he did play. By the way, did you ever get to see "A Guy Named Joe"? – I had seen it in Africa about a year ago and wrote you about it being a good picture.

That was a tough thing for Mrs. Emmer to have lost a son and then learn that her other one was also killed. I didn't know any of them, but it is a hard thing to take and I offer my sincere regrets to her. There are going to be a lot of sorrowful stories yet to come out of this War.

I still don't know if I'll go to the dance this evening. It will probably be our last one that we will give in the European Theatre. As you probably have heard, there is a definite restriction of fraternization with the people in Germany, so that is why I say that this is probably the last one to be given in this theatre.

Well, Darlings, I guess that's about it for today – so regards to all of our friends and love to the folks – and millions of extra-tight hugs and extra-long kisses for the baby and you –

With All My Love,
Your Dave

Saturday – 31 March – 1945
Somewhere in Eastern France

My Sweetest Darlings,

With the War going Eastward so very fast, it is necessary to try to keep up with them. We have been busy as bees all day long again. I can tell you that Louie, one of our Supply Clerks, is no longer in France and he will be having company soon, so we are quite a busy lot packing up.

This evening, I decided to take in a show to relax. Fay, Okma, Winikoff, and a few others and I went to see "Woman in the Window," with Edw. G. Robinson and Joan Bennett. We all thought that it was a very good picture and liked it. As I had read in the write-ups about it in magazines, the ending was supposed to be the best – it was! If you haven't seen it, do so, as I think that you will enjoy it.

Say, did I tell you that I received your package the other day with the fruitcake, Cheez-Its, canned boned chicken, anchovies, Vienna sausages, and the checker game in it? Well, I did and it all came in fine – I already won two games on it. Yes, as you assume, the Cheez-Its are already gone.

Well, Darlings, as it is now past midnight – a very happy Easter and April Fool's Day. I'll be home next year at this same time – so just hang on a little longer. Regards to all and love to the folks - A billion hugs and kisses for Carole and you –

With All My Love,
Your Dave

Dad protects Nancy from an overly amorous dog at Castle Edenkoben, Germany (Spring 1945). Nancy was Dad's constant companion – and the favorite of everyone in his unit.

Dad feeds Nancy at the Shell station/garage/auto dealership his company occupied in Schwabisch-Hall, Germany (May 1945).

Portrait of Dad taken in Schwabisch-Hall (May 1945).

Clockwise from top: Dad, Nancy, Hicks, and Ellison at Schwabisch-Hall (June 1945).

Group shot of the 346th Signal Company Wing outside the mess hall at Schwabisch-Hall (June 11, 1945). Dad (holding the ever-present Nancy) is near the left edge of the third row from the bottom. Lieutenant Rodger and 1st Lieutenant Lonnie C. Temple are the two officers in the center of the bottom row.

Dad and Nancy at the cathedral in Ulm, Germany (June 1945).

Dad, Nancy, Joe Dines and Sergeant Donal J. O'Connor atop the cathedral in Ulm (June 1945). While up there, Dad felt a sudden, inexplicable compulsion to climb over the wall and jump. Thankfully, he restrained himself.

The ruins of the main street in Ulm (June 1945), taken from the top of the cathedral.

Three of Dad's pals from Supply – Hicks, Louie Lonigro and Sergeant Fay – Darmstadt, Germany (July 1945).

Dad's "home" in Darmstadt (July 1945). Standing in the doorway is a fellow who got drunk and jumped out a 3rd-floor window of this building – and who "emptied his carbine" at a German plane that was 20,000 feet above him during the invasion of Southern France. Dad had serious concerns about this guy's mental health –with good reason.

Bob Hope rests before going on at his USO show in Darmstadt (July 24, 1945). Dad had a great seat. At one point, Nancy leapt from Dad's arms and ran across the stage during a woman's tap solo, prompting a memorable quip from Hope.

Bob Hope in his natural habitat at the same USO show.

Comedian Jerry Colonna before his appearance at Bob Hope's USO show in Darmstadt (July 24, 1945). Dad asked Colonna to wiggle his moustache and he complied.

Jack Benny takes a pratfall at his USO show in Darmstadt (August 2, 1945). Because Dad had to stay behind for an inspection and then run errands in his jeep, he missed Benny's show – which was reportedly "ten times better" than Hope's. As a consolation, one of his Supply buddies shared this photo with him.

Dad also missed out on seeing Ingrid Bergman at Benny's USO show. He'd seen her in Saratoga Trunk *a few months earlier and had recommended it highly to Mom.*

Dad at Piccadilly Circus, London (late August 1945). This was in-between the massive nighttime celebrations of the Allies' recent victory over Japan and the official end of the war.

The leather photo wallet that Dad carried throughout the war. This picture of Carole was the last one Mom sent him before he returned. There are still a precious few fine strands of baby Carole's hair tucked into the lower left border.

*The Spoils of War: The letter opener Dad took from a German
bank executive's desk; the mezuzah given to him by a rabbi at the
synagogue in Nancy, France; the Prussian cavalry saber with which
Dad threatened two German youths who were playing with a flare
gun in Schwabisch-Hall.*

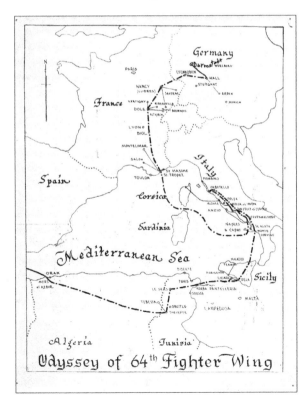

Map tracing the
Odyssey of the
64th Fighter Wing,
*beginning in Oran
and ending in
"Darmstadt" (Dad's
handwriting).*

The 64th Fighter Wing coat of arms. The Latin motto MORS SEMPER TYRANNIS *translates as* DEATH ALWAYS TO TYRANTS.

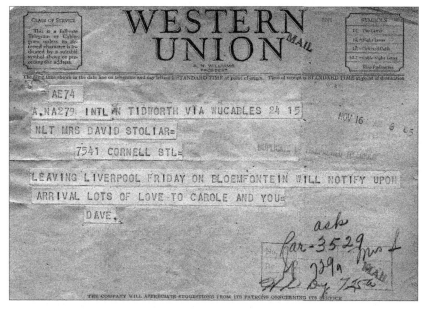

After all the lengthy, eloquent letters, this terse telegram was Dad's last communication with Mom before shipping home in November of 1945.

6. GERMANY

Wednesday – 4 April – 1945
Somewhere in Western Germany

My Darling Amy and Carole Frances,

It has been so long since I have written you that I don't know how or where to begin, however, as you see by the above phrase, I am no longer in France. The evening before we left, I went over to the Mougins and told them that I thought that that evening was the last time that I would see them for some time. They were very much put out about it and told me to be sure to tell you that they enjoyed being a friend of yours and mine and hoped that they both will be able to get to see you and me after the War. They couldn't fully express their feelings as to my leaving and it was very hard for me to tell them, as they were very nice to me ever since I arrived in the Nancy area. I told them that if I get near the place that Mr. M. was in, I'd try to find out if he is still there, as it isn't too far. They both said that they felt that they had known me long enough to embrace me and kiss me on both cheeks (as the French do) as a farewell gesture.

Well, the next day, we took off for other lands. Okma and Mullen and I rode in a jeep and it was a very chilly ride. We went thru a lot of French towns that were badly beaten up and had very few buildings left, but as we approached the German line, you could see the intensity of the increased bombings that smashed most of the buildings. Once across the line, we completely ignored the people and smiled as we drove thru their broken towns and villages. It must have burned them up to think of "Der New Order" and what it has brought them. I thought that no place could possibly be as badly smashed as Terracina or one of those towns also along the Tyrrhenian Sea, but this was as bad and worse in most instances. It is amazing to see some of the people trying to pick out an item or two from all the rubble – Each and every wall is completely smashed and yet they seek remains. There are, no doubt, quite a number of dead beneath the ruins at this time. It would take a long time just to clear away the mass of rubble. We saw Jerry equipment every fifty yards all along the way. It is an amazing thing that they have enough equipment to carry on a War after seeing so much destroyed and thrown away. Huge trucks lie along the roads either burned or without wheels, after running out of gas. I saw piles of Jerry clothing along the road and shoes to go with it. In fact, along one railroad siding, I saw cars full of Jerry clothing and equipment that were abandoned in their hurried retreat. They must have stockpiled for twenty years before for this War, if they are still wearing clothes and using equipment.

The cities as a whole are drab as the people and aren't lively at all. There is an entirely different feeling present in Germany than there is in France. I realize that one is a liberated country and the other is conquered, but the impression that one would get even before the War would be that of sadness and cold reception. As we drove along the highways, which were in pretty good shape, we saw a lot of very fertile country that will never produce another morsel of food for the Nazis.

Well, when we finally got up here, it was getting dark and we had to set up our cots without any lighting. After that, we decided we had better fix something to eat – so we opened some cans of bacon and a preparation made up of ham, eggs and potatoes and made some coffee and really had a feast – with bread and fresh butter. Well, after that, we decided that as long as we had no lights and there wasn't anyplace to go to – we may as well hit the hay, so that we'd be fresh for a nice, full day's work this morning.

We have a large room in which there are about fifty men. To tell you the truth, it is the second floor of a former stable. Can you picture that? Here we are, an army which has come in as conquerors, and the enlisted men sleep in a barn! As you probably have guessed, the officers are sleeping in nice places as usual. Boy, what a great day that will be when the War will end and we won't have to put up with that sort of "democratic" treatment. I can tell you very sincerely that there are a great many men who have said that they wouldn't spit in a man's mouth if he was dying of thirst – if that man had been an officer during the War. Oh well, it will all be over very shortly.

We got up early so as to get all the things off the trucks and placed. After it was over, I was a tired duck, however, I had to get out and find a quartermaster laundry and get some other information, so I took off in a jeep this afternoon with one of the other fellows – Oscar Larsen. It is ordered that everybody will go in pairs any time they leave for anyplace. Well, I found the laundry and got some dope and then ran across a find. There was a Jerry warehouse that was being cleaned out to make way for American supplies, so I finagled the fellow out of about 4,000 boxes of matches, some soap, some honey, and 600 pounds of Jerry sugar. It so happened, we are low on sugar and would have had to sweat it out until we drew rations again. Anyway, the Mess Sergeant was one happy guy when he learned that I had brought that back. Of course, honey is something which we haven't had since we have been in the Army and we will have it with pancakes soon. I'll have to go back there and see what else I can dig up.

Boy, every time I think about this setup, I laugh all the harder. Why, we even have one faucet for all the men to wash out of – Just think of that! If you want to get washed up in the morning, you get in line or else wash later in the day. Last night, it did get cold, too, up there, as there is only a wood roof between you and the weather. When we all awoke this morning, it was harder than h. . . to get out of our bedrolls, as the cold just clung there. Well, maybe only the better horses were allowed to sleep upstairs before we got there – That is some sort of consolation.

I have here, before me, your letters of the 20th-21st-22nd and 24th, so I will take just the first two and the V-Mails and let the others hang on for tomorrow. It was a tough thing that I couldn't get Germany's surrender as a birthday gift – but I'll be satisfied to get it at any time now. You must have been psychic when you wrote that you wondered where our next move was going to be, as we had been in Nancy for a long time – Now I can blame you for this move.

Say, if you make any strudel, send me some. It used to come in in pretty good shape. Don't forget to send me some Hydrox cookies, if you can find them. If you think that I'm going to even try to get out of your sight after I get back – sister, you are crazy! Just think – all that meat and no ration points!

So we come to the end of my first letter from Germany – and not my last one. However, I do hope that I won't send as many from here as I did from France. I do miss you and the baby very much and find great consolation in knowing that I have a fine wife and baby waiting for me when I get back there. I do love both of you very much – so don't wonder about it.

Well, Darlings, say "Hello" to all our friends and love to the folks – a million hugs and kisses for the baby and you –

With All My Love,
Your Dave

———

Thursday – 5 April – 1945
Somewhere in Western Germany

My Dearest Darlings,

Our advance is still going on unhalted and gaining momentum in some areas. The British have certainly bottled up a large number of Jerries up in the Holland area. Along with the Ruhr Valley being cut off, it will be a great factor in ending this War. I also read that the Russians were only 11 miles from Vienna – Little did I know that when I said last week that soon the Russians will be on their way to Vienna that they would really be up there so far. After capturing the Austrian capital, they can swing Northward and cut off the Jerries from the South. It would be a great climax if Patton were to meet them in Czechoslovakia.

Say, did you see the article about the movie starlets playing strip poker for the clothing drive for the liberated nations? I'll bet that the newspapermen really were on the edge of their seats. What else will they think of for the War Effort? I forgot to tell you last night – I spoke to a fellow while back in Nancy who had just come over from the States as a replacement. He said that of all the towns that he had been in, St. Louis was the worst as far as morals went. He said that the girls were absolutely man-hungry and were easier to take out and sleep with than any other city's women. I was one surprised guy as he told us that. I'm very sorry to hear it also, and hope that the V.D. rate is not as high as it was when I left. What is the latest situation from the viewpoint of a St. Louisan?

Today, I drove the Mess Sergeant over to that place I went to yesterday and we picked up some more honey – about 200 lbs. of it, in fact. We had pancakes with honey this morning and everybody really enjoyed them immensely. That was about all that we could use from that place as most of it had already been cleared out.

By the way, did I ever tell you I have a picture that was taken at the Passover services in Nancy? Les knows one of the fellows who was taking pictures and he got him to take a shot of Les, Winikoff, Ellison and me. It is a good picture and as soon as the time limit is up on this shot, I'll send it to you. You don't know it, but all pictures made by the "Stars & Stripes" aren't given out until made public or thirty days have elapsed. They weren't printed in the "Stars & Stripes", because there is a slight scratch over Les' body, which made it worthless for publication. Otherwise, they would have run a story about the meeting in Nancy.

So, Darlings, that about winds up the day and its activities. Send love to the folks – regards to all our friends – and a billion hugs and kisses for you and Carole Frances –
With All My Love,
Your Dave

———

Friday – 6 April – 1945
Somewhere in Western Germany

My Darling Wife and Baby,

Well, I crossed the Rhine today! No, it wasn't hard at all and it was like riding across a bridge over the River des Peres. I can't tell the place at which I crossed, but it was as easy as eating chocolate pie. I got some information about places for which I have been looking. I took another fellow who works in the Orderly Room – Watkins, who lives in Illinois – and we first went to that town where Mr. Mougin was supposed to have been. Well, I first looked up the Allied Military Government Office and learned that he had been moved on the 16th of January to an address in that same town. We finally located the house and, to our disappointment, nobody answered the door. Well, at least I found out that he was alive up until the 16th – That is something heartening to write to the Mougins. They can now follow it thru by writing the A.M.G. and getting them to try to trace him from there.

After that, we drove to one of the large twin cities on the Rhine. As we passed thru, it looked like a huge foot of a tremendous giant had stepped on the city at one time and smashed every building there. The destruction is beyond description and imagination. Can you picture a city of about 400,000 completely in ruins? Well, we crossed the Rhine and saw its mate – another city of about 500,000. This was also in complete ruin and lay like a smashed doll after being run over by a car. You have no idea of how our bombers have smashed these cities to bits. It will be an impossible thing for the Germans to forget the Allied bombings after the War. Some of the people tried to act as friendly as though nothing had happened – but we ignored them completely. There are thousands of liberated Russians, Poles, French, Italians, and other nationalities, running around these bombed-out cities and picking up whatever scraps they can find. I stopped in at a Military Police Headquarters to get some information and the lieutenant showed me some pistols that were turned in today. One was from a German

General. He also showed me some liquor that had just been turned in and was suspected of being poison.

Just as we were leaving, two M.P.'s took a Jerry, in civilian clothing, out into a jeep and drove off with him. We asked what it was all about and were told that he was one of Himmler's SS men, who had just surrendered a few minutes before – giving himself up as he had had enough of War. As to the War news, it is still going very well and I hope the supply lines will be able to stand the rush and keep up with Patton. Thus, we come to the end of an adventurous day and are ready to hit the well-known hay. There was a movie at the headquarters, but I didn't think that Jack Haley and Jean Parker would be too good, so I'll be patient and sweat it out, as I have done for all good things, including a discharge. Ah, what a day when they say that I have graduated to the status of a civilian!

Give my regards to all our friends, love to the folks, and lots and lots of love and kisses for Carole and you –

With All My Love,
Your Dave

Saturday – 7 April – 1945
Somewhere in Western Germany

My Sweetest Darlings,

Well, [Mess Sergeant] *Carlin and I left about 9:00 and we must have stopped in at least ten different cities before we finally located what we were looking for. Luckily, we ran across an abandoned warehouse of a plant that had manufactured face powder and rouge. In there, we found some beautiful aluminum pots, which were even better than anything we had expected to get from our own depot. After we had loaded the jeep trailer to capacity, we took off and it was one noisy ride back here. The pots made so much noise that they sounded like a tank was coming down the road. Incidentally, we drove on Adolf's super-duper Autobahn and it is pretty good.*

I never had any idea that I would be so lost over here, as I have found it. You see, in France, I could at least read the signs and other printing that was other than English. However over here, I can't even pronounce the stuff – let alone read it. I understand such words as "strasse" – "schule" – "bier" and a few others, but generally speaking, I am lost. Gosh, you could really go to town with what you know of the German language. Well, the less I hear of it, the better off I'll be. I always did think that it was a harsh-sounding tongue and haven't changed my mind about it. Say, please don't teach the baby any of that type of singing. If necessary, teach her to sing in French or pig Latin.

Last night, I wrote to the Mougins and told them of my vain attempt in trying to locate Mr. Mougin. I made it as easy as possible and tried to convince them that he is probably still very much alive and perhaps on his way back to them. As I had to go that way again today, I stopped by that same place and had just as much luck in locating him. It seems that nobody ever heard of him being there. Of course, I wouldn't put it past the Nazis to make a false entry in the records to confuse those who managed to get hold of the papers.

Rodger came back about an hour ago with a truckload full of captured Jerry equipment, including an elephant gun, radios, a teletype machine, steel measuring instruments and many other pieces that will be found in the garbage dump a couple of days from now. I don't see what he would want with all that sort of junk – It is only a headache to haul around with you. As to souvenir hunting, I value my legs and arms and life too much to pick up that sort of stuff. Too many men have set off booby traps with that same sort of thing for me to repeat the gesture.

I guess that is about all the new for today – so love to the folks – regards to all our friends – and beaucoup hugs and kisses for the baby and you –
With All My Love,
Your Dave

Sunday – 8 April – 1945
Somewhere in Western Germany
My Darling Amy and Carole Frances,

One of the fellows put in a line to this room so that I can now work by electricity instead of lamplight. However, I'll have to put up more of an obstruction in our window, so as to black it out completely. As it is, I have a couple of pieces of cloth, but they are insufficient for the time being, so I'll take care of it right now – Excuse me, please. Well, it is now OK and I have that off my mind. As you know, it is against the law to fraternize – including talking to these people – so it will be pretty hard after a while not to talk to anyone but the men around you whom you have seen every day. I hope that they will start to issue more Paris passes, so that the morale will hold up. With the War fast coming to a close, I guess it will end before any of *us dare to go out in the evening just to go for a walk. It isn't worth it. I see that the British are close to Bremen and Hanover and still going strong. No news has come from Patton's way, so he must be going along well. I suppose it will be necessary to move again in a short time, as we are now too far from the front again. As long as Wurzburg has been taken, and it is a fairly large city, I hope that we go there.*

As to helping to clear up a question as to "that place I have been going" – it was St. Dizier and I couldn't tell you at the time because of censorship. Now I can tell you about those moonlit nights in December also. It was the 24th when we had a number of alerts and we saw a few Jerry planes fly over. On this occasion, one dove down and passed directly over our heads just about thirty feet above. In fact, he had to pull up in a hurry or else he would have crashed into the trees. Well, we expected him to return the next night and drop a few greeting cards, but I suppose he was detained elsewhere or shot down on his way back. Well, it was during a blackout due to an alert that De Filippo was injured in falling down a hill and breaking his leg. Also, it was during one of those nights that a plane swooped down on the road below us and strafed a jeep along the road, injuring one of the officers who was driving with his lights on. Then, in February, I heard a long roar of Jerry motors one night as I was walking back from the show. It is very funny, but we can detect a Jerry plane from a G.I. just from the roar of the motors. The American planes have a steady roar and the Jerries have one that gets strong and then weak. Anyway, it has been a long time since we have seen a Jerry plane up in the air – Most of them are battered hulks on the ground. That was what I meant by those moonlit nights – Are you relieved now?

We have one of the classiest setups in the way of latrines that you can find outside of any home. We have portable toilets which were brought to the requesting person's rooms. They are box-like affairs with nice covers. In fact, some of them are leather-seated. Well, Mullen and Okma worked on them and got about five holes dug and placed one box seat over each. Of course, a latrine is not a latrine if there are not others to sit and talk to you as you go about your business, so they arranged the seats in an alternating fashion, so that a man wouldn't be too self-conscious about the whole thing. Then, all around the whole area, they placed a nice, wide piece of sackcloth that was found around here. That, of course, makes it private. For a trough, they got hold of a portable tub which is made of galvanized iron. It has a hole in the end so that it drains down into one of the holes under one of the boxes – It is quite a setup and should be seen to be appreciated. Sorry that I don't have any film left or else I would take a shot of it. I suggested to Mullen that we place pinups on the sacking, so that it would be more of a pleasure to go to the toilet than an effort. Then again, we could also put up eye-test signs for those who are hoping to be discharged from the Army because of their eyes. In other words, all the comforts of home, right out here in the wilderness. What a tough War!

And as the sun fades in the West, we leave the sad-sack land of der fuhrer and sing to them, "It Should Happen To You." Regards to our friends, love to the folks, and lots and lots of hugs and kisses for the baby and you – and I do love and miss you both very much –

With All My Love,
Your Dave

———

Monday - 9 April – 1945
Somewhere in Western Germany

My Darling Wife and Baby,

I put together a package which Fay took with him to Nancy. I asked him to stop in at the Mougins' and give it to them. I had accumulated a few cartons of cigarettes along with the various candies, so it was a nicely assorted box. I also sent one of the cans of gefilte fish and the box of bouillon that you sent in your last package. They ought to get a lot of enjoyment out of it, as everything in it is unavailable in France at this time.

I had to make another trip and Micka's jeep was the only thing around at the time, so I took Winikoff and another fellow named Abrams (not Jewish), and we took off at about 10:00. I decided to go into the advance location of the outfit to which Les is attached. I learned that what I am looking for will be up in this vicinity in about four days, so there was nothing more to be done about it except to try to chisel some noon chow. As we started to eat, Winikoff exclaimed that Les was sitting over at the other side of the table. I looked and sure enough, there he was. I had just written him a letter, too, last night. They have taken over a former German barracks and headquarters. That is what we should have done, but no, we have to sleep in a cold stable.

On top of seeing him, I also acquired a new friend – a dog. It is a very lively white dog with black markings on his head and eyes, also being *spotted all over with tiny black spots. He looks as if he was half bird-dog and half-Dalmatian – Anyway, he is a very likable dog and smart as they come. He took to me as soon as we saw each other – It must have been love at first sight. Anyway, I don't know which he is – French or German – but I'm going to bring him up to understand English, as he is still young – about four months old. Before I go any further, I had better straighten it out – He is a she, and I had a hard time trying to think up an appropriate name for her. As we had recently spent a nice time in Nancy, I decided that that was a nice name to remember – so Nancy she is. So far, she answers to that name and a whistle, so we ought to get along. I just tell her to stay by my side and she does that; I point to a chair and she jump up onto it; I ask her to stand up and she does that – Isn't that a smart dog for her age? Anyway, after I brought her back here, another, much larger and older male dog made friends with her and is outside the Supply Office door at this time, trying to get Nancy to come out to play. This afternoon, Nancy really jumped all over the other dog and the larger dog is now scared of Nancy. The other one is so large that Nancy can walk underneath the other's body without touching. So Nancy will stay right with us until we leave for the States and then I'll try to take her along with me. At this time, she is sleeping on one of the Supply shelves, but I have a box upstairs for her beside my bed.*

[Dave's] Aunt Ruth didn't have much to say in her letter, except that she would deem it a great favor if I could write to an outfit to which her nephew was attached and try to learn what had happened to him, as he was last reported missing in action and they haven't had any word from him since. I think that I'll write the First Sergeant of that outfit and see what I can find out about him.

Well, Darlings, I certainly wish that you both were with me somewhere in the States, enjoying another honeymoon. Well, it won't be too long – So regards to all our friends, love to the folks and a billion hugs and kisses for Carole and you –
With All My Love,
Your Dave

———

Tuesday – 10 April – 1945
Somewhere in Western Germany
My Sweetest Darlings,
I just heard the nicest song I have heard in a long time – "He's Home For a Little While." It is being played on a rebroadcast of Dinah Shore and Frank

Morgan's program. She sang it – and how! The lyrics are really terrific! Now there is a program of music by Tommy Dorsey and one of the Eberly boys is singing "My Prayer" – a very pretty rendition, too. Of course, I always cared for your singing a lot more and especially right now. See if you can get a special pass to come over this way to visit relatives and then you could very casually drop by and we'd ahem! Anyway, it was a nice thought.

Nancy is really a smart dog and seems to understand everything that I say to her. I found out that she likes raw hamburger and will not eat cereal in the morning. I give her water from a water glass – some style, eh? The amazing part of the whole thing is that I can't go anyplace at all without her hanging onto me. She even sits by me in the Mess Hall. The funniest thing happened to her this morning. I left her to sleep in the Supply Office and locked the door. When I opened it and turned on the light, she got so excited and jumped all over the place. Well, you know that some children get so excited that they wet their pants – Well, Nancy was so excited that she wet all over the place at one time, as she jumped up and down and across the chairs, so she must be quite attached to me. I just have to move a foot and she is up and alongside of me. Everybody comments on how she is even getting to look like me. I take her with me when I go out on the road and she barks at all strangers – Isn't that good for a dog about four months old? At times, she boldly walks across the seat and lays down on my lap as I'm trying to drive. I know that you and Carole Frances will like her when and if I can get her home.

I just heard the news and it is still going well all over this theatre. It won't be too long before they will announce that all of Vienna has been liberated. That was really a great push up to the capital of Austria and will be a great threat to the Nazis from the South. As it looks now, it will be no surprise to anyone if Patton meets the Russians in Dresden. It certainly is a matter of weeks before this will all come to an end. We are going along at will and nobody is attempting to stop us, so it can't last more than another four weeks. It is rumored by the Germans that it will be over on the 20th of this month – I don't know where they get their date. As long as it is soon, I don't care.

Well, Darlings, that's about it for today, so regards to all and love to the folks, and many, many hugs and kisses for Carole and you –
With All My Love,
Your Dave

[LETTER FROM JANINE MOUGIN DATED APRIL 7, 1945 – NANCY. FRANCE]

Dear David,

I have good news to tell you today. I am almost certain that you are guessing! Yes, my father came back from Germany yesterday afternoon. He was during fifteen days in the woods at the right of the Rhein.

He was very happy to find the bottle of champagne you gave to us for him.

I shall write you a longer letter when we shall have news from you. I shall put this letter at the post office this afternoon in order that you receive it soon.

Sincerely,

Janine

Wednesday – 11 April – 1945
Somewhere in Western Germany

My Dearest Amy and Carole Frances,

The sun shown all day long and the heavy bombers were over in huge numbers again, so it looks like the Reich got a helluva blasting again today. It's a marvelous sight to see – the batches of white planes moving along in formation like a chorus of trained birds. Every now and then, a few fighters would dart in among them and they looked like tiny flies alongside the heavies. Well, just so the weather holds up and we are able to get gas up to the front, everything will be OK and it will end darned soon. Vienna has about fallen to the Reds. With Holland about cut off, there will be about 200,000 Nazis cut off in those two sectors alone.

This morning, Fay came in from that trip back to our old area. He told me that he delivered the package that I made up for the Mougins and wasn't able to see Janine, but did see her mother, so, in the best French that he was able to muster, he told her about my endeavor to locate Mr. Mougin. Well, the amazing thing about the whole affair was that her husband came back to Nancy last Friday. That was the day before I first stopped in there and tried to find him. Anyway, I'm glad to hear he is home and well. They will, if they haven't as yet, break open the bottle of champagne that I gave them expressly for the day when he returns. I know that their family is very happy at this time and will drink a toast for me and you when they open the bottle. Fay told them that I wrote just the day before and that they ought to receive my letter any minute. They, in turn, had written me and told me that Mr. Mougin had returned – so it looks like our letters crossed. So now it looks like I will never get to see him, unless I have to make a trip back that way sometime in the near future. I never even have seen a picture of him, but Mrs. Mougin told me that he was of a short stature – so perhaps he and I are similar.

So you were amazed at my impressions of Lauren Bacall – Well, have you seen her picture and if so, what did you think of her? I think that after two pictures, she will be finished. Have you seen many pictures with the gal with the hair drooping over her eyes [Veronica Lake]? That is a very similar case. So I still like the reliable types like Claudette Colbert and Greer Garson. Were you able to see "Rhapsody in Blue" as yet?

Glad to hear that [radio commentator] Gabriel Heatter is so sure about more men getting more and longer furloughs after the War is over here – I'd like to be in on the deal. As to going to the Pacific, I still think that we will go there, but only after a furlough in the States. By that time, I hope that men over 28 are reassigned to a station in the States – what a dream! With the recent attacks and landings on those islands South of the Japanese islands, I hope that Paul is safe and sound. Has Beulah heard from him recently?

Today, we had a little excitement as three Jerries were captured in the hills near us. They certainly did not look like any Supermen. They were glad to be captured, so that they could get something good to eat and a place to sleep. It wasn't anything serious or else I wouldn't have told you – so don't worry about it.

Say "Hello" to all our friends and love to the folks – Nancy also says "Hello" to everybody. Tell Carole that I'll try to bring this dog back with me, as she would really like her.

Billions of hugs and kisses for he baby and you –
With All My Love,
Your Dave

⎯

Thursday – 12 April – 1945
Somewhere in Western Germany

My Most Adorable Wife and Baby,

With Nancy at my feet, trying to go to sleep, I begin this letter. I worked all this morning trying to get this stable in decent shape for the inspecting officer. That is just like the Army – They give you a stable to live in and expect *you to have it as neat as a pin. We had to sweep out the manure, pile old furniture, drag out electric turbines, dust the cobs off the walls and windows, sweep the moldy piles of dirt from the floors and just about redecorate the place for the Germans. Well, it really doesn't make a damned bit of difference to me if they intend to have men sleep and live in stables, so if my bed isn't made up in the morning, they can send me home as punishment. Anyway, we won't have to put up with this much longer – This will be the last time we'll be in buildings until we hit the States, I think. Don't worry about me, as we will always be safe and sound. By the time we get to where we are going to go, the front will be way beyond Berlin. After all, you know that the 9th Army is now about 50 miles from the capital now – It won't be long now. As to Patton, only God knows, and he is taking good care of him so maybe this month will bring about the end of the War. As you may know, most of the big events of this War have happened during the month of April – so who knows?*

It's amazing, but the people are starting to come back slowly, and they all smile and try to be so friendly with us. However, we still ignore them and go about our business. We stopped at a place into which a G.I. outfit was moving and I picked up a couple of souvenirs including an air-raid warden's helmet, a silver letter-opener, and a pair of spurs. I found most of it in a former bank building in which there were loads of blank paper money, ready to be printed into currency. There were a great many Russian women there, cleaning up the place for the Americans. They are waiting only for that day when the armies link up, so that they can go back to Russia. They asked me something in Russian and all that I could do is say, "Nicht verstehe" ["I don't understand"].

Say "Hello" to all our friends and love to the folks – a million and one kisses for Carole and you – I do love you two very much, too –

With All My Love,
Your Dave

———

Saturday – 14 April – 1945
Somewhere in Western Germany

My Dearest Wife and Baby,

After evening chow yesterday, I received the "Stars & Stripes" which headlined the death of FDR. We had heard a rumor of it that morning, but nothing definite until later in the day. It was very hard to even think that he was gone. Just the other day, I wrote that all big things happened during the month of April during this War – but I never dreamt that it could have been his death. Now the War will have to end this month in order to make up for the tremendous loss which we have suffered. As a man, he was no different than any other man who comes from America, however, as our president and a symbol of free-thinking people, the rest of the world has lost more than we. They were counting heavily on him and his influence on all the other Allied countries. In one case in particular, France has lost its greatest chance for a quick recovery when De Gaulle failed to visit Roosevelt when invited to do so. That was one of the many mistakes that he is guilty of and will affect France after this is all over.

As to FDR, we, the Jewish people in particular, have lost a representative voice. We will miss him greatly and will never again find a man from another faith who will do so much to try to beat down anti-Semitism as he did. I don't know what others say about it, but I felt that he was doing us a great favor in being our president again – not that we were doing him a favor by reelecting him to that unthankful office. Now that he has worked himself to death, as Wilson had done after the First War, I hope that the Allies will not repeat the mistakes which they committed during Wilson's time. They owe that much, at least, to his memory. I'm afraid that the Americans will never fully realize how great a man he actually was. It is only after one gets away from his home country that he is able to see how popular the American and his ideas are in other lands. The Italians will miss him most of all the countries who looked to him for aid. I guess many South American countries will alter their views after the European War is ended. I doubt very much if any of them will wage war in the Pacific Theatre in person. Well, international politics were never my line – so why worry about them? As an individual, there will be nothing that I will be able to do about it. However, I do hope that they don't forget the man who helped to save their countries from invasion, while his own countrymen were calling him a warmonger.

As to Truman, as a president, we cannot look forward to any greatness coming from him. In the first place, he is stepping into a pair of shoes that are large enough to drown him. Secondly, he isn't the aggressive type of diplomat that his predecessor was. Last, he was launched into a political career by a "boss" who later was convicted on a Federal charge, so it looks like Truman's term will be a similar one to Grant's.

At this writing, Nancy is below the desk going away at three hambones that I gave her yesterday. We had ham the other day and included were some hams which were made by the Heil Packing Company of St. Louis. Those homemade foods always taste better somehow. I ought to be getting some packages any day now. You may send me some jars of pickles, if you wish.

So, my Darlings, that is about the dope for today – so regards to all and love to the folks – a great big hug and kiss for Carole and you –

With All My Love,
Your Dave

————

Sunday – 15 April – 1945
Somewhere in Western Germany

My Darling Amy and Carole Frances,

Last night, I received a package from you and a letter dated the 4th of April, which is very good. The package contained two boxes of Cheese Tid-Bits, a package of caramel-covered puffed wheat, a package of Pretz-Stix, a can of tuna and a can of sardines. It was all a very welcome sight and I offered the Pretz-Stix to our Mess Sergeant, who is also from St. Louis, and he went wild over them. He said that they were the first that he had had since he was overseas. On top of that, they were made in St. Louis, which makes them twice as good. Mullen also helped to get rid of them and we enjoyed and made away with them in a hurry. As I was going back to our area, Ellison stopped me and hopped on me for the bag of caramel-covered wheat, which was also very good. So now I have the Cheese Tid-Bits, sardines and tuna left. I'll hang onto them for a while.

I'm sorry to hear about the meat situation being so critical now. I really don't have to have any salami, if it takes away from your table. After all, we do get most of the fresh meat that is slaughtered in the States and you have to search for hours at a time to locate a wee bit. Why, just the other day, the Ration Depot had some frozen hogs, which were captured from a German dump, and they gave us a whole one, so we had pork sausage patties one night, ham the next, and meat and beans the next. Then tomorrow, I think that we will have pork. We got a lot of good bacon out of it also, and some fat for frying, which is always a good thing to have around. And you are having a helluva time getting any sort of meat – so forget about sending me a salami – I don't need it. By the way, does that butcher still resemble me? Don't go telling him that.

That was nice of you to tell Carole that the Easter Bunny from France left her the eggs which she found. Were you able to color them this year? I recall giving you a gift of something inside an egg – what was it? I think it was a bottle of "Toujours Moi."

I see that the War Department is a lot more optimistic than most of us about it ending in a very few days. It is a lot more cheerful than at any time previously, but how can it end in a few days? I give it until the end of the month and that will be good. As it is, we are not far from the Russians North of Czechoslovakia. After that junction and the one in Berlin, a general mopping up will be the finishing touches. So at this very time, the Army is probably planning the shipment of the Air Forces and attached units to the South Pacific. I hope that they don't exclude a furlough home first. As to the capture of [former Vice-Chancellor Franz] *von Papen and the three Generals, I think that it was the plainest case of being purposely placed in an area that I have ever seen. After all, you don't think that the Nazis would allow a man of his ability to be captured in an area that was certain to be cut off. It was a plain, out-and-out case of a put-up job. I guess that is the way in which we will capture the villains – one at a time, in scattered parts of the Reich.*

As you know now, Mr. Mougin was liberated and has returned home to his family. As to his being captive in the first place, the Germans took many thousands of Frenchmen and young girls as slave laborers to the Reich factories. Now that many of the larger cities have been liberated, there are thousands of people of all nationalities wandering about, waiting to get back to their countries. We even have some Russians working at headquarters. The situation is probably very similar on the Eastern Front and there are probably many American and British prisoners wandering about.

As to the champagne that we bought for Fay, we got rid of that before we left Nancy and it was good. We still have one bottle which we may open this evening when Dines and Fay get back from a dance that is being given for the liberated people down in the village. There will be a lot of husky Russian and Polish women to dance the polka with – so why go? They decided that they wanted to see what it was like – so why try to stop them? After all, they are single. However, neither of them speaks Polski or Russian, so where can they get?

Well, Darlings, that just about winds up another day's activities and I do miss all of you very much – but love you and Carole more than you know – regards to all and love to the folks – a hug and kiss for Carole and you –
With All My Love,
Your Dave

———

Monday – 16 April – 1945
Somewhere in Western Germany
My Most Beloved Wife and Baby,
    The Mess Sergeant and I just got back from a nice long drive back to some point in France. After we left Landau, the roads were as bumpy as a bed with cracker crumbs in it and as dusty as a Spring wind in Kansas – so it was no picnic. It was about 70 miles from where we are now and we were really worn out when we got there. It was my first time in that area and we passed thru Haguenau on the way. If you will recall, that was the city which we took and the Germans later retook and then we recaptured again. All along were battered German tanks and armored vehicles. Now and then, there was an Allied piece of equipment, but the bulk of it was Jerry. Why, even the greater part of the ammunition fired was American, as shown by empty cases. There were many small German villages that were smashed to rubble and the only inhabitants were cats and dogs. If the people back home think that they are having a tough time of it with rationing and brownouts, they ought to see the damaged cities and then realize that they have 1,000 times as much as the French, Italian, English, and German people. Why, in some cities in France and Germany, the people certainly don't have any future to which to look forward. If they do have the money, they can't buy any furniture, as they have no home to place it in. If they do have a piece of a home, there is no furniture to buy – so tell the people at home to be thankful for what they have and that they are in America and Americans.
    I just hooked up our loudspeaker to the radio that is in the Orderly Room, so now it is going full blast with a program called "Downbeat" and it features Paul Whiteman this evening. Nancy is lying down underneath the table and trying to sleep with all the music going full. Maybe after our next move, we will be a lot better off – I think that we will. Anything will be better than a stable. Why, even back in Italy, the French had better places to sleep in than we Americans, and here in Germany, they are once more getting the better of all the setups, including some of the captured vehicles. I

just this minute had a helluva argument with Mullen over supplying some liberated Polish men, who have just come to us to work as KP's. In Italy, we furnished the clothing, bedding which included cots and blankets, and even paid them and fed them and gave them our PX rations. Now they came in and asked me if I had five cots to give them. It has been holy hell to get cots around here for a long time and I do have them, however, if one of the men's bunks rips, he'll need one in a hurry and I'd have to take it away from one of the Pollacks. So they took them and then asked me to give them a tent. Here we sleep in a stable and we have to give them a tent for themselves – That was the last straw and I hit the ceiling. I told him that if he wanted a tent, to go ahead and take it, but I wouldn't sanction it. Boy, what a relief it will be when we get back home and out of this Army!

We are now listening to an address by Pres. Truman, which is being delivered to the Congress. It is a simple but effective speech and a reminder to the Axis Nations that we are still fighting for an unconditional surrender, which was Roosevelt's aim. I suppose Truman will serve out his term, but he won't be reelected, as there are others who are more informed about government ins and outs. The news is still going well on all fronts – so maybe it will end over here soon. I'll bet that the 3rd Army men are getting instructions on Russian ways and customs and language. What a day that will be when they meet! I remember when the Americans met the British in Africa; when the Seventh Army met the 3rd in France, and when the 1st and 9th Armies met East of the Ruhr. Those were great moments in this War and very important in bringing it to a quick ending. So it will be a terrific meeting when it comes off.

Well, Darlings, I want to tell you that I miss you and Carole very much and love you twice as much as yesterday. Won't it be a grand day when we can sit at home with just the three of us and relax and listen to the radio and know that we are at last at home? When we wish to go for a walk – all we will have to do is walk out. When we want a hamburger – all we'll have to do is to go up to the corner. Well, it won't be too long and we'll really appreciate our homes when we all come back to them.

Regards to all of our friends and love to the folks – a billion hugs and kisses for Carole and you –

With All My Love,
Your Dave

Tuesday – 17 April – 1945
Somewhere in Western Germany

My Darling Wife and Baby,

Well, we have come to the end of another day of War and separation and closer to the end of this whole affair. The 3rd Army is still blacked out, so we must be a lot further East than we know. With wholesale surrendering of Nazi troops, it can't last any too long. Even Hitler is warning the rest of the troops not to retreat or surrender – so it must be a critical situation in the Berlin area. If it is true that the Russians are also starting up their offensive in a direct line for Berlin, the vise ought to be closed in a week or ten days. It is a shame that we have to take prisoners and feed, clothe, and pay them according to the international agreement which the Axis Nations don't look up to.

Fay and a couple of other boys asked me if I wanted to go along with them for a drive in one of the captured vehicles, so the four of us took off for a point on the Rhine. There was Jerry equipment all over the area. In fact, I didn't see one piece of Allied equipment destroyed anywhere. We came to a Russian refugee camp where there were some Russians outside, waving us to come in. We went in and tried to speak to them in a nice mixture of German, Yiddish, Russian, French and English. We were really lost when they rattled Russky off at us in a hurry. There were about a hundred women and about twenty-five men. We met a lot of big, husky, strong and ugly women. I never saw such specimens of the human race as these. They were almost grotesque. I showed your new pictures around the table and they were all so enthused over the baby and jealous of you. When I told them that my father and mother were born over here [Eastern Europe], *they cried out that I was a comrade. Well, we were lucky to get out without having to stay all night with those Amazons. The men were young and strong as oxen – most of them with blonde hair and high cheekbones. While there, a few other G.I.'s came in also who are attached to the Wing and we all had a grand time trying to do a Russian Polsky dance.*

At about ten, we took off as thunder and lightning lit up the sky ahead of us. We reached camp just as the rain started. So there you have a full description of my first meeting with Russians from Russia who were prisoners in Germany. They were so grateful to the Americans for liberating them that they couldn't do enough to show their appreciation. All that they are waiting for now is the day when we meet up, so that a thru passage to

*their home can be made. However, some of them told us that they know that
their homes are burned to the ground, so they really don't have much to go
home to at this time. It's a sad case.*

*Well, that brings us up to the moment and I'm tired and ready to hit
the hay. So hope that our darling daughter is getting bigger, prettier and
smarter each and every day. Regards to all – love to the folks – and a billion
and one hugs and kisses for you and Carole –*

With All My Love,
Your Dave

Wednesday – 18 April – 1945
Somewhere in Western Germany

My Most Adorable Darlings,

*The radio is carrying a very pretty arrangement of an old favorite of
mine, "Indian Summer," and I feel like I was back home getting ready for
a date with you. I always seem to connect all the pretty songs with you
somehow – why? I guess I really didn't have such good times until I went
out on dates with you. Remember how we used to laugh so much at things
which only you and I could see were so funny? Gee, what would we ever do
if we ever forgot to laugh? If we have learned one thing in our married life,
it is that we are able to laugh at some things which had been thought pretty
bad at one time or another, so I'm looking forward impatiently to having
another laugh with you soon.*

*I just got back from the evening show at headquarters. They showed a
picture which I had missed while in Nancy, "Keys of the Kingdom." It is,
indeed, one of the great pictures I have seen. Even though we are of the
Jewish faith, I can still appreciate the theme of the picture, because we also
have a similar tension between the Jews and the gentiles. However, I was
happy to see that a note of cooperation was introduced into the story to show
that Protestants and Catholics can live together very happily. With pictures
and books such as this to be introduced to the public, perhaps in the future,
faiths will only mean a different type of worship, instead of criticism. When
that day comes, and if permanent peace is attained, then we can say that we
are living in a world to be proud of.*

I just heard that [war correspondent] *Ernie Pyle was killed on Okinawa
Island by Japanese machine-gun fire. As you know, he was a great friend of
the G.I. ever since he entered the War picture. He really wrote articles that*

everybody appreciated and liked. He typified the doughboy and his woes. I recall his writing, after he left the theatre over here, that he would go home and then, in spite of himself, go to the Pacific Theatre to continue to write about War, as it was still his job as a War Effort. However, there was that same fear that he had always possessed of getting killed. Well, I guess he knew that that was the way he was going to die. It is a very tough blow to the enlisted men to lose two very great friends in FDR and Pyle all in one week. Perhaps God has given us these losses to make up for the great gains which we will also get during this month. After all, we must always take the bitter with the sweet.

Over here, we aren't allowed to send packages home, because the postal authorities seem to think that we have confiscated German property and are attempting to send it on home. How very ridiculous we are at times in being just in our treating of war criminals. Why, I know of actual cases of Polish and Russian laborers who have gone into German homes, deliberately taking furnishings without even a murmur from the Jerries. After all, that was what the Nazis had been doing for years. Certainly a taste of the same medicine can't be so bad. I admit that the old story of an eye for an eye is not very modern – but after all, neither is warfare.

I suppose you really have your hands full with the actual running of the house and the baby to take care of. I don't relish your job at all – Mine is a lot easier to handle – and you don't get to see the various lands which I have seen neither – so there! On the other hand, I can gladly tell you that I'd rather be right there, back in St. Louis, and seeing nothing but America at all times.

I guess that's about all for the day, so say "Hello" to all our friends and tell them that I'll be home sometime this year, so save a day for a grand reunion. Love to the folks and many, many, many hugs and kisses for the baby and you, because I love you two very, very much –

With All My Love,
Your Dave

———

Thursday – 19 April – 1945
Somewhere in Western Germany

My Darling Amy and Carole,

Today has been a very pretty one, with the sun out all day long and the mercury about 50. As you may have expected, we had planes galore out today to take advantage of the weather. As we get further East, it is getting harder to find decent targets to knock out. I imagine that it gets pretty lonesome up there when there aren't any enemy planes to tangle with. The Western Air Forces had long ago met the Russian Air Force over German targets and I suppose they had to argue over who had the priority to attack. Well, as long as we keep going Eastward, that means that the end is very close. The 7th Army has entered Nuremberg and will probably take it in a week. Along with that, the 3rd is in Leipzig, which is a great advance and will be meeting up with the Russians in a very short time. As they have already crossed over into Czechoslovakia and are still going, they may meet the Russian forces in that country also. When that happens, the War is at an end, except for a few spasmodic uprisings, I suppose. Anyway, the Reich is now a very small affair, geographically speaking.

I hear that tomorrow is to be Hitler's birthday and we are to be especially alert for any outbursts. Well, after seeing the effects of our bombings and shelling, I don't think that there will be anything brewing, even if these people were ordered to do so. They fully realize that the War has passed their homes now and that they are well off. The radio just said that the Russian armies are about 20 miles from Berlin now. What a helluva headache the Nazis must have now with the Allies coming in from the West and East at the same time. Even if they do have the reserves in that area, they will have to be placed at only one front, which makes it easier for the other. Now that the Ruhr pocket has been cleared and many thousands of prisoners taken, the Nazis don't have a thing left to send them equipment and munitions, so it can't be too long.

I see that baseball season has opened and we split even inasmuch as the Cards lost their game and the Brownies won theirs. However, since then, I learned that the Brownies lost the other day and are now even. Well, as I've written before, the Cards will repeat, but the Browns will not. Did they have a large crowd out at Sportsman's Park – or don't you know? Well, I hope to be there for the Series this fall.

I had better end this letter, as there isn't anything else to say – except that I love you and miss you very, very much – (They are playing "All the Things You Are" on the radio right now – A coincidence – eh?) Well, say "Hello" to all and love to the folks – a billion hugs and kisses for the baby and you –

With All My Love,
Your Dave

Friday – 20 April – 1945
Somewhere in Western Germany

My Darling wife and Baby,

I got a letter yesterday from [Amy's cousins] *the Terhochs in France. They ask for soap and cigarettes as a favor. As I had written you and Aunt Otty before, they would appreciate these sorts of things and clothing in preference to money. As you know, there were a great many soldiers court-martialed for selling cigarettes to the French in the black market. Well, since then, nobody has been able to send any smokes or other PX items by mail, so it is impossible for me to send them a package including these items. However, you in the States may be in a better position to get them for these people. If I was able to get down that way, I'd bring something with me, but it is impossible now.*

Today has been another very pretty day and the bombers and fighter-bombers really gave Hitler a big birthday gift. They must have hammered the devil out of Germany and Czechoslovakia today. I heard that the armies are still pressing forward, although a slight stiffening has been seen on the 9th Front. Of course, the Russians are increasing the pressure from the East, so it will be a matter of days before Berlin falls. After the Elbe has been crossed on a broader scale, we'll walk in.

Earlier today, Nancy came running over to me and I noted that she limped a bit and pulled her rear left leg in a peculiar manner, so I picked her up and, with the help of a fellow who had some veterinary experience, we located a tiny thorn in the paw. We got a tweezers and finally got it out – and off she ran to jump around some more with a huge red dog who has been after Nancy ever since I brought her here. However, I think that he has finally been convinced that she is still too young. You ought to see the way they throw each other around.

I heard that we will be paid in marks from now on. I don't know what difference it makes, because we aren't allowed to go into stores and buy merchandise anyway. If we did go in, that would mean fraternizing, which is dead against the law for American G.I.'s. However, I and others have seen English soldiers and American officers associating with the Germans on various occasions. If a G.I. were to do it, he'd get a nice, big fine and a few months hard labor. That is just another one of the many things that create such a hard feeling between us around here.

Well, Darlings, that is about all for today – so hope that all is well at home. Regards to all and love to the folks – a lot of hugs and kisses for Carole and you –

With All My Love,
Your Dave

———

Monday – 23 April – 1945
Somewhere in Western Germany

My Most Beloved Wife and Baby,

Before I go any further, I want to mention that the radio is carrying a very pretty rendition of "All The Things You Are." It is still a very pretty number and brings me such nice memories of us together. However, a song isn't necessary to make me remember you – I think of you and Carole at all times. It is one of the things that makes this War endurable. I hope that we will soon be together and forget all about the War and its cruelties.

Okma and I just got back from Nancy. I had some business to clear up and the only way to do this was to go down there myself and see that it was done. I had been on the road between Landau and Haguenau and it did not appeal to me again, so I thought that a better route would be from Landau to a town to the West and down, into France. Well, we had wonderful sailing in Germany on excellent roads, however, when I took that turn toward France, that was when it got bad. We got lost in mountainous regions that took us up and down about a thousand hills. We went thru some towns that never had seen Americans, I think. At one village, we met some American G.I.'s who had been left behind to mop up and haven't been picked up for eight weeks. Anyway, they said that they weren't any too anxious to get out or else they would have asked us to take them.

(We interrupt this program to announce that we just had a mail call and I received one letter from Mrs. Mougin, two from Janine, and four from you, along with a nice package. What a haul that is – eh? The package had the pretzel sticks, potato sticks, chili and tongue in it, and I want to thank you for it – a very nice assortment indeed.)

Well, Okie and I decided to head up in the general direction of Bitche and Sarrebourg. We got into a stretch of ups and downs and were really on the racing derby. When we went up, we figured that that must certainly be the last hill, but when we got to the top, lo and behold, there was another higher one, but we finally got into Nancy at about six in the evening. The first place

I went to was the Mougins' and they were really a surprised lot to see me walk in. They couldn't get over the idea that I had returned and went to see them first. Mr. Mougin came and I met him for the first time. He seems to be a very easy sort of person, a likeable guy and not overbearing. He is about the same height as I, about 135 lbs., grey hair, a sallow complexion, and well and neatly dressed. He said that he had known me for a long time, as the others had spoken often of me. We spoke of the places in Germany which we had both seen. He told us that he had hid in the woods for 15 days while the Jerries were out looking for them and the Americans were approaching the Rhine. After that sector had been captured, he came out and got a ride toward the border. He found four Jerries who wanted to surrender, so they threw down their guns and jumped on the same truck upon which he was riding. He had returned on the same day that I had first gone to look for him. We joked about the sizes of the Russian women's arms and breasts and about the War situation. I asked him if he had ever seen any of the atrocities that were committed upon the American soldiers and he said that he hadn't. Oh yes – I asked about the bottle of champagne which I had given them and they answered that they had opened it that same night that Mr. Mougin had returned and drank a drink for me also. They thanked me so much for all that I had done for them and said to be sure to thank you and send their best wishes to you and Carole Frances.

(THE FOLLOWING MORNING) Okie and I hit the hay and had a real night's sleep for a change and did not awaken with a sheet of ice over us as we have here. Well, he got his work done and I packed all of my bedding and we took off with another fellow who came back with us. We stopped at one of my points of business and got whatever they had and took off. On the way, we saw a PX attached to one of the outfits and decided to try to get some rations from them. We were able to argue the Sergeant out of it and bought some candy, chocolate, and Coca-Colas. These were the first Cokes that we have had since we were stationed in Naples, waiting for the invasion of France. The unfortunate thing about it all was that we were unable to take them with me and had to drink them right there, as they wanted the bottles back.

So Otty already sent a package to the Terhochs – That was quick work. Did you send any soap? That is one of the things that they asked for in their letter. Send some laundry soap and toilet, as both have been so inferior during the past five years. I'd suggest that she send some Cashmere Bouquet as a toilet soap, as it lathers so much easier and will last longer. As I told you, their letter was from Annecy, so they are still there and they didn't say anything about going to Paris.

Yes, the break between Russia and Japan is a real break and will help us in a big way when we start putting the pressure on the Japs. With all the landings going on in that area, the Burma Campaign going well, perhaps we will get a break and go back home for a 30-day furlough.

As to sending [Fresno friends] the Evensons Carole's old and outgrown clothing, it is a very charitable gesture, but I don't like the idea. After all, if you were to add up all that we have spent on the baby and we do expect to have another, it will be an additional expense to replace those same items which you have sent to Fresno. It isn't that I don't appreciate their position, but I also am thinking of us and after the War. I don't know; maybe since I've been over here, I may have lost all sense of sympathy for anybody. I hate the damned Germans more and more every day, especially after seeing more of the pictures of the prison camps and the Nazis' crimes. Darling, how in the world can anyone or anything ever allow even a dog to starve. They simply starved, killed and raped without any hesitation. If we were to do anything that would seem uncivil, we'd be called savages. So if a German came up to me, asking for food or water, I don't think that I'd flinch in shooting him right between the eyes. If only we were able to wipe them off the face of the world and not have to worry about them making War again in a hundred years. They just aren't any good in a peace-loving age and will never be.

How in the world did I ever get off on that subject while speaking of the Evensons? Anyway, as long as you have already sent the package, I hope that they will appreciate it. Well, Darlings, that takes care of another letter, so I guess I had better hang onto the other two and answer later in the evening.

Say "Hello" to all of our friends, love to the folks and beaucoup love and kisses for the baby and you –
With All My Love,
Your Dave

Tuesday – 24 April – 1945
Somewhere in Western Germany

My Darling Wife and Baby,

During the past few days, there have been established various rest camps for the 1st TAF, among which is the city where the Terhochs live. Well, today there was a listing of the men to go there and the first one is a fellow who had been the principal of a small school in Kansas and who had gone to Missouri U. I spoke to him and he is going to take a package down to Eric and Edith [Terhoch] for me – That is nice of him, isn't it? So I am going to make up a box and put some soap and cigarettes in it. Wasn't that a bit of luck?

Sorry I wasn't able to be there in your dream that night – I'll try to make it the next time. You said that Carole had awakened from a bad dream – What does she dream about? I often wondered what a child would dream about. As to my being disappointed in the house (in the dream), I'm certain that it must have been a dream, as I do like it and I'm sure that I will after I see it. Not until you mentioned it did I realize that we had been overseas 15 months already. At that rate, we'll be ready for "rotation" in July. Gee, if only they would revive that plan for the Air Forces. I wasn't surprised to hear that Paul expected to be back home this summer, as the Navy always did allow their men to get home sooner and more often than the Army.

As to [comedian] Jerry Lester, I have never seen him, but if he looks like me, he must be funny. Where did all of these doubles come from all of a sudden? Maybe I'm really back home and these guys are supposed to be over here. After all, there could be worse things than that.

As to your letter of the 11th – The Yanks were 63 miles from Berlin at that time. Now we hear so many rumors about them meeting on the Western edges with the Russians that we just take it with a grain of salt. It may be true that they have met on the Southwest side, however. As you have seen in the papers, we are heading down towards the Czechoslovakian and Austrian borders, hoping to meet up with the Russians in that direction. If the Allies in Northern Italy are able to gain momentum, it may turn out to be a triple meeting.

As to Lilly [Otty's sister], I don't know what to say about her desire to go to Palestine after the War. She seems to be very much interested in the movement and it may be the best thing for her. As it is, she will have a hard time finding a husband – and you will agree with me on that. So perhaps over there, she will be more appealing to the men and will find more happiness than she'd find here.

Well, Darlings, that brings us to the end of the day's activities and I guess I ought to get to bed – so regards to all – love to the folks – and a bushel of hugs and kisses for the baby and you – I do love and miss you two so very much –
With All My Love,
Your Dave

Thursday – 26 April – 1945
Somewhere in Western Germany
My Dearest Darlings,

As I write this letter, the Russian Armies are quickly moving Westward in taking Berlin and possibly Hitler and some of his rats. As yet, it is only a rumor that he is there, but we do hope that it is true and that the trap is already sprung and that he is caught. Along with that, the American Armies in the South are really putting on the steam and heading towards Munich. It is now a race between three armies – the 7th, 3rd and the French 1st, who have suddenly entered the picture with a quick advance. So the picture gets better and better as time goes on. All this, of course, will help to get me back home a lot sooner. I still don't like to hear about all those Air Force units going directly to the Pacific Theatre, however. It certainly is no morale booster to have that staring you in the face.

At the last minute, I decided to go with Joe Dines to the Wing theatre to see "Woman in the Window." He hadn't seen it and I had, but I liked it so much that I went again. However, we had a special short subject for G.I.'s only, which was an all-around short with news (?) cartoon and a miniature on "Nostradamus," who had prophesied Hitler and the War and almost all other events dealing with this period. His latest prediction is that Hitler will be destroyed by either Himmler or Goering. All these prophesies were made back in the 1400s when he was a scholar. All have come true so far and it can happen as he had predicted. After all, Himmler is a powerful arm in the S.S. – In fact, he is their head and can order them to kill Hitler and still get away with it. At this time, nobody would really be bothered if Hitler was murdered, so we'll wait and see what happens.

Well, Darlings, I hope that our darling daughter is well and gaining steadily every day in weight, beauty and mentality. Oh – regards from Nancy.

Say "Hello" to all our friends and give my love to the folks — and oodles and oodles of love and kisses for the baby and you —

With All My Love,

Your Dave

———

Friday — 27 April — 1945

Somewhere in Western Germany

My Darling Amy and Carole Frances,

I had to go down to Haguenau on business this morning, so I took the Mess Sergeant, Carlin, with me and also one of the other boys who was not on duty at the time. All along the road, there were Jerry prisoners filling in the holes. They were guarded by French Moroccans who didn't seem to give a damn if the Jerries smoked while working or not. If an Allied prisoner did that, he'd be shot down at once. I don't know why I don't accidentally run over a few of these damned s__ __ _____. It would be such an easy thing to do — and a great favor to society.

Holy smoke! Do you mean that Carole is already holding hands? She'll be dating before I get back home at that rate. Well, at least we know that she has sex appeal already. That puts her about ten years ahead of the other girls her age. I wonder if that is my strain coming out, because I fell for Goldie Zweig when I was five or six.

It was announced that the Russian and American armies had lined up two days ago. That must have been some occasion! Also, it was rumored that Mussolini has been captured once more. Well, it wouldn't be much to have him in captivity, except as a specimen to examine for the sake of science. He certainly has been a liability to Hitler ever since the Allies landed in Italy. Yes, I agree with you that it will be a great relief not to have the shadow of War hanging over us after it is all over.

I was wondering if you had seen some of those pictures of the prison camps. As you say, I already have told you about my thoughts on it — so why go any further? Just so long as the people back home are getting acquainted with these conditions.

Well, Darlings, I guess I had better get some sleep now — It's late and I'm worn out from that trip. So excuse me and say "Hello" to all and send love to the folks — billions of hugs and kisses for Carole and you —

With All My Love,

Your Dave

Saturday – 28 April – 1945
Somewhere in Western Germany

My Sweetest Angels,

I just got back from the Wing theatre where I saw "Experiment Perilous" with Hedy Lamarr, George Brent and Paul Lukas. It was really entertaining and I was surprised with her acting – sort of good. It was one of those pictures which Hollywood is making in its usual cycle – this one about psychological murders. Of course, it keeps the audience guessing right from the beginning, but I had an idea about the villain from the start. I think that I got that idea from the picture "Gaslight," which was along the same lines as this one.

There are many being sent to the Pacific Theatre directly from Europe. I certainly hope that they overlook our number when the selecting comes up. After all, there are so many other nicer and younger fellows who want to see the world. Put an ad in the Sunday paper for a person to relieve a G.I. from active duty. Maybe a WAC will answer – who knows? As the end to this War draws nearer and nearer, that possibility looms bigger and bigger to us. In fact, there was a pretty good rumor today that Himmler offered to surrender unconditionally to the Americans and the English, but they refused on the basis that any surrender will be made to all the Allies and not to any part of them. So if it is true, the surrender will probably be made to the Russians also any day – In fact, it may be going on now. It would be something if the organized (?) resistance were to end on May Day – the birthday of the Reds. They would raise the roof off the Kremlin. Of course, it would be celebrated all over the world as the halfway mark and the biggest problem out of the way. It has been a long and hard grind and, at times, it looked as though the Jerries weren't going to have any trouble in their conquest of the world. However, we can now say that we are a free people and will always be free! Gee, it was only a few years ago that the Nazis were flaunting their power about most of Europe and threatening our very shores – Now look at it. There is no Reich!

You really can't imagine how proud I am to be able to say that I am an American. It should be something to instill upon the children in schools after the War. I can assure you that I will do my utmost to try to make Carole understand the honor and privilege of being an American. Back in the days when I went to school, some of us thought that giving the Pledge of Allegiance and the singing of the Star-Spangled Banner were a lot of nonsense and a bit old-fashioned. However, it is one of the finest and most-effective gestures that a schoolchild can make. I suppose that this seems like a lot of flag-waving to you, but it is true and I mean every word of it.

Say, I suppose you had better start to slow down sending me any packages, as I may either be on my way home or to another theatre – and not to see a movie. Gosh, I hope that the men already over there are coming along well and will end that War a lot sooner than was figured. There are so many other outfits in this same Wing which have been over since the invasion of Africa and now don't have any hope of getting back until after the Pacific is finished. That is a crime and very unfair. However, in War, everything is unfair, so we aren't surprised at anything that happens. The one thing of which I am certain is that I will be home at some time and safe and sound, so whatever happens, just remember that we will be back together again sometime – for all time. Gee, I wish that we get a 30-day furlough after it is over. They'd have to dynamite me out once I get home.

So say "Hello" to all and love to the folks – a lot of nice, bug hugs and kisses for Carole and you –

With all My Love,
Your Dave

Sunday – 29 April – 1945
Somewhere in Western Germany

My Sweetest Sweethearts,

Well, from all the flashes which we have had in the past twenty-four hours, it's a wonder that we haven't decided that the War was ended already. There have been so many unconfirmed reports of unconditional surrender that when it does come, everybody will be used to it and it will not even faze them. All day long, the radio has carried these reports and the news from Italy that Mussolini has been executed by the guerrillas. Well, it is good riddance of bad rubbish, but tough that the Allied Military Court couldn't try and convict him and his men. That is what will probably happen to Hitler and a few other loyal Nazis. Himmler is the power at this time, because he is the head of the S.S. and the Army is no longer able to stand up as a unified force, so he will be able to surrender on the part of Germany. Today's teletype news carried a report, unconfirmed of course, that Himmler has killed Hitler. So from here on in, it will be a matter of what is and what is not true. Either way, the War is over at this time and all that remains is the official papers stating so.

I certainly hope that we are given some consideration in the designation for the Pacific Theatre. This whole Wing and Air Force has been overseas on steady duty ever since the invasion of Africa. There is one attached Fighter Group which has been in about two months longer than that, as they were giving air support to the British Army when Montgomery was having such a hot time of it at El Alamein. Gosh, that seems like ages ago. So they certainly deserve to get home for a rest, even if they are sent to the Pacific. So let's hope and cross our fingers – maybe our eyes, too, if it will help.

I received a package from Aunt Mary which contained a nice, large salami which was well-packed in wax and waxed paper. That really is the only way to send something like that and expect it to arrive in good shape. She also sent a can of sardines in soybean oil. Those things really come in handy late at night. I received two letters from you, finally. The first one was written on Friday, the day when Roosevelt died. I can imagine what an effect it had on the American public. Your impressions are probably typical of the nation at that time. I don't think that I told you when I first heard about it. We had just gotten up in the morning for breakfast and some of the boys, who were on the midnight shift, came in with that news. Of course, at first, we thought that it was just a piece of propaganda from the Nazis, however, as the day grew older, the radios carried the news as correct and we all were none too happy to hear about it. There are so many men who had never even heard of Truman that they are leery about his ability. Anyway, the War is about over and they don't think that it will make much difference who is president now. However, there was a certain sense of assurance which we had while he was our C-in-C. Roosevelt was mourned all over the world and certainly deserved all the tributes paid him. Perhaps the world will also do the same to Churchill, but before he dies. He also has done a great job, as has Stalin. It is so much nicer to pay tributes to men before they are dead.

Your letter had the first inkling of your receiving my mention of helping my dad. Perhaps we can do something to help. After seeing so much of War, and everything through which we have gone in the past, we now see that money is nothing but a means. No, don't misunderstand me – I wouldn't throw it away. But I have gotten a different slant on its value since being over here and seeing what people have gone through. Billions have been thrown to the winds in various manners and thousands of well-off people *are now paupers due to the War. Perhaps I may have been influenced too much by the War – who knows?*

Well, Darlings, that is about it for now. Hope that everybody is well at home and that I'll be there with you soon. Say "Hello" to our friends and love to the folks, and for Carole and you – an enormous hug and kiss –

With All My Love,

Your Dave

———

Wednesday – 2 May – 1945
Somewhere in Western Germany

My Most Beloved Amy and Carole Frances,

It has been a long time since I wrote to you – in fact, about three nights ago, to be exact. Since then, lots has happened. One thing, in particular, is that we are no longer in the same place from which I last wrote you.

On Monday night, I managed to obtain four bottles of champagne from a few of the boys in another outfit. Fay and Joe Dines had another, so that night, we, including Louie, our other Supply man, all had a time. Of course, the evening couldn't have been complete without the salami sandwiches that I made from the salami that Aunt Mary had sent me. Along with that, we had some sardines that I had from a package before – Then Joe brought down some tuna. It was a grand time and we really cleaned the five bottles in a hurry. It is a funny thing, but Louie is about the easiest thing to get tight. After two or three sips, he was way up in the air. On top of that, he was reading a humorous book and laughing out loud, so I wonder if he ever really knew what he was reading.

The next day, I had to make a trip down to Haguenau again and I took a couple of the boys along. As we got about ten miles out, up came the clouds and rain. To add to our discomfort, it turned to sleet and snow and froze on the windows, which had no workable wipers. So there we were – trying to drive on a slippery road and keep the window dry at the same time. On top of that, it is hard enough for two people to be dry in an open jeep – let alone three – so the older fellow's arm and leg got all wet. When we finally got to Haguenau, we headed for the stove so that he could get dried off and we could get warm. Then the snow started once more for about the fiftieth time and we had to wait for it to slow down before we decided to get on our way again. We finally got back at about 3:00 in time for about ten more minutes of sunshine and then it turned ice cold.

While I was gone, Fay and Louie loaded up the balance of the supplies and we were ready to push off that next morning. I went in an open jeep with Mullen and another fellow – with Nancy as my traveling companion. It was a cold ride and we were lucky that Mullen had taken his blankets along in the jeep, as Nancy wasn't warm enough with what I had brought along. Well, we drove through such cities as Speyer and Heilbronn and finally landed at another town further East. Speyer was the most completely overlooked large city that I have seen. It may have been because the French had it picked out as their headquarters and wanted to spare the large buildings for themselves. However, when we saw some of the other cities, they were just the opposite – completely smashed to bits. Heilbronn was especially battered. There is absolutely not a building standing – not even the walls.

We finally got to our destination at about 5 in the evening and had dinner. After that, we looked at the place which is supposed to be for the men. It is a kindergarten. There are still papers, toys and all the other things lying about to indicate that children had been taught there. In the back is a little garden where they had outdoor classes. As we rummaged through the rooms, we found many things to show that the children were being taught that Hitler and Nazism were the right and only things in the world. They even had a few pictures which were cut from an issue of "Life" magazine to show that most of the women in America were man-crazy; that the people were immoral; and that there are wild animals roaming all over America. To illustrate these points, they showed pictures which were from a revue on Broadway and the ballet numbers had sailors dancing with their hands over the rearmost posterior of some girls. Anyway, it was right in the schools that Nazism was born and it is right there that it will have to be killed.

The funniest things have happened – Whenever a German passes, Nancy barks like the devil at them and chases them – only the Jerries. She must sense it or else she is a Super Dog. However, this afternoon, she was bad. I have been afraid of dogs crossing the street ever since my other dog, Buck, was killed while crossing the road. Well, Nancy ran after a horse and I called after her to come back. She started back and then turned around and ran after the horse again. Well, when she came back, she crept up to me and I whacked her good across the rear end. She started to whimper, but took it like a big dog. After that, she stayed close to me as we walked back.

All we do now is ask, "Is the War over today?" So far, there have been so many unconfirmed reports that we aren't very excited about the prospects of the end. It means that we will have to start worrying about direct shipment to the Pacific then. However, one thing is certain and that is that we will not do any more moving into Germany – This is our last. We may go back to France or home or to the Pacific.

Well, Darlings, I hope that all is well at home. Say "Hello" to our friends and give my love to the folks – a billion and one kisses for the baby and you – and I want to remind you that I do love you very much –

With All My Love,
Your Dave

———

Thursday – 3 May – 1945
Somewhere in Western Germany

My Darling Wife and Baby,

I am now possessor of a cavalry sword. I found it this afternoon right outside this place. It has a wonderful sheath made of a highly polished metal. The sword has a carved hand-guard and a lion's head as the decoration. The eyes of the lion are red jewels. There's a small animal's head at the bottom of the handle. The blade is highly tempered steel and etched about ¾ of the length of the whole thing. Rodger walked in later and saw it and was his mouth wide! He said that he was looking for something like that to send home.

All that we have been doing so far is looking around and seeing what is what in this vicinity. Fay and I took a walk in the afternoon and went to a gasthaus [tavern] which was recommended by a Frenchman. It is called "Drei Kunig" – the "Three Kings," as you know – even if the German spelling isn't correct. There, we found Russian liberated people galore, also some French soldiers and WACS. The beer wasn't bad at all – dark in color. It cost us about ½ cent per glass. I spoke Yiddish, which is similar to German, so we were able to be understood. Gee, what a linguist I'll be when I get back home!

I don't think that I told you about the setup which we have here. Well, it was formerly a filling station – a Shell Station, incidentally. There are four stalls for autos, a showroom for the Mercedes automobiles which the owner sold, and offices on the lower floor. Upstairs, he lived with his family. The usual thing over here is to select whatever place you think suitable and have the A.M.G. move the people out. They go out, leaving 90% of their *belongings behind. However, there is nothing which any of us want, so we just throw it aside into one corner. In the room where I have the office, there are still all the parts which the former occupants sold. The shelves are full and all his records are intact. However, we threw out a lot of stuff which cluttered up the office. It will be one big headache for him when he has to straighten out everything. In fact, we found his credit paper – a value of about $20,000 at this time, so to make it all the more difficult, we tore up the paper. We did that just to be spiteful. We found that this yokel had been a very devout Nazi, so we are doing everything possible to make it difficult for him. This guy had many conveniences in his home – two electric iceboxes, intercommunication systems, radio and other smaller things, but in order to obtain these things, one had to be a big Nazi and he was definitely!*

All over the streets, you see white displays of cloth ranging from bed sheets to panties, indicating surrender. From every window and doorway, you can find these fluttering in the breeze. At least these people realize that they have definitely lost the War and that we are conquerors. The Poles and Russians who walk the streets spit on the Germans and take whatever they want. We have about 15 Poles and Russians at our disposal, if we need help. They cleaned out the school into which we moved and are helping with the Mess Hall. As you know, it is hard for some of the boys not to be able to speak to anybody while in Germany. When they first came up, there were a number of Russian and Polish girls who took a liking to the G.I.'s and they were invited into the girls' homes. Well, after the Wing got all set up, the officers saw that the enlisted men were on the inside and that the officers were on the out, so they told the girls that if they (the girls) were caught speaking to any of the G.I. enlisted men, the girls would be shot. The idea of shooting, of course, is only to frighten the girls. If true, that is about the lowest thing for any man to do.

We did receive the "Stars & Stripes" which carried the headline, "Hitler Dead!" That is really something, isn't it? At this time, I don't know what to think about it, because the Jerries are liable to come up with any sort of a story possible. If he is dead, he probably was killed long ago, as the rumor went. As it is, [Admiral Karl] Doenitz came out with a statement that he died fighting in Berlin – which, of course, glorifies Hitler as a martyr. However, it probably was true that Himmler killed him and started the surrender procedures. Since Doenitz took over, no peace offers have been mentioned. According to the story, he died on May 1st, which was the Reds' birthday – Ironical, if true, eh? At any rate, the War is already over, except for the official notice, so now it is whether or not we are going to the Pacific and when.

Well, Darlings, I hope that all is well back home. No doubt, there was a celebration on the streets when it was announced that Hitler was dead. Along with the surrender coming up soon, they will really be happy. Well, let's hope that we all get home sometime this year.

Nancy, our dog, is getting to be a big gal now and says "Hello" to all. How is our darling daughter getting along these days? Well, say "Hello" to all of our friends and love to the folks – a billion and one hugs and kisses for Carole and you –

With All My Love,
Your Dave

———

Friday – 4 May – 1945
Somewhere in Western Germany

My Dearest Darlings,

Today, I received a letter from my dad, two from you, and a package from Syd. In his package was a jar of herring spread, a few cans of sardines, and a salami. Well, I unwrapped the salami and, much to my disappointment, it was spoiled. That was the first in about a year that came in rotten. After I peeled off the wax paper, I knocked off the wax and there was a stinky scum on the salami. I washed it off, hoping that it was only bad on top, but then the skin came off and I knew that it was bad all the way thru. That is a shame, because it takes so many points to get one of these. Otherwise, the package was in good shape.

As to that school for the rest of the outfit, it is now occupied and we have most of the company up here now. The men have a captured Jerry radio for entertainment and a couple of speakers, so we took the other radio which we had received from Special Service for this place. On top of that, today I got hold of a new Jerry record player, so we have all the requirements for a nice day room, however we do need some new records, as those which we brought over from Africa are about worn out. We keep nagging the office for them, but so far – no luck.

You certainly saw a very good play in "Blithe Spirit" – I recall that it was a hit on Broadway when I was a civilian. I'm surprised that Noel

Coward's plays are still being shown in the States, because he caused quite a disturbance with his feelings on the War when he was in England.

Well, say "Hello" to all and give my love to the folks and bushels and bushels of hugs and kisses for the baby and you –

With All My Love,

Your Dave

———

Saturday – 5 May – 1945

Somewhere in Western Germany

My Darling Wife and Baby,

At this moment, it is raining cats and dogs. Speaking of dogs, Nancy sends her love. Oh yes – one more thing – We now have a bar of our own – for the 346th men. We took over a bar and made the people move to the rear. Today was the first day and they were short on beer, but had plenty of wine, as a couple of the boys had found a cache of captured wines which the Jerries had taken from France. So now, the only problem is to locate a beer source of supply.

We aren't worrying about the War, because we have heard that the War is over except for two small pockets – in Czechoslovakia and Norway. After that, it will be actually ended. However, now the rumor runs different from yesterday – Those men who have been overseas less than one year will go back to the States for a 21-day furlough and then go to the Pacific Theatre; those with 1-2 years service will stay as Occupation Troops; and those with over 2 years of service overseas will go back home for good. It is a fair idea as far as squareness goes, although it deprives us of going back at once. However, at the same time, it will not expose us to any danger.

Now for your letter of the 28th of March – my birthday – Sorry that I wasn't on hand to receive the congratulations – Next time. By now, you ought to have received that Passover picture – like it? That night was the first in a long time that my dad was at Baba's for Passover. I recall when I was about five or six years old, we were at Baba's for Pesach and I got drunk on wine. That was nice of the maid to stay with Carole while you went to temple, and your meeting with [Dave's Aunt] Molly and [Uncle] Ben at the Seder was a nice coincidence. The temple services on V.E. Day is the best idea in the way of celebrations that I have heard of and I hope that everybody who had planned on getting drunk will show up at temple.

Well, so our darling daughter really knows a lot of songs. I never heard of some of them – I guess they are new ones which have come out since I have been overseas. From what I hear, this "Rum and Coca-Cola" is supposed to be pretty good. Of course, your piano playing helped her to remember these songs quite a bit. Well, that about does it for today – It is getting very late and I'm all wet – So regards to all and love to the folks – a great big hug and kiss from Carole's daddy and yours truly – I do love you –

With All My Love,
Your Dave

———

Sunday – 6 May – 1945
Somewhere in Western Germany

My Sweetest Darlings,

With all the armed resistance about ended, it looks as though we can declare the War at an end. As we had expected, they are surrendering in groups and it will be a day or so before all the groups have laid down their arms. Now, the Peace Conference at San Francisco will have a golden opportunity to do a big thing. As to getting lost whenever I go out on a trip, that is impossible as long as one has a map or signs on the highway to direct you. After all, this country isn't backward at all. They may have been narrow-minded, but they were also far-sighted.

As to Nancy, she is doing very well and today I taught her a new trick. I have her jump up to the top step and then onto my back. From there, I pull her tail and when she turns around, I pull it again from over my shoulder. However, after a few times, she slipped down over my side and fell on her back – so that was the end of the tricks for the day. She is so well liked by everybody. She comes to whomever calls, but she leaves when I whistle. At this writing, she is sleeping like a babe in the corner. You have no idea how much the companionship of a dog adds to life in the Army. She is really like a very good friend. You ought to see her when I leave to go to chow – She runs to the window and whines like a baby. I can't take her into the Mess Hall any longer, because the Adjutant, Lt. Micka, doesn't approve of it. She is so much cleaner than a lot of the people around here. I know that Carole would really like her a lot, if I were able to get her home with me. As to sending any dog food, thanks, but we have enough around here.

As to the blackout which was enforced at our old location, it was necessary because the Jerries at that time had a few places with which to make some nuisance raids on the Rhine bridges near us. So, in order to avoid being their "Target For Tonight," we adopted the blackout policy very strictly. However, we still had a couple of scares. So it wasn't that we were trying to hide; it was as a protective means. I'm glad you liked the description of the latrine, because they are really funnier than words can describe.

Well, Darlings, I guess that's about it for now – so regards to all – love to the folks and lots and lots of love and kisses for Carole and you –

With All My Love,

Your Dave

Monday – 7 May – 1945

Somewhere in Western Germany

My Dearest Darlings,

I guess today is the day for which we have been waiting so long. As to the date of May 7th, there is no great significance and it doesn't impress one as a date to remember. Of course, we can always connect it with December 7th as a convenient way of remembering it. I wonder how the world is reacting to the official ending of the War on this continent? I suppose the folks back in the States are really going on benders and some to church. Well, as long as they celebrate in their own ways – I guess you can't take that from them. We certainly have waited long enough for it come around. Do you think that it will be remembered as Armistice Day was remembered? Today, we went about our business as though nothing even happened. In the afternoon, some Russian girls who were passing the station stopped in and gave us some nice purple and white lilacs, which I have on my desk at this very moment – They smell pretty nice, too. These liberated workers would do almost anything for the Americans now that they are free again. Well, almost anything.

It was a very pretty day right from the start. The sun was out early and it was beautiful – a real day for the end of the War! I was able to take Nancy walking with me when I went out and she also felt the difference in the weather. I never saw a dog that was so human in actions.

Well, now for the bad news – I have to make a trip down to Nancy tomorrow morning. That is one trip all the boys just live for, however, I have to go there on business and also to Haguenau on the way back, so with the boys who will go along on a two-day pass, we will have to make it a four-day trip. That means that I will not be able to drop you a line for the next four days. I will drop in to see the Mougins and give them your regards.

By this time, they ought to be all set up and in the old routine of family life once more. Say, who knows – maybe Janine will be married while I'm there.

Oh, before I forget, Jarvis, that fellow who went to Annecy on a pass, got back late last night and he came in and saw me. He also gave me a letter from them by Eric, as he is the one who speaks and writes English. He gave them the package which I had made up for them and they said that it was greatly appreciated. Jarvis told me that they planned to move back to Paris very soon. He intends going back into the business of raising snails, which he had done before the War. He told Jarvis that he has been trying to keep one step ahead of the Nazis ever since France fell. I don't know if I will ever have the opportunity of going down there, but I will try to send packages with those men who do go.

Well, Darlings, I guess that is about all for now – so regards to all and hope that everybody is well at home. Love to the folks and lots and lots of hugs and kisses for the baby and you –

With All My Love,

Your Dave

⸺

Sunday – 13 May – 1945

Somewhere in Western Germany

My Sweetest Darlings,

In your letters, I learned that the baby had gotten that skin disease, impetigo. I'm still stunned and unable to figure out how on earth she ever got in contact with the germ in the first place. I've heard about men getting that in cutting themselves after shaving – but not a child. Were you able to figure out how it ever happened – so that you can prevent it from reoccurring? That's why I yearn to be back home with you – so that I can watch over you. After all, you do have a tremendous job of looking after the house and the baby, so you are pretty well occupied throughout the day, so here's hoping that the next letter tells me that she is all healed.

We made Nancy at ten in the evening. That was the day the surrender was being celebrated. We went to our old spot – the university – and found that it had been taken over by that Section which is now in control of Nancy – The Lorraine Base Section. Well, we convinced them to allow us to stay there, even though we were not Infantrymen. After that, we all wanted to go out and celebrate the Victory also – so we all had friends in Nancy and went our different ways. I, of course, went to see the Mougins. They were sitting in their window, trying to get some relief from the evening heat. They were certainly surprised to see me. It was a very appropriate day to show up – wasn't it? Well, we sat and talked and I brought a few little things for them, for which they were so thankful. We then opened a few bottles of sweet white wine, which was delicious. At one o'clock, I was amazed how the time had flown and didn't want to be a bore, so I said that I had better be off and then was answered with an invitation to dinner the next night. I accepted, as I figured that it would be the last time I'd see them. Well, after leaving them, I ran across a dance on the street about three blocks from their home. It seems that all of France was staying up that night to celebrate and they threw their doors wide open, so I stayed and danced – being a wee bit under the weather. I must have gone to four dances before I realized that it was five in the A.M. and I hit for home. I was really fatigued when I lay down to sleep.

The next morning, I got up and took the Motor Sergeant with me as the driver – and we went to Haguenau over that damned highway which is probably the worst in the ETO. I think that the Jerries probably tortured their prisoners by taking them over that road. After getting my business all finished, we returned to Nancy a couple of hot, dirty men. I went to see the Mougins and we had a very enjoyable meal of about six courses. I explained that in the States, we placed bowls of potatoes, salads, vegetables, and a platter of meat on the table or buffet and in that way, eliminated all the trips to the kitchen that the French women make in serving a meal. I stayed until about one and I told them that the next trip to see them would probably be in about 15 years, when the baby was 20. We said goodbye and they wished you and the baby a lot of luck, and me also. After leaving them, I went by one of the places where I had been the night before and there was another dance, so I stayed for an hour and then hit the hay.

The next day, we had to go to one of the Supply Depots at Toul and after driving out there, we learned that they had moved to Metz, but had left all their carried-over work with another outfit in Nancy. We then went back to Nancy and got our work finished there. It was about noon, so we took the rest of the day off. We went to some bars and had beer. All the time we were in Nancy, it was as hot as St. Louis in July – You can imagine! Well, we got back that evening at about midnight after going to another dance in the market square. They all celebrated for three days and all the shops were closed. The next day was the last for those men whom we had taken with us on pass, so we also took a pass. I went to the Red Cross and had some stripes sewn on my shirt. While there, I had some doughnuts and coffee. I left about noon and on the street, I ran across a fellow I had known in St. Louis, Harry Steibelman. We stood and talked about half an hour and he told me that he had been in the hospital in Nancy after being shot in the foot by a sniper in Germany. Well, while there, he really got sick and caught pneumonia. He is certain that he's going to the Pacific. We were ready to hit the road again and it was one happy truckload that headed back to Germany.

I do hope the baby is all healed and enjoying her swing and slide, so hoping that all is well at home now – regards to all and lots of hugs and kisses for the baby and you – love to the folks – and I do love and miss you very much –

With All My Love,
Your Dave

———

Monday – 14 May – 1945
Somewhere in Western Germany

My Darling Amy and Carole Frances,

Well, I hope that the baby has long ago gotten over that impetigo and is back to normal. It must have been a pitiful sight to see her watching all the other kids playing and she all alone with her toys. It hurt me to even hear her cry when she was an infant – so you can imagine how I would feel if I were home to see her with her face, neck, arms and legs all broken out. So I'm very anxiously waiting for your next few letters, telling me that all is well once more.

I had forgotten all about my prediction that the War would end in May. However, I didn't miss it by very much – about 12 days to be exact. Now that it is over, we are all asking what will happen to this outfit and nobody seems to know yet, so we are kept on edge – but the Supply Section keeps on working anyway. There will be inspections from now on until we get home or to the Pacific. I thought that we'd leave all that sort of stuff back in the States when we shipped out – but it is even worse. Well, now I can't say that the War will be over soon, as it is over and it is worse than before, as the men haven't as much to do now, so the inspections are to take up the day. If anyone even mentions Army to me when I get back home, I'll get up and walk right out of the place.

As to the address of your aunt in Vienna, I'll hang on to it, but I doubt if I'll ever go any further than the place in which we are now. If any of the boys does have an occasion to go down that way, I'll give him the address and have him try to locate the family at the Institute for the Blind. I do hope that the Nazis left the blind alone while they occupied the country. As to your little request to be careful of the Nazis in Germany, I am and I don't fraternize one iota – so don't worry.

I do hope that everybody is well at home now and that the baby is back in stride. Tell her that her daddy doesn't like to see her sick at any time, so be careful at all times. Say "Hello" to all our friends and love to the folks – I do love and miss you so very much – millions of hugs and kisses for the baby and you –

With All My Love,
Your Dave

———

Tuesday – 15 May – 1945
Somewhere in Western Germany

My Darling Wife and Baby,

From the very beginning of this day, I have been on the go. There is so much work around here to be done, now that the War is ended, and a lot of accounting to be done that I go about in circles and wonder how and when it will all clear up. Most of the equipment which had been in operation is now coming back. On top of that which we own, we have acquired property of other organizations and now it is necessary to clear it all. You can imagine what a job that is – all the way from Italy. In some, there are parts or accessories missing or broken and they all have to be accounted for – That is my job. I think that I ought to have it all cleared in about two or three months.

It seems that you and I were of the same opinion as to our thoughts on Mr. Mougin's safety before he was liberated. I also thought that he was a dead man a long time ago – either from American bombings or the treatment in the Nazis' camp, however, I didn't want the family to lose faith and he finally returned in good health. One thing that I'm glad to see is that the people back home are really seeing the atrocities which the Nazis had committed. It is ridiculous now when I read in the paper that three Nazi prisoners were given only ten years for various forms of sabotage against us in the States. When will we start to mete out treatment which they will understand more clearly? You would be very much surprised if you really knew how deeply rooted the Nazi theory is embedded in their minds. It has been a matter of years of extensive propaganda and we can't knock that influence out in kind treatment. They only understand atrocity and cruelty – so that is the way we ought to treat them.

That must have been quite a relief when Aunt Ruth called up and told you that her nephew had been liberated. He must have gone thru a lot to be in the hospital now. It's a wonder that they didn't kill all the Jewish prisoners. As to the Pacific, we are still in a quandary and don't know which end is up. Whatever has been decided in Washington about the 346th, it certainly hasn't been handed down to us as yet. All we can do is hope that they lose our outfit in their vast files until after the War is over in Japan. By that time, we would be back in the States for good.

Well, Darlings, it is now 11:35 and I am dead tired, so I'll close and send regards to all and love to the folks – and a great big extra hug and kiss for the baby and you –

With All My Love,
Your Dave

———

Thursday – 17 May – 1945
Somewhere in Western Germany

My Most Beloved Wife and Baby,

In the morning, I had to go to Stuttgart on business and we didn't get away until about 9:30. It is a large city and very industrious before the War, however, there is not a single building of any manufacturing importance that had not been touched. There is extensive damage all over and the people who have already returned to the place stand and look at us as though we brought the War. I had to make another trip, so I took Louie with me and also Nancy. One of the other boys wanted to come along for the ride, so there were three of us in the jeep. We finally got back at about 9:15 and a bunch of weary dogs we were, including Nancy. After that, it was too late to write and I was really too tired from all that driving – so am I excused?

In addition to getting two letters from you, I got a package in which you packed a can of cream of mushroom soup, a jar of soluble coffee, packages of popcorn, potato chips and pretzels. So far, we have done away with the pretzels, as we took them up to the bar and had beer with them. Now we are on the potato chips. Mmmmmm – They are good! Just send a bag or two of chips with each package and I'll be happy. You must really think that I'm going batty if I'll be happy in this Army by just receiving potato chips. Anyway, thanks a million for the package.

As you know now, we have been in Germany over a month and so far, nothing has happened to me or any other member of our organization – so please don't worry about us unnecessarily – We are careful at all times. It was true that there were cases of men being murdered by small boys and young women when we first moved in, but that has all disappeared. However, we still are alert for a reoccurrence.

Today was taken up mostly with clearing up a lot of the property around here. We also had to do the housework around here, as I got rid of the Poles, because they were too stupid, so it looks like all the boys will have to do the work around here. If I had my way, I'd get a few Jerry soldiers and work their heads off. I scared the hell out of six of them this afternoon when they stopped in front of our place to rest. I told the bastards to get the hell out of here in a hurry and they really took off. I hate them and everything about them.

So, with another wish that the baby and you and everybody else are all well and enjoying as nice weather as we – regards to all and love to the folks – and billions of hugs and kisses for Carole and you –

With All My Love,
Your Dave

Friday – 18 May – 1945
Somewhere in Western Germany

My Dearest Darlings,

Two more trucks rolled in this evening from our place back at Edenkoben with all the rest of the men. I was all in and decided to go upstairs and sleep, but I found two of the fellows out on the porch, showering with the hose. It was so inviting that I put away all the mail and took a very refreshing shower – in the nude! I know that some of the German people must have seen me out there, as there are other homes around – but what do I care about them? It was refreshing and I washed with soap, too!

You wrote that now, all of you were waiting for the announcement of the joining up of the Reds and Americans – That seems so long ago now. In fact, so does the War. I just don't seem to have any conception of time anymore. As you know, we didn't move any further after we got to our second place in Germany, and it looks as though we will be here for quite a while. At times, I think that I'll purposely screw up the works and just relax like so many other men are doing at this moment. However, you know me – I can't do a bum job, even if I attempted to do so. If I didn't know that the extra 50-dollar allotment would be cut off, I'd do just as I have written – Really I would. I'm so sick of this Army and what goes on in it that when I think of it, I get quivers in my stomach.

Well, Darlings, I guess that we have come to the end of another day of peace in Europe. Little by little, the Jerry soldiers are returning to their homes and their families are getting back to their normal routine – all except us. We have to sit by and see it all. And to think that we won the War! Well, hope that I get to see you by next Xmas, as I had promised last year. So hope that everybody is well and send regards to all – love to the folks – billions of beautiful hugs and kisses for the baby and you – I love you very much –

With All My Love,
Your Dave

Monday – 21 May – 1945
Somewhere in Western Germany

My Dearest Darlings,

In the morning, I got one of the jeeps and took one of the boys with me on a trip to Stuttgart. Nancy also wanted to go along, so she climbed into the front seat with us. It started to rain and it was chilly all the way back. We got back about 3:45 and after unloading the supplies, we had to go up to the medic's office to have an inspection. I don't know what the doc said about me, but he did point out that I had a slight case of flat feet. Say, who knows, but maybe I'll be home before I know it.

That was a terrible thing to broadcast [prematurely] over the radio that the War had ended. They really broke all rules for reporting and they are still in hot water with correspondents all over the world. The report about Hitler's death about that time was about true, I think. There was a report that Himmler had killed him, which I think was what actually happened, so that the Allies would not be able to catch him and convict him.

Gee, I was really sorry to hear about Howard Leeser being killed in Italy. With what she (Flossie) has gone thru – that must have really hit her hard when she did learn of it. How is she now? Still in a daze, I suppose. Have *you found out how he was killed yet? Well, that is the way of wars – you don't know where they will hit next.*

Say "Hello" to all and love to the folks – loads and loads of hugs and kisses for Carole and you –
   With All My Love,
   Your Dave

———

Tuesday – 22 May – 1945
Somewhere in Western Germany
(First uncensored letter)

My Most Beloved Wife and Baby,

   Today has been one of various climatic conditions and mood for me. I got to the point where I thought that I would be a lot better off if I were transferred out of this outfit. I have been in it so long and I've seen all the things wrong with it, that I have gotten to a boiling point. Certain members of this organization seem to dislike the authority that I carry and are trying to do whatever they can to get the rest of the outfit up in arms. Well, last night, they almost succeeded, but I told them off at the bar. I said that I never liked the job I had and never wanted it. I also said that if there was any other fellow who wanted to take over the job, that he was welcome to it. I also said that as long as Micka was right there (he was), that I would just tell him that I was no longer to be the Supply Sergeant. Well, after that, everybody seemed to quiet down and I left. This morning, after cleaning up the place, I went over to see Micka, as he is the Adjutant of the company. I asked him to send in my request for a transfer to Capt. Temple, as it would be for the best of all concerned. Well, he said that if it were up to him and he were the Commanding Officer, he would absolutely refuse it. He also said that he was positive that Temple would not allow it also. However, I asked him to tell Temple anyway and also say that I want to definitely get out of the company. I don't know what will happen to my request for a transfer, but as long as the men know that I don't want to remain, perhaps that will make them a bit happier.

   As to Hitler's death, I saw in yesterday's "Stars & Stripes" that he had asked to be killed by a member of the S.S. That coincides with what I had written some time ago – that he was probably killed by Himmler, so as to escape capture by the Allies. Perhaps I am right – who knows? All that remains now is to see what penalty the War criminals pay for their crimes.

I hope that all of them are hung by their tongues until they strangle to death. That sort of treatment would impress the German people more than anything else on the fact that we mean business in this Occupation business.

For the past week, the Zuper-Dupermen have been returning in huge Supply trucks and unloaded at central points throughout Germany. In this case, this city is a central point of debarkation for them. You should see how the people look out from their windows, stand on the streets, climb all over them and throw bottles of wine to them and kiss them as if they were conquering heroes. It is a joke to see them now. Not too long ago, they were the high and mighty and now they click their heels and come to attention when they are approached by any Allied soldier – no matter what rank. They have certainly fallen a long way. They walk by us and look so pitiful – ragged and forlorn. Their only happiness comes when the people welcome them. On the roads, you can find thousands of them wending their way home on foot. Now they know that somebody else has taken their place – but definitely! These people have never seen so much equipment as when some of the convoys go by. It looks like a parade put on by General Motors to display their products.

Yes, I agree with you that it was most unusual that the Jewish prisoners in the camps were allowed to live. Well, God was probably watching over them.

Hope that I haven't caused you any anxiety as to my request for a transfer – but don't let it worry you any. So regards to all and love to the folks and loads and loads of hugs and kisses for Carole and you –

With All My Love,
Your Dave

———

Wednesday – 23 May – 1945
Somewhere in Western Germany

My Darling Angels,

You enclosed an article on the child as a three-year-old. The funny thing about the paper was that on the reverse side was an article on the appointment of Doenitz as the head of the Nazi Government. Then in your letter, you said that your dad asked you to ask me what the real lowdown was on that deal. Well, as you already know, the death is still something to be doubted until the body is actually found and identified as that of Hitler. However, I do think that he was done away with by the S.S. As to Doenitz, he was about the only man who had not let Hitler down in a military way. He was the one who was responsible for most of the submarine warfare and its success against the Allies, so Hitler asked that he be appointed as his successor. As you know now, Doenitz is no longer a power and is being held as a P.[O.]W. I have been saving the "Stars & Stripes" from the day that the first announcement of Hitler's death was made until after the War was officially declared over with Germany's unconditional surrender. Carole will get a kick out of them when she is studying World History and comes to the subject of the Second World War, its causes and its effects. I certainly wish that I could figure out the last part of that phrase. I suppose that you have read that a lot of the 5th Army is being sent to the Pacific. About the 20th of June, we expect to learn of our designation – Here's hoping.

As to your impression that with all the troops which have already been sent to the Pacific and those to be sent from the ETO, there ought to be enough men to handle the War efficiently without calling on us – well, that isn't the case. The main idea is not to try to send as many men home as possible, but to end the Pacific War as quickly as possible, with as few casualties as possible. After that, everybody will be able to go home. As much as I want to get out of this damned thing and home for good, it is beginning to look as though we are South Seas bound.

Incidentally, what did you do on V.E. Day? Go to temple or get drunk? Well, no matter what you did, I was only kidding, as I know that you were thanking God that it was over finally and that it helps to bring us closer again. Well, Darlings, I guess that is about it for now, so regards to all, love to the folks, and lots and lots of love and kisses for the baby and you –

With All My Love,
Your Dave

———

Thursday – 24 May – 1945
Somewhere in Western Germany

My Darling Amy and Carole Frances,

We have been busy all day with Supply details and then at 4:00, we all had to go to a G.I. movie. I think that it is being shown to all civilians also in the States – "Two Down and One To Go" – Have you seen it? Well, it will answer a lot of questions as to whether or not I will be coming home soon. As Gen. [Henry] Arnold said, there will be very few men going back to the States at this time, as most of them will be going to the Pacific. After replacements have been sent to the various organizations, then all men who are deemed as nonessential will be allowed to go home. Well, I think that we (Supply) are classified as nonessential, so I hope that it won't be too long. Anyway, I think that we had better forget about a discharge and hope for a furlough in the States as the best thing. The Pacific is about definite – I can't keep that from you. It is just a matter of when and how now, I think. I know that you will be let down, but you always asked me what I thought and that is it.

It is a funny thing, but you said that the whole country was building up to the final announcement of the surrender, while over here, we weren't even fazed, as it was expected for such a long time that it was another day. Today's teletype news said that von Rundstedt and Goering were both taken to England and nobody seems to know why. That is another one of those difficult things to figure out.

As to that canned tongue, if I forgot to mention it, I have already eaten it and it was good, however, please don't send it anymore, as we get that stuff in our meals and we are tired of it after a while. Also, don't send any soluble coffee or tuna or salmon, as we get plenty of all those things. I do appreciate them, but we have them here, so why go out and pay money and valuable points for them? As to the cookies, no, I haven't received the packages – but I'm expecting them soon.

Well, Darlings, say "Hello" to all and love to the folks – millions of hugs and kisses for the baby and you –

With All My Love,
Your Dave

———

Friday – May 25 – 1945
Somewhere in Western Germany

My Dearest Darlings,

At the very start of the day, I awoke. No, it wasn't at six or seven, but at about one or two. One of the boys had a dog which gave birth to five puppies about a week ago, and all of a sudden, out of a clear blue sky, the mother started to bark last night – or morning. Well, she must have kept that up until about four – I fell asleep about an hour later. During the night, Nancy came upstairs and jumped on top of my bed. Well, when the barking started, Nancy started to bark also and that awakened me. I put Nancy back downstairs and then went to sleep again. It was about 7 when I got up.

I forgot to tell you about a funny incident yesterday. There are many German people who come in here, thinking that this is still a civilian gas station or garage and ask for the proper things which one usually finds in a station or garage. Well, a tall, grey-haired man came in and, in accented English, asked if there was a mechanic here. I assumed that he was another German and said very harshly that there was not and that he would have to leave. Well, he didn't say anything but thanks – in a very sarcastic manner. I forgot all about it until I was walking up the street towards the Orderly Room and I noticed an auto across the street with a passenger sitting in it who was all dressed up as a typical diplomat would be dressed for a formal ball. He had on a tailored coat, gold-braided collar, a distinguished-looking face and everything else to go with it. As I looked further, I saw that his driver was the fellow whom I had very impolitely thrown out of the place about ten minutes before. Then I saw that there was a foreign flag on the auto – that of Switzerland. Then, on the front bumper, was a sign "Consul General de Suisse," which means that this guy was the Consul-General of Switzerland. Well, I quickly thought over the situation and decided to go back and apologize for the way I had treated the driver and asked if there was anything that I could do for them. They said that all that they wanted was to have a mechanic look at their car. The Consul-General said, in good English, that he appreciated my offer, but there wasn't much to be done – so I took off. I didn't want to have them get a very unfavorable impression of the American Army – especially the enlisted men. Well, c'est la guerre!

That remark which the baby made about the "kop" ["head"] must have floored my dad when the baby answered that she drank out of one. Punning at her age – what a gal! Well, she is definitely your and my child at that rate.

I'm sorry that you had yourself worked up to such a high pitch about me coming home to be discharged, because I definitely think that we will go to the Pacific. The only thing for which we can hope is a furlough back in the States first, before going there.

So, as the sun fades in the West and the dark of night creeps up from the East, we bid you adieu from this distant land of Germany, where there are very few large cities to which to go visit and fewer bridges over which to cross the rivers. Anyway, say "Hello" to all our friends and love to the folks – lots of love and kisses for the baby and you –

With All My Love,
Your Dave

Saturday – 26 May – 1945
Somewhere in Western Germany

My Dearest Wife and Baby,

Well, we have been busy as a beehive today with inventory and at times, it seems that we will never be able to get it finished. In spite of the War ending, the Administrative Section, including the Orderly Room, Mess Section, Motor Pool and Supply, are up to their necks in work, while the others sit back and play ball in the afternoons.

Yesterday, just before I was ready to go up to our room and hit the sack, Nancy saw another dog across the street and took off. I whistled and whistled and she still wouldn't return. Prior to that, she'd run as fast as she could as soon as she heard me call. About 30 minutes later, Louie brought her in and said that Nancy had come in, up the back porch, and was creeping in with her tail between her legs. She came into my room and I picked her up and spoke to her and then gave her a terrific smack on the hind end and she didn't even murmur. She looked at me as though she was about to burst out in tears and I whacked her again and then took her downstairs where she stays. I think that she may have finally had sex relations with another dog. She really took a liking to that dog and didn't even pay any attention to my calling. Now I'll have to wait and see. She didn't seem as spry today as she usually is – Do you think that it could be?

So regards to all and love to the folks – I love and miss my darling wife and baby very much – lots and lots and lots of hugs and kisses for you both –
With All My Love,
Your Dave

———

Monday – 28th May – 1945
Somewhere in Hall, Germany

My Sweetest Darlings,

Don't be in hopes of me having a summer furlough – I'll be lucky to get one at all. As to sending packages, you had better tell all the others to hold up on sending them until we get some more dope on our whereabouts in the near future. As to our going to a bar in Germany, it is approved by the Military Government – so it's OK. As to speaking to the civilians at times, it is necessary to ask where we can obtain certain items in town – verstehen [understand]? So that is not fraternizing.

Have you received that money order I sent for the baby's birthday? Please don't buy a bond – get her something out of which she can get some pleasure. Perhaps a 2-wheel bicycle for when she gets older. I'm sure that we have enough War Bonds by now – so get something for her alone. In fact, ask her what she would like to have – maybe she'd hit on something we have not even thought of.

Since yesterday evening – after chow – I haven't seen Nancy. I thought that perhaps she was about the neighborhood and would return last nite. Well, she didn't, but I saw her pass in one of the Wing vehicles – so now I'll have to try all the Motor Pools to see where I can pick her up. I really miss her – One gets attached to a dog after a time.

Well, Darlings, say "Hello" to all our friends and love to the folks – for the baby and you, many, many, many, many hugs and kisses –

With All My Love,
Your Dave

———

Thursday – 31 May – 1945
Somewhere in Western Germany

My Darling Amy and Carole Frances,

I had planned on sending Louie to Heidelberg and Mannheim on a Supply run, however, in the morning, I decided that I'd make it up there, as I wanted to get hold of a few other things that I had thought about. So a driver from the Wing came up and he had a topless jeep with him and nothing else. On the way there, we stopped behind a truckload of Security Police (same as M.P.'s) and they gave us a large jar of pickles. They were really delicious, too. Well, after eating in Heidelberg, we took the superhighway up to Mannheim and then we went up to the place where we picked up the supplies. While up there, I talked them out of a half of a pup tent. With that, we tied it over us and that kept the rain off of us, which started about 2 minutes after we had gotten it tied on. The rain was still coming down hard, however, we wanted to get back here before dark, so we took off. We, of course, finished the jar of pickles on the way and they were good. There is a warehouse full of them, if I can ever remember which village it was where we stopped and picked them up.

However, the biggest and best event of the day hasn't been told. The driver who took me on that trip yesterday told me that there was a small black and white female dog in their tent area. Well, I was certain that it was Nancy.

So this morning, I asked one of the boys to drive me up to this place. I got out of the jeep and gave one whistle and out she came – flying like the wind. She just couldn't keep her tail still and jumped all over me, licking and chewing me. Well, I must say that we were both very happy to find each other again. She didn't look so full, so I gave her a can of C-rations as soon as I got her back. You should have seen her go thru it! Well, all day long, she has been licking my hands and jumping all over the place. Of course, everyone was as pleased as I to see her back again. She is such a likable dog that everybody likes her and plays with her.

So now the company is back to normal and I still haven't heard anything on a transfer. During my absence yesterday, there was a general meeting held. One of the boys asked Temple what the latest rumor was and he answered that it was hot off the latrine that we would be home in 60 days. Well, that is a definite impossibility, because there is too much red tape involved to get us back that soon. However, don't get me wrong – There is nobody who would rather be home than yours truly – and in a big hurry, but I don't want to give you too much hope and have the bubble burst. So just take it easy and if I'm heading West, I'll let you know.

I received one package in which Beulah sent me a good salami, a jar of Guava Jelly, a can of fruit cocktail and a can of tuna. As you can see, the salami will be the first to be consumed. Joe Dines was around already and he is licking his lips fast and furious. I may start it tonight.

Well, Darlings, I guess that about winds up another day in Germany, so regards to all and love to the folks – lots and lots and lots of love, hugs and kisses for Carole Frances and you –

With All My Love,
Your Dave

—

Friday – 1 June – 1945
Somewhere in Western Germany

My Dearest Darlings,

Well, here it is June and the birds singing, the sun shining, and I'm away from you and the baby – what a situation! Well, at least I know that I won't be in this theatre next year at this same time. In fact, I'm very certain that the War in the Pacific will be won by this same time next year. So even those boys who have been sent there already will probably be on their way home in 1946. As to us, I'm sure that I'll be coming home by Xmas.

Now we have another group of reports to make out to cover various items which have been lost during the course of the War. It's a very funny thing, but here we have won the War and have to account for lost property. It would be the easiest thing in the world for everyone involved to just drop them, as a reward for winning the War – but no, the Army has to keep up its traditions and send thru millions of pages of reports and which involve millions of man-hours. I don't know how in the world we won the War – but as long as the Jerries did not either, what's the difference?

Today, I received two very well-wrapped packages from my favorite brunette. They were the Tollhouse cookies for which I have been waiting so impatiently. I just opened them – that is, one box – and there are two cans empty already. All the boys raved about them and were begging for more. Joe Dines, of course, made a hog of himself. I haven't even started on the salami yet – what will power! Meanwhile, regards to all and love to the folks – beaucoup love and kisses for the baby and you –

With All My Love,
Your Dave

Sunday – 3 June – 1945
Somewhere in Western Germany

My Darling Amy and Carole Frances,

Here it is Sunday and a very pretty one at that. In the morning, I saw the civilians going to church in great throngs. At times, I wonder what in heck they pray to. I know that there are still churches around here and I have seen nuns walking about. However, how could God-fearing people ever allow such a creature as Hitler to get into power and still believe in God? He not only persecuted the Jews, but he also mistreated the Catholics in his early years in power. Now, everybody goes about as though nothing ever happened to affect their lives. I'd like to have seen and heard a gentile sermon when Nazism was in full bloom. I recall the period during the early thirties, when Hitler had just been "voted" as Chancellor of the Reichstag, that the people also were guilty of looting the homes of the Jews who had been thrown out and beaten to death. They are these same people who are in these same cities today – and that is one thing I will never forget. I can assure you that I will make things as difficult as possible for them as long as I have to stay here. At times, I have a great desire to wear a "Juden" ["Jew"] band on my arm and see what the effect will be. Well, this was the day of prayer for them and I hope that they didn't pray for another Wehrmacht [German army] *in about twenty years.*

This afternoon, I decided to go out with Ellison. We went for a walk to a stream not far from here. We walked down to a point where the stream narrowed down to about five feet and where there were many rocks upon which we could walk to cross over. We sat down and chewed the fat for a long time and then decided to get back, as it was after five. We were too late for dinner, so I gave Ellison a bit of the salami which I had been saving for him, as he always gives me some of his when he gets a package. Then Dines and I walked up to the bar, where we had a couple of glasses of champagne and then called for Ellison and went to the show to see Bing Crosby in "Here Comes The Waves," which we all enjoyed very much. The take-off on Sinatra was really a lulu. After the show, we went back to our room and it seems that everybody was hungry, for some unknown reason, so I opened the other box of cookies and now I have one can left. Dines brought down a can of sardines and I went out into the garden we have in the back and got a head of lettuce. So we wrapped a sardine in a couple of leaves of lettuce and had a very tasty sandwich. However, we were still hungry, so we went downstairs to the Supply Room, where I had some eggs. We boiled them and had crackers and Tokay wine jelly with it. After that, we were all well satisfied, so we retired to our rooms.

As to Max [Sarver]*'s outfit, I guessed right if he is on his way to the South Seas. I was surprised to read that Max wrote from where he was leaving and how they were going, as that is definitely forbidden. In fact, we cannot even tell you where we are going when we leave Germany. You see, certain P.O.E.'s mean where we are headed, so you can see why the censors want to keep it quiet. After all, the Japs are still operating subs and can take advantage of a slip of the tongue. Well, Darlings, say "Hello" to all our friends and love to the folks – a great big hug and kiss for the baby and you –*

With All My Love,
Your Dave

———

Monday – 4 June – 1945
Somewhere in Western Germany

My Dearest Darlings,

This afternoon, I decided to call up one of the Supply points and see if there was anything around there for us. The driver of the truck took one of his friends and I took Nancy. Well, it so happens that the "driver" hadn't done much driving in civilian life; he certainly did not know much about the type of truck he was handling; and he didn't know what driving was all about in general. He knew that his brakes were bad and was bitching about them all the way down there. On the way, a couple of fast-moving trucks passed us and the "driver" decided that he was as good as the others, so he stepped on the gas. We finally came to a populated section where we could see these other two trucks stopped at an intersection. Well, when we were about 100 yards from the rear of the second truck, he decided that it was time to step on the brakes. As I said before, the brakes weren't any good, so in spite of his desperate pounding on the pedals, we just kept on going and finally crashed into the rear of the truck ahead of us. Luckily, I was able to place my hand on the dashboard to avoid the shock and the only thing that happened was that my knee came up and hit the dashboard. Everybody came out well – even Nancy. We were on our way thru Stuttgart and there before our very eyes was a bridge crossing a fair-sized river, which was completely out. Even a blind man could see it. Well, our "driver" just kept on going about 35 or 40 until I very casually said to him, "I think that you had better turn left or else we will all be in the water." He was dumbfounded and woke up just in time to turn and avoid running off into the river.

Well, we had a few more close ones after that, but we finally made it back. Fay told me that there had been lots of activity about. First of all, two German women decided to thrash a Russian girl. The action took place right across the street, so some of the boys saw it. After the Russian girl had been cut above the nose, she turned on the German women and was knocking the devil out of them before they ran away. A couple of German men stopped the girl from chasing the two women and that was when some of the G.I.'s stepped in. They threatened to kill these two German men if they didn't allow the girl to follow the two women. Well, it was too late for her to chase them, as they had gone a long way by then. The Russian claimed that the other two had stolen her wristwatch before the beating. A couple of the boys took her to a civilian hospital close by where a couple of stitches were taken in her head. After that, the two men were apprehended and locked up. I don't know what happened since that.

Later in the evening, one of the boys found a 10 and a 15-year-old boy playing with a flare pistol. It isn't the idea that it is not dangerous, but that perhaps they were possible saboteurs. You can't trust the youngest German child in Germany today. So we took the gun and flare away and questioned them. I decided to put a scare into them, so I took out my sword and started waving it about – pointing the end at their bodies. You should have seen the older one sweat! After that, I phoned the Occupation Authorities and they sent a Captain down in a jeep and took the boys away. Well, that was the second incident of the day.

About 9:00 P.M., an AMG car drove up and out jumped about 4 plainclothes men and a couple of G.I.'s (one was a Sergeant from the AMG with whom I had previous dealings). A number of us walked across the street to where these men had gone and started getting inquisitive. Well, the Sergeant told me that they were looking for an S.S. man who was supposed to have just returned to his home at this place so we decided to go up and try to find him. We spent about an hour looking about, but he probably found out that he was heard of and took off.

Well, I was in the midst of that first page when Mullen phoned me that I had to go up to a Quartermaster meeting in Heidelberg. The purpose of the meeting was to associate all Supply Officers with the correct methods of fitting the men in their organizations with the new "Eisenhower"-type jacket. It is a short-waisted jacket with fly front. We were passing thru one small village when I started thinking about those pickles we had picked up on our last trip up there, so we stopped a number of G.I.'s and asked them if they knew of any pickle factory about. Well, we were lucky to be in the very same place, only about 100 yards from it, in fact. We went in and we bought 4 cans of good pickles (55 to 60 to a can) for the Mess Hall and one can for myself. That is, for the boys in the Supply Section. After that, we drove out to this place where the meeting was to be held. A Lt. Col. opened it with an introduction to the subject and also a Lt. Schwartz, who would demonstrate the "proper fitting of the ETO Jacket."

We got back to Heidelberg, then we hunted for a place to get some beer. Well, most of the places were closed, so we found a bar about 10 miles out. We drank him out of beer and it was good, too, and then asked where we could find some wine, champagne or schnapps for our bar. They showed us a place and we figured out that we only had room for one keg and they only had red wine – so it was a jeep-load with four men, 5 large cans of pickles, 10 gallons of paint, and a jug of wine. You can imagine what a picture that made. We must have stopped at least ten times on the way back to have a wee nippy, however, I didn't indulge, because I didn't feel much like drinking. Well, we finally got back here and we were one tired lot.

Well, Darlings, I guess that's about all for now, so regards to all our friends and love to the folks – a billion hugs and a trillion kisses for the baby and you –

    With All My Love,
    Your Dave

         Wednesday – 6 June – 1945
         Somewhere in Western Germany

My Dearest Sweethearts,

Here it is about a year ago today since we made the first landings on the French coasts, in Normandy. If you will refer to a map of Europe and Africa, you will see what a tremendous job it has been and how it was accomplished in a comparatively short time. In 1942, the Nazi holdings extended over most of Europe and Northern Africa. If they had been successful in going on thru to Alexandria, a possible linkup would have been made with their armies coming down from the Crimea. What a situation would have faced us at that time with our backs to the wall in the Pacific. So you can see that in a very short time, we have not only stopped the threat, but we have completely destroyed it in Europe. If you will recall, I wrote in Italy that when the end would come, it would come very fast and that was how it did happen. We can thank our God that we lost as few as we did in this campaign. It was considered quite a feat just to have made the landings, let alone defeat the Nazis within a year afterwards. Well, once again, I thank God that we are Americans and that we are living in America.

As to the recent Jap balloon attacks (?) on the West Coast, it is unfortunate that those people had to be killed when one balloon exploded. As everybody knows, it is just a psychological threat to us and a gesture to increase the home morale in Japan as our air attacks increase. With bigger and better raids soon to bomb their islands into the ocean, we may as well expect any sort of attempt to make us jittery. However, a Jap submarine has not operated successfully in the Eastern Pacific for a couple of years, and it will be a long time before one does. At the same time, their ability to send balloons all the way to the Coast is really something to figure out. As most of us know, we own about all the helium in the world and that means that the Japs must be using a new type of gas. However, these "attacks" can never reach a dangerous stage, so don't become excited. As long as we are on current events, I may as well go into the Okinawa Campaign. It has certainly been a costly one for us so far and it will be even costlier the closer we get to Tokyo. That is why we are mainly interested in knocking out as much of their power by air, so that we won't have to lose as much on land later. The airfields were completely smashed so that it was impossible to take off and attack our ground forces. We, in this theatre, can appreciate that fact more than anyone else. Now, the doughboys praise the help rendered them by the close support given by the various Fighter Wings. Also, we are as thankful that they took these fields, from which we could fly, so that we could hit deeper into the enemy territory. Well, I hope that the Okinawa affair will end soon and then we will be in a position to carry on a tremendous Air War with a huge number of fighters to support the super-fortresses coming out from islands further away. That is why the Japs are fighting so fanatically to prevent our taking the island.

Today was the first time that the German public have been shown some of the atrocities at the various concentration camps. The AMG had pictures on its walls, but today was the first time that these same pictures were posted for public consumption. I wonder how they feel when they see things like that for which they are responsible. I just walked across the street where they are being shown and the people just stand and don't even seem to be affected by the pictures of these men tortured to death by their fellow Germans. These people are nothing but a lot of cold, bloody and heartless killers, even though they don't wear uniforms. I hope that the American Occupation authorities come out with the same policy as the Russians – that is, that for every shot fired at any military or civilian American in this territory, fifty German hostages will be shot. That is the only treatment these people seem to understand and that is the way we should treat them. Why, if an American prisoner did not feel like working, he was taken out and beaten to death. We are too "humane." Just how much of that sort of stuff can the soldiers take after giving their lives for a cause that is slowly dying away?

So far, every day seems to point to going back home for a furlough – Hope that I'm right in my calculations. We have seen three boys home already on the point system – They flew home and are probably civilians now. All I can do is hope for a break after we get to the States. Well, Darlings, I guess that's about it for now, so say "Hello" to all and love to Mother and Dad – and trillions of hugs and kisses for Carole and you –

With All My Love,
Your Dave
P.S. I love you both very much.

———

Saturday – 9 June – 1945
Somewhere in Western Germany
My Sweetest Darlings,
    As I was walking back from the show one evening, I happened to notice a place with mosaic work on the wall. At first, it didn't even faze me, but after realizing that there aren't many such places in Germany, I looked again and, going up to the second floor, I saw that there was a Star of David built into the wall. It had been a Jewish synagogue at one time. The windows have been walled up and some still have sand bags in them. I tried to see inside, but all that I could see was a lot of bags and boxes, so it must have been used as a warehouse for the Nazis after they ran the Jews out and took whatever they wanted. The surprising feature was the fact that the building was still standing and not burned to the ground. Isn't it ironical that Nazism is dead now and the synagogue is still standing? Right in Germany, too.
    I didn't mean to frighten you about those nuisance raids which the Nazis put on, but as long as the War is now over, you know that all is well and that we were never in any danger. However, there was one case where an officer was strafed while he was driving on the road, near Nancy. He was supposed to be driving with blackout lights at the time, so it was his fault that he was injured.
    Well, Darlings, say "Hello" to all and love to the folks, a trillion and one hugs and kisses for the baby and you –
    With All My Love,
    Your Dave

———

Sunday – 10 June – 1945
Somewhere in Western Germany
My Dearest Darlings,
    Your first letter was of the 8th – the day after V.E. Day. As you and I both felt the same about celebrating, I suppose there were many others who felt the same as us. If the downtown section was dead, most of the people must have gone to pray, as I had hoped they would. I was glad to hear that special services were held for the temple congregation in celebration of V.E.

Day. That was the best way to show their respect for that day and those who helped to make it all possible. I can imagine what an effect your folks must have made on the temple when all of a sudden, they got up and walked out. Well, it was very nice of so many of them to phone and inquire as to her health. Now that she is all well, I hope that all illness has left the premises of 7541 and that all of you will have a most enjoyable time up in Michigan.

I certainly do agree with you that refugees are the nerviest people in the whole world. I think that we agreed on that long ago, after we had gotten acquainted with Mrs. (Gee, I forgot her name – She had a daughter, Stella). Anyway, she was about the worst of all.

In one of your letters, you enclosed some pictures and I want to say that I am very much disappointed in those of the baby. I have seen other pictures that were a lot cuter, but I guess you can't have her look pretty all the time. Try to get her to smile when she looks into the sun, instead of frown, as that makes her look like an old hag. By the way, try to use F11 and 100 when you take shots in bright days and perhaps they will come out better. Anyway, take your time and set the lens before you snap the shot.

Today's "Stars & Stripes" carried a very heartening story about the big possibility of the point minimum being lowered to 80 or 75. I'm holding my fingers and eyes crossed and hope that they bring it down low enough for me to get out of this damned thing. If anybody even mentions Army to me in civilian life, I'll scream. Incidentally, we are losing another man tomorrow – to be transferred to another outfit, so it looks as though the remnants will go back to the States for a furlough and reassignment to the Pacific. Somehow or other, I had always had a similar idea about the future of this outfit and it seems that it is coming true now.

Well, Darlings, regards to all and lots of love to the folks – much more for the baby and you with beaucoup hugs and kisses –

With All My Love,
Your Dave

———

Monday – 11 June – 1945
Somewhere in Western Germany

My Dearest Wife and Baby,

During the day, it was very routine and rained on and off. However, after lunch, it was decided that the Wing photographer come over and take a group shot of the boys for a snapshot book that is being made up of odd *snaps of the company. Sooo – in spite of threatening weather, we had our picture taken in front of the Mess Hall. As you expected, I had Nancy on my lap – so if I can get a copy, you will know how she looks. Everybody keeps asking me if I'm going to take her back to the States with me. I'm seriously thinking about it, too. Well, after that, a whole regiment of returning Nazi soldiers came riding thru the streets on horseback. It is bad enough that they are allowed to roam about now, but they also have horses, which they no doubt stole from the Frenchmen and Russians. I don't know when we will ever learn – but we are still being too lenient with these people. All that I hope is that we haven't won this War in vain again.*

As to your writing that Beulah deserves a D.S.C. [Distinguished Service Cross], *yes, perhaps she does – but I think that every mother with one or more children should get some sort of a consideration if she had to bring up a family all alone. That means you, too!*

By the way, I played a little poker in the afternoon and won $20.00!!!

Sooooo, say "Hello" to all – love to the folks and loads and loads of hugs and kisses for you and the baby –

With All My Love,
Your Dave

———

Thursday – 14 June – 1945
Somewhere in Western Germany

My Dearest Sweethearts,

Just got back to our room after seeing a USO show – for the first time since we were in Italy. It was pretty good, too, and the show was packed. It included an M.C., an accordionist, a song-and-dance girl, a male dancer, and a girl vocalist who was very good. She sang a lot of popular songs and included was "Rum & Coca-Cola" – which was the first time I had heard it. I can't see why or how it ever became No. 1 on the "Hit Parade." Well, all in all, it was a very enjoyable show and we were surprised with a movie afterwards – "The Falcon in Hollywood." It's better it should have stood in Hollywood! It stunk!!!

How is everything coming along back home? Hope that Carole is spending a lot more time outdoors, too. Does she still ask why I don't come over for a visit? Tell her that I'll try. If they decide to lower the mark now, I'll be ready to pack up my bags and be off in a cloud of dust. I don't want to work

*up your enthusiasm, but it is looking pretty good at this time. All I'm doing
is crossing my fingers at all hours of the day.*

*Well, Darlings, say "Hello" to all our friends and give my love to the folks
– billions and billions of hugs and kisses for Carole and you – I do love and
miss you both very, very much –*

> *With All My Love,*
> *Your Dave*

———

> *Friday – 15 June – 1945*
> *Somewhere in Western Germany*

My Sweetest Sweethearts,

*Just got back from a trip down to Stuttgart and am ready for a rest. After
unloading the new jackets, I tried one on and they really look terrific. We
were given some 9th A.F. patches at the same time, which I didn't like to
see, however, we are under them only for administrational purposes at this
time. I hope that we aren't transferred into that unit permanently, as that
would mean Occupation, I think. However, I shouldn't worry because after
July 16th, I'll have 85 points and be ready for discharge. What a nice word
that is, all of a sudden! So let's keep on hoping for a break and maybe you'll
be getting out my civvies soon.*

*By the way, did you read about Gen. Patton's little speech to some
schoolchildren in California? He told them that there will be more wars in
the future, because, simply, there have always been such things. I have also
said that there have been wars and there will always be wars – until all
traces of envy and jealousy are erased from every man on earth – and that
is an impossibility. So I hope that his little note didn't put a damper on the
San Francisco Conference – at least, it didn't help it any, I know. However,
might is and will be the only way to keep peace in the world, so I hope that
sufficient allowances will be made for its maintenance. With a huge Allied
Air, Ground and Naval Force, no nation would even think of going to War
again. However, one of the larger nations could possibly enter into a dispute
with another larger member, bringing about another War. Therefore, I do
hope that the delegates to this Conference are the most brilliant in each
nation and that they will do as good a job as expected of them.*

*Well, Darlings, hope that all is well back home. Say "Hello" to all and love
to the folks – oceans of love and billions of kisses for Carole and you –*

> *With All My Love,*
> *Your Dave*

Monday – 18 June – 1945
Somewhere in Western Germany Still

My Dearest Darlings,

If this sort of thing persists, I'm going to look up the Postmaster himself and find out what in all hell is holding up our mail for such a long time. I can understand that perhaps men returning to the States have taken up the space in planes going Westward and that delayed my letters, however, nobody is coming over this way except idiots – so why the delay? It was bad enough when there was a War on, but now I can't understand it at all. Oh, yes, I do get newspapers, but they aren't one-one thousandth as nice as receiving a letter from you.

At 2:00, there was a meeting in Temple's office. All the Section heads were there and so were two other officers. The main idea was to put up a bitch about not getting enough passes for the men. It seems that a lot of the men were rather burned up at Temple taking off for Paris last week for about 8 days and here a number of men still hadn't gone away on pass, so some of the other sergeants asked me to also show up and put up a bitch. Well, as it is, I don't have much of a bitch, as both Fay and I had already been to Paris and Fay just came back from a four-day pass with his brother, so I just stood around and listened for a while.

In the evening, I decided to go to see "Hangover Square" with Laird Cregar and Linda Darnell and George Sanders. It's better that I should have stood in bed, because it was a putrid picture. It strived so very hard to make it into a thrilling murder picture, but failed so very miserably. However, we also saw a combat short subject, which was interesting. It was a wee bit late, as it showed the advance of the British into Cleve and the Allies into Haguenau, which was about last November, I think. When I got back here, I found a nice-smelling aroma filling the air. I saw a number of the boys in the kitchen frying some deer meat - without ration points, too. We have a nice, wooded area around here and there are beaucoup deer to be had, so in the past three weeks, a few of the boys have shot three of them and we have been noshing in the evenings. It is really good and I like it very much.

Hope that all is well back home. Well, say "Hello" to all and love to the folks – a billion hugs and kisses for the baby and you –

With All My Love,

Your Dave

—

Tuesday – 19 June – 1945
Somewhere in Western Germany
My Most Beloved Wife and Baby,
 In the evening, after chow, we read that there was going to be a French traveling stage show in town, so we took off early so that we would get a good seat. The show was pretty good, even though the chorus consisted of only four girls. However, they were quite versatile and one put on a specialty number which wasn't too bad. They had a couple of comic teams which were good. Then the Master of Ceremonies was a former vocalist with Tony Pastor's Orchestra and he sang on the order of "The Voice" – which made many fellows in the audience yell, "Oh, Frankie."
 Gee, I had no idea that I was writing such disheartening letters and telling you how badly off I was. Perhaps I was a little on the fidgety side and was popping off too much. I can assure you that in spite of all the bad things around here, I will come out OK and not be too affected by them. It is now at a stage where I don't give a damn and don't hold back on my words and thoughts, so I repeat again that the only and foremost thing in my life now is my wife and baby and am living only to get out of this damned Army and back to civilian life. I realize that this is slander, but that is exactly the Army today. Well, anyway it won't be too long before I'll be coming back – I hope.
 As to my reaction towards Carole's impetigo, I must have been too worked up, as I knew you wouldn't tell me about it if you weren't sure that it was about finished. No, I want you to tell me about those things – Next time (God forbid) I won't be so excited over it. Say "Hello" to all and send my love to the folks – a billion hugs and kisses for the baby and you – and I want to tell you that I love and miss you both very much –
 With All My Love,
 Your Dave

—

Friday – 22 June – 1945
Somewhere in Western Germany
My Darling Amy and Carole Frances,
 I want to tell you about that other dog which we had here. It was brought over here by one of the boys while she was pregnant. Well, about 5 weeks ago, she gave birth to five puppies. Yesterday, the original owner of the dog came and took her away. Prior to that, whenever Nancy would come up on

the porch and come near the pups, the mother would bark and almost run Nancy out of the place. Well, for the past two days, Nancy has sort of adopted the pups and plays with them all day long. It is wonderful how a young dog can naturally acquire a maternal care for some other dog's pups. The pups also like to play with Nancy – so it is one happy family now. Oh yes, while we are on the subject of dogs, I noticed in the "Stars & Stripes" an article saying that it was against Army regulations to take pets of any kind with you on a plane or boat returning to the States. However, I'm certainly going to try to bring Nancy across with me, as she is too good a dog to leave here. She really understands what I say to her and she is such a nice companion to have around in this damned country. I'm sure that once I get her home, you and the baby will take to her in a hurry. The first thing that she will do will be to probably wet the floor, as she does that whenever she gets excited. It all happened back in Edenkoben when she was hit on the spinal column with a horseshoe – Ever since then, she wets when she gets excited or scared. Otherwise, she goes regularly outside in the morning – afternoon and night – just a regular gal.

I guess you are about ready to take off for Frankfort right now. I don't recall when you said you were leaving, but by the time this letter arrives, you will be up there, I'm sure. So I want to take this opportunity to wish the baby another very happy and enjoyable birthday and party. I hope that I will be back there with her for all the rest of them for a long time to come.

Well, Darlings, say "Hello" to all of our friends, love to the folks and so very many hugs and kisses for the baby and you –
With All My Love,
Your Dave

———

Saturday – 23 June – 1945
Somewhere in Western Germany
My Dearest Darlings,

Fay and I were bawled out for one of the men going to lunch with his sleeves rolled up, his collar unbuttoned and without a cap. Well, that was too much! So now we tell the men to be careful when they leave and to be on the ball so that we won't get our rears chewed and we won't have to chew theirs.

I wrote you that there was a USO show in town last week. Well, one day, the accordionist came in to the Supply just to sit and bat the breeze with us. He was here about four hours and we all had a very enjoyable time. Well, the day after that, the Master of Ceremonies came over and we sat and talked. He said that in all his visits, he had never run across such an unfriendly bunch of officers as those in this Wing. He said that usually, the Commanding Officer comes up and thanks the USO unit for their performances and tells them how much they appreciate it. But not this outfit! I was amazed to hear it coming from this one fellow, as I didn't think that they could be that rude. After all, these USO people don't have to do this. That is why the performers like the enlisted men so much and would much rather be with them than with officers.

As for us, I think that we will just take it easy for a while and rest our carcasses in Schwabisch-Hall. I am not in any position to tell you anything as yet, but I will as soon as I can. I already know – but it isn't to be let out as yet, so you will just have to sweat it out for a while until we are able to give out that sort of information. I have already told you that we are in the 9th Air Force – so that will help you in your calculations.

Oh, before I forget, I am going to Lindau – I think – which is located about 150 miles southeast of here. It is right on the border of Switzerland and Germany, southeast of Constance and Friedrichshafen. It will be an all-day trip and perhaps it will take two days, so don't be surprised if you don't get any letters from these two days. I have invited two other fellows to come along, beside the driver. They will be Dines and another fellow who is a nice sort of a guy and who seems to be a better type of person than the general run of G.I.'s. These two are bringing along their cameras and we ought to get some very beautiful pictures out of it.

I hope that you were able to get hold of a puppet performer for the baby's party. Gee, it may have been today, in fact, as you said that you may have to push it up a week. If so, I hope that everybody had a wonderful time. Well, Darlings, say "Hello" to all and love to the folks – and for Carole and you, a million hugs and kisses –

With All My Love,
Your Dave

Tuesday – 26 June – 1945
Somewhere in Western Germany

My Dearest Darlings,

Well, here I am – back again and safe and sound. On Monday, the driver, "Tennessee"; a fellow from Chicago named Oleck; another fellow from Chicago named [Sgt. Donal J.] *O'Connor; Joe Dines; and Nancy and I drove to Schwab-Gmund and then to Goppingen. All this time, we had been driving in French-occupied territory. Well, it was about lunchtime and we saw a French non-commissioned officers' mess in town. I went in and gave them a very sad sack story and we were invited in for lunch. Well, it so happened that Nancy made quite a hit with all the men there. We had a very delicious meal served to us, including wine. The French had just gone in and taken over a restaurant and they prepare the food while the Jerry women serve it – and also clean up the place.*

We arrived in Lindau and as we neared the city, we could see snow-capped mountains in the distance. These are the Swiss Alps. Just below the Alps lay the lake which was really something to see. It was tremendous and had very pretty and colorful homes lining the edge. These towns along the lake were not touched by bombs, so you can imagine how nice it all looked. We drove up to Friedrichshafen (where the huge zeppelins were stored before the War) and then up to Waldsee. It was dark when we got there, so we decided to try to get some rooms in that town. Luckily, I ran across two of the Frenchmen with whom I had spoken that same afternoon, and they found rooms for all of us. I didn't sleep very much, because some of the Frenchmen were a wee bit high and loud. Also, the jeep was parked just below and I was worried about it. I slept off and on and finally, at about 7:00 A.M., Joe Dines came over to awaken me. We drove out to a farm about 15 miles out. We got the farmer to fry us two eggs apiece and heat some water for our packages of Nescafe, which we had brought along, so it wasn't a bad breakfast at all. Even Nancy had a time – chasing chickens and cats.

Well, we drove to Ravensburg and up to Ulm, which is a very old city which had been bombed time and again. The mass of rubble and twisted steel girders reminded me of Mannheim. The amazing thing about the town was that there were thousands of people walking about the streets – shopping at the very few shops that had escaped our bombs. They seemed like a lot of mice coming out of their holes. We stopped for a while at the well-known cathedral. It was only hit by a single small bomb – but all around it were signs of destruction. We decided to walk up the tower and get a bird's-eye view of the destroyed city. The stairs wound and wound up to about 250 feet and we came out on a ledge from which we were able to look all around. The people were tiny specks on the ground, but the masses of rubble stood out like sore thumbs. It's a very funny thing, but when I look down from a high place, I get the urge to climb over. However that doesn't hold true in an airplane – Can you explain it? Maybe I'm ready for the booby-hatch?

Anyway, we walked back down and took off for Stuttgart – driving on the Autobahn all the way. When we got there, it was lunchtime, so we went to another non-com's mess which is run by the French and we got fed. We got in about 4:00 and the first thing that Dines and I did was to get under a cold shower. It was just what I needed, as I was not only dirty, but drowsy also. I dressed and had chow. After that, I took Nancy out for a walk, as she had ridden for the past two days.

Today was a gorgeous day for traveling and Nancy didn't shiver as she did yesterday. I had a heavy jacket to cover her with and it really came in handy. She is such a thin-haired dog that one would think that if a slight wind came up, all her fur would be blown away. However, she is such a smart dog that she'd probably find a way to keep warm if she was out on her own. Well, Darling, that about winds it up for now – so say "Hello" to all – love to the folks – a billion hugs and a trillion kisses for Carole and you.

With All My Love,
Your Dave
P.S. I do love and miss you very much!

———

Wednesday – 27 June – 1945
Somewhere in Western Germany

My Sweetest Darlings,

Last night, it really poured and did it lightning and thunder! There was one bolt of lightning and then a blast of thunder that about threw everybody out of bed. It continued on thru the night and I heard almost every roar of thunder. In the morning, it was still pouring, so I didn't go to chow, however, I had a few places to go to, so I had to go out in the rain anyway.

I drove to a shoemaker's to pick up my shoes, which I had left there to be shined. I knew that this fellow made shoes and boots, but never was interested in ordering any, as you must provide the leather. Well, the driver told me that he knew of a place where we could buy some – so we drove down there – about 22 miles away. We bought a couple of skins in reddish brown and in black. After chow, I took my brown and one small skin over to the shoemaker. I asked him if he could make me a pair of boots and two pair of low quarters. The shoemaker said that the skin I brought in was one of the finest he had seen. Well, I took off my shoe and he measured my foot, so *now, I'm having one pair made on a strap style and another on a lace model. The boots will be calf high, as they are a lot more comfortable that way. We'll pay 20 marks, which is $2.00 today to us – but to the Germans, it is about $7.50 – so it is pretty good, isn't it?*

So give my regards to all – love to the folks – and a great big birthday kiss for Carole's forthcoming birthday – a million more hugs and kisses for the baby and you –

With All My Love,

Your Dave

———

Sunday – 1 July – 1945
Somewhere in Western Germany

My Sweetest Darlings,

This afternoon, I had a few places to go to in town and get some questions cleared up. Well, at one of the other organizations, I took Nancy into the place with me and the Captain and Warrant Officer there both played with her. It seems that everybody wants to have her and take her back home. I certainly picked a likable dog!

Well, in the evening, while at chow, the mail was delivered – and what do you think? Yes, a letter from you – finally! I also received a package from my mother – 3 lbs. of pretty good cookies. For chow, we had fried chicken, but I didn't feel hungry, so I put my part into my mess kit and brought it down to Supply. I also brought along about six other portions in a can, so if Fay hadn't eaten, he could have some of it.

About 6:25, I decided to go to see "Cinderella Jones" – with Joan Leslie and Robert Alda. It was really one stinking picture. After "Rhapsody in Blue," they should have waited a bit longer and selected a better story. When I got back here, I went down to the Supply Office and there was Fay, gnawing away at some chicken bones – so I joined him and Hicks in my portion. Of course, Nancy, the chowhound, was right there to beg for some – so I gave in and gave her a bit. She is some gal, as she can eat 24 hours a day and not gain weight. Fay told me about his trip, which was uneventful except for the fact that they stopped at Dachau, but were refused admittance because it was said that typhus was prevalent there. He did say that he saw one fellow who was on a detail there not long ago and he had to assist in cremating 1400 bodies at one time. He said that he still does not know what kept him from going out of his mind while there.

I was surprised to read about the parade in honor of Gen. [Omar] Bradley – He is from Moberly [Missouri], isn't he? The crowds must have really mobbed the streets, because he is about the best-liked General of all the top men in the services. He seems to understand the G.I. and tries to help him in every way. It was in Africa that he made a strategic move that saved thousands of lives.

Well, Angels, that about winds it up for the 1st letter of the 18th month we have been away. It really doesn't seem that long and I'm sure that we'll both be able to forget it after we are together again – for good! So, regards to all – love to the folks – and so many, many hugs and kisses for Carole and you –

With All My Love,
Your Dave

————

Monday – 2 July – 1945
Somewhere in Western Germany

My Very Dearest Wife and Baby,

Temple took off for Darmstadt, where he will stay until we all join him up there later. He always has done that before we move – so that he could pick out the best spots for us when we get there. Tomorrow, Mullen, the Mess Sergeant and I are supposed to go up and look it over and size it up in our minds, so that leaves Rodger here, who is so very much unacquainted with the administration of the company that it is pitiful. Oh well, why should I worry about it – All I'm worrying about now is when I'm getting out.

I wrote you about my having some shoes made – Well, it seems that the original owner of the place was a Jew. When the Nazis were starting their purge, one employee saved this Jew's life and that of another. Out of gratitude for what was done, he gave the whole works to the present owner. Today, the liberated Jew came back just to visit. He is living in a prison camp still but expects to get out soon. He dropped in just to say "Hello" and is giving his former employee a hand while he is here. That is the very first case I have heard of a German saving the life of a Jew. The Jew isn't even from Germany, as he was born in Rio de Janeiro. What do you think of that?

Regards to all and love to the folks – and a billion kisses and hugs for Carole and you –

With All My Love,
Your Dave

————

Tuesday – 3 July – 1945
Somewhere in Western Germany

My Dearest Darlings,

I just got back from a French USO show and it was really good. Considering the fact that they are not very well acquainted with "swing," the orchestra wasn't too bad. There was a Mistress of Ceremonies who had as much personality as a stone – She stunk! Then there were two separate acts of solo dancers – These girls were really good and could pass in the nightclubs back home. Then there was an elderly juggler who was mediocre. However, two acts were very good – one a man and woman doing one of those almost-nude athletic dances. The others were two brothers who were as limber as a blade of grass – They were very funny, too. So all in all, it was an entertaining show.

Gee, it was exactly a month ago that I asked for the transfer – Well, I'm still around, as you may have noticed. Speaking of the time element, I read that almost everybody will have a holiday tomorrow, as it is the 4th – So far, we have heard nothing pertaining to us. Therefore, I suppose we will work as usual.

Holy Smoke! Do you mean that that puppet performer actually wanted 15 bucks for 30 minutes' work? It's outrageous! If you finally hired her, I do hope that she was thoroughly enjoyed by all the kids. As to sending the baby to dancing school – I'm all for it. It gives her poise and a very good sense of rhythm. It may not seem so important now, but it will have its effects later. I know that she'll enjoy every minute of it and make rapid progress.

So you, too, are sort of disappointed by the way France has been acting since the end of the War in Europe. Well, that is just one argument and there will be so many that will arise. Even though the San Francisco Charter was signed by most of the nations of the world, it will not end wars – so we had better not fool ourselves with it. I don't enjoy writing this, but it is the truth and we may as well face it. Why, right now, the Germans are all asking the Americans if we will replace the French in that area. The reason behind that is that we are far too lenient with the Jerries and we'd give them a damned good opportunity to rearm and start a revolution. So I say again that force is the only method these people understand and that should be our method of Occupation for at least 50 years. The Jerries were never to be trusted and never should be, even with their arms in the air.

Well, Darlings, that about winds up another day in Germany, so say "Hello" to all and love to the folks – a trillion hugs and kisses for Carole and you –
   With All My Love,
   Your Dave

————

Wednesday – 4th July – 1945
Somewhere in Western Germany

My Dearest Beloved Wife and Baby,
   I just returned from a musical program which was put on by the Special Service Unit of the 1st Armored Division, which is also located in this town. It was made up of the men within the organization and they were all pretty good. The orchestra was about eight pieces and heavy on the brass, so that any mistakes could be drowned out. The M.C. was also the vocalist and he wasn't too bad, except that he was nervous as all hell. All in all, it was a pretty good program.
   After breakfast, I couldn't find Nancy and I didn't think anything of it until she came running in – wet and shivering. She was soaked to the skin and whimpering, so I bawled her out and placed her on the radiator to dry off. At first, she couldn't get used to it, but afterwards, she wouldn't get off, as it was too comfortable. She was so grateful for my taking such good care of her after she was dry that she was constantly licking my hands all the rest of the day. I think that she has learned her lesson now and will not venture off in the future.
   I went for a walk over to the shoemaker's place. I saw that liberated Jew there and we spoke for a long time. Another fellow walked in and he was introduced as the other Jew who was protected by the German who now owns the shop. After a long talk with him, I decided to get back, as it was time for lunch.
   In the evening, we received some mail and among the letters were two from you – also one letter from the Mougins in Nancy. They are almost positive that their future son-in-law is now in the States, as they received some regulation form to be filled out by Janine and sent back to the American Government, so I guess the wedding will take place after all – perhaps in America, however.
   So that about winds up another day's activities in the European Occupation. Hope that new point system will be announced soon, as I am

*on pins and needles waiting for it to be announced. So regards to all – love
to the folks, and beaucoup love and kisses for Carole Frances and you –
With All My Love,
Your Dave
P.S. Je t'aime tres beaucoup!*

[LETTER FROM ERIC TERHOCH DATED JUNE 8, 1945 – ANNECY, FRANCE]

Dear David,

*We have received your kind letter of Mai 31st for which we thank you
very much. We are very glad to hear that you are in good health and now
the war being finished you think certainly to return to the States. We should
be very sorry if we should not have occasion to get your acquaintance – the
opportunity is now the best – because you are in Europe, so if you can have
holidays, we hope you can arrange it to spend them in Annecy. Meanwhile,
I have been in Paris and I was very sorry that I could not find an apartment
so we are obliged to stay here longer but we trust to go back latest about end
of August. You will certainly know that the Germans have plundered our
apartment during the occupation of Paris – so we must first find anything
else before we can return.*

*Last week we had a long letter of Aunt Otty and Lilly – they have sent a
package with very good things and we have been very glad. Our American
family is very good for us – we have another uncle in New York, who is
helping us too.*

*Have no pity with the Germans. They have stolen all we have had and
my poor mother, two sisters and a brother and the father and the mother of
my wife have been deported by them and until now we have never had any
news.*

Perhaps you can let us know in what town you are staying at present.

*Thanking you once more and trusting that you will come soonest to Annecy
– my wife and myself we are wishing you a lot of luck.*

*Very sincerely yours,
Eric*

Thursday – 5 July – 1945
Somewhere in Western Germany

My Dearest Sweethearts,

This morning, I ate breakfast, returned only to find that Nancy had taken off again. However, about 10:00, in she strolls and dirty as a rat. I bawled her out and told her to get into her box – and in she went and went to sleep for the rest of the morning. After lunch, I went to a lumber mill to pick up some lumber. I was the only one around who could speak to the owner, so I had to go along. We filled the truck, but still have to come back tomorrow to get the balance. We had the Jerries do all the work, however. The fellow who was in charge had been discharged from the German Army in 1941 – after he had been wounded outside of Moscow. I told him that the only good Germans were the dead ones – and he agreed. See how easily they will turn against their own people?

When I got back, it was time for chow and mail call. I received six letters from you – and one each from the Terhochs and my Aunt Ruth Fiman. The Terhochs are still in Annecy and are expecting me to visit them as long as I am still in Europe. Well, I hope to get a pass as soon as we get up to our new place. They also said that they heard from Otty and are awaiting her packages.

So Carole keeps saying that I'm coming home soon – hope that she's right. Do you think that she'll recognize me when she does see me? As long as you are satisfied with me coming home by Xmas, I am also, as it takes the Air Force so long to handle administrative affairs. As to any more packages, no, don't send them, as I still don't know when I may be off. One thing is certain and that is that I'll be over here for 3 more months at least. As to my getting to the States and the points being lowered, that is impossible as we are now Occupational.

This is really something! You will be in Frankfort the same time as I, because I expect to go up to Frankfurt (Germany) very soon, after we move to Darmstadt.

Well, hope that all is well up North. Be sure to bundle up warm and stay out of the wind, as it can give one a sore throat in a hurry. So regards to all – love to the folks – a million hugs and a billion kisses for Carole Frances and you –

With All My Love,
Your Dave

Saturday – 7 July – 1945
Somewhere in Western Germany

My Dearest Amy and Carole Frances,

I went over to the shoemaker's to find out when I could expect my shoes. Well, I met this Jewish fellow while there and he told me that he had word that one of the big S.S. leaders of this city was back in town – so he wanted my suggestion. I took him over to the CIC [Counter Intelligence Corps] (sort of FBI) and he was interrogated there. The fellow (Jew) said that in a couple of hours, he could get more people who knew more about it and also the names and addresses of the men who helped in the concentration camp which was not far from here. He also said that there were 183 Jews buried in that vicinity and that these men were responsible for these crimes. He said that most of them had been shot in the back of the head; those who were wounded were shot again while on the ground. Well, it was about noon, so the CIC told them to be back at about 3:00 and they would look further into it. After lunch, I went up to the CIC and found two of the Jewish fellows there whom I knew – and another new one. Finally, an American civilian (in civilian clothing, too) took us into his office and he went into the questioning more thoroughly. It seems that he wants everything in black and white – He wants written or seen evidence of maltreatment. He isn't any too convinced about the fellows who were mentioned by these Jews. However, personally, I think that it is a lot better to go out and bring in a suspect and question him, rather than suspect him, build up a case and then find that he had fled. So Monday, these men are to return to the CIC and perhaps they will go out to pick up the suspects. Can you picture the Gestapo allowing such a thing to carry over for two days? So I guess I'll be around if and when they drag these Jerries in and I hope that the CIC tortures them.

As to your letter of the 6th, that was the day you received your own package – the cookies that never caught up with me in my travels last Fall. Even if I received the package now, I may not have been able to eat the cookies – but the shrimp would have been nice. I still have a can, but no sauce – so I'm waiting for somebody to get a can or jar of sauce.

As to my dog, Nancy, no, she isn't expecting – so I'm relieved for the time being. As to her periods, I'm afraid that she hasn't shown any indication of it – and she doesn't use the "Regular" size. Nancy has been back for quite a while and we've had no trouble with her since.

As you know now, we are Occupational and will be around for a while. I hope that you are not waiting in St. Louis for me to come in. After all, if I knew right this minute that I was to be discharged, it would take about 3 to 4 months for me to be a civilian again. There is just too much red tape in the Army to allow a quicker changeover. So that draws this 7th day of the 7th month of 1945 to a close. Regards to all and love to the folks – very, very many hugs and kisses for Carole and you –

    With All My Love,
    Your Dave

———

Tuesday – 10 July – 1945
Somewhere in Western Germany

My Dearest Darlings,

    Well, we started packing up on Saturday and continued on thru Sunday and yesterday. We still haven't loaded most of our supplies on trucks as the vehicles just returned from Darmstadt last nite. We went ahead and packed the typewriter and all the paper with the idea that we were pulling out tout de suite. So-o-o we waited and waited – expecting to load up and get out – however, we are still around. So Temple instructed me to stay here until each piece of equipment was taken out of operation at Headquarters and that I should see that every piece that was ours came back to us, so it looks as though I'll be around here (with four or five others) until about Friday or Saturday. Therefore, I opened the box which had the paper in it and decided to get off a letter to you before you think I am on the way home.

    Your next letter was the first information that I received about Paul's coming home. I wrote him some time ago that he'd probably be home a lot sooner than I – so here he is! Well, he has seen a lot more action than I and he deserves a rest. It came up so suddenly that I'm led to believe that his ship was probably hit. I hope that he is OK, however, if that is the case. Paul is probably home at this very moment – and I'm still sweating it out. As to reassignment after his furlough, he'll probably go back to sea duty, unless he is physically unfit – God forbid.

    Yes, I agree that separation makes insignificant things seem unimportant now. So here's hoping that you all are well and having a wonderful time. I wish I was there – regards to all – love to the folks and so very many hugs and kisses for Carole and you –

    With All My Love,
    Your Dave

Tuesday – 10 July – 1945
Somewhere in Western Germany

My Dearest Darlings,

I suppose you will think it rather unusual, but yes, this is the second letter for today. The first, which I wrote in the morning and afternoon, was to make up for the ones I missed the previous two days. Well, after I went up to our old Headquarters, we went to chow at the 63rd Fighter Wing Mess Hall. That is the new outfit that moved in here, but I think that they may also move up to Darmstadt. They took over a German restaurant with Jerry waitresses and plates – and that is how they eat – in fact, that is how all American troops should be eating now – not out of mess gear. Well, the idea of eating out of plates and drinking coffee from cups is the only good feature of the whole thing, because the food was very scarce and not too well prepared. However, the main thing is that the Jerries wait on you and they realize that we are the victors – not they. Our Wing is the opposite – just a big bunch of appeasers.

I'm so glad that everybody had such a good time at Carole's birthday party. The kids must have really gone for the puppet show. Did Carole understand it? You said that you had cake and ice cream – Gee, I'd like some chocolate layer cake, with a slab of chocolate ice cream across it, right now. Does that make you smack your lips?

As to that driver who gave me such a scare, it isn't my idea to take a driver – it is Temple's. I always want to do my own driving, as I feel a lot safer. I'm afraid that your imagination ran off with you once more, because even though we carried wine and drank beer, I did not get drunk, as you thought. The last time when I was high was the last day we spent in Edenkoben, before we moved to Hall, and that was the end of April. So please don't get the wrong impression – I'm not an old soak. The beer around here is weaker than water and the wine is weaker than the beer.

Well, my Dearest Darlings, that about winds up a very sunny day, which is now being threatened with rain. In fact, it was so warm that I gave Nancy a bath and she took it like a veteran. So hope that all is well – regards to all – love to the folks – and many, many, many kisses with lots of hugs for Carole Frances and you –

With All My Love,
Your Dave

Wednesday – 11 July – 1945
Somewhere in Western Germany

My Sweetest Angels,

Well, I'm still writing from the same place, as we still have about 7 truckloads of equipment left to be moved. That is really going to be some job, because each switchboard weighs a couple of tons and there are 3 of them to be moved out of a small room – down a flight of stairs, outside, down 2 more flights of stairs, and then loaded up on trucks.

The biggest rumor came in the evening, when Fay phoned to tell me that Temple was made Communications Officer for the 63rd Wing, which is also moving up there. Then he said that Rodger is supposed to be the new C.O. – Well, I don't know if it is all true, but if so, that's a good break for him and a bad one for me. I say that because he'll expect me to go right on handling the Supply and will not demand that Micka take his responsibilities as he should have long ago. I'm so damned sick and tired of the job that I'd rather be a private now and take it easy. After all, I've seen the War through and am as much entitled to relaxation as the others in the outfit. Don't mention the rumor to Mary as yet – until you hear something more official.

As to the balloon scares, I haven't read anything in the papers for quite a while – Have they stopped publicizing them or aren't the Japs sending them?

So that brings us to the end of another day and I hope that tomorrow brings news that I'm eligible for a discharge – I hope. So have a good time and say "Hello" to all – love to the folks – and many, many thousands of hugs and kisses for Carole and you –

With All My Love,
Your Dave

Sunday – 15 July – 1945
Somewhere in Western Germany

My Dearest Darlings,

Well, here is my first letter from our new location in Darmstadt. I'm seated in a nice room on a soft armchair at a tablecloth-covered table which acts as a desk. In front of me is an open window thru which I can see a large open court on which is a huge ball field. It had formerly been a parade ground, I think. All around this court are large, four-storied buildings – one of which we are occupying. The 64th Headquarters Squadron occupies a building; the 63rd Headquarters Squadron another; the M.P.'s another; the Operations still another, and we have one. It's a pretty nice setup, except that it will take a lot of work to get it clean and in shape. We have showers, too – but they are only cold water at this time. However, that's OK, because it has been about 80–90 degrees for the past 48 hours anyway. We have a Supply Office downstairs with a couple of adjoining rooms in which we store items we use every day. Then we have some heavy equipment in stalls of a former stable, but they are clean. Then we have a couple of vans in which we packed some equipment that we will never touch again. So all in all, it will turn out OK – if I can get some locks and hasps for the doors.

We finally pulled out of Hall and we had gone about 3 miles when we had to stop to pick up a trailer which had broken down the day before and which was left at the side of the road until we came back for it. Well, it was an hour later that we got on our way again and then one of the trucks had a little trouble. We finally all met in one small town where I went into a bakery and bought some buns and a loaf of bread. Right next door was a butcher shop (metzgerei) and I bought a whole salami – Everything cost me a grand total of twenty cents – and it was good, too! We drove in at midnight and most everybody was asleep, and I couldn't find the Supply Rooms to get a cot upon which to sleep, so I did the next best thing – I slept out in the jeep – with Nancy. Luckily, it was warm and dry, but Nancy heard the most distant barks of dogs and in answering, she woke me about 6 times.

This evening, after chow, I saw a pilot getting ready to go up – so I asked to go along and he said OK. I took Nancy with me and she really loved it – except when the pressure started to hurt her ears. This was a test flight as some cylinders had been replaced in the motors of the B-25 and they wanted to see if it was OK. In this sort of a situation, it is necessary to wear a parachute and I was really uncomfortable sitting on it. When we got down and out, Nancy was as spry as ever.

Now for some late news about the 346th. Rodger is no longer the C.O. – nor is he any longer in this outfit. Micka is no longer in the 346th – nor is Temple. Rodger is in the 582nd Signal Air Warning Battalion, which has been overseas for quite some time. Micka is now in the 927th Signal Battalion – the same outfit in which Maddox is now located – still a 1st Looie, incidentally. Temple is in the 63rd Fighter Wing, however, that does not leave us without an officer, because the Message Center Officer, Lt.

Shannon, was transferred into our outfit. He is absolutely hated by the men who worked under him. It is rumored that he will become the C.O. – but the men hate to even think of the idea and are seriously considering asking for transfers. In fact, a couple are reportedly transferred already, so it looks as though I should have insisted on a transfer a month ago – The officers seem to have thought the same, because all of them asked to get out. Now the hell of it is that I'll have to find an outfit that wants a Supply Sergeant if I'm to be transferred. As it is, if Shannon becomes C.O., we will never get along, because we didn't formerly. So I had better be on the lookout for an opening in an outfit that isn't as bad as this one.

Well, Angels, regards to all and love to the folks – a billion and more hugs and kisses for Carole and you –

> *With All My Love,*
> *Your Dave*

———

> *Monday – 16 July – 1945*
> *Somewhere in Western Germany*

My Dearest Wife and Baby,

I had my first contact with our new C.O. – Lt. Shannon. He didn't have much to say, because he knows absolutely nothing about what is going on and has to rely on us for the transaction of business in this company. Lt. Shannon asked me how everything was coming and I told him and then I figured that now was a good time to ask about that pass to Annecy, so I explained that you had relatives down there and that I'd like to see them, as long as I'm in Europe. Shannon asked if I could leave with everything as it was and I explained that Fay was a more experienced fellow who could handle the job, so he said that it was OK. Now here's the tough part of the job – I don't know if there is plane service there anymore – so I'll have to call and find out tomorrow. If there isn't, I'll have to hitch a ride to Nancy or Lyon and catch a ride to Annecy. Joe Dines wants to go along with me – so I'll probably know more about it tomorrow. I hope that the Terhochs are still in Annecy since I received their last letter.

I agree that we both need each other very much at this time. Gee, recall how you'd want to sleep late on Sunday mornings and I'd want to _____. Oh well, those were the days! I'll be seeing you again and I don't think that you'll want to sleep late again. I think that you now will agree that sleep

is time lost – right? So regards to all – love to the folks – and so very many hugs and kisses for Carole Frances and you –
  With All My Love,
  Your Dave

———

Wednesday – 18 July – 1945
Somewhere in Western Germany
My Dearest Sweethearts,

  Well, I suppose I ought to warn you not to look for yesterday's expected letter – it ain't! I spent the evening with a fellow named Ed Olech (from Chicago) and we talked until midnight. After evening chow, I decided to lie down and read awhile. When I finished, it was about time for the show – They had "Circumstantial Evidence" and I liked it, in spite of its impossibilities. There was a short subject before the main feature which disclosed the invasion and capture of Angaur Island from start to finish – very interesting. After the show, Olech came in and we started talking about the War and its effects and the post-War – So you can see that it must have taken up a lot of time. So when he left, I was really worn out – Am I forgiven?

  Well, this morning started off with a bang with me having to get 80 telephones ready to go to Nuremberg – two requisitions to type up – and a trip to Heidelberg to pick up a truck, which was left down there. Before chow, I decided it was time to take a shower on account of working and sweating down near Heidelberg, so I also shaved and took Nancy into the shower and she loved it – after she got used to it. So we are both a couple of clean kids now. She's sleeping on my cot at this moment, but I'll take her downstairs before I go to bed.

  Incidentally, we caught two mice yesterday down in the Supply Office. Fay and Hicks had seen mice, so I set the traps the night before. We must have hit the jackpot, because none have shown up all day – but I still have a couple set – just in case.

  Sorry that you didn't get out to celebrate the 4th as in former years – Maybe after I'm back, we'll resume those picnics. Yes, our big worry is about over – going to the Pacific is forgotten about, so that's a consolation, at least. I suppose that Beulah is no longer impatient, because Paul must be home by now. Hope that all is well with him.

Gee, Amy, I never thought that you were among those in the States who was affected by the high-powered propaganda that the "Isolationists" and "America Firsts" are now throwing up. It is this very same clique that wanted to sell us short to Hitler, who is now a forgotten stump. So now, they are preaching possible war with Russia. Please don't let such rabble-rousing affect you – It is all a bunch of lies. Russia will line up with America before she'll align herself with any other nation. It is as I have written before – She wants to take this opportunity to clearly and definitely establish herself as the Number 1 power in Europe today – Can you blame her? England and France and the States had always been allied, so now, with De Gaulle leaning toward Stalin, England is left alone to fight for her position in Europe. That is why Churchill is clambering for recognition of Italy as an Allied Nation – so that she will be the one friend England can have in that area and on the continent – outside of possibly the Netherlands and Belgium. However, the one thing about which I am certain is that Russia will not go to war against the States!

So, my Darlings, regards to all – love to the folks - - oceans of hugs and kisses for Carole and you –

With All My Love,
Your Dave
P.S. I love you both very, very much.
XXXXXXXXXXXXXXXXXXXXXXXXXXXXXXXXXXX

Friday – 20 July – 1945
Somewhere in Darmstadt

My Very Sweetest Angels,
Your letter of the 7th of July was the first from Frankfort this year. Gee, that delicatessen stuff you bought downtown must really have been delicious, because Chicago is known for that type of food. My lips are watering now as I am thinking of it. Does the baby like corned beef and salami? I know that she likes Tollhouse cookies, because there's chocolate in them. As to the "dinner on the liner," I suppose the food is pretty bad nowadays with so many returning servicemen riding the trains. As much as I know that you all needed a vacation and rest, there was a slight feeling against your taking a train at this time. I've seen pictures and heard so much about the way the returning men have been crowded into old and hot parlor cars on their way home. I'm sure that you wouldn't want me or any other serviceman to

ride that way. However, there aren't enough civilians to feel and think that way to make any great difference – so please don't feel too badly about it. I just want to bring out that point so that you can pass the word along when you are back home and somebody mentions a possible train trip for pleasure purposes. Perhaps it will help to curb the unnecessary trips and make it a bit more comfortable for the veterans.

Today has brought about many changes. There are supposed to be about 29 men shipped into the outfit and the same number leaving for destinations unknown. Included in the departing group are Ellison and Louie, the fellow who worked in Supply. The reason those two are leaving is that their Army Specialty Number is that of a clerk and they are in demand at this time by other outfits being redeployed. Mullen told me that the only ones who are considered absolutely essential now to this outfit are a clerk-typist in the Orderly Room, me and Mullen. Even the Mess Sergeant is up for possible shipment. Well, now I don't know what to do or say – so I'll just sweat it out and hope for a break.

So, hope that all is well up in Michigan and that you are all having a wonderful time – regards to all – love to the folks – a billion hugs and a trillion kisses for the baby and you –

With All My Love,
Your Dave

———

Saturday – 21st July – 1945
Somewhere in Darmstadt, Germany
My Darling Carole and Amy,

Just as I started to get out my fountain pen and write, Ellison came in and we sat and talked until a late hour. He is shipping out in the morning and he came to tell me that he considered me a friend of his and that he was sorry to leave. I told him that he should be thankful, because he's going into an outfit that at least has a good chance of going home first before going to the Pacific – if they go to the Pacific at all. Louie came back from Nancy and he was surprised to learn that he was shipping out also. It was a shame and he hated to leave, although he didn't say it. He brought back a bottle of good cognac and gave Fay and me half of it.

You were really hot under the collar about our outfit being designated as Occupation. After all, as you later admitted, it is a lot better than having to go to the Pacific Theatre. There are still many men with over 100 points and who have been overseas for about 35 months who are being held here indefinitely, because they are listed as being essential. That is a lot of hooey, because they can replace any man — no matter what he does. One fellow who is with us has 124 and he has no idea when he is leaving — overseas 35 months, too. So you can see that my case isn't as bad as a lot of other fellows. I am still wondering how I will get down to Annecy. All I have to do is to find a means and I will leave — but I haven't found out a way of getting down there, so I'll be around for a while yet, I guess. Louie told me that the Mougins are still trying to locate their future son-in-law's outfit. They haven't heard from him in quite some time and they are wondering where he can be at this time, so I am going to try to find out for them.

As to your interest in the possibility of the wives and children of servicemen coming over here to stay with their husbands and fathers, I am definitely against it. You don't know what all is involved — You haven't the slightest idea of the inconveniences involved in your living in Germany. You see, since we were in Africa, Italy, France and Germany, we have become acclimated to these various hardships and don't even think about a tiny discomfort. Why, if you wanted to go down to the corner drugstore and buy an item, all you had to do would be to walk about a block or two. Here, we can't. There are no modern conveniences anywhere at all. To take a shower, you would have to walk to the next building and shower in an open room where you could be seen by anyone else in the room or outside. Amy, you just don't know how many smaller items there are that, to me, I may not even think about — but the main thing is the unhealthy conditions around here. The cities are all bombed out and there is a great chance of disease starting up. I certainly do not want my wife and baby exposed to any dangers unnecessarily. Even if all I had to do was to wire you to come on over, I would not do so. So please don't even think of that possibility, as it is out. I can wait awhile longer and get home for good — so I'm sure that after thinking it all over, you will agree with me that that is the way to look at this situation. I don't think much of any man who would have his wife or child come over here to live under these conditions. So let's sweat it out awhile longer and we can be together again back home.

As to your request that I request some more packages, I guess I will, as long as I think we will be around for a while. Send me some potato chips, sardines, Hydrox cookies, chili sauce, shrimp, anchovies, oysters, and anything else but coffee and salmon and tuna. As to salami, if and when the red point situation eases, you may try to get a small one, so that it will not set you back too much in the rationing. Also, send me some kosher pickles. Is that enough?

So, once more, regards to all – love to the folks – so very many hugs and kisses for the baby and you –
With All My Love,
Your Dave

Monday – 23 July – 1945
Somewhere in Darmstadt
My Sweetest Darlings,
I was up early this morning so as to clear some of the records for a few of the boys who had to go to their new outfit, which is located in Nuremberg. Fay stopped by in Frankfurt and picked up some Coca-Cola – the first in a long time for me. We are now allowed two bottles per man per week. On top of that, we received some PX rations this week and we got 2 bottles of beer with them, so our refreshments ought to hold out for a while. The only bad feature is that they are sending over a lot of cheap candy, such as "Hi-Mac" – it's really lousy! However, we did get some tea biscuits this time and they are good – made by Nabisco.

Well, what do you know? We will finally get a chance to see Bob Hope and Jerry Colonna. They and their show are coming out to the airfield where Baron is stationed – tomorrow afternoon. So I suppose there will be trucks to take the men out there, so that they can catch some big-time stuff for a change. Say, his program is broadcast on Tuesdays – isn't it? Well, maybe they will rebroadcast it back to the States – Could be. No, I guess not, because it would be too early in America. Anyway, I'm going to try to see it and take some picture out there.

Nancy seems to be the one who is having the time of her life. She stays down in the Supply Room and sleeps on my old clothing that may be about. In the morning, I let her out and she lays with some other dogs all day long, coming in only occasionally to get some water and to be petted. In the evening, she comes upstairs and lies on my bunk until nearly dark, when I take her downstairs again. She has had quite a lot of companions lately, because many fellows have brought in some various breeds of dogs and they all have one great time. One Colonel has a tremendous German shepherd dog whose head is larger than all of Nancy – but she bites and jumps all over

this dog and they get along quite well in general. Of all the dogs in the area,
Nancy seems to be the favorite of most of the fellows.
   Well, Darlings, that's about it for now – so regards to all – love to the folks
and a great big hug and kiss for Carole and you –
   With All My Love,
   Your Dave

———

Tuesday – 24 July – 1945
Somewhere in Darmstadt

My Dearest Wife and Baby,

   Well, about 11:30, I asked the Mess Sergeant if we (Fay, Hicks and I)
could eat early lunch so that we could leave early for the Bob Hope show.
He said that it was OK and that he'd like to go along, so we took him and
another Mess Sergeant and drove out to the airfield where the show was to
be held. It was an open-air area with an amateurishly constructed stage. We
swiped some chairs and sat down on the left-hand side of the stage. We were
seated about 10 feet from the stage and at the place where the entertainers
would have to come on to perform. Otherwise, in the center, left-center, and
right-center, the men had to sit on the ground for about a hundred feet back.
In the rear, the men were standing, sitting on rooftops, trucks, or anything
else that would help them.

   Before I go any further, I had better tell you of the incident when I first got
out of the jeep. I saw that there were a lot of command cars about a certain
area, so I figured that some of the performers must be there. Well, just then,
Jerry Colonna came near and I asked him if he'd pose for a picture and he said
that he would be glad to. So I snapped his picture after I asked him to wiggle
his moustache. I certainly hope that it comes out good, because he was right
there next to me and there shouldn't be any excuses for it not being any good.

   Well, the orchestra was supplied by the Air Force and it was darned good
– especially a G.I. vocalist – He must have been a professional before the
War. Then Hope came on and it was really a howl from there on out. He
really did harp on the setting – out in the forest. The second performer was
a well-stacked tap dancer who was pretty good. Well, near the end of her
dance, Nancy heard the clicking of her taps on her shoes and ran up on the
stage. The dancer stopped a few seconds, as she probably figured that Nancy
was going to bite her. However, I called her and she ran into my arms. After

that, Hope came out and said, "You better hide that dog, because if Crosby sees it, he'll throw a saddle over it." That made the crowd roar.

There were numerous performers, including a very good pianist and an accordionist who could sing also. In fact, she sang "That's How I Subscribed to Liberty Magazine" – except when she came to that last line, she sang, "And it had nothing to do with Liberty Magazine." Then there was a Hollywood starlet named Gale Robbins (hear of her?) who had a fair voice. Then Jack Pepper, who has traveled in the Hope show for a long time, sang. All in all, it was really a darned good show and I'm sure that everybody enjoyed it. They do 3 shows a day – all in different cities. Well, we saw their C-47's out on the field, so we decided to drive out to see them off after the show. We came to the strip just as the plane with the performers was taking off, so we were out of luck. They took off at 2:50 and had to be in Nuremberg by the 4:00 show – a distance of about 200 miles – so you can see that these shows don't have an easy time of it at all – and the men do appreciate it. I know that the folks at home have no idea of what USO performers go thru to reach as many G.I.'s as possible. If they did, they would certainly contribute more to the activities of the USO and Red Cross.

So-o-o-o-o, I guess that is about it for today – wish I was there – regards to all – love to the folks – a billion and one hugs and kisses for Carole and you –

With All My Love,
Your Dave

————

Wednesday – 25 July – 1945
Somewhere in Darmstadt

My Darling Amy and Carole Frances,

After evening chow, I went up to my room and rested a bit and read a couple of comic magazines – the bestselling papers in the Armed Services. Then I decided to go over to the showers and cool off and get cleaned up. Nancy came up with me, but after seeing the water, she got cold feet and backed out of a possible shower. She still remembers her last one, when I had to get her used to it at first before she would stay under the water. Lately, she has been running about with a lot of other puppies on the post and I think that another shower at this time would do her a lot of good, so maybe tomorrow I'll give her one.

The damnedest thing happened this morning. One of the boys who is at the radio transmitting station not far from here asked me if I had seen the plane accident. He told me that there were two planes above them, a P-38 and a P-47, which were having a practice "dog fight" and diving and chasing each other, as in actual warfare. Well, all of a sudden, one of the planes (P-47) dove downwards and went into a spin. He failed to come out of it and crashed into the forest and made a path right through the trees, diving into the ground and bursting into flames. This fellow who told me about it was one of the first two men over there to see it. He said that after the fire was burnt out, they were able to extract what was left of the pilot – a charred mass of bone. The arms and legs had been cut off from the impact. This is about the most discouraging thing that could happen to an outfit after seeing the end of the War. Well, I guess it was his number and it was up. It's tough that a fellow goes through combat and then has to lose his life.

That is why I get so damned disgusted when I see drivers speeding on the highways – You'd think that the War was just at its height, instead of being ended two months ago. So many useless accidents have occurred on the highways due to speeding that it is a wonder that these fellows don't just commit suicide with a gun, so as to save the trucks. There was one place on the Autobahn where a bridge was dynamited by the Jerries and it rests over the highway – with leeway on one side only. Well, there are signs to tell you to cross over, because of the bridge – but do you think that they pay any attention to the signs after having a few shots of schnapps? I saw one truck try to go under and it came out with a bashed-in windshield and the driver suffered cuts and bruises. Later that day, another fellow in a command car belonging to the 63rd Fighter Wing tried to go through and the car was completely smashed up and the driver killed. So you see, there are so many careless people that the War casualties would be cut down considerably if they were only a bit more thoughtful and sober.

I saw that the new mark will be announced at the end of this month, however, even if I am eligible for discharge, how long will it be before I am alerted for shipment back home? Well, I suppose you are as anxious to hear the answer to it as I – so why worry you with it? We'll just bide our time a bit more – eh? I guess that is about all the news for today – so say "Hello" to all and be sure to see that the folks rest as they should – love to them – and so many hugs and kisses for Carole and you –

> *With All My Love,*
> *Your Dave*

Thursday – 26 July – 1945
Somewhere in Darmstadt

My Dearest Darlings,

I don't know how I stand this damned job – I get to hate it each and every day twice as much as the day before. It gets on your nerves and there is no thanks for it, so the hell with it. I'm tired and want to go swimming like all the others do. Tomorrow, I'm going to Hanau again for some supplies – just to get away from the place. We have a trip to Nuremberg to be made, but that is too far, so I am sending Hicks. There are some very heavy items to be unloaded and I do not feel like helping to do so.

I just got back from the bar that the Headquarters Squadron has built, where I had some beer with two chaplains – yes, two chaplains. One was the one who used to be at Pinedale at the same time we were stationed there, and the other was a Jewish chaplain who was down today to conduct services for the Jewish men on the post. However, I didn't learn about it until after it had started and I wasn't dressed for it. This Jewish chaplain is from the Humboldt Park section in Chicago. He is with the 12th TAC and will come down here every Thursday to conduct services. The other one will remain here as the chaplain of the Wing. He is a nice guy and he and the other chaplain drank with the enlisted men as though they preferred their company.

I rather expected you to say that Nancy was the best of all, because everybody who sees her wants to take her away from me. I have to turn down about ten offers per day. At this time, I'm looking for a suitable breed with which to breed her. You see, she is a small dog and has a lot of Dalmatian and bird dog in her – so I want to find a similar strain so that we can get a pretty good result. After all, if I were to breed her with a huge dog, she'd have a pretty hard time of it, I'm afraid. Anyway, it won't be for a while.

So Carole Frances had her first shampoo! I can imagine how frightened she must have been when she first saw all the machinery with which the beauticians work, but I guess she is a woman after all, if she liked it so much after it was all over.

Well, Darlings, I want to wish you all a very enjoyable stay up there once more. Be sure to take it easy in the sun, however, as it is too easy to become sun-stricken. Well, regards to all – love to the folks and many, many hugs and kisses for the baby and you –

With All My Love,
Your Dave

———

Friday – 27 July – 1945
Somewhere in Darmstadt

My Darling Angels,
 I got hold of Ed Olech and another fellow named Abrams and we took a jeep up to Hanau. We went up to Frankfurt and we almost had some lovely fox skins to send home to our families. On the superhighway, right ahead of us, were three very nice-looking young foxes. Unfortunately, I nor the other two had our guns with us, so we failed to get such nice prizes.
 As to what [commentator H.V.] *Kaltenborn said about the War in the Pacific being over within 3 months – well that could happen, but I don't think so. I have always been of the opinion that we will not have to invade Japan, but can defeat them by air. As you now see, their cities are in ruins and they are feeling the effects of our bombings to a great extent, as indicated by their radio broadcasts. So I insist that we will not make an amphibious invasion of the islands, but will pound them from morning through the night – into the next day – until the surrender. It may be won before Winter sets in, because at that time, the Japs will have absolutely no place in which to live and keep warm. So I say that it could end in December or January. December 7th would be a most appropriate date on which to surrender and we could make that date the official date of surrender, if it lasts that long. After all, it was almost on the anniversary of Hitler's proclamation of War that we won over here.*
 So take good care of the folks – Carole Frances and yourself – Get a lot of rest – Regards to all and love to the folks – many, many thousands of hugs and kisses for the baby and you –
 With All My Love,
 Your Dave

———

Sunday – 29 July – 1945
Somewhere in Darmstadt

My Darling Amy and Carole Frances,
 I had figured on writing you last night, after the show. The picture was "Objective – Burma," with Errol Flynn. It was very, very, very good and I hope that many people see it in the States. In fact, it was the first picture that

ever made me sit on the edge of my seat, waiting to see what happened the next moment. Of course, there will be people back home who naturally will say that it is 100% a propaganda picture. It may be that, but at the same time, it succeeds in showing you how tough a tiny part of the CBI [China-Burma-India] *campaign was. So if you multiply that by a thousand, you may get a mental picture of what the men are going through in trying to put away our enemies in the Pacific.*

To add to the ridiculous statements which are being made by our "brilliant statesmen" at home, they are requesting more thorough investigations be made by company commanders before approving furloughs for troops in the States. Amy, when I read that, I almost boiled. No doubt, these two statesmen (?) will receive many letters voicing disapproval. It is a thing like that which makes it tough on men returning home from a Theatre of War. After all, just because the War is ended, that doesn't mean that it is now necessary to forget about the men and let them go to hell. Now that that is off my mind, I will get on with this letter.

It was a long picture and it was about 11:00 when we got out of the show. Olech, Dines and I went down to the Supply Office and we sat around discussing the picture. We drank some of the Cokes we were issued the other day and we had a late snack of a steak sandwich, which I had taken with me from the evening dinner. It was 11:30 when we decided to close up and I was really tired – so I went right to bed. So, after hearing my story, do you forgive me?

I was a bit peeved this morning when Nancy came in with some kind of dirt all over her hindquarters, smelling nasty. I brushed her off and poured some DDT powder on her, so as to disinfect her – just in case. Ordinarily, she is such a clean dog and everybody wants to take her, so this must have been one of her bad days.

Now that it is about over, I'll tell you something. I had a peculiar irritation in my throat a number of days ago. I hadn't slept for three nights on account of it, so I finally decided to go on sick call and get it over with. My throat was slightly swollen on the right side and a pressure was felt on the right ear – through the Eustachian tube – so I explained the trouble to the doctor. He diagnosed it as trench mouth of the tonsil. He swabbed the spot in my throat with some kind of acid and then with peroxide. Each application almost made me vomit. However, I guess it has helped me, as the swelling has gone down and my throat is well again. On top of that, I had to chew tablets of sulfanilamide to counteract any secondary infections. So now, I am about as good as new, so please don't worry one little bit – I'm safe and sound.

I guess that Paul and Beulah must have really had quite a time together after such a long time apart. Have you heard by now where Paul is to be stationed? I hope that he doesn't have to go back to sea. (Dinah Shore is now singing "He's Home For A Little While" – and it is good – but good!)

By the way, wasn't that a tough thing to happen in New York – the B-25 hitting the Empire State Building? I guess they were lucky that not more damage was done than did occur. Well, that is included in the huge cost of this War.

I'm sorry that you had to go to the trouble of finding a history of Darmstadt, because that was before the War. If you go into Darmstadt today, you ride down huge piles of rubble and smashed buildings. That is Darmstadt since the War. Oh, there are a few homes on the outskirts of the city, but the center and outer areas are smashed to bits. In fact, the other day, after a drizzle, the smell of the dead, who are still buried under the debris, came up into the air – It was enough to make you vomit. So what you learn about German cities is all ancient history – They have had a remodeling job.

Well, Darlings, I guess this is about it for now, so regards to all – love to the folks – and have a wonderful time – lots and lots and lots of hugs and kisses for the baby and you –

> *With All My Love,*
> *Your Dave*
> *P.S. I do love you both very, very much.*

<hr />

> *Monday – 30 July – 1945*
> *Somewhere in Darmstadt*

My Most Beloved Wife and Baby,

This morning, I took Ed Olech with me and we went up to Hanau for some supplies. At lunchtime, we went over to their Mess Hall and ate. I had Nancy along with me and she ate the ham which they had, even though it was salty. Ordinarily, she doesn't like ham, because it is always so salty overseas, so she must have really been hungry at the time. I don't know what I'd do without her – She has gotten to be a real companion to me. She is so likable, too, that everybody wants to take her from me, but she will only answer to my whistle.

This outfit is really getting me all bawled up. This evening, I saw a fellow in the hallway and asked him if he was "Perkey" – a fellow for whom I have been looking for the past three days. This fellow answered in some of the best Polish language that he worked in the garage. Well, you could have knocked me over with a feather, because this guy had on G.I. clothing that was washed and pressed and looked just like a G.I. At this time, there is a definite shortage of Olive Drab clothing in this Theatre. Here, the liberated people run around in G.I. clothing, while the G.I.'s are anxiously waiting for theirs. That is definitely a damned shame and the fellows themselves are to blame for most of it. I know that some of them have probably sold or exchanged articles of clothing for schnapps or some other item. Then, some of the officers give the foreigners their old clothing to wear. Then, there are some "liberated" girls who act as "interpreters" for some of the officers and they are given clothing. It is a dirty shame – especially when the men need these same items. Well, thank God that this can't last forever.

Well, regards to all – Love to the folks – Lots of nice, warm schmooshin' for you and the baby –

With All My Love,
Your Dave

Tuesday – 31 July – 1945
Somewhere in Darmstadt

My Dearest Wife and Baby,

It so happens that this organization has a quota of two men to go to England on a seven-day rest trip. Well, as so many are alerted at this time to be sent to other organizations, Shannon is reluctant to send any men out on pass, so I decided that as long as I couldn't get transportation down to Annecy, I may as well try to go to England on pass. Well, Shannon OK'd the trip. Right after that, the Motor Sergeant asked Shannon if it was OK to let me have a jeep with which to go down to Annecy. After thinking it over, Shannon said that it was OK to do that – Now what in the world am I to do? I do want to see the Terhochs – but I also want to see England. At the same time, if I take a jeep down to that sector, I will have a helluva time locating a G.I. place to get some repairs done in case something happens to the jeep. After I got there, I would have to worry about the jeep at all times, because there are numerous cases of jeeps and other vehicles being stolen. If I went to England, I would fly and then have a hard time getting around once I was in London, as it is a lot better if you have a vehicle in such a large city. I am going to have to work it out as well as I can. However, at this time, I think that I will take the England trip and hope to see the Terhochs at some other time. What a tough time I'm having – eh? Having to choose between a trip to England by plane or a trip to Southern France by jeep.

Well, Darlings, hope that all is well at home – Regards to all – Love to the folks – And many thousands of hugs and kisses for Carole and you –

With All My Love,
Your Dave

———

Thursday – 2 August – 1945
Somewhere in Darmstadt

My Darling Amy and Carole Frances,

After eating evening chow, I took a jeep up to Frankfurt. I picked up a G.I. who was on the road. He was a refugee who left Germany some years ago and went to the States when the Nazis moved into power. He was just coming from Hamburg, where he was visiting his mother and brothers. He said this his mother fainted clean away when she saw him walk in the door. She hadn't heard from him since 1939 and hadn't the slightest idea that he was in the ETO. He said that he had studied medicine in Berlin during his visits back to Germany. At this time, he is with a medical unit under the 7th Army and he said that he acts as an interpreter. I dropped this fellow off at a refueling point where there is also a Red Cross doughnut truck – so I naturally took advantage of the situation and filled the jeep and my stomach. These mobile units are really a tremendous help to the boys when they need a snack.

I was disappointed when I learned that the Jack Benny show was shown again this evening in Darmstadt. The boys who had seen it in the afternoon said that it was ten times better than the Bob Hope show – so I really felt badly. We were told that inspectors were definitely coming around this afternoon or tomorrow morning for sure – so we have had to sit and sweat it out while the others went to the show. As I was typing this, the radio announced that there was to be no change on the points for the time being. Well, this is really a morale builder for the boys. After waiting for two months for the "new" mark to be announced, they come out with something like that. I suppose you are as disappointed as I, so I won't say any more about this in this letter.

I went over to the medics to have my throat swabbed again – just to prevent any future infections, so don't worry. The doc thought that it may have been diphtheria – but the result was negative, so we just kept on with the sulfadiazine tablets – but with soda bicarbonate tablets thrown in. So I am OK now and will remain well – so don't worry.

Once I get back, if the weather is nice in St. Louis, we will just sit in the house and rest. That is all that I want to do for about three months. I wouldn't know what to do if I were to go right back to work. Of course, there will be many other things that will seem strange to us again. For instance, if our trousers wear out, we will not be able to just bring them down to Boyd's and get them exchanged for a new pair – We'll have to buy a new pair. Also, all we do is drive into a station and fill up the tank – no money or ration tickets – How will I get away with that back home? However, with all those little, strange things, I'd be the happiest guy on earth to have to learn all over again, if it meant that I was to be a civilian for a change.

So say "Hello" to all – Love to the folks – and bushels and bushels of love and kisses for Carole and you –

With All My Love,
Your Dave

———

Friday – 3 August – 1945
Somewhere in Darmstadt

My Dearest Darlings,

Just got back from the show where I saw Jack Benny in "Horn Blows at Midnight" – It was pretty funny. A most unusual picture, too. It had a very good supporting cast with it. I hadn't heard of the picture until it arrived, so if it is new, try to see it – It may be good entertainment for the baby, too. The picture was here last night, too, the same night that his troupe played in Darmstadt. It would have been something if he had shown up at the theatre to see his own picture.

I see that they have sent only 235,000 men home from the 800,000 expected. That would mean that it will be about six months at least to get the balance, or 565,000 men, back home. When that time rolls around, it will be after the first of the year before any new announcements can be made, so it will be about June or July before I will even have a chance of seeing the States again. By that time, the War in the Pacific will definitely be over, so once more, I can say that I am totally disgusted with the whole setup. I have about given up all hope of getting home by Xmas of this year.

I received a letter from the Mougins in which they told me that their future son-in-law was back home in Pennsylvania for a 30-day furlough before getting ready to go to the Pacific Theatre. They hadn't had any word from him for over two months. They hoped that I get to visit them once more before going home. Well, from the looks of things, I will probably be over here for a while and have enough time to visit them. Speaking of visiting, the jeep in which I was supposed to go to Annecy was in an accident – so I think that it is off for the time being. Another thing is that the Terhochs had figured on moving back to Paris in August – so if I did drive down there, I'd be taking a chance on finding them gone back to Paris. So I think that as long as there is an opening to go to England, I will take that on the 9th.

You must be psychic – dreaming that I was in the hospital with throat trouble. As you know, I did have trouble with my throat – but that is about over now. Well, Darlings, that is about all the news for the day. Nothing ever happens around here – so regards to all – love to the folks – many, many hugs and kisses for the baby and you –

With All My Love,
Your Dave

———

Saturday – 4 August – 1945
Somewhere in Darmstadt

My Dearest Wife and Baby,

We are now having to stand reveille and retreat every day except Sunday. However, after the first night, I decided that I had had enough and I sleep while the others stand reveille. So if they catch up with me, I'll be a private tout de suite! There is absolutely no need for any of us to be here. There are sufficient numbers of troops of the other Allied nations to take care of any territories we could give up. This continent is no longer a danger zone to the safety of the United States as it was in 1941, therefore, why must we keep Occupation Troops here in the first place? We have certainly given them enough food and clothing by now to allow us to return home and let those other countries take on those responsibilities. Some people will argue that we have to stay in order to create a good-will policy and give us a good foundation for our world trade. I say that we are far ahead of the others and now, we should let the Europeans do something for their "fellow *countrymen."* There are so many railroad men who are aching to get back to work – That is damned idiotic! What a relief it will be to stay at home with you and Carole Frances, not worry about falling out for retreat, etc.

I decided to rest awhile and then take in a show. They had "Enter Arsene Lupin" with Charles Korvin, Ella Raines, and J. Carrol Naish. It wasn't too bad. The only funny thing about the whole picture was when the hero kissed the girl. The whole audience roared and Nancy ran down the main aisle, barking as loudly as she could. She gets excited whenever she hears any disturbance that is not a natural one – What a watchdog she will make back home! So now that the show is over, I am down in the Supply writing you the very uninteresting events of the day. Oh yes – there is one more thing – Some of the high-point men who were transferred into our outfit are going back to the States tomorrow, rather, they are going to Paris and then catch a boat from Le Havre, I think. At least they are starting an evacuation – That's something to think about for the time being.

Well, Darlings, I suppose I have worried you enough for one day with all my bitchings, so I had better turn in and call it a day. So hope that all is well at home and that the weather is nice. Regards to all our friends and love to the folks – Many, many, many hugs and kisses for the baby and you –
    With All My Love,
    Your Dave
    P.S. Ah loves you'all.

———

Sunday – 5 August – 1945
Somewhere in Darmstadt

My Darling Amy and Carole Frances,

After reading your mail, it was time for evening chow, which was awful – We ate liver for about four days straight last week and today we get it again. Since the Mess Sergeant was shipped out, we have not had very good meals as a whole. One fellow, who we just sent back to the States, was a former teletype operator who turned cook – so as a cook, he is an excellent teletype operator. Oh well, it can't last forever – or can it?

Incidentally, I asked Shannon if there was a possibility of letting Ed Olech and I go to England together on the 9th. He said that as soon as we were finished with the inventory, I could plan on going to England on the 9th – However, he didn't say anything about Ed – so I hope that he will be able to swing it.

So you didn't like the idea of my taking Nancy up flying – Well, after all, she never had that thrill before. I can assure you that I will not go up for a test flight anymore – Those parachutes are too bulky anyway.

As to Micka, he tried to get into the same company as Maddox, because he knows nothing at all and Maddox would protect him if he screwed up at any time. I hear that Micka is the Adjutant of that company now – That is really a laugh, because he is an imbecile. As to Shannon, he hasn't been such a bad Joe up until now – I don't know if he will stay the same, but I think that he will, because he depends on the men in the Orderly Room and Supply a helluva lot, because he knows nothing about either.

Yes, I really do like flying – There is nothing like it. When you are up in the air, there is a certain feeling which is very difficult to describe. However, as to buying a plane, I'm afraid that it will be a long time before they will be offered at popular prices and emergency fields have been built all over the country. Then, they will have to have gas stations all along the ways and so many air-maintenance plants – So we'll be riding in autos for a while yet.

Well, that about winds up the day – so hope that everybody is well at home. Take good care of yourselves and say "Hello" to all; love to the folks; and oceans of love and kisses for the baby and you –

With All My Love,
Your Dave

———

Tuesday – 7 August – 1945
Somewhere in Darmstadt

My Most Beloved Darlings,

Yesterday, the doc decided to try penicillin in a last effort to knock that irritation out altogether, so he gave me a shot at about 9. An hour later, my throat felt a little more swollen. I waited until 11, when I had to go back for another shot, and one of the enlisted men there gave it to me. I returned to the Supply Office and started working, and I felt worse and it was harder for me to swallow. About noon, I phoned the Major and asked him if the shots would swell my throat and he said that they shouldn't. He didn't seem worried, so I went up to eat lunch. While sitting there, I broke out with chills and shivered as though it was 10 below in that room. I decided to go up and lie down and rest until one, when it was time to go back for my third shot.

I explained to the Sergeant that I had chills and now it felt as though I had fever – so he took my temperature and phoned the doctor after seeing that I did have fever – I learned today that it was 101. The doctor told him to forget about the other shots and to give me some ephedrine capsules, and that I should lie down and drink as much water as I could. I got a pitcher from the Mess Hall and I must have drunk about twenty quarts of water during the day and night that followed. As I lay there, it felt as though I was burning up and I started to perspire – and I do mean that I sweated it out. My blankets were wet through and through. I awoke at various intervals – just in time to go to the bathroom and to drink more water. I felt as woozy as the drunkenest drunk on Sixth Street in St. Louis. It was about 6:00 A.M. when I awoke, and it seemed like a different world. However, my legs were as weak as a day-old duckling's and I wobbled into the bathroom. When I walked downstairs, my legs were still very, very weak, but I managed to drink a cup of coffee and piece of toast. After that, I went downstairs and had to go to work, as we sent out three more men to other organizations. At nine, I went back to the Dispensary and the doc was surprised to see me looking so well. He explained that mine was the third such case that he had seen in which men reacted to shots of penicillin by getting chills and fever. He swabbed my throat with a different solution this time and I almost vomited again. However, he decided to start giving me vitamin pills – So today, I started with one brown, ball-type pill and three of a smaller, white tablet per day. So I am really getting the doc's full assortment of wares.

Anyway, today, I feel better than I have felt in the past eleven days. It is as though a terrific weight was lifted from my shoulders. So, once more, I say that you should not worry, because this time, I am definitely well and am making plans to go to England in the next couple of days. I think that I will have to borrow some money to avoid any financial embarrassment – I do have about 35 bucks, but they say that it takes at least 100 to have a good time.

About those people whom you met who came from Germany, I can see their reaction upon finding such a high degree of anti-Semitism in the States. It is a shame that such things are still in existence after so many have died to do away with just such feelings. However, the anti-Negro problem is going to be another tough situation with which to deal after it is all over – so it isn't going to be all a bed of roses after we are all home again.

Hey, please don't let Carole go riding her bike "lickety split" around the walks. In the first place, it is dangerous for her, in case she should fall; another

thing is that she might ride into a child and injure him. I get so nervous when I read that she rides so well, because I immediately think that she may get too confident and fall – Well, thank God that she hasn't hurt herself. Well, hope that all is well back in St. Louis and that the weather is nice. Regards to all and love to the folks and for my darling wife and daughter – the nicest, biggest and fondest hug and kiss in the world –
    With All My Love,
    Your Dave

———

Wednesday – 8 August – 1945
Somewhere in Darmstadt
My Darling Wife and Baby,

Well, I just heard something over the radio that seemed like a ray of light out of the dark clouds over the Pacific. Russia declared war on the Japanese as of tomorrow. The War is certainly to end before the end of this year – With attacks from the West as well as the East, Japan has no possible chance of standing up against us any longer than four months. It was funny that the Russians were going through so many strenuous maneuvers in Siberia ever since the end of the War in Europe. Now we can see the reasons – The equipment was on its way to attack Japan. I can truthfully say that I didn't expect Russia to declare war, but it is a relief to have her on our side at this time. So perhaps we will have a celebration on December 7th, after all, as the date of the surrender of the Japanese. I know that the people back home are going to take this news even more enthusiastically than I. With this declaration of war, we should now try to get as many men out of the ETO and back home as possible, because the Russians are going to supply many more men than we will be able to get over there in the next six months.

This morning, I had to have the Major look at my throat. He is really a good surgeon and he really never had any opportunity to do the type of work for which he was seeking while in the Army, so he asked to go to the Pacific and he left today. Anyway, he told the Colonel about my throat and they both looked at it and suggested that I take an intravenous injection for the gland that remains swollen. He said that I had a spirochete (?) type of tonsillitis infection. I also got the injection and he gave me a bottle of peroxide with which to gargle three times a day. I told him about my possible trip to England on the 9th, but he suggested that I stay and get this all cleared up and try to go again later. I told Shannon about it and he said that it was OK with him – so I guess it will be the 16th when I leave. It seems that when I try to get away on a pass, there is always something to hold me up.

Hope that everything is OK back home. I am a lot more enthusiastic about seeing you soon than I have been since the end of the War in this Theatre. So say "Hello" to all and love to the folks – and so many great, big hugs and kisses for Carole Frances and you –

With All My Love,

Your Dave

P.S. I do love you so very much!!!

Thursday – 9 August – 1945

Somewhere in Darmstadt

My Dearest Darlings,

The Colonel said that my throat was much better and that tomorrow, he was getting in a new medicine with which to swab my throat, and that ought to do away with the infection at once. He is almost certain that it is about finished and the only reason that I have been coming back was to see that it is going away, so please don't worry about me, as it is just about well now.

The other night, we opened our bar – up on the 3rd floor of the building we occupy. Well, one of the fellows decided to help celebrate the opening, so he had a few too many and jumped out the window. Luckily, he landed in the grass or else he would have hit the concrete walk and certainly been killed. He suffered internal injuries. He was always a little on the dopey side and was a wee bit slaphappy. You could wave a cork under his nose and he would be drunk in no time. He was the one who emptied his carbine at a Jerry plane that flew over the landing in Southern France at about 20,000 feet. When a fellow does that, he certainly isn't all there – so perhaps that will prevent him from going to the Pacific, where he was supposed to go. Since that opening, the bar has been closed – so I guess Shannon isn't taking any chances again. That is typical of this outfit – They will always screw something up for themselves.

Well, that was a very smart answer that Carole gave when you told her about the letter advising you against coming over here. She must realize that things aren't any too comfortable over here. So, my Darlings, that about winds up the day's activities in the Darmstadt area. It is still drizzling and looks good for all night. So hope that the folks are well and resting a lot at

home – Say "Hello" to all and love to the folks – a million hugs and a trillion kisses for the baby and you –
    With All My Love,
    Your Dave

———

Friday – 10 August – 1945
Somewhere in Darmstadt

My Most Beloved Wife and Baby,

    Well, today has been one for which we have been waiting a long, long time. Even when the Jerries surrendered, we were not as enthusiastic as we could have been, because there was always the reminder that the Japs were still ahead of us. In a very short and most unexpected time, we have brought them to the point of surrender. I can truthfully say that this was certainly not expected so soon. Even with the declaration of war by Russia and the atomic bombing of Japan, I didn't think that the end would come so soon. At this very time, there is still no news as to the verified acceptance of the surrender by the United States or any of the other Allied nations. In fact, the radio says that Washington is still waiting for the offer of unconditional surrender to be given them, so it will probably be a couple of days before the end is official. The only exception so far is that the emperor remains as the head of the Japanese people. That will be a point to be discussed, no doubt, in the surrender terms worked out later. Anyway, we can now see a definite end to all hostilities throughout the world.

    Well, it is like a weight being lifted from our shoulders all of a sudden. As to us, I don't think that we will get home this year, even with the War over. There are still so many men overseas with over 85 points and who are sweating it out that it will take at least six months to get these men home. So, we won't be home until next year – I'm almost certain of that. Gosh, it's almost impossible to believe that it has happened. This does bear out what I have advocated – that we will not have to invade Japan to defeat it. When I think of the statements that high military officials have made, saying that the War was liable to go into 1947, it made me laugh. However, I was only laughing to make myself confident that it would end long before. Well, Darlings, it is here now and we can all thank God that he has brought this whole damned affair to an end and that he has brought us the victories. I am so thankful that I am an American, even in spite of all the minor faults which we have back in Washington. So, Darling, we do know that we will be back together again and much sooner than we figured last week.

Well, we had a lot of work to do anyway, as there are still reports to be made out, even though the War has ended over here a long time ago – three months, to be exact. We also have men still going and coming in the organization, so that takes a lot of time.

Well, once more, I want to say that with the news about the Jap surrender offer, I feel a lot more optimistic. It was such a dark subject before – but I think that we can now see a chance of getting back by next Spring. However, it won't make me mad if we get home this year. The people back home will probably really go up in the air when it becomes official. So regards to all and love to the folks – a million hugs and kisses for Carole Frances and you –
With All My Love,
Your Dave

—

Saturday – 11 August – 1945
Somewhere in Darmstadt

My Darling Amy and Carole Frances,

We just came out of the theatre and I want to tell you that we really had some high-class talent to entertain us this evening. Paul Robeson was here. Along with him were Eugene List, a noted, young concert pianist; a talented violinist named Miriam Solovieff; and Robeson's accompanist, Lawrence somebody. Robeson came out and immediately started out by singing four numbers, including a couple of ballads. The audience, which numbered about three thousand, was a very receptive one and appreciated each number very much. After he finished, he introduced Miss Solovieff, who had the honor of having List accompany her on the piano. She played some very difficult numbers, which were well received by all.

Well, after she was finished, List played his part of the program. As you may have read, he is the one who played for the Big Three in Potsdam as a favor to Truman, who requested it. He did play very well and everybody showed that they liked him. After he finished, Robeson came back out and sang some more – including "Ol' Man River." He ended with one which is an old favorite among his followers – "Ballad of an American" – and I enjoyed it very much. The program, as a whole, was so very enjoyable that nobody wanted to leave after it was over. Back home, you wouldn't be able to get such talent together for one concert unless it was for a charitable purpose. Why, just to hear Robeson would cost you five dollars – another three to hear List and perhaps as much to hear Miss Solovieff after the War. So we really had the class this evening.

Now here is the unexpected thing that happened this afternoon. I was on my way down to the large Supply Room that we have in the rear of the area, and on my way down, I saw some USO uniforms outside the theatre. So I went over and sure enough, there was Robeson standing there, talking to a couple of G.I.'s. So I also joined in and it ended up with just him and I talking. I told him that I really admired his work – especially considering how hard it is in the States for a colored person to make the grade. He told me about his last role that he played before going overseas – "Othello" – and said that he missed St. Louis on that trip, however, he had sung at the Municipal Auditorium at various times. I also told him that he had been a favorite with my dad for many years, as he used to hear him over the radio very often. I asked him if he would sing "Ol' Man River" and he said that it would be worked into the program. He told me that he expected to be here tomorrow – so I think that I will try to get a few shots of him and the others. I only have three rolls of film left and when I go to England, I want to have enough to make a pictorial history of the trip, so I can't afford to waste them now.

I went over to the doc's and he said that by Monday, I ought to be entirely finished with him. However, he told me that there will be a slight depression in my throat where that ulcer was. You see, they had to use some sort of acid with which to treat it – so I guess the acid ate away the flesh – at least the ailment will be gone, however.

I just heard the "Hit Parade" and it had some songs on it with which I am unfamiliar. The ones I know are "I'm Beginning to See the Light," which was No. 1; "Candy," which was No.2; "Sentimental Journey," which was No. 3; "All of My Life," which was No. 4; "My Dreams are Getting Better All the Time," which was No. 6; "Laura," which was No. 7, and "Dreams," which was No. 8. The ones I don't know are "Just a Prayer Away," which was No. 5 and "I Should Care," which was No. 9. I really do like "Laura" and "Sentimental Journey."

We have been listening to the radio all day to hear if the War is ended, but it looks like we are going to ask for a definite unconditional surrender – no strings attached, such as the Japs' request to retain their emperor. That is a very delicate thing to iron out. In the first place, he is the only thing to which the Japs look for their lives and religion. However, he is also the one who was responsible for the decision to go to War. Then, on the other hand, the Allies ask that all freedom of religion be restored to Japan. If that is the case, then they cannot ask to do away with the emperor, who is exactly that. In the meantime, I heard that we are continuing to use the atomic bomb on the Japs. From a righteous point of view, that isn't the best thing to do at a time when they are asking for a chance to surrender. However, they did exactly that while they were in Washington negotiating "peace." We are certainly doing them a thousand times as much damage as they did us. Well, I guess there is no wrong or right in War.

That is about all the news to relate today. I just took that old picture out of my bag – the one of Carole which we took in Fresno – remember? I have that one and also the one I got for last Xmas on top of my table in my room and, after looking at them, I think that I will have a hard time recognizing the baby when I get back. Well, I hope not. So, say "Hello" to all and love to the folks – lots and lots and lots of hugs and kisses for you and the baby –

With All My Love,
Your Dave
P.S. I do love you both so very much and am aching to get back.

———

Sunday – 12 August – 1945
Somewhere in Darmstadt

My Dearest Darlings,

I expect to go to Nuremberg tomorrow to pick up some supplies. I made arrangements to get a jeep and Joe Dines asked to go with me – so we will probably spend the night there and return the following day.

So far, there have been no new developments on the Japs' surrender – but I expect it to end any day now. The longer they ponder the issue of whether or not to retain the emperor, the more they will be bombed and wiped out. With the Japanese newspapers playing up the crown prince, that is certainly an indication that they expect to replace Hirohito. I have been sitting with my ears pinned to the radio most of the day and am expecting the announcement to be made any minute. I suppose those at home are doing the same. The tension is terrific with me, but many of the men don't seem to be affected by it at all. Perhaps they have been overseas too long to appreciate such a time. Well, I hope that I am wrong about not getting back until next

Spring. Perhaps the Army will do something where there will not be so much red tape and we will get back by Xmas.

Last night, Joe Dines told me that he had received some salami, so I demanded that he bring it down and we cut into it – so I had a midnight snack and it was really good. As long as we are going to be here for a while, if it will not cut into your meat ration allowances too much, see if you can scare up a salami and send it over here. The thing that we never see and which we would like to have are potato chips – Try to send me a couple of boxes of them. Also, some of those potato waffle-shaped affairs. That ought to take care of the Request Department for a while.

How are the folks doing these days? Hope that all is well at the store. Also, with the War almost at an end, there will no doubt be a relaxation of materials and plenty of piece goods should be available. This season ought to be a tremendous one with the woman dolling up for her man and he buying new clothes. Well, Darlings, say "Hello" to all our friends and love to the folks – and for Carole and you, a tremendously huge hug and kiss –

With All My Love,
Your Dave

Tuesday – 14 August – 1945
Somewhere in Darmstadt

My Dearest Amy and Carole Frances,

Well, we finally got back after a long, tedious, and rain-filled trip. As it was chilly and threatening rain, I decided not to take Nancy along and she definitely didn't like to see me leave without her. We drove up to Darmstadt and then took the highway up to Aschaffenburg. That is the city that was first taken by the 3rd Army and then had to be recaptured by the 7th. It is really battered up. We drove on to Wurzburg and that is also smashed to bits. There is an old and famous castle up there that still is standing, however. Otherwise, it is almost impossible for you to conceive the damage done over here, unless you saw it all. We left for Nuremberg and arrived about 3:30 that afternoon. We had to refuel, so we went down to the gas dump, which is located right next to the well-known Soldiers Field, at which the Nazi Youth used to meet. The gas is laid out along a tremendous stretch of great blocks of granite. I think that Hitler probably landed his plane on this stretch, as it was close by the Field.

Joe Dines said that he had some relatives who were supposed to be near Munich, so we headed that way. (I forgot to tell you that that afternoon, we had stopped along the way and I bought a salami and a loaf of bread. That was our lunch – with a glass of beer.) About 9:00, we decided to get rooms at one of the small villages along the Autobahn. We found a very nice room – a double bed and one single – so we parked the jeep inside the barn area and unloaded our things. We washed up and then walked over to a "brauerei" and had a bottle of beer. It was about 10:00 when we hit the hay. We had one helluva time trying to fall asleep, because of the mosquitoes. Well, after we finally fell asleep, we were awakened by a couple of Jerries running down the street and yelling. None of us knew what it was all about until we stuck our heads out the windows and saw a lot of people running up the way. There was a bright reflection in that direction and, occasionally, I could see flames reaching above the houses. We later learned that it was a barn full of straw – 40 tons of it – and it did go up fast! There's nothing much that one can do in a case like that, so we just jumped right back into bed. We finally got some sleep and awoke at about 6:30. We had told the woman in charge to fry us some eggs the night before – so we had eggs and a couple of slices of salami, with coffee made from corn kernels. We drove on to Munich in between showers. We drove to the Deutsche Museum where they were supposed to have all the names of the displaced persons in that area. Well, Dines didn't have any luck in locating them – so we went to the gas dump to refuel. It was there that we were misinformed by a Lieutenant that the War had officially ended at 8:10 A.M. this morning. It sounded like good news, but we later learned that he was all wet. We decided to head back, so we headed for the Autobahn.

As there was a show being put on by the G.I.'s of the 19th TAC, I decided to go. I'm glad that I did, because there was some unusually good talent in it and a couple of very funny comedians. The audience was always in an uproar and the whole program moved along very quickly. It was 9:00 when we got out and I went up to the bar to get my ration of Coca-Cola – 2 bottles per week – and came down to my room. It is now 10:35 and after that 630-mile trip, I am tired. Meanwhile, Darlings, I hope that all is well at home. So, regards to all – love to the folks – and so very many hugs and kisses for Carole Frances and you –

With All My Love,
Your Dave

Saturday – 25 August – 1945
Somewhere in Darmstadt

My Most Beloved Wife and Baby,

Well, here is the first letter since I have been to and returned from England. The first morning was the 15th and Joe Dines and I got up at 6:30 so that we would be out at the field in time. We flew on a direct route, passing over the Main River and on to Holland. Down below, we saw what appeared to be a body of water, but upon closer study, we saw that it was the flooded region about which you have no doubt read. It was back in March, I think, that the Nazis flooded that part of Holland in order to hamper our crossings of the Roer and Upper Rhine Rivers. Well, at this present time, this sector is still water-covered and it will be years before it will be ready for cultivation again. As we came closer to the English cliffs, we all were straining our eyes to see the White Cliffs. Sure enough, there they lay before us – a long line of high, white cliffs, marking the Isle of Great Britain. They were as if molded out of clay and set into a miniature sea. We flew directly to London, passing over many old English villages and hamlets. We landed at an airport about 15 miles from the city.

The first thing that we had to do was to get in line – the very typical G.I. procedure. It was to show our passes and to get our money changed from marks into pounds. The pound is equal to about $4.03. Well, I borrowed 40 bucks from Joe, so that I would be sure to have enough. So we changed our money and got on the bus which was to take us to the city. That was where the fun began and continued as long as we had to put up with English traffic. As you know, they drive on the opposite side of the road than we – so here we were, driving along the left side and the driver was about the nerviest guy I have ever driven with. He must have just skinned at least 10 buses, about 25 people, and 35 streetcars on our way. We decided that it would be a good idea to get away from the regimentation and get a room for ourselves, so we walked the streets for about two hours before we finally landed a place. It has a general bathroom adjoining, so we just locked the outside door and it was practically ours all time we were there.

We went out and walked down Marylebone Street and found a Czechoslovakian restaurant. It was run by refugees, as are most of the better restaurants in London. We enjoyed a good meal of wiener schnitzel – topped by apple strudel. However, it was there that we learned that a pound note is *the quickest thing to lose track of. It cost you at least 10 shillings, or 2 dollars, every time you go to eat. On top of that, the service is so darned good that you have to tip at least a shilling (20 cents), so that really leaves you almost nothing.*

It was the second night of the V.J. celebration, so we went down to see what it was all about. We were told to go to Piccadilly Square, as that was supposed to be the place for celebrating, so we took the subway (a very good subway system, too) down there and got off in a mob of people. The streets were jammed to capacity for blocks and blocks. All that you could do was to stand there and let the crowd push you around. There were fireworks all over the place, with many of them falling right into the crowds. I know that many must have been injured that night. We were hugged, pushed, offered drinks, winked at, asked to join parties, and so many other things for which Piccadilly is popular. Well, at about 12, the subways stop, so we decided to head for home. We got there OK and hit the sack – a couple of very tired babies.

The next day was our first actual day on leave, as the pass didn't begin until that morning. That afternoon, we went for a walk to Westminster Abbey and the Houses of Parliament. It was the opening of the new government and the public was being allowed to visit . We went back down to Piccadilly, because we heard that there was going to be more celebration down there. We were once more pushed about, and about 9:30, we got a bit thirsty and hungry, so we went up to a very smart-looking place and found a long line waiting to get in. However, your Uncle Davie didn't like standing in line – so I asked the headwaiter if "Colonel Ashby" was seated yet, as he was expecting us. That must have made an impression on him as he let us in and we went into the dining room at once. It is called "Veeraswamy's" – an Indian place. The waiters and waitresses are all dressed in native Indian costume and the interior was as if you were in a Hindu spot in Calcutta. I know how much you like atmosphere and this was it!

The next day was drizzling. We found a very nice kosher place at which to eat and let me tell you that I made a pig of myself. We had real corned beef – they call it salt beef over there. We ate kosher pickles and real Jewish rye. We had a very nice meal and then we decided to go to a show and rest our legs, as we had been walking all day long, so we went to see "Affairs of Susan" – It was really good.

The fourth day, we had a little better weather, so we went over to 10 Downing Street – the home of the Prime Minister, as you know. We found

a place called the "Austria House" – also run by refugees – and they served
real kosher food. The clientele was all Jewish and continental. It was really
very tasty and we enjoyed it a lot. After that, we went downtown to the
Regent-Plaza and tried to get a room but no luck, so we just stayed there
and drank for the evening. We met a few refugees there and had some good
talks about the Jewish Problem. If you think that the anti-Semitic feeling
is bad in the States, you had better not come to England. It is three to four
times as great. That is a very conservative estimate, too. I never heard such
open expression of opinion as I did in London. I was told how Sir Oswald
Mosley, the Hitler Representative in England, took his many followers
into the Lower Eastern section of London and were on the way to beat
up the Jews in that part of the city. Well, the Jews had caught wind of it
and were ready with their Christian friends and they beat the devil out of
the attacking force. It is certainly amazing that such outright expression
is allowed to flourish in England. Even Churchill, upon the murder of
the anti-Semitic military governor in Palestine, said that each Jew in the
British Kingdom, no matter whether man, woman or child, will be held
responsible for that action. That shows you just how things are over here.
With [Prime Minister Clement] *Attlee in now, the Jews hope to get a*
better deal, because they are well represented by the unions.

The fifth day, we went out to the Pall Mall. That is where the Buckingham
Palace grounds begin. We went over to the palace gates and took some pictures
there and then we heard a lot of bagpipes coming down the way, so Joe took
a shot of me in front of the bagpipe band. It was about lunchtime, so we
went down to Piccadilly Square and walked around until we came across a
nice French restaurant – "Restaurant des Gourmets" – and we ate a couple
of delicious meals. Well, Joe and I walked around the Square awhile and
then went into a couple of bars and had a few drinks. If you are wondering
why all the drinking – well, that is all that you can get in London. You
never saw so many drinking persons in all your life. You can't get Cokes and
chocolate sodas as you can in the States – so you get liquor and wines. In all
my stay, I promise you that I did not get lit up once or even close to it.

The last day was spent in trying to locate some gifts for you and the baby
and also for Joe's sister – but we were both out of luck. We ended up at New
Bond Street, so we went over to the celebrated Savoy Hotel to try to get into
the restaurant – but no luck, as it was filled up. There was a dinner there for

the Russian Ambassador and the dining room was full of long beards, so we went over to the Strand and had an excellent meal there.

The next day – yesterday – was the day we were supposed to leave. We showed up at the registration place at 8:00 A.M. and we waited outside until noon. At that time, we were told to go to lunch. We returned and sweated it out until 3:00 and our names were still not called to leave that day, so we were given passes until the following morning at 8:00. You see, the weather has been very bad for flying, and if the clouds break for just a couple of hours, they will send up as many planes as possible. So we took off and went downtown to a Chinese restaurant for a good Chinese dinner. We really wanted to get the things we are not able to get over here, so we had shrimp and lobster chow mein and Joe had chicken chow mein. However, we didn't go out for any drinks, because the night before we left Germany, Joe had taken a few and he was one sad sack on the way across, so we decided to get a good night's sleep and be ready to take off in the morning.

Well, this morning, we reported again, but this time it was a clearer day and more planes were up, so we were called and loaded onto trucks. We drove to the field and registered to go to Germany, and then changed our money from pounds to marks. I had about 30 dollars left – so I was sorry that I didn't spend it all on a gift for you. This time, we flew faster and made it in two hours and ten minutes. When we arrived, it was the same old story from everybody – "How was England?" – and we have to answer the same thing fifty times. The best part of all was receiving 17 letters, of which nine were yours up to the 16th of August, which isn't bad at all. However, I'll start on them tomorrow.

So, my Darlings, there you have my little story of my visit to England and I am now a worn-out guy. Ten pages of typewriting is tiring and a lot of reading – so you ought to be well occupied for a while when you get this letter. I do hope that all is well back home. Say "Hello" to all and love to the folks – and so many millions of hugs and kisses for the baby and you –

With All My Love
Your Dave

———

Sunday – 26 August – 1945
Somewhere in Darmstadt

My Dearest Darlings,

There have been so many things that have happened since I have been away that I have to catch up on what is happening to men going home.

From the strong rumors that are going around, the whole 64th is going home next month and so are other high-point units under the Wing, however, yesterday, the 63rd Wing took over operations and we are the only Signal Unit around here to handle the communications for them – so our outfit will probably be on hand for a while yet.

Well, so you sent me a package from Frankfort – and with all those nice hors d'oeuvres. I should be getting it any day now. Now that the restrictions have been lifted on canned foods, I'm glad that I didn't make it too difficult on you as far as points go. Can you imagine going into a grocery and buying what you want without worrying about points? Gee, you will be able to buy as much gas as you wish, too! Well, it won't be too long before all the nice things are available once again. Speaking of doing away with rationing, you are lucky that you were not in England when the announcement was made that Lend-Lease was to be discontinued at once to England. You never saw and heard such degradation of the United States Government – Most people seem to think that we did it to hinder the success of the new Labor Government in England, however, they seem to forget that we certainly could not go on feeding the entire world forever and not get paid for it. I argued that the Prime Minister should have foreseen such a possibility and made arrangements for it when it did come. Now, they are slandering us left and right and sarcastically saying that they can get along quite well without a shipment of Spam. There was a headline in the English papers saying that tires, nylons and gas were now available in the States. You can imagine the effect that it had on the people over there – They still are rationed as before. I tried to buy a pair of shoes so that I could change, but I was told that I needed points. So England now is not too warm towards us.

So our darling daughter did a striptease at the beach. I'll bet that she had all the people wide-eyed at such a shape of things to come. By the way, while in London, I read about the girls in San Francisco who danced nude right out in public – What in the world has happened in the States to cause such demonstrations? I guess such a thing as morals is a long-forgotten subject. Wars seem to cause just such a condition all the time.

The next letter was of the 7th – the day when the atomic bomb was announced. I guess it made quite an impression on the world and the Japs especially. From the newspaper accounts, it was terrific and is still having its effects due to the radioactivity. A scientist in the States was criticized when he said that it was his opinion that this would happen and he was right. What the future uses of our control (?) of the atoms will be is too hard to visualize. One slight mistake and it could destroy America – so it is more to be feared than anything else. Yes, I know that it could replace all other means of power – but it is so far from the control stage that it is frightening. I'm afraid that we have hooked onto something that may be a little too hard to handle.

Yes, the baby will have a couple of good references in her parents to help her with recent history. I could tell her so much about what I have seen of the Old World and the effects of the War on it; the many old and historical places I have been to and seen. You could describe the difficulties involved in buying food with ration points. Well, Darlings, that leaves me with ten letters of yours to be answered on top of nine other people, so I will have to end this now and try to get a couple of others out. So give my regards to all and love to the folks – a billion hugs and kisses for Carole and you – I love and miss you two more than you will ever know – but am in hopes of seeing you by Xmas again –

> With All My Love,
> Your Dave

———

Sunday – 26 August – 1945
Somewhere in Darmstadt

My Sweetest Angels,

Just got in from seeing the show on the post – "Weekend at the Waldorf" – and it was really most enjoyable, so much so that I was sorry to see the picture end. If it hasn't been released in the States, it is with Ginger Rogers, Walter Pidgeon, Lana Turner, Van Johnson, Robert Benchley and many other good supporting players. As an added short, we saw the invasion of Iwo Jima and it was very impressive – especially as it was in Technicolor. The naval gun attack was beautiful to see – as was the erecting of the American flag on Mt. Surabachi – the famous shot made by Joe Rosenthal of the AP. It seemed just a couple of months ago and now we see the pictures of it. I only hope that friends, relatives and sweethearts don't see these pictures of the men who were wounded.

Right at this very moment, I am blue as blue can be. Some of the shots in the picture sort of reminded me of us when we went dancing at the Chase Club. We certainly did have some very enjoyable times together – hope that we'll be able to pick up where we left off very soon. The sooner I get away *from this damned continent, the better I'll like it. It will be so nice to have you and Carole Frances beside me again. There is an indescribable feeling of security that one gets when he has his family with him. You say that there is no competent head of the family there now – What do you think you have been doing these past two years? I'd say that you have been doing a terrific job!*

As to those services every Thursday, they fell through, because the chaplain has to come from near Nuremberg and it is too hard. On top of that, there aren't enough Jewish boys around here to have a big turnout, so we would have to go to Frankfurt to attend services, I think. With the [Jewish] holidays almost here, I guess there will be transportation available for that.

Louie, the boy who worked in Supply, sent me a ten-dollar money order on a bet we made. I said that the War in the Pacific would end before May of 1946 and he didn't agree – so I won. However, I am not going to keep it, as the odds were so much against him.

The next letter was of the 8th – the day you learned about the Russians declaring war on Japan. Since that day, they have literally walked into Japanese-controlled territory, capturing thousands of men and materiel. Of course, the Japs had no fight in them after the atomic bombs were dropped, so Russia cashed in on our campaigns. As to any prevention of future wars as long as we have the atomic bomb, I'm afraid to express my opinion. Anything can happen. As to seeing Truman when he was in Darmstadt, I missed him, as I was driving back to our area when I saw the 3rd Armored Division lining up for his inspection. I didn't know about it until the next day and that was too late.

Well, Darlings, that takes care of three more letters and I still have seven more of them to go – and so many from other people – that I don't think that I'll ever catch up again. Meanwhile, say "Hello" to all and tell them that I may be home soon – Love to the folks and many, many hugs and kisses for Carole and you –

With All My Love,
Your Dave

———

Monday – 27 August – 1945
Somewhere in Darmstadt

My Darling Wife and Baby,
In your next letter, you and the all the rest of the world were waiting for V.J. Day to be announced. It is funny, but even at this late date, the War

has not officially ended in the Pacific. Today's radio news said that the ships entered the Tokyo Bay this morning, so it is the beginning of the end. I hope that the Japs do not have any treachery up their sleeves this time. By the time you get this letter, it should all be over. We have been through it a long time and now we do deserve some uninterrupted happiness together. Today's "Stars & Stripes" said that all 85-pointers will be out of the ETO by the end of October. If that is so, we who have between 85 and 75 points will be out by Xmas – or am I shooting too high? Now that September is so near, I am starting to get a wee bit nervous about it all. Before, it was all so very far away that I didn't think of it – but now, I am on the verge of leaving the ETO and it feels great.

That commentator who said that if the Kaiser [Wilhelm] had been left at the head of the government, there would not have been a Hitler, must really be a nut. Doesn't he realize that popular opinion means a lot and that the Kaiser was being held directly responsible for that War? That is exactly the situation today, and we are holding Hitler directly responsible, along with so many of his stalwarts. With Wilhelm, there were the Junker generals about whom we have forgotten all too soon. Sure, Hitler would never have been able to gain power, but it would have given the Kaiser another chance to wage war and that is the ultimate goal of all Germanic peoples - to wage war successfully. That is why we must do away with not only the Nazis, but also with the Junkers. In Japan, we must rid the islands of the War Party and the Jap industrialists. It was they who asked for War and it was they who have suffered in the end. Count Mitsubishi, who makes most of the planes for the Japs, was a prominent member of the War Cabinet and one who will be held as a war criminal – I hope. There you have the main reasons for the War with Japan and Germany.

Pertaining to that article you sent about getting pets home – I will do everything I can to bring her along with me. One of the boys told me that the day after I left for England, he was up in the room next to mine. Well, Nancy walked into my room and sniffed around and realized that I was gone, then she ran out into the other rooms, looking for me. Then she went out in the halls and whined – Wasn't that real friendship? When I got back here, she jumped all over me and nearly wagged her tail off. She seems to be such an understanding canine that at times, I think she is human. This morning, however, she was a bit shaken up. I saw a mouse in here and set the trap for him. Well, Nancy is an excellent hunter and she ran around sniffing all over the place for the mouse. When she got to the trap, she must have sniffed the cheese there, as it went off and I was startled by a loud yelp. She ran around the room and whined. At first, I thought that it had caught her on her paw, however, her left eye was closed – so it must have swung over and hit her above the eye. I put a damp cloth on the eye and she finally went to sleep. She was a bit weary when she got up and she was trembling all over. I decided not to give her anything to eat and I was lucky that I didn't, because she got ill in the afternoon and vomited what she had in her stomach. After that, she lay down outside, in the sun, and regained most of her vitality. She was lucky that she didn't get her head bashed in, because that trap is a large one. I know that she and the baby would become great pals and that Nancy would protect her with her life. Now that we do live in a home, it is nice to have a good dog about. At night, she never whines or howls and she is housebroken, too. What more can you ask of a dog – cooking and baking?

As to meeting me in New York, Darling, I'm afraid that I wouldn't know when we were to leave or dock so that you would be on hand in time. However, if I can find out, I will certainly wire you from France, but let's not count on it. After all, can you picture each and every man on each and every ship wiring his wife and sweetheart to meet him in New York? Along with the normal population, there would be about 20 million in New York every time a batch of ships arrived. Hotel reservations are hard to find as it is now – so you would have a helluva time.

Say, Darling, I am certainly serious about taking it easy for a while – if it will be OK with Dad and Joe at the store. If I could just relax for a while, I'm sure that I could be converted back into a civilian again very easily.

You wrote that you hoped that I wouldn't get the notion to phone long distance – Well, I did get the idea, but we would have to place a reservation with the phone company one day; return the next to find out if we can get our call through; and then make arrangements for a convenient time. Well, after asking the price, I learned that it was awful high and we would want to speak for a long time – so I decided against it. As to sending any Xmas gifts to me, please don't, because I think that I'll be home about that time – so save them. So that about winds up the news for today, so say "Hello" to our friends and love to the folks – A great, big hug and kiss for Carole Frances and you –

With All My Love,
Your Dave

Tuesday – 28 August – 1945
Somewhere in Darmstadt

My Dearest Darlings,

Your next letter was of the 14th – the day you were awakened by the loud criers in the automobile, shouting that the War was over. As you later learned, it was the same old stuff from Domei [Japan's news agency] and not quite official. Sorry that you were awakened by it. Today's news told of the arrival of the surrender fleet in Tokyo Bay – so it won't be long now. As you know, I was still in Germany when it ended – but celebrated in London.

The next letter was of the 15th and you finally learned that the War was over in the Pacific. Did you remember that Sunday afternoon, while we were listening to Sammy Kaye's Sunday Serenade, when all of a sudden, the program was interrupted and the announcement was made that unidentified planes had attacked Pearl Harbor? It seems just a couple of years ago – but it is 4-1/2 to be exact. Well, time has gone by quickly and it won't be too long before we will be back together again. You were really being a bit too optimistic, however, when you said that I ought to be on my way within 60 days. It takes you that long to just get from here to the actual loading aboard ship, so if I am back in time for Xmas dinner, I will thank God a thousand times.

I guess the East Shore Hotel was just like all the large cities throughout the world, if everybody was kissing each other. If you thought that Frankfort made a lot of noise, try to mentally multiply that by a million and you will get an idea of the noise in Piccadilly Circus on the 16th and 17th. It must have been twice as bad on the 15th – We didn't know, because we were sound asleep in Darmstadt.

Yes, the Pacific War did fold up in a hurry, much to everyone's surprise. I guess I wasn't quite as correct as I thought as all I forecast was that we would not have to invade Japan. That in itself was better than most people thought, so we did save many thousands of lives. As to the atomic bomb for Germany, at this time, I am glad that we didn't use it, or else we would be sleeping in tents and in a pile of dust. Of course, that is the smallest way of looking at it, as it would have saved millions of lives, as you said.

Well, in spite of all the worrying about Joe being drafted, he was able to stay out and now he is able to forget all about ever being drafted. It was a *big help at the store, no doubt, and I hope that he decides to confine his efforts to the store in the future. I don't know what to think about getting back into the store – I feel that I have lost all knowledge of what it is all about.*

Well, Darlings, hope that all is well at home and that you will all have a very enjoyable holiday. Give my regards to the friends and relatives and love to the folks – oceans of love and kisses to Carole and you –

With All My Love,
Your Dave

Wednesday – 29 August – 1945
Somewhere in Darmstadt

My Beloved Wife and Baby,

As you now know, the surrender negotiations are being signed today in Tokyo Bay – so the end ought to be announced officially any day now. Funny as it may seem to you, I am more interested now in what the Cardinals are doing, now that they are only 2-1/2 games behind the Cubs. To expect the Brownies to come through is too much, even though they are only four games out.

So you are planning on my trimming Carole's Xmas tree – Well, I hope that I can make it. It will be very nice to be on hand this time, as she is starting to appreciate Xmas now. Say, maybe I can really be Santa Claus and get a costume and all. As to our 5th anniversary, I'm sure that we can arrange it once I am back. However, we can plan on seeing a play at the American, have a few wee nippies at the Chase Bar, dinner in the Club, and then – well, maybe a brief spin in Forest Park. What do you think of that?

I haven't had baked ham since I left the States. However, there are so many more important things which I haven't had that ham will be the last thing for which I will ask when I get back. One thing that I definitely do not want is lamb in any shape or form. We had so much of it over here that we are beginning to baa when we start to speak. As long as we are on the subject of food, today we had our first bananas overseas and they were really good. We really can't say that the Army hasn't tried to get us what we have missed.

This evening, I went to the show to see "Dangerous Passage" – but I may as well warn you that it stinks from the acting, not the background, which was in the Panama area. There was a short subject which was a British-made film and it was a propaganda picture to get the English people acquainted with America. They started out by showing a couple of shots from a gangster film and then proceeded to tell the audience that we are not like that after all. Anyway, it was a very weak effort, but it had its good intentions and it must have been shown in England when the Yanks first came over. Well, Darlings, regards to all and love to the folks and huge, gigantic, stupendous and overwhelming hugs and kisses for the baby and you –

With All My Love,

Your Dave

Thursday – 30 August – 1945

Somewhere in Darmstadt

My Dearest Darlings,

As I read in today's "Stars & Stripes," they are to lower the mark to 80 as soon as MacArthur says that he no longer needs combat troops. With the men going as fast as they are now, there is a very excellent chance of me getting back by Xmas – so let's cross our fingers.

As to that fellow who walked out of the third-floor window, he suffered a broken ankle on it and is in the hospital still, even though his outfit left for the Staging Area. Now, they are probably heading for the States and he is here in the hospital – That shows you that you should let nature take its course and make the best of things. You said that he must be a mental case – Well, in Africa, he was under observation, but the docs said that he was normal. However, we thought differently.

As to the newspaper situation in St. Louis, I saw that they have been on strike for some time and that there is a great possibility that a new paper will be seen there. I can imagine how that has affected the community – no news, except what you get over the radio. Well, I hope that it is over by now. Those damned strikes were bad enough while the Wars were on – so I hope that the veterans do something about strikers.

Well, now I am waiting for a package from you and one from my dad – His has some salami in it, too. However, I will enjoy the seafoods that you are sending as much. I hope that you sent some sauce with it. So-o-o-o, I had better get some shut-eye. Say "Hello" to all and love to the folks – lots and lots of hugs and kisses for Carole and you –

With All My Love,

Your Dave

P.S. I do love and miss you very much – am very anxiously waiting to get back.

Saturday – 1 September – 1945
Somewhere in Darmstadt

My Most Beloved Angels,

Well, I just did something which I have not done since we all were in Africa – I marched in a formation. Yes, it has finally come to that . It so happened that today, one of the boys in the 63rd Wing and who was formerly in the 45th Infantry Division was decorated with the Silver Star for Gallantry in Action last September. Well, after the decoration was presented, all the men passed in review. However, I think that tomorrow will bring a notice to all personnel on the post that no dogs will be allowed on the post. I say that because after I locked Nancy in, she jumped out one of the windows and followed us all around the place. She even ran after the Color Guard and was right in the middle of the award. If I know Col. Jackson, he will issue an order like that very soon.

Have you heard "Nancy With The Smiling Face"? – It is being played quite a bit over here – sung by Sinatra. I happened to get in on the "Hit Parade" this afternoon and heard the three top tunes – all of which I am unfamiliar with. They were 1. "If I Loved You" 2. "I Wish I Knew" and 3. "Till The End Of Time" – Where in the world did these songs come from? I don't know if I like them, as I haven't heard any of them often enough.

Well, well, so you are sending me a salami – potato chips – shrimp – sauce – and Hydrox cookies. That, indeed, is a package to prize very highly in the ETO. I told the boys that if I am on my way home when it arrives, they can open it and have a feast on me – Is it OK with you? I also have that one you sent from Michigan on the way and one from my dad as well – What price popularity!

They are now playing "The Missouri Waltz" and it really makes me homesick. With the battleship Missouri and Truman in the limelight, Missouri is finding her place in the sun after all these years. Well, it won't be too long before I will be back there and the ETO will seem so long ago. So regards to all and love to the folks – and many millions of marvelous kisses for Carole and you –

With All My Love,
Your Dave

Sunday – 2 September – 1945
Somewhere in Darmstadt

My Dearest Darlings,

Fay and I just got back from seeing – what do you think? No, you are wrong – We went to see a circus. The soldiers all had reserved seats and we had the choice of sitting on seats just surrounding the ring or in the boxes immediately behind us, so we took the boxes. It was lucky that we did, as there were horses and elephants who didn't have much respect for the spectators. The ones who were seated in front of us were made very uncomfortable a couple of times, due to the animals relieving themselves. There were two acts in which children were featured. As a personal display of appreciation, some of the G.I.'s threw bars of candy and packages of chewing gum to these kids after their acts. They really treasure that more than a thousand marks, because they cannot obtain candy in Germany at this time. There was one tiny girl who was an acrobat who was watching one of the G.I.'s give some candy to a small child next to him. It made a lump in my throat to see the look on this girl's face as the other child received the candy – I wished that I had some to give her at that time. She made me think of Carole Frances, as she was only about four and slim in build.

I am starting the "Fall of France," by Paul Reynaud. With most of the War Criminals now captured, there will be many stories coming out about who was responsible for what. In the first article, Reynaud accuses [Vichy Chief of State Philippe] *Petain of previous knowledge of the fall of the French Army long before the attack by Hitler. That is, he knew that the Army was too weak to hold the Germans and, as head of the Army, he should have informed the people. So we will get a lot of conflicting stories on War responsibilities now that it is all over. Why, even a dirty rat, who is writing for the "Chicago Tribune," has accused the late president of being responsible for the attack on Pearl Harbor. That is about the lowest thing that can be said by anyone – especially after a man has died in striving to bring us Victory. With such things as that happening, the returning veterans will become so damned disgusted with the States that they will have a hard time getting acclimated to its free speech.*

Well, with the end of the War almost an actuality, we will be in line for a discharge soon. So say "Hello" to our friends and tell them that I'll be back soon. So love to the folks and many, many, many hugs and kisses for the baby and you –

With All My Love,
Your Dave

———

Tuesday – 4 September – 1945
Somewhere in Darmstadt

My Most Beloved Darlings,

I read that there were 34,000 people out at Sportsman's Park to see the double-header between the Cards and the Cubs. Gee, I hope that I can get home to see at least one of the games, if the Cards win the pennant.

I was lucky to receive your letter in the morning, as in it was the request to try to locate Bertha Rothschild or Mrs. Ross' lawyer in Frankfurt. This morning, I asked the Motor Sergeant for a jeep to go up to Hanau, as I had left a typewriter up there yesterday. However, as he always screws up the works, he wasn't able to give me a jeep – so I had to take a weapons carrier and drive it myself. After getting my work completed, I went on back to Frankfurt to try to find these people. Well, I decided to try the lawyer first, as I had his address and, as he had married a gentile, I figured that he had a good possibility of still being in Frankfurt. I finally got to Uhland Strasse and then looked for 54. I found 55 and looked across the street and saw a large apartment completely destroyed and thought that that was it – but I went a little further and found that it was the next building to it. I asked where I could find the Kahns and was directed to the second floor. As I walked up, I saw a Star of David posted on the wall, saying that this was a Jewish home. I wonder if that has been there a long time. I rang the bell and a young girl answered the door.

Well, a little after I was ushered into the apartment, a tall and elderly woman came out and took me into a study. We introduced ourselves and then I told her the story of your letter and the people involved. Fortunately enough, this woman spoke English, so that I was able to converse a lot better than if it was to have been in German or Yiddish. She said that this Mrs. Ross must be the same woman whose name was Rosenberg or something like it and she changed her name when she went to the States – Is that correct? She took the information and told me that she didn't think that there was much likelihood of locating Dr. Maas' sister if she was at that camp in Czechoslovakia, as there weren't many who have returned up until now. However, she is going to speak to her husband about it and then ask the rabbi and see if he knows anything about them, as he was at that camp.

She asked me to return next Monday afternoon and she may have some information on Mrs. Rothschild. The home in which they lived was not the prettiest, but I guess they are fortunate to even have a place, compared to what the other German Jews have now. So I guess I will be back there to see them next Monday. As to the package that is being sent me for Mrs. Rothschild, if I am on my way home when it gets here, I will instruct Joe Dines or one of the other Jewish boys about it and he will carry out your instructions.

It must have felt good to be able to buy a lot of canned goods without worrying about the points. Gee, then to be able to make a devil's food cake with icing, too! Gosh, prosperity is back to stay!

So you just want me home to shovel snow — Well, just for that, I'll come back twice as fast, because I haven't seen a good snow since last Winter in Nancy. Little did I know that a year from last December, I would be home. It was so very far from us at that time. We were still being bombed and strafed in Nancy, so Jerry still had a little left to throw at us. That was also the time of the Battle of the Bulge. However, as you now see, it was a costlier venture for the Germans than they had figured. Von Rundstedt gambled everything on that one shot, but he didn't have enough to put behind it, so now we are going home a lot sooner, because von Rundstedt took that chance.

The time certainly has flown this past year. Why, it seems only a few months ago that we landed in Southern France and made our way up the Rhone Valley. Then on to Dole and Nancy. Edenkoben seems just yesterday and Schwabisch-Hall this morning. Well, that will be the same way it will feel after we are back together again — as though I had never gone. The only noticeable difference will be the size of our daughter. Well, Darlings, I guess that about winds it up for now, so say "Hello" to all and love to the folks — and many huge hugs and kisses for Carole and you —

With All My Love,
Your Dave

———

Wednesday — 5 September — 1945
Somewhere in Darmstadt

My Darling Amy and Carole Frances,

There wasn't much doing in the morning, except to get some of the boys ready to leave. We are sending them out fast and furious now and they will be down in my category soon — I hope. They are sending out those who had over 85 still, before the new change. However, as long as they are down in the 80 group, that makes me feel fine.

As to that package that you were holding up, I hope that you went ahead and sent it. Even if I am not here, it will be a nice treat for those who are still around. However, please instruct all the others not to send any packages.

From what the car manufacturers have said, there will be plastic cars for sale very soon. I am still intent on buying our own car, so that we won't have to depend on the folks all the time.

Well, Darlings, I had better start getting my things together, so that I can be ready in a moment's notice to push off. There is a very strong rumor that those with above 80 points are taking off next week – but do not put too much faith into it. I'll write each day and when I finally hear definitely, I'll tell you. However, as to when I will arrive, I'll try to inform you from England, as that is where we go from here. So say "Hello" to all and give my love to the folks – oceans and oceans of hugs and kisses for the baby and you –

With All My Love,
Your Dave

—

Thursday – 6 September – 1945
Somewhere in Darmstadt

My Beloved Wife and Daughter,

I received a package which you had sent from Michigan. Yes, it was the one with the olives, sardines, cheese, anchovies, lobster, and the napkins – I don't know if the napkins were to fill up space or not, but they are the first that we have seen overseas. I have already opened the olives and they are about finished at this writing. However, I have placed the other items up in my room until another day.

I am trying to find out what the procedure is on getting Nancy back to the States. I'm very intent on getting her back home, as I know that Carole Frances will like Nancy a lot and they will be great pals. Also, Nancy would certainly protect Carole with her life. She always barks at anybody who happens to be walking around late at night. So many times, she acts so very human. All the boys want her and Okma says that I should leave her with the outfit instead of taking her home, as it will never be the same without her. Nancy and I are having a great time down here in the Supply Office. It seems that we have had a few mice running about. I took out the traps and caught three of them, breaking their backs. Well, after I figured that that was all, along comes another and now we are having a time in catching him. I can't leave traps down here during the night, because I did that one day and Nancy was caught in it and hurt her eye, so I have to take her out and try to catch the mouse during the day. I think that I'll let Nancy stay up in my room for one night and see how many mice we will catch. I just saw him and he ran into some corner and we can't seem to locate him now. I left my PX rations down here last night and sure enough, he had eaten a corner of one of the Oh Henry bars, so I have a personal grudge to settle with him when I catch him.

One of the boys in the Orderly Room told me that there are 14 men who have between 80 and 95 points on the old basis and who are eligible for discharge now. So that means that if the quota is large enough, I may get in the next shipment or the next after that. Anyway, things are looking rosier than they have ever seemed since I left home. I hope that I am not being too optimistic about this thing, but I do think that I will be home in time to carve the turkey. Well, Darlings, send my best wishes to all our friends and love to the folks — and a tremendous hug and kiss for the baby and you —

With All My Love,
Your Dave

7. ENGLAND

4 October 1945
[Somewhere in Southampton]

Well, My Darlings,

I guess we are really having our difficulties in getting back together again. You are as surprised in receiving this letter as I am in writing it. We were near Stone, England in an Air Force Staging Area camp. We were all told that we'd stay no longer than a week, so that was why I didn't write, as I figured that I'd be home long before the letter arrived. Each day, we all figured that we were leaving, as every so often, a shipment was awakened at 2:00 A.M. or 10:00 P.M. and told to get ready to leave. We were told that we were going directly to Swansea (in Wales) and load on the "James W. Fannin," a ship waiting for us. Well, we ended up down here in Southampton. Things were going along very well and we expected to be out in about 4 to 5 days.

Well, as it is my luck, that damned throat started acting up again, after a damp spell up in Stone. At the same time, a rash broke out over my arms and shoulders – so I was immediately sent to the Dispensary. The doctor there told me that it was necessary for them to send me to a hospital so as to clear it up, before allowing me to leave the United Kingdom and enter the States. They said that it if was any communicable illness, that they would be held responsible for the consequences if anything broke out aboard ship. I was sent to a hospital about 8 miles from Southampton. So here I am and they are taking blood tests galore to find out what it is all about. So it may be 7 to 10 days before I am out and ready to board ship and get back home for good. You can readily imagine my disappointment, which we are both experiencing at this time. However, as long as I'm back before Thanksgiving, that won't be too bad. The hell of it is that I think my shipment probably left on the Queen Elizabeth, which left today. Well, in spite of everything, we will be together again very soon – so let's just have a bit more patience.

I guess you want to hear all about what has taken place since my last letter. Well, two days prior to our leaving Darmstadt, I went up to Frankfurt for services at a very nice Jewish synagogue, which is still standing – much to my surprise. While seated there, I casually glanced around – and lo and behold – who was sitting in the rear – [Dave's uncle] *Sol Axelrod! I was amazed and he almost jumped out of his seat when he saw me. He is now with a Machine Records Unit and he has a wonderful setup in a private home. There are about 40 men in the outfit and they took over about 3 homes – new ones, which formerly belonged to Pro-Nazi Germans. Sol and I spent the evening there that night and the next day, he came down with me to Darmstadt and slept there. He was really startled at finding me right next door to him, practically. I was under the impression that he was on his way home long ago.*

Well, the next day (the 10th), we all boarded trucks and drove to Furth, which isn't far from Nuremberg. We got there about 11:20 P.M. and found an empty home on the airfield – so hit the sack on the cold floor. The next morning, we drove to the airstrip to which we were to go and found about 2,000 other men waiting around. There were only about 10 or 12 C-47's, so the rest of the men were told to go to the railroad yards. We were assigned to beautiful, exclusive and luxuriously furnished 40 x 8 cars. Yes, we lived for 3 days and nights in cattle cars. We ate C and K-rations all the way, except for 3 occasions where we stopped along the way and washed and ate. Every so often, the train would stop, so that the men could relieve themselves. Well, we finally arrived in Le Havre and were then taken by truck to Camp Philip Morris. Well, we sat around there for a while, figuring that we'd probably leave from there, as that is a big shipping point.

One day, we finally were taken down to the locks. There, we boarded Victory ships and took a long trip – right across the Channel. We landed at Southampton and boarded a train. It took us about 125 miles Northwest, to Stone. We unloaded there and were taken by truck to Nelson Hall. Each day, there was another line to sweat out – if it wasn't a physical, it was to change your money into U.S. currency.

All this time, I had carried Nancy with me without running into any trouble. However, just before we left Darmstadt, she had her first monthly and then she came into heat. You can imagine what a large masculine following of dogs she had running after her, sniffing. In Le Havre, there must have been about 6 or 8 dogs whom she chased away. However, when we got to Stone, she finally ran across a nice-looking red dog named "Dammit." Well, Dammit finally seduced her one morning when she was out alone. I decided that as long as she had finally been gotten to, there was nothing for me to do about it. So on several more occasions, they had their little get-togethers and Nancy really loved it.

Well, getting back to the Customs, I was told that I'd have to have Nancy put up at a vet's for about a month or two and then have her inoculated. Then she would be shipped to the States about a month after that. All this would cost me about 55 pounds ($220.00) [more than $3200 today] *– so I decided to find a home for her in England. It so happened that one evening, I went into Hanley on a pass and she saw me leave. The next morning, the fellow in the room next to mine told me that he was sitting in a pub in Hanley that night before and in walked Nancy. In the course of the evening, he took her to the Red Cross. While there, a civilian employee happened to say that he'd like to have a dog like her, so I left my address and asked that he come out to camp if he was seriously interested in having Nancy. The next morning, I got a call to go to the Main Gate – so I took Nancy with me. It was this Englishman and I asked about his home. He has a yard and two children who are crazy about dogs – so I thought that they would take good care of her. The man seemed very serious and assured me that she would have a good home with him. So I told her to get into the waiting cab and I locked the door after her. You should have seen her – It was a pitiful sight to see that look in her eyes and to hear her whimper as the car drove off. Well, Dammit certainly did miss her and he followed me wherever I went – always with the hope that I'd lead him to Nancy. He even slept in our room – as Nancy did. Well, the day we left Nelson Hall, Dammit also cried the way Nancy did when we loaded onto trucks.*

That brings us down to the beginning of the letter when we were told that we were going to Swansea and ended up in Southampton. So all we can do now is to wait a bit longer and I'll be back with you and Carole Frances for all time. As to answering this letter, I don't suppose it would do any good, as I'll be out of here before you ever receive this and I'd never get your letter while over here. So as things progress, I'll write and then try to wire again on the day I board ship. If we go by Liberty, it will take about 12 days – if by a liner, 6 days. So I'll let you know in the wire – if I know. However, as I've written you before, I'm to be sent to Jefferson Barracks [Missouri] *after debarking – so I'll phone from there as soon as I can.*

*Well, my sweethearts, that about winds it up for now – so don't worry –
I'll be aboard ship coming home by the time you get this. Say "Hello" to all
and for the baby and you – a billion hugs and kisses.*
    With All My Love,
    Your Dave

6 October 1945
Still in Tidworth

My Dearest Wife and Baby,
    *I guess you are as surprised and disappointed at receiving this letter as I
am at this time. Yes, I also thought that I'd be on my way back by now – but
it's the same old story of a snafu'd situation – typical of the Army. The Queen
left on the 4th and only WAC's, nurses, men with 95 or more points, and
a few men with less were on it. It seems that I'm in the next group and on
which they are working now. That may mean anywhere from 3 days to 2
weeks more in this one spot – just waiting. I haven't even left this camp,
because I have always been afraid that we may just be that lucky to get a
ship all of a sudden, so I'm just hanging around, taking it easy and hoping.
I know that you would like to receive a daily letter from here – but since all
these disappointments have come up, I don't feel like writing anybody one
line. That is why I wait and try to write one a week to you, at least, so that
you know that I'm still alive and waiting to get back home. With no mail
coming in, it is damned hard to write you an interesting letter without
including at least a couple of "bitches" about this Army life, so in order to
avoid that, I try to hold off my writing to a minimum. However, as I have
told you before, I will wire you just as soon as I hear when and how we are
to go. I must have certainly built up your hopes about the Queen Mary –
Well, so did I build up mine. However, there is still the Europa, which is
coming in soon, and one aircraft carrier – so maybe?*
    *Since having my shipment cancelled, I feel as though my whole attitude
has changed. Maybe it is my imagination – but I just don't have much
ambition to do anything. I hope that I change when I hit the U.S. again.
I keep pulling out the pictures of you and the baby and talking about some
of the times we all had together. I guess we should be thankful that I'm
home this year as it is – so let's thank God for that. After all, there are
many thousands of men who will never return to their homes again. Well,
Darlings – Hope that my next line will be a telegram – So say "Hello" to*

all – love to the folks and hope they are both feeling very, very well – and a billion terrific hugs and kisses for Carole Frances and you – I do love and miss you both very much –
    With All My Love,
    Your Dave

13 October 1945
Near Swindon, England

My Dearest Wife and Baby,

    Well, I'm back to where I was about a month ago – in another Staging Area camp. Yes, it seems as though I've lost a month in getting back to the States and all on account of a simple throat ailment. Since the last time I wrote you – about 10 days ago – I had blood tests taken almost every day. Well, they finally decided to give me some penicillin, in spite of what I told them about the last experience I had with it. Well, after the second shot, and almost to the exact minute as my first go with penicillin – I broke out with extreme chills and then a high fever – It went to 100. I told the nurse about it and she called the doctor and he said to continue the penicillin, but to apply cold cloths to my head. I felt a lot better in a couple of hours and then I started on the road to recovery. Well, they still were unable to learn the cause, but as long as it cleared up, I'm glad and won't have to worry about how much longer I'll be in England.

    During my stay in the hospital, we listened to the direct broadcast of the World Series games and really enjoyed them. When the last game came up, I decided to bet with a very loyal Cubs fan – so I took the Tigers and we bet the high sum of $4.00 (1 pound). After the 1st inning, we were ready to call it a day. A number of the nurses in our ward lost on the Series.

    Well, yesterday, I received my clearance at the hospital, a ride to the railroad station in Southampton, and a ticket and orders to report to the 98th Reinforcement Depot in Ogbourne St. George. Today we were given a lot of processing to straighten up our service cards and given influenza shots. Now all we have to do is to have a clothing check and we'll be ready to go to Southampton once more and try again. Now with the strikes tying up loading and unloading at docks in the States and England, that means a little more delay. However, I think that I ought to be in the States by Nov. 1st. It was hell when I heard the news broadcast about the Queen Elizabeth docking in N.Y. – That should have included me, but it didn't. However, it is still a lot better than we figured last August – so let's be grateful for that. I suppose Carole Frances is being asked daily when her daddy is coming home. Well, Darlings, it's a shame that I can't receive any letters, as we're supposed to leave here in 5 days – so keep well – regards to all – love to the folks – and a billion hugs and kisses for Carole and you –

    With All My Love,

    Your Dave

—

                                             20 October 1945

                                        Tidworth, England

My Dearest Darlings,

    Since my last letter to you from Swindon, a bit of everything has happened. First, the Queen Elizabeth and the Aquitania are withdrawn from our service; then I am put on guard duty for 24 hours; then, to top it all off, while at the guardhouse, we heard a few explosions and I heard something whiz by my head. At least, it seemed close to me – but I later learned that it was 100 yds. from me. Well, it so happened that there is an English camp located not far from us and they were practicing mortar fire. Well, they overshot their marks (accidentally?) and about 7 men in our camp were hit – a couple seriously. Well, investigations are still going on, but nothing but an apology will come of it. You see, there is an extremely high degree of jealousy existing in England – mainly from the way the English women have fallen for the G.I.'s. Naturally, many happy homes have been broken up – or love affairs – and, as a result, the English soldiers and G.I.'s are constantly having fights. It's a wonder that War isn't declared once more. When the Yanks first came over to help, the English couldn't do enough for them. That resulted in many close friendships and marriages. Well, now that the War is over, the English seem to have forgotten all about our help and, with Lend-Lease stopped, they don't give a damn what happens to the G.I.'s. So I wonder if the mortar shells hit accidentally. .

    So, to bring you up to the present, we left Swindon yesterday, under the load of a field bag, blanket roll, and a duffel bag, and were taken by truck to this place, which is about 20 miles from Southampton. This is the last time we will be moved until we load in the ship to take us back, so I am now back to where I was a month ago. This camp is huge. There is a beer parlor across the street, a Coke bar a block away, a donut dugout a block away, PX a block

away, and a gym right across the street. I can't tell you now when we're to leave, but we will be told far enough ahead of time to let you know – so do be patient and I'm sure that we'll be eating turkey together on Thanksgiving. Well, Darlings, hope that all is well at home and that Carole is getting bigger and better all the time – Regards to all – love to the folks – and billions of hugs and kisses for the baby and you –
With All My Love,
Your Dave
P.S. Try to send one letter to this address.

---

26 October 1945
Still in Tidworth, Eng.

My Dearest Darlings,
This past month has been one of tension and nerves, but I don't think that it will be repeated again. The very latest rumor (and it seems to hold water) is that they are finally going to break up all these shipments and send the high-point men ahead. So as they work down, we will be sent to the ships as they arrive in Southampton. That's where I am now. Well, with all the protests being voiced both over here and over there, the higher authorities are finally getting on the ball and doing something about getting the high-point men home before the lower. This delay has caused such a definite dislike for the Army and everything that goes with it, that there will be no great rush for ETO veterans to enlist.
The wind has been at gale strength all week and I'm sure that that has made it harder for ships coming this way to meet their schedules. Then again, storms on the seas may have caused damage to some, which will mean additional delays. Therefore, even with all their planning, I'm afraid that all the 80-pointers will not be out of the ETO by the end of October, as previously announced. I don't know when I'll ever get out of here. And all the while, I was so darned certain of having Thanksgiving turkey with you – Now it is very doubtful. However, I'm not going to give up hope until after the Queen Mary leaves. I've really been lonesome as all Hell for Carole Frances and you. Everything could have been so nice if that damned throat condition had not come up and detained me. Well, as you always have said, the best things in life have always been the hardest to attain. I'm certainly going to appreciate my family, once I'm back home. We'll be about the most secluded family in St. Louis, I think.

I just looked at the last letter you sent me – or rather the last one I received – and I noticed that it was written on the 1st of September. I don't think that I ever did answer it, as I was getting ready to leave Germany when it was received. You wrote that the last mile is always the hardest – Gosh, I can't even get that far.

Then, with all the families clambering for their men to be cleared out of the ETO, they allow thousands of dock workers to strike, tying up hundreds of ships, which otherwise could have been carrying thousands of men back to the States. You know, Darlings, I get so damned disgusted with our government and its stupidity. In fact, right in Congress, we can find the cause of all this redeployment trouble. Instead of immediately getting idle cargo ships and Liberties converted into transports for hauling men from Europe, they sat on their asses and begged England to lend us their liners. It took only 5 days to convert the carrier Lake Champlain into a troop carrier – so they could have done a Liberty or cargo in 1 day or less. Now, we are paying the English government 100 dollars for every enlisted man carried by them and 110 for every officer. On top of all that, they recently declared about 300 ships worthless for warfare – but they certainly could have been repaired and fitted as troop carriers, instead of wasting away in dry dock. Well, I guess I've gotten it all off my chest by now - so I feel a bit better – but no closer to home.

Well, my Angels, I do hope that you haven't forgotten me by now – It has been such a long time since we've been together – but it won't be long now. As I've written before, I'll wire as soon as I know when I'm definitely leaving – so here's hoping! Meanwhile, say "Hello" to all our friends and hope that all is well back home – love to the folks – lots and lots and lots of love and kisses for the baby and you –

With All My Love,
Your Dave

—

27 October 1945
Still in Tidworth

My Sweetest Wife and Baby,
I decided to drop in at the Main Headquarters and try to get some dope on shipping. I went into the Personnel Section and explained my case and was told that the Commanding General of the United Kingdom Base had cancelled all shipping orders and that all men are to be sent out according to

their points. I am in the next group and they will probably go in the next seven days – So we will be very lucky to catch the Queen Mary. However, that is some information that I never had before.

This afternoon, I walked up to one of the Red Cross buildings here on the post – called "Tidworth House." It is the former home of Lord Tidworth and seems to be of Colonial architecture. There is a huge ballroom, with the skylight as a ceiling and a huge chandelier hanging in the center. There are private tennis courts, croquet courts, billiard rooms, and music rooms. There is also a snack bar downstairs and I see that they sell hamburgers – so I'll try one for a change.

Well, Darlings, I'm getting more and more impatient as each day goes by – but it won't be too long now. As I've said before, I'll phone you from J.B. [Jefferson Barracks] as soon as I can – so be patient. Meanwhile, take good care of Carole and yourself and send my regards to all – love to the folks and a billion and one hugs and kisses for the baby and you –

With All My Love,
Your Dave
P.S. I do love you so very much.

[TELEGRAM]
OCT. 28 1945
ST. LOUIS, MO
EVERYBODY FINE WAITING ANXIOUSLY TO SEE
YOU HOME
LETTER FOLLOWS LOVE
AMY

[TELEGRAM]
NOV. 16 1945
TIDWORTH
LEAVING LIVERPOOL FRIDAY ON BLOEMFONTEIN
WILL NOTIFY YOU UPON ARRIVAL LOTS OF LOVE
TO CAROLE AND YOU
DAVE.

AFTERWORD

A sudden, abrupt ending to their lengthy, detailed "conversation." When I came to those two brief telegrams and realized they constituted the final written words exchanged between my mother and father during the war, I was left with so many questions for him: Did anything interesting happen during your long voyage home on the *Bloemfontein*? What was it like seeing Mom and Carole again after so much time had elapsed? What did you do your first day home? Was it a difficult adjustment shifting from military to civilian life? What was it like going back to work at Henry Schwartz & Co.? Did your wartime experiences impact your outlook on life and the world? Did you often reflect on all you had gone through or did it rarely enter your mind? Etc. etc. etc.

Sadly, my dad died before I read the letters, so I'll never have answers to most of those questions. We would sometimes discuss his wartime experiences and I often looked through his scrapbook of snapshots, fascinated by the dead Nazis, humiliated collaborators, bombed-out buildings, and photos of Bob Hope, but none of the Stoliar children ever opened up those black blinders to read our father's letters. They remained in our garage for many years and then Carole took possession of them after our mom and dad died. I think there were so many pages, with so much dense handwriting and single-spaced typing, it didn't seem like something we ever felt like tackling. Also, I think there was a sense that it would somehow violate the intimacy of what we assumed were very personal letters that this faraway soldier had written to his young wife. Technically speaking, they really weren't any of our business.

For whatever reasons, we didn't get around to actually reading them until the Stoliar children got together to celebrate Carole's 70th birthday in 2012 – and even then, we only gave them a cursory skimming, just to get a sense of what they contained. It was then that I began to think that some of them – with their detailed reportage of World War II as it was happening, plus my dad's ruminations on politics and mankind, as well as his little side adventures – might be of interest to more than just our immediate family, not unlike those diaries left behind by random Yanks and Rebs that manage to vividly capture what daily life was like for a soldier during the Civil War. When I was a kid, most of my peers had dads who had served in the war, so it didn't seem particularly noteworthy that my father had been in it. Now that I'm in my late sixties and most of "The Greatest Generation" is gone, I've come to appreciate this remarkable archive, which remains intact after more then 75 years.

In terms of my questions about what happened after those two terse telegrams were exchanged, I do have a few tantalizing puzzle pieces to work with. In February of 1992 – the year he died – my dad, in a video interview, provided a couple of answers to questions I had yet to formulate. He said that the day he returned from Europe, he and our mother opened that bottle of champagne he'd sent her from France and they drank to his homecoming – in their new home. (I guess she had stored the bottle correctly after all.) Also, three-and-a-half-year-old Carole Frances greeted him that day by singing:

Kiss me once,
Then kiss me twice,
Then kiss me once again.
It's been a long, long time.

That song – written by Jule Style and Sammy Cahn specifically for wives to welcome home their war-weary husbands – was #1 on *Your Hit Parade* the week that my father returned to the States.

I also know, from what my mother told me, that my dad was very self-conscious about letting Carole see him without his clothes on, because she'd grown so much older while he'd been away. Additionally, my mom had been expecting my dad to come home looking haggard and undernourished after fighting a world war. Instead, he'd gained enough weight that she had to let out his old clothes.

Apart from those fragments, other details about his return and readjustment to civilian life are lost to the ages, since Carole was too young to remember. She did, however, astonish her 3rd-grade class one day by informing them that she and her mother had lived in France during the war. Wow! Imagine living in a Nazi-occupied country during World War II! It was only upon further examination that Carole realized she'd confused "France" with "Fresno." At that age, they sounded so similar – how much of a difference could there have been?

There were a few of my dad's wartime adventures that I knew about, because he'd *told* me about them, but which weren't reflected in his letters. For instance, when he was still in Basic Training, he was awakened one night by the distinctive sound of one of his army buddies drunkenly peeing into one of my father's shoes next to his cot. In a similarly scatological vein, he also told me about the latrine conditions aboard the Liberty ship that took him across the Atlantic to North Africa. He said there were long rows of wooden planks over a large trough, with holes cut out every couple of feet. Each man would sit back-to-back with another soldier and, as the ship rocked back and forth, everyone's crap would slosh up against their bare buttocks. Lovely image, that.

When my dad was in Oran, he had a problem with one of his molars, so he saw the camp dentist, who fashioned a crown and placed it over the tooth, admonishing him, "Now remember, this is only a temporary crown. When you get back to the States after the war, be sure to see a dentist and have him replace it with a permanent one."

When my father died nearly fifty years later, he was buried with that same temporary crown on his tooth.

Another war story my dad told me: One day, when he was stationed in Germany, he was sent on a Supply run and instructed to take a dirt road that curved around a large field. Once my dad got to that location, he thought, "It's silly for me to take that road. I can make the trip in half the time by cutting through the field." And so he drove his jeep directly through the center of the field, indeed in half the time. Once he got to the far end, he looked back and saw a sign posted at the edge of the field. In large, black letters, it warned: *"ACHTUNG! MINEN!"* I suppose he didn't mention that incident in his letters, because he didn't want to worry my mother – or provoke a stern reprimand – or both.

One of the stories my dad enjoyed telling was about Nancy upstaging Bob Hope's USO show in Darmstadt in 1945. In a strange twist of fate, I found myself inside Bob Hope's house in 1990. Dick Cavett was going to interview him for his CNBC talk show and, since Dick and I are longtime friends, he allowed me to tag along. During a break in the taping, I told Hope the story about Nancy running across the stage and I quoted his quip about Crosby and the saddle. Hope chuckled – getting a kick out of his own cleverness – and asked, "Did I say that?" It was truly surreal, being able to relay this incident back to Hope nearly half a century after it happened.

As a side note, I have a theory that the tons of telephones and switchboard equipment being trucked to Nuremberg in July of 1945 were in preparation for the landmark trials that would begin there a few months later. After all, the eyes – and ears – of the world would soon be trained on those historic proceedings, which would require a great deal of communication equipment. That's just my theory; I can't be certain.

As they had discussed, my parents went about the happy task of providing a sibling for young Carole Frances and, on August 6, 1947, Patricia *("Isn't that a pretty name?")* Jane Stoliar was born. In 1952 and 1953 respectively, Stephanie and Henry Schwartz died, and so, when my parents had a son on September 30, 1954, he was named Steven Henry in their honor.

In the late '50s, eclipsed by department stores and direct sales to customers, Henry Schwartz & Co. went out of business and my father eventually went to work as a salesman and then a sales manager for the National Chemsearch Corporation, training new salesmen. Perhaps his wartime experiences shepherding that flock of younger, less-dedicated Supply men prepared him to oversee the training of novices. In 1962, he was asked if he wanted to start a West Coast branch in Los Angeles, and so we packed up the contents of the Cornell Avenue house and departed University City, getting our kicks on Route 66. Years after we'd moved to California, my dad told me that he'd left his Army uniform in the cedar-lined closet in the basement of the Cornell house, because he figured, "What am I going to do with it?"

For all I know, it's still there.

My mother died of cancer in December of 1969 at the far-too-young age of 49. Afterwards, my father remarried twice, retired, and died of Advanced Respiratory Distress Syndrome at the age of 76, shortly after returning from a trip to Israel in December of 1992.

There was one other element in my dad's letters that I was curious about: The fate of Janine Mougin and her family, whom he befriended in Nancy. Since neither my mother nor my father ever talked about the Mougins, I figured that was a dead-end in terms of updates. Nevertheless, I decided to cruise down the information super-highway and see if I couldn't pick up a clue or two. This led me to Matt Mackensen, a Pennsylvania man who was the son of Janine Mougin and her G.I. husband, Richard, who had become a veterinarian after the war. So they'd married after all and had moved to the States! Matt was touched by my father's narrative of his helpful interactions with his family, and he was grateful for a copy of the photo Janine had sent to my parents, because his own family photos had been lost over the years.

He confirmed that his mother was, indeed, a skilled pianist with a special fondness for Chopin. Although he wasn't familiar with the incident in which Janine and Madame Mougin were injured by broken glass, he did say that his mother spoke of a time when the Nazis rounded up the locals – including her and her mother – and herded them into a cellar to be gassed. The arrival of the Allies forced the Germans to flee, allowing the imprisoned villagers to return to their homes. She also told Matt that if one German soldier was attacked by French Resistance fighters, the Nazis would round up ten random villagers into the town square and shoot them.

Matt was old enough to have heard firsthand his grandfather Henri's stories about being held prisoner in the Nazi labor camp, and to have known Madame Mougin – Germaine – an indomitable, chain-smoking force of nature who lived until the late 1980s. Sadly, Janine died in 1986 – before Germaine – and Richard in 1991. It does not appear the Stoliars ever followed through on visiting the Mackensens – or vice versa.

Before closing, it seems altogether fitting and proper to include a few words from Carole Frances herself, since she figured so prominently in our father's letters – as well as in his thoughts:

I had no preconceived ideas on what his letters would contain – likely just "Miss you" and life in the Army in general. I figured they'd be of interest only to Mom and family, but he was much more observant than I would have anticipated. I enjoyed hearing of his various interactions with others, helping kids along the way, adopting Buck and Nancy, descriptions of remnants of beautiful buildings and trips taken. I was taken aback by the hatred he held for the Germans, although seeing the atrocities and devastation, it's understandable. Nonetheless, I didn't get that impression in St. Louis. I never thought of Dad being particularly religious, but his Judaism seemed more pronounced during his service. I guess with planes dropping bombs and bullets whizzing by, one finds religion.

The "Dad" in the letters was a very different person than the one I came to know later. Although he always had a sense of humor, "my" Dad seemed more cool and aloof. In general, he wasn't one for showing emotion; he was rather stoic. Since we knew them as "old, married folks" – not the newlyweds of his letters – I was never aware of the deep feelings he held for Mom. I often reflected that his love for [his second wife] *Penny must have been greater than for Mom, as I never saw that caring and passion shown, which we did see between Penny and him. But his letters showed the depth of his love for Mom and me. I was, however, disappointed with his harping on her "dating" other men in his absence, preaching on what to send to him and putting her down on her prowess (or lack thereof) with a camera. But I can understand how important news from home was to a G.I. half a world away. You hung on every word you read, connecting you to those dear ones at home.*

Our sister, Pati, and I concur with Carole's reactions to the "Dad" in the letters. While some of what we read was clearly written by the man we knew well, there were a lot of powerful passions – from deep yearning to unflinching hatred – that felt foreign to us, since, as Carole said, he wasn't one for showing emotion. He also seemed to have hopes and ambitions during the war that were tamped down, if not extinguished entirely, by the time he reached middle age, perhaps because he had to be more focused on feeding us and keeping a roof over our heads, rather than honoring his own desires and aspirations. I hope he felt the sacrifice was worth it. I suspect he did.

I do have a few tangible mementos of his war experiences – in addition to the hundreds of letters and dozens of photos – among them, the Prussian sword with which he threatened those two German boys who were brandishing a flare gun; the mezuzah he received at that temple in Nancy in December of 1944; and the silver letter opener he took off the desk of a banking executive in Germany. I also have a Nazi officer's cap and a German magazine with a photo of Hitler and Mussolini on the cover, neither of which he mentioned in the letters.

In rummaging through a box of miscellaneous items, Carole unearthed the fragile, mimeographed program from the Passover Seder in Nancy that our dad attended in March of 1945, signed by some of his fellow Jewish buddies. She also found the photo wallet he carried with him throughout the war. It contained the last photo of Carole that our mom had sent him. Still tucked into the leather that bordered the vinyl photo window were a few, precious, soft and slender strands of hair from her young head.

I hope you have enjoyed this journey through the Second World War, as seen through the eyes of a young Jewish husband and father from the suburbs of St. Louis. I still disagree with his assessment: *"I don't think that my letters are any better than anyone else's,"* but then I'm hardly an objective observer.

INDEX

Made in the USA
Middletown, DE
26 February 2022